Six Therapists *and* One Client
2nd Edition

Frank Dumont, EdD, and
Raymond J. Corsini, PhD

Editors

SPRINGER
PUBLISHING COMPANY
PAPERBACK

Raymond Corsini, Ph.D., has been a clinical psychologist for over 50 years. He started as a prison psychologist (15 years), then was in private practice in Chicago (5 years), then was an industrial organization psychologist (10 years), and finally was in private practice in Hawaii for 25 years. He was trained by Carl Rogers, J. L. Moreno, and Rudolf Dreikurs. He has published considerably in this specialty.

Frank Dumont, Ed.D., is a full professor in the Department of Educational and Counseling Psychology at McGill University (Montreal). He has worked at McGill since 1972 in the capacity of teacher, researcher, chairman of his department, and coordinator of the Ph.D. program in counseling psychology.

Springer Publishing Company, Inc.
11 West 42nd Street
New York, NY 10036

Acquisitions Editor: Bill Tucker
Production Editor: Jeanne W. Libby
Cover design by Mimi Flow

06 07 08 09 / 5 4 3 2 1

New ISBN 0-8261-0264-6 (pbk.) © 2006 by Springer Publishing Company, Inc.

Library of Congress Cataloging-in-Publication Data

Six therapists and one client / Frank Dumont and Raymond J.
Corsini, editors.— 2nd ed.
p. cm.
Includes bibliographical references and index.
ISBN 0-8261-1319-2 (hardcover)
1. Psychotherapy. I. Dumont, Frank, 1928– II. Corsini,
Raymond J.
[DNLM: 1. Psychotherapy—methods. WM 420 S625 2000]
RC480.F5568 2000
616.89'14—dc21

99-058723

Printed in Canada at Transcontinental Printing.

CONTENTS

Contributors

Shawn Blau, *Fairfield University, Fairfield, Connecticut*
Raymond J. Corsini, *private practice, Honolulu, Hawaii*
Frank Dumont, *McGill University, Montreal, Québec, Canada*
Albert Ellis, *Institute for Rational Emotive Behavior Therapy, New York, New York*
Betty Alice Erickson, *private practice, Dallas, Texas*
Stephen Lankton, *private practice, Gulf Stream, Florida*
Arnold Lazarus, *Center for Multimodal Psychological Services, Princeton, New Jersey*
Barbara McCrady, *Rutgers University, New Brunswick, New Jersey*
Harold H. Mosak, *private practice, Chicago, Illinois*
Nathaniel Raskin, *Northwestern University Medical School, Evanston, Illinois*
Alice Goodloe Whipple, *private practice, Princeton, New Jersey*
G. Terence Wilson, *Rutgers University, New Brunswick, New Jersey*
Fred Zimring, *Case Western Reserve University, Cleveland, Ohio*

Preface

We have chosen the therapeutic systems represented in this book because we believe they will dominate this discipline in the approaching decades. An important problem that remains unresolved in our field is that different therapeutic systems not only provide different approaches to treating very similar disorders, they also conceptualize these disorders differently. The question we ask here is: how would six eminent therapists using six different contemporary psychotherapies differentially handle one and the same client.

Six Therapists and One Client is a partial response to this question. The contributors to this volume have demonstrated in as precise and concise a manner possible how they, individually working within the framework of six different theoretical orientations, would have treated the same person. Their distinctive approaches are immediately apparent and comparable. The central protagonist of this book is Don Green, a complexly troubled (and historical) person, for whom an evolving assessment and treatment is concurrently provided by six therapists. An intake interview (chapter 1) presents him as he originally presented himself, troubled by a number of fears, shackled by dysfunctional habits, confused and drifting through life, relatively friendless, vocationally misplaced, sexually compromised, self-doubting, and buffeted by time and life. He is a prototype of "clinical" Everyman, a client that might enter into any therapist's office, male or female, Black or White, straight, gay, or bisexual.

A major task in developing a second edition of this book was ensuring that truly contemporary and influential systems of psychotherapy were presented for examination. Thus the reader will find a chapter on Multimodal Therapy and another on Ericksonian Hypnotherapy, neither of which appeared in the first edition. The structure of each chapter remains the same. The chapter on Rational Emotive Behavior Therapy has been revised to reflect the latest thinking of Albert Ellis. The chapter on Adlerian Therapy has been fine-tuned, but the chapters on Cognitive-Behavior Therapy and Rogerian Therapy are largely as they originally appeared in the first edition of this book.

There is an initial segment in each chapter entitled, "Something About the Therapist." This is followed by "The Setting for the Therapy." The case "histories" that follow not only present the "classic" structure for the therapy being used but the covert reflections of the therapists as they explain what was going through their minds as they made one or another intervention. Each chapter terminates with a brief commentary and critique of the therapy presented, written by another expert in the system that was used.

A close reading of this book will affect every therapist's thinking and procedures to some extent. Reading these chapters written by therapists and theoreticians (who are committed adherents of the systems they espouse and use) cannot help but provide insights not only into the therapies at issue, but the individuals who practice them. Additionally, students, people in need of therapy, and all who have curiosity about the vagaries, paradoxes, and vicissitudes of the human condition (and how others attempt to alleviate human psychological suffering) cannot help but benefit from it.

Frank Dumont
Montreal

Ray Corsini
Honolulu
Summer of 1999

Introduction

Psychotherapeutics has evolved over the past 100 years as rapidly and dramatically as has medicine. Were therapists to practice psychotherapy today as it was practiced, say, by Forel, Bleuler, Janet, Freud, or Jung at the height of their popularity, one might suspect them of suffering from the Rip Van Winkle Effect. The half-life of our field, viewed as a scientific discipline, is not measured in centuries; it is measured in decades. Some would argue that at least half of the substantive material found in the textbooks of psychotherapy of even 35 years ago has, for all practical purposes, been superseded by new theoretical and praxiological material. One of the major reasons for this is that revolutionary advances in the psychoneurological, perceptual, developmental, and social psychologies on which a sound psychotherapeutics must be founded have necessitated radical adjustments in the way we work with our clients. Psychology was in its infancy in the late nineteenth century. In consequence, the nineteenth century science on which the psychotherapies of 100 years ago were based seriously compromised most of them.

Political factors provide equally compelling explanations for the radical changes that have taken place in psychotherapeutics. There has been a continental drift away from the male-conceptualized systems of the late 1800s, not only because they were formulated in terms of a flawed understanding of what a normal human being is, but because it has become politically untenable to postulate a uniquely male template for normality. The vision of the great pioneers of nineteenth century dynamic psychiatry was largely constrained by the belief systems and cultural templates that were regnant in various parts of central and western Europe at that time. They fearlessly, that is, unknowingly, fashioned architectonic systems that they presumed were applicable to all peoples in all times and places. In short, they developed nomothetic systems. These systems may have had some internal validity, but they had very little external validity, to borrow terminology from experimental psychology. To the extent that their concepts of human nature were largely a reflection of the tacit assumptions of the cultural enclaves in which each of them was born and raised, their theories were not generalizable to the world at large. That effect was certainly heightened by the peculiar patterns of their personal, family histories. Nietzsche asserted that every psychological theory is autobiographic. The truthfulness of this unsettling aphorism has been confirmed over the past century. The models that prevailed in the Salpêtrière, or the Burghölzli, the Viennese Psychoanalytic Society, or the Nancy School are no longer considered normative by serious psychologists. The result has been a dramatic shift, in construing the principles of human development, away from the grand nomothetic systems of the nineteenth century to contemporary emic models.

There have been other major changes in the theoretical foundations of contemporary psychotherapy. It is not possible to enumerate, still less discuss, them all here, although the six distinctive modern approaches presented in this book vividly reflect these changes. It will be useful, nevertheless, to indicate what some of them are and the reasons why we have chosen the theories for this book that we have. To begin, contemporary theories reflect a lifespan approach to understanding how humans develop. Consequently, the arrested-development model epitomized by classical psychoanalysis is in rapid decline. The six widely espoused theoretical orientations included in this volume are evidence that the rigid stage-formulations of earlier systems of personality development required severe modification, if not rejection. As long as there is life, there is potential for change and development. A benign environment will not only allow human potential to effloresce at all "stages" of life; it will catalyze it.

The basic science of human development and the applied science of psychotherapy are tightly enmeshed. We have discovered that the proper treatment of all clients needs to be nicely related to the developmental level, neurological, educational, and physical, to which they've attained. The Rankian principle, that we must abandon a therapist-centered therapy for a patient-centered one, has come to dominate the field. It found its most eloquent statement in the work of Carl Rogers. On the other hand, a one-size-fits-all approach to psychotherapeutics is no longer seen as professionally acceptable. The multimodal approaches of Arnold Lazarus and Albert Ellis, among others, make this vividly evident. We have included these three approaches in this book.

There is an important corollary to this principle. The authoritarian attitude of the past has ceded, by and large, to a more egalitarian model for therapist-client interaction. It is largely recognized today that individuals know more about themselves than does anyone else in the world, no matter how wise. No longer are clients dragged forcibly to admit they have fears, convictions, beliefs, wishes, and simple ideas they have no cognizance of but that their therapists suspect they have. It is widely recognized that interpretations of patient mentation proffered by therapists may reveal more about therapists' belief systems than about their patients' realities. Transference flows both ways. Moreover, the broad sweep of millenia-old constructivist philosophies have moved the theoretical focus onto how individuals construct their reality. Although this principle (generally recognized today as Kantian) is implicit—in uneven proportions—in all of the therapies of this book, it is especially evident in the Ericksonian model, as exemplified in Steve Lankton's treatment of his client. This therapy postulates that it is the clients themselves who are the wellsprings of the creative and healing remedies for their difficulties and sufferings.

The single-principled, reductionist systems of the past are also in eclipse. No longer are models of human development accepted that postulate a single principle, such as sexual libido, or reason, or emotion, or genetic variables, or training, or familial relations, to account for the variability in human personality and behavior patterns. Holism is in the ascendancy. Our understanding of the multidimensionality of the human personality and the complex dynamics that shape it (as Antonio Damasio, for example, eloquently explains in his book, *Descartes' error: Emotion, the brain, and human behavior*) has revolutionized our approach to psychotherapy. No matter how ardently we have sought simplicity in our models, it has proven to be as mischievous an objective as complexity. Ockham's Razor has never truly been useful, as his proviso, other things being equal, (i.e., ceteris paribus), has never existed. Human beings have ever been more complex than our simple paradigms of yesteryear would have supposed. But as in other realms, virtue lies in the middle way. Though mindless complexity must still be eschewed, our models must be more holistic and encompassing of the elements of our universe than we ever imagined in the past that they might be.

Although the psychotherapies of Ellis, Lazarus, and to a lesser extent Adler can be characterized as behavioral as well as cognitive, we decided to retain in this new edition the chapter on Cognitive Behavior Therapy by Barbara McCrady and Terry Wilson. On the other hand, like most other therapies, it has evolved in a holistic direction. As McCrady states in one of her reflections: "For a cognitive behavior therapist, defining the antecedents, consequences, and thoughts and feelings surrounding a problem is essential to developing a plan of change" (p. 281). It was also important to retain the chapter on Adlerian therapy, demonstrated by Ray Corsini, as it reflects one of the most powerful modern developments of twentieth century psychotherapy, the movement away from a largely intrapsychic treatment of the client toward a more socially based one. His community-oriented theory is not only viable in itself, but it has contributed in signal ways to such different theorists as Karen Horney and Albert Ellis. The former can be truly considered an Adlerian in Freudian clothing; the latter a cognitivist clothed in Adlerian accouterments.

The psychotherapies that have been selected for this volume represent some of the more representative contemporary approaches to what Ellis calls, "treating Nice Neurotics," clients who do not have serious personality disorders, still less psychotic symptomatology. (Ellis nevertheless surprised us by diagnosing Don Green, our historical client of choice, not as a nice neurotic, but as a personality-disordered person.) We have continued with a simple model for displaying the strengths and contrasts that exist among some of the most powerful therapeutics at our disposal. In our judgment, the systems illustrated in this volume will be the dominant ones in the decades ahead.

We have chosen to retain a simple plan for this book. Don Green, the central figure in this volume, is historical. He was treated, successfully, by Ray Corsini. But we have asked all six therapists to treat this same client. This allows the readers to contrast more clearly their divergent diagnostic and therapeutic approaches to working with an individual who had a multitude of problems. It provided a level playing field for the six therapists. Their construal of the task, their selection of data for their problem formulations, their assessment of the client's problems, and their approach to (re)habilitating an individual (who, in fact, finished therapy to lead a productive and personally satisfying private life) give us multiple perspectives on the resources at our disposal. The readers will individually judge which approach suits them best. Favoring one approach, of course, does not exclude recourse to strategies that are found in various other models. Chapters 2 through 7, demonstrating broad divergence, schoolwise, in helping a complexly troubled person, can be read with profit by those who are most committed to one or another approach, (and, indeed, to some that are not represented in this volume).

We trust this will be an instructive and pleasurable read for you.

Frank Dumont
Montreal
Summer, 1999

1

An Intake Interview With Donald Green

By Raymond J.Corsini

After my 1 o'clock client left, I looked at my schedule and noted that my next appointment was with a person who wished to have therapy but was uncertain whom he should see. The purpose of this meeting was to determine whether he would continue with me or whether I would refer him to a colleague whose theoretical orientation seemed to better fit his needs. His name was Donald Green. I had no other information about him.

When Donald Green arrived, I saw he was a bit shorter than average and somewhat pudgy. He was wearing a brown suit and glasses. We shook hands, and I noticed that he had a firm, warm, dry grip. I waved him to the chairs and couch in the room and walked over to my chair. He took the seat farthest away from me, and we looked at one another a while, sizing each other up. I got the impression he was a bit more uncomfortable than the typical first-time client.

I said, "I'm pleased to meet you," and waited to see what he would say in reply.

Mr. Green took an envelope out of his inside coat pocket and offered it to me. "I have here a psychological report done on me, which you may want to see," he said.

I reached over, took it, and put it on my desk. "I'll look at this a bit later," I said, "but right now I'd like us to talk a bit. Will you tell me the reason for this appointment?"

He answered, "I've been having problems on my job, so my supervisor suggested that I see a doctor. I went to my regular physician and he ordered all kinds of tests. When he got the results he told me he could find nothing physically wrong, and he thought I should see a shrink. So I looked in the telephone directory, and selected this clinic."

"Tell me something about yourself," I said.

"Well, my problem is that I come in late to work practically every morning. I'm an engineer for (mentioning a large manufacturing company). I'm in charge of waste disposal systems and controls for emissions from smokestacks, pollution, things like that. I've been with this company since I graduated from engineering school 17 years ago, and I've had this particular job for 6 years. I work on my own and report to the chief engineer, but I hardly ever see him or bother him. Every evaluation I've had has been very good. In recent years, though, there's been one black mark on my job ratings—being late for work."

"Can you tell me more about that?"

"As I said, I'm late almost every morning. I always was sort of a sound sleeper. In college I had an alarm clock. Now, I have three alarm clocks, two electric and a windup model. I set them at 5-minute intervals, and every night I hide them in different places, one in the bathroom, one in my living room, and one in my bedroom. I also have an arrangement with a neighbor to call me on the phone and keep ringing until I get up and answer—the phone is in the living room. And finally, the paperboy comes and I pay him to keep knocking at my door until I open it and get the newspaper from him. And after all that, I still get in late."

"I see. Can you tell me any more?" I asked.

"I like my job, and I've always been punctual about almost everything. This coming in late started about 3 years ago and has been steadily getting worse. It's not at all like me. But I usually stay after regular hours to make up for coming in late, and sometimes I go to the office on weekends and don't ask for overtime pay, though I live out in the suburbs. I don't think my job is in real jeopardy, but people are talking about me. My supervisor likes me and is worried. He thinks I should do something about the problem, and that's why I'm here."

"Well," I said, "I want to ask you some questions. But first, do you have any questions to ask me?"

"Just how confidential is therapy?" Mr. Green asked.

"According to the ethics of my profession, I am obligated to give no information about you to anyone unless you give me permission to do so, or unless I learn something I clearly believe would be dangerous to you or to other people."

"Oh, there'll be nothing of that sort, I assure you."

"Good. Let me ask you this: Have you ever had any personal counseling or psychotherapy before, or have you ever thought of having any?"

"I guess everyone has problems or thinks of discussing matters with therapists. I *have* thought about it, but I never really considered it seriously. No, I've never seen any professional person about personal problems, but I'm sure I have some, like anyone else. I suppose the reason I have such trouble getting up in the morning has some psychological basis, but I can't figure what it might be."

When I asked "Now can I ask you some personal questions?" he nodded his agreement. I asked, "What's your present family situation?"

"I'm not married, never have been. I have one sister but I haven't seen or heard from her in 10 years. I don't even know where she lives or if she is married. We never got along and never liked one another. She's 8 years older than me, just 50 years old now, and I'm 42. My parents are dead. There are some uncles and aunts but I have never really had anything to do with them. I live alone."

"How about your social life?"

"I have two pretty good friends, Jim, an artist about 20 years older than me, and Mary, his wife, who is a bit younger. I have dinner at their home every Thursday night. I usually bring some of the fixings, like a steak, and she cooks while Jim and I play chess. Then we eat, talk, and I walk home."

"Is that your entire social life?"

"Practically all. We have a company picnic and a Christmas party that I go to, but I usually go alone. I just don't do much socializing. I even eat at the company cafeteria by myself, but usually I brown-bag it, bring my own lunch and eat it in my office. I guess you could call me a loner."

"Do you date?"

"No, I've never dated. Look, you'll ask me this eventually, but I'm not gay. Just never dated—well, once, at the senior prom in high school. I like women, but I'm just shy with them, I guess."

"Ever have sex? With anyone?"

"Never."

"Tell me about the family you grew up in."

"I more or less grew up as an only child, since my sister was so much older, and she didn't like me. My father was 15 years older than my mother; he was 40 and she was 25 when they got married. I was a so-called change-of-life baby, born when my mother was 41 and my father was 56. He was a strange man, liked to be by himself a lot. I saw very little of him. He worked as a bookkeeper, and he would come home for dinner, go into his room—he had a separate bedroom—and that was that. Our family hardly ever did anything together. My sister was usually with her friends—she had lots of them. My mother used to try to get her to take me along but she wouldn't. She had her own life."

"What can you tell me about your mother?"

"She was a saint. Quiet, always working. If she had nothing else to do, she would knit. She had a few friends who would come to the house, but not when my father was home. He didn't like strangers coming into the house. She was loving but not affectionate."

"How did your parents get along with each other?"

"They rarely talked to one another. I never saw them even hold hands or anything. When I learned the facts of life I couldn't believe they'd ever slept together—you know what I mean?"

"Yes, of course. So, essentially, they ignored each other?"

"More or less. I know my mother liked to talk and socialize, but not my father. She was a kind of martyr, but I think she loved him."

"What was your relationship with your father?"

"Distant. We practically never talked or did anything together. He just avoided me—but then, he avoided everyone."

"And what was your relationship with your mother?"

"She took good care of me, like nursed me when I was sick. But she was not really affectionate. I don't think she ever hugged me or kissed me."

"Are you more like your mother or your father?"

Mr. Green looked up to the ceiling and thought for a moment. "I guess I'm a bit like both of them—solitary like my father and a hard worker like my mother. I'm always busy. Besides my job, I have a paying hobby fixin' up used cars."

"I'll want to know more about that a bit later," I said. "First, tell me something about your sister."

"Oh, Diana. She was wild, rebellious, sociable, just as different from me as possible. I was obedient, tried to please my parents. Neither of them could do anything with *her.* And, as I mentioned, she ignored me. I was good in school and she was not. My mother wanted my sister to take me out so I could be with her and her friends, but she never wanted to. There used to be a lot of arguing about that. I didn't want to go with her, anyway. She had lots of friends, but I usually had just one."

"Can you tell me more about yourself as a child?"

"I played a lot by myself. I did my chores. I did my homework. I didn't want to go to summer camp after the first time. I was a Boy Scout for a while, and I always did a lot of reading; I still do. I did well in school, better than my sister. And I helped a lot around the house, while Diana went out a lot. She got yelled at and punished often, but not me. She was very competitive with me, I thought."

"Is there anything about you that you might want to change, besides this matter of not getting up in the morning?"

"Well," replied the client, "yes and no. I realize that I'm different from other people, and I wish I were more sociable. Still, I feel I'm a success and get along OK. I sometimes feel lonely and depressed and wish I had more friends. Sometimes I think I would even like to get married and have children." He paused, took a breath, and then continued. "Actually, I feel trapped in my lifestyle—the way I live—and I don't know how to break out of it. Sometimes I get a desperate feeling. I've even had thoughts of suicide. Deep down, I'm lonely. I've never talked so much about myself to anyone else in my life as I'm doing now with you. I don't really have any confidants. Even Jim and Mary, my friends, they really don't know much about me, and I don't know much about them, either."

"So there is more that concerns you than just getting to work on time?"

"That's right. I don't know much about therapy, but is it too late for me to start being more—well, like other people, more normal? Or am I doomed to be a loner all my life?"

"That's a question that can be answered in therapy," I said.

"I suppose it is kind of a dumb question. I really want to know what makes me tick. Do you think you could help me?"

"That's really a judgment you must make yourself," I replied. "I can assure you of only two things: What you tell me will be treated as confidential, and I will try my best to be of help. But if I think someone else can be of more help to you, I'll refer you to them."

Mr. Green looked me in the eye and asked, "But how about you? Do you like me?"

"As of this moment, I simply need to get to know more about you," I replied. "I want to keep any feelings out of the situation. We are now more or less sizing each other up to see whether we can work together, and I am only interested in getting more information from you. Is there anything else I should know about you?"

"Well, I have sexual feelings for women. I subscribe to a couple of men's magazines. I take care of myself sexually. You know what I mean?"

"Of course. That can be dealt with later as well, and in depth if you wish. Anything else?"

"Yes, there is. I am ashamed to tell you about it."

Mr. Green looked up to the ceiling, contemplating this confession. I wondered what it could be. When he began to talk, it was evident that whatever he was going to say bothered him a great deal.

"You'll think I'm crazy," he began. "Every once in a while I go into a kind of panic about something, and then it turns out that there was no need for the panic. But these things I imagine are so real . . . so real." He seemed to be struggling for self-control. For a long time he was silent, while I waited to hear what was bothering him.

Finally he said, "I fantasize catastrophes. They become real, and I act in weird ways. And I do it again and again and again. I don't learn from my experiences; it happens over and over. I imagine something, always terrible. I exaggerate whatever it is. It keeps me from sleeping sometimes, I get so worried." And again he was silent for a long time. I waited patiently to see whether there was more to follow.

When Mr. Green started talking again, he said, "Let me give you an example. I buy cars, fix them up, and then sell them at a profit. I live in a small house, but it has a large heated garage that can take four cars. I have a lot of machinery, a metal lathe, and other equipment. I look up ads for cars for sale by owner, and if I find a model I like I call the person up and arrange to see it. If I like it I buy it, take it to my garage, and fix it up. Then I resell it. So, as I told you, I have a paying hobby.

"About a year ago I saw one of the cars I had sold in front of a garage. I began to think that the woman who bought it from me had taken it to the garage because it wasn't working. I decided she was angry with me; maybe she was going to sue me or have someone beat me up for selling her a lemon—that sort of thing.

"So I began to keep away from the part of town she lived in. It got so I avoided going to town at all, afraid of meeting her. This went on for months. I couldn't sleep, was in constant fear. I even thought of giving up my job, changing my name, moving to another state. One evening I was in line to go to a movie, and someone tapped me on the shoulder. I turned around. *It was her!* I wanted to run away, but I controlled myself. She just started talking about the movie, and then I asked her about the car. She said she was happy with it and it ran fine.

"I then mentioned, as casually as I could, that I had seen the car in front of a garage. She said she had never had to take the car in to be fixed—she drove it all over, and nothing had ever gone wrong with it. I was so relieved, I can't tell you. But then I started concocting another and even worse imaginary catastrophe. I hope you can understand that they become more real to me than reality."

"I can certainly understand fantasizing of this kind," I said. "But you said you had another fantasy?"

"Yes, one right after another; it's been like that for many years. Here's another example. One year I didn't send in my income tax return on time. I kept delaying and started to think that if I did send it in I would be penalized or even jailed. The longer I waited, the more I became certain that I was getting into deeper trouble . . . some day or night the IRS would break into my house, and arrest and prosecute me. For months I agonized about this. Finally I told Jim, my friend, about it. First he laughed at me and told me there was nothing wrong with what I had done. He said lots of people miss the deadline, and the IRS simply fines them for being late. But I would not believe him. Finally he practically dragged me to an IRS office; I wouldn't go alone. I was positive I would be put in handcuffs."

"What happened?"

"The woman I talked to at the tax office was actually very nice. She told me a lot of people for one reason or other didn't send in their returns on time, and there might be a small penalty, a fine or something. But you know what happened? Actually, I had a refund coming. Instead of being prosecuted and going to prison, I got money back. The company had taken more money out of my paychecks than necessary. Can you beat that?"

"So, you scare yourself about things that are not real?"

I guess that's so, but they sure are real to me at the time. Very real, very, very real. Does this sound crazy?"

"No more than children being afraid of ghosts and hobgoblins living in closets. Well, I think I have a good deal of information about you. Is there anything else you want to tell me or ask me?"

"I already feel better having told you all this," Mr. Green said. "I think you should read the report I gave you, however."

"We'll get to that," I said. "But first, I'd like to know if there's anything else about you that you think I should know."

"My job calls for me to give directions to foremen and mechanics about manufacturing to specifications. If they start to argue with me, I usually don't make a fuss over it or stand up to them. I feel that they're more powerful than I am, even though I have authority over them in these matters. I'm afraid of them; I even have done work myself rather than make a fuss about it. I guess I'm kind of a coward. At times like these I feel worthless. Deep down, I have a fear of other people."

"Is there any fear of anything right now?" I asked.

"No," he replied. "I'm between these crazy fantasies right now. When I finally find out how nutty I've been, like seeing that woman on the movie line or the IRS agent, then I feel OK. But I wonder about my imagination, my growing fear, my inability to tell anyone about it, my unwillingness to do anything about it. Like, it seems I just want to stew about it."

"Anything else?"

"I do have a strange phobia—fear of dogs. No, not of dogs, but the barking of dogs. Even a little puppy, if it starts to bark, I get all upset. I'll be walking down the street and sure enough, if I hear a dog barking—even if I can see it and know it's tied up or behind a fence—I will either cross the street or turn around."

"How about dreams? Do you dream often, do you have a recurring dream?"

"There are two dreams that I have over and over. One is that I have just failed a crucial exam and will not get my degree. It is so real that when I wake up I have to assure myself that it is not true. The other one is that I am somewhere with no money and no place to go; sometimes I'm even naked. I'm just lost.

"Oh, some years ago I had absolutely the most unusual dream of my life. To understand it, you have to know that I am not at all musical. I like music, but I have never been able to learn to play any instrument. In this dream I was in an opera house. I think I was alone. And—here's the unusual part—I could hear the beautiful music and when I woke up I was angry because I wanted to hear more of it. What's funny about this dream is that I never dream sound, and certainly not music."

"We may go into dreams later, but now I'd like to ask you about your first memory."

"My first memory? . . . Well, yes, there is one I think about once in a while. I think I was about three years old. I was standing on the roof of an apartment building we lived in, looking down to the street. I was with my mother, who was waiting for my father to show up. Finally she saw him, and she pointed him out to me, saying he was carrying something, and she hoped it was ice cream."

"Can you tell me more about that first memory?"

"Well, I could not see my father, and I guess the reason is that I'm shortsighted. You can see I wear glasses. I remember thinking how wonderful it was that she could see him, and I remember hoping that my father would be bringing ice cream, since she wanted it."

Looking as though he were about to cry, Mr. Green said, "I came here because my supervisor suggested I see a doctor and then the doctor suggested I see a psychotherapist. This was about my getting to work late, but there are a lot of things that bother me. I feel I have been a failure in life: living like a hermit; no real friends, no women friends, no possibility of ever settling down, getting married, and having children; being scared of dogs barking; the fantasies that become so real. I am even worse off than my father was. At least he got married and had children. Do you think there's any hope for me?"

"Yes, there's always hope. People *can* change. And psychotherapy can make a difference. Whether it will in your case, I certainly don't know at this time. But let's look at what's in this envelope you gave me. This industrial psychology firm has a very good reputation. How did they come to evaluate you?"

"Well, my company decided to have every person in the organizational structure at certain salary levels evaluated for managerial potential. The way it worked was like this: First, all who were eligible had to volunteer to be evaluated. It was only suggested, not required, that you have this evaluation, whether or not you wanted to become a manager. The evaluation was to go to us personally and not to the company. The only thing the company would know would be whether or not we were considered to have potential as managers. The company would then decide which employees should be sent for further training. I didn't want to be a manager but I wanted the evaluation, so I went through the 3-day program. They gave us all kinds of tests, and we had stress interviews, role-playing, sensitivity sessions, that sort of thing. I finally got this confidential report, which they promised went only to me. I wish you would read it. We were told that if we went to any therapist, like I'm doing now, the psychology firm would give you fuller information—exact scores on tests, that sort of thing."

I took out two sheets of paper imprinted with the name of the industrial psychology firm and noted the name of the psychologist who had written the report. I read it quickly, while Mr. Green waited.

CONFIDENTIAL REPORT ON DBG

This report is written at the request of an industrial organization which will be given a recommendation relative to our estimate of the managerial potential of the above employee, identified by initials only. No other information on the employee will be given to the employer. This report is given to DBG, the person evaluated. No other copies are made or kept. As a matter of company policy, we will not discuss the report with DBG or provide him with any further information about our evaluation procedure. However, any professional licensed in this state to practice a helping profession may be given, with DBG's written permission, copies of documents relating to the report, including objective test scores, projective materials, etc., within one year of the above date. After this date, all such materials will be destroyed.

At the time of this evaluation, DBG is an adult male who states that he is in good physical health, takes no medication, and is a moderate drinker and a nonsmoker. He has a B.Sc. degree in engineering and has taken additional courses in his specialty. He graduated from elementary school, high school, and college at the usual intervals and went to work for his present employer immediately after graduation from college. He obtained his job through his father, who had worked for that company for many years.

He has moved upward within his specialty and is considered a good employee who can be depended on. His direct supervisor states that DBG frequently is late coming to work, but in view of the nature of his work, and his tendency to work overtime without compensation, this is no problem. Nevertheless this supervisor, who is planning to retire soon, believes that DBG may have difficulty with a new supervisor because of his lateness. We have not explored the reasons for this behavior.

DBG states he has no interest in becoming a manager. He has taken this evaluation mostly for the purpose of knowing more about himself. We find that he is relatively unambitious, at least as far as further advancement in this company is concerned. He intends to remain with the company, in which he has been employed 17 years, until retirement.

In discussions with others about DBG, a part of our usual procedure, we find that he is thought to be peculiar. From all we can learn, this opinion is based primarily on the following facts: He has no close associates in the company; usually eats lunch alone, frequently brown-bagging it from home; does not participate much in company parties or picnics; and does not engage in social relations with anyone in the company, either on or off the job.

He has never been officially reprimanded (except advised relative to his lateness) and maintains a kind of protective shield about himself. In talking with this evaluator, DBG answered all questions completely, volunteered little, and did not appear to be hostile or anxious. He seems to have a lot of self-control. In a word, his relationship with the evaluator was formal and neutral.

Test Results

Intelligence. Two tests of general mental ability, a group and an individual test, put him in the top decile of adult males. He functions well in both verbal and nonverbal areas.

Interests. A test of vocational interests shows a preference for person-centered activities, especially sales. Because this finding is in decided contrast with both his training and his stated preferences, a second test of vocational interests was also administered, with the same results. There is a secondary interest in mechanical work.

Personality. On the basis of a questionnaire, a multi-choice test of personality, nothing significant stands out, and the same is true for a projective test. He falls well within the limits of normality, showing a considerable degree of creativity and imagination on the projective test. In discussions, he states that he has no artistic or creative capacity and does not do any writing or painting.

Leisure-time activities. He spends most of his free time repairing and refinishing automobiles. He purchases cars and then resells them. He does some fishing and a great deal of walking. He takes walking tours on his vacations and has taken some cruises.

Summary

Overall, DBG is a self-contained individual, of above-average intelligence, but within the expected limits for his profession, a person with creative capacities and social potentialities, who seems to have established himself comfortably in a position for which he has been trained. He seems to have no desire to move either horizontally or vertically in this company or to seek employment elsewhere.

This writer would say that DBG has found his niche and seems content on the job and is well suited for his work. He may benefit by having some personal counseling in view of his solitary habits. He is not recommended for managerial training.

Neil D. Griffin, Ph.D.

I put the report down and said, "Seems rather complete and well done. What about it? Anything you want to discuss?"

"I thought it all fit in quite well, but I wonder about the item that says I have an interest in selling. I've never sold anything in my life, and I don't particularly like the idea of selling."

"All I can say about that is that apparently you replied to the questions in the vocational-interest tests in the same way successful salespersons do. This may be worth examining in greater detail later on. Anything else before we discuss whether you'll start therapy with me or not?"

"Yes. . . can you tell me anything about the therapy?"

"I will, but not today; we just don't have time. I'll get back to you tomorrow and we can make a final decision as to who you'll work with. Then a schedule can be established. Days and hours to meet, how often, and then matters bearing on insurance, the payment schedule for therapy, and so on. OK?"

"Fine," said Mr. Green. "I'll wait for your call."

Milton H. Erickson developed a system of psychotherapy that has found wide acceptance and has, as well, provided the foundation for several successful derivative approaches developed by those who have studied his work. Erickson's methods are useful for both brief therapy and for the long-term treatment of serious mental illness.

Erickson believed the limitless varieties of human behavior and thinking could not be encapsulated in a single theoretical framework. He proposed a model emphasizing strengths and wellness rather than pathology. It is predicated on an understanding of normal behaviors and of the developmental phases of psychosocial, cultural, and familial life.

The unconscious is understood as the repository of a lifetime of learnings that are influential in ways we're not aware of. The therapeutic use of these resources is an integral part of therapy. Hypnosis is a vehicle for communicating with the unconscious and conveying information that can be used both consciously and unconsciously. Erickson's psychotherapy is reality based and future oriented; but "insight" as such is not considered necessary. While direct interventions and assignments may be appropriate, many issues are better addressed indirectly. Clients are experts on their own persona. An indirect intervention gives the client the flexibility to use what is most helpful at any moment and to remember and understand other parts of the intervention on deeper levels at appropriate times.

It is the responsibility of an Ericksonian therapist to create a psychotherapeutic climate, to initiate change, to provide encouragement, and to use a broad range of ethically effective resources in achieving the client's legitimate goals. Careful observation and utilization of whatever the client presents is vital. This is a therapy of expansion, not of taking away, and one of using the client's own world as a tool for healing.

Betty Alice Erickson

2

Ericksonian Hypnotherapy

SOMETHING ABOUT THE THERAPIST • *Stephen Lankton*

When I reflect back on the experiences that I've had that were important in developing my ability to function as a creative therapist, I think there were as many that were purely personal as there were that were just academic. I grew up in a rural part of lower Michigan and, as a result of that, spent a good deal of time inventing my own methods of entertainment. I spent a good deal of my childhood doing scientific investigations in chemistry, astronomy, physics, electricity, electronics, and optics with materials that I purchased and built and accumulated in the basement of my house. When I wasn't involved in those sorts of curiosities, I was disassembling and reassembling anything I could get my hands on to find out how it worked. While I was curious about how people conducted mental activities like so called "thought," I couldn't get much reliable information about that area. Answers in physical science were easier to obtain. For a long while I expected that I would become an engineer or scientist as I grew up. I, along with two classmates, graduated from our high school with more mathematics credits than anyone had ever previously accumulated.

So I began my career in college in a mathematics and engineering orientation. My college experience was shaped by the socio-political climate of the mid-sixties, and a couple of events in particular. One of my friends from high school had come back from California with a noticeable and disturbing personality change that was a result of taking street drugs. That opened my eyes to the difficulty that many youths were facing. At exactly the same time, a very influential teacher I had announced the beginning of a "crisis and intervention center" for helping youths who had been exposed to psychedelic and hallucinogenic drugs. This was a psychology teacher and I was really quite impressed with her. She taught psychology and did counseling at the psychology clinic. She was very good at explaining aspects of personality that I had always been rather confused about. Engineering topics, mathematics, and chemistry topics no longer really fascinated me because I already understood the building blocks for those fields. But the events that had to do with psychology were a domain I had never really looked into, and I was quite amazed to learn what she was teaching.

Partially because of my admiration of her and partially because of my recognition of what drug use had done to one of my friends, I attended the meetings of this newly formed crisis and intervention center. I soon became one of the principal players in its development and coordination. This center was one of the first on the eastern side of the Mississippi, and it operated somewhat like the San Francisco Suicide Prevention Center. And our training came from a number of professionals in the area of empathy skills, crisis theory, depression and suicide, problem-pregnancy counseling, poison control, drug abuse, and so on. Our association with this crisis center, The Listening Ear, gave us valuable exposure to the work, personalities, and professionalism of many individuals like Drs. Bill Kell, Dozier Thornton, Norman Kagan, Dick Pierce, and others in the Michigan State University area.

I learned a great deal about crisis theory and empathy skills, and one of the things that was crucial in this learning was the manner in which rapport had to be built rapidly with people who were taking LSD and having a bad trip. With anyone who came to our door, you had to very quickly grasp the reality they were explaining to you, and you couldn't disagree with it in an adversarial or contentious manner. It was necessary to adopt their view of reality, at least for a short period of time, and to reemphasize aspects of it that they had felt were negative or disturbing.

For example, if someone came into the room and felt concerned that the walls were moving, it could be advantageous to quickly move beside them and look where they were looking and say, "Oh yes, I see what you mean about the walls moving. I can see them right over there." But when I look at it more carefully I realize it was just the shadows caused by the curtain as the sunlight passed through it. "Yes, the sunlight gives a warm glow to the curtains and a feeling of warmth and comfort, like the sunlight coming through my clothing, or coming through a window, cascading on the carpet where you're sitting comfortably. Do you like that kind of feeling?" And in that manner, I took their perception of reality and their moving walls and quickly changed that to shadows and sunlight that created the shadows, the warmth of the sunlight, and how the warmth of sunlight is enjoyable. And before very long, I'd have the person sitting down remembering what comforts they've had sitting in the sunlight.

I didn't think much about the utility of that sort of learning at the time. Eventually, I changed my majors from engineering and mathematics to psychology and ended up graduating from undergraduate school with degrees in anthropology, psychology, linguistics, and history. I went in my employment hours to a boys camp where I did street work with delinquents at risk. I had to rapidly build rapport and hook them up with community resources. From there it was a natural step for me to consider going to graduate school in social work at the University of Michigan. I concentrated most of my clinical efforts on outpatient psychiatric work. Simultaneously I enrolled in a postgraduate training program in Gestalt Therapy and Transactional Analysis training that I continued after graduate school for over 4 years.

Graduate school became an excellent opportunity to integrate behavior modification, Gestalt Therapy, and transactional approaches to personality change with psychodynamic case work theory. Drs. Frank Maple, Charles Garvin, and Richard Stuart at the University of Michigan continually encouraged me in this direction by such activities as having me conduct monthly teaching sessions for other graduate students relative to what I was learning from the extracurricular clinical training.

By the time I graduated from the University of Michigan with an M.S.W. degree in social systems in 1972, I had accumulated a reputation around Michigan for my clinical work. I continued work at the crisis center, my work with delinquent youths, and some teaching programs I had developed on the topic of youth crisis and its genesis. Soon I got a wonderful job at a family service agency supervised by

Lloyd Demcoe. There I honed my perception and skills for the next 5 years working with families and individuals. For several years I was able to enjoy further intense training in Gestalt Therapy, body therapies, psychodrama, Transactional Analysis, and even Rolfing. I met Dr. John Grinder, a linguist, and enjoyed working with him as he and his associates and I developed the early foundations of what they later came to call Neuro-Linguistic Programming (NLP). By virtue of those combined experiences I became a clinical member of the American Association of Marriage and Family Therapists and, over the years, subsequently became an Approved Supervisor in family therapy.

In 1975 I began to journey to Phoenix to study with Dr. Milton H. Erickson, MD. I had heard about Erickson from a luncheon discussion I'd had with Dr. Gregory Bateson at a therapy conference. Dr. Bateson suggested that my theories on families and symptom development were something I should speak about with Dr. Erickson. I promptly called Dr. Erickson and was invited to come to Phoenix to study with him. I have many stories to tell about studying with Dr. Erickson. A curious aspect of those stories is that for several years I couldn't understand them nor his approach to people—until it finally dawned on me that the skill I had learned long before in approaching college students who were having LSD trips was of the same nature as his. That skill was essential to understanding Erickson's approach.

This approach that proved so effective was utilizing the behavior that clients present and matching their reality and perception so I could communicate with them in their own language about what they experienced. Helping them use those perceptions and memories to retrieve desired experience was exactly the same procedure that had worked with the LSD clients. It was the same behavior that was essential to understanding Erickson's work and to replicating his methods with people who were being seen in the context of hypnosis (Lankton, Lankton, & Matthews, 1994) or were being seen in other kinds of face-to-face therapy. While that therapy might not be hypnosis in the proper sense, it still employed the same principles that were foremost in hypnotic work: the principles of meeting clients at their model of the world, using their perceptions and talents to help them retrieve experiences from their own life, and connecting to those experiences in the context in which they needed to find them.

I continued studying with Dr. Erickson regularly until his death in 1980. Over that period of time I began writing about his work and, over the years, continued to train and write several books that pertained to his influence in various therapeutic areas. It was especially interesting to try to put together an approach that could be learned and replicated and researched that had to do with the work of a man who was not well understood. When I first met him, concepts like metaphor , suggestions, anecdotes and binds, paradoxical intervention, utilization, goal-directed work, ambiguous functions assignments, goal-directed metaphors, building a social interface, and multiple embedded metaphor were phrases that were not well systematized or in some cases not even invented.

While he, of course, used words like utilization, suggestion, and hypnosis to describe his work, he had only written one article about complex stories. Many people, including myself, had never seen it. Some of these interventions and concepts had been used by others for years (e.g., Victor Frankl and paradoxical intention, Albert Bandura and representation systems, Jay Haley and assignments and utilization, etc.). However, they had not become popular or well researched, and they did not hang together by a common thread of logic, nor appear to be more than disconnected tricks. As regards Erickson's written explanations of his own work, there were no easily obtainable sources until Dr. Ernest Rossi published his collected papers in the 1979 and early 1980s time frame. Even then, we still didn't see the more comprehensive theory that we've since been able to piece together from our own critical observations (Lankton & Lankton, 1998a).

I assume it was because of my contribution to this body of theory that the Milton Erickson Foundation presented me with their Life Achievement Award to the Field of Psychotherapy in 1994. Having made contributions to the handbooks of marriage and family therapy, clinical hypnosis, social work, and other writings in body therapy, brief therapy, and therapeutic epistemology, I was able to extend the influence of Dr. Erickson's work into a number of different areas of psychotherapy. As a result of my work in explicating the contributions of Dr. Erickson in these areas, I became an Approved Consultant for the American Association of Clinical Hypnosis and a Diplomate in Clinical Hypnosis, awarded by the American Hypnosis Board for Clinical Social Work. I have now become the President of this Board.

The final aspect of my development that I feel was crucial to my professional growth has to do with the pervasive sense of awe and curiosity I've always experienced in the face of the things that surround me. Living at the time I did and the place I did, I was always fascinated by the ability to do anything and create anything. If it was possible to make a motor out of nails and wire, I wanted to find out if I could do that. If it was possible to take the air out of a tube and create a vacuum or add a filament and create a light bulb, as Edison had done, I wondered if that was possible for me and how that would work. If it was possible to make an arrow and glue feathers to shafts and shape with a hot wire, I wondered what that would be like. I wasn't really interested in accomplishing any of the goals for the sake of obtaining the end product—I was interested in performing the activity that would lead to the goal and see whether or not that activity would, in fact, lead to the goal. That is to say, my goal was never to think "I want to have an arrow," but to discover a process for producing an arrow. I was interested in how to make things happen. And it was the accumulation of that knowledge and my penchant for experimenting, modifying, and trying all over again that I found useful. With that same orientation toward clients, I'm more interested in working on our relationship, experiences, and communication, and learning how they go together. What I learn is what works and what doesn't.

This orientation leaves me in a comfortable mode. I can make video tapes to help people get over their pain or panic attacks using hypnosis, without having any anxiety myself because I'm not working to accomplish the goal of getting rid of the anxiety so much as I'm working to experiment with how a particular process will work or how another process will work for them. I'm not basing my success on some particular goal but rather I'm basing my actions on the possibility of one process or another being more fruitful for them. So, I never have quite the same anxiety that other people have reported having as a result of that. I experience the joy of learning—anything and everything. In some ways Dr. Erickson had that same joy, and it was his recognition of that joy in me that I think attracted him to me. It was certainly that which attracted me to him. I wonder to what extent it is my seeing that in my clients and their seeing that in me that creates a mutual inspiration and a mutually rewarding experience for those clients whom I learn the most from and who probably learn the most from me.

Most recently, my efforts to spread the influence and benefits of Dr. Erickson's work have led me to work on improving the way information flow or knowledge flow is engineered in large corporations. I have been able to see the result of this same thinking taken to the organizational level in the work I've done for large insurance companies, financial institutions, and health care companies. Ironically, what I attempt to do again and again in corporate consultation work of that caliber is not the accomplishment of specific goals. It is, rather, improving the complex processes of corporations' problem solving routines, as they try to accurately and efficiently use their resources to improve the lives of their customers, investors, and employees. So I find there is a strong parallel between (a) what individuals do in changing process to control their comfort; (b) what couples and families do to implement processes to improve their communication, experience, and love, and (c) what these corporations are able to do—all using these same principles.

The Setting for Therapy

While I travel frequently to conduct clinical training and corporate consultations, I maintain an office with a full-time office manager for my clients' convenience (and, of course, that of my colleagues who share this space). My office is inside a larger office that appears from the outside to be a cozy two-level home nestled in a wooded area. Surprisingly, it's in a very busy part of Pensacola, Florida, by a shopping mall. Many people have expressed astonishment at how it is hidden from the hurly-burly of this area. A wooden porch leads to the waiting room door. It is well appointed with couches, chairs, popular magazines. A glass window opens to the office of computers, files, printers, and so on. My office is on the second floor that is reached by climbing a turning staircase past a window revealing a charming tree that always sports a few squirrels. This office has a cute wooden balcony that I sometimes use with clients. Two walls are entirely windows. The remaining space is shared with plants, books, chairs, end tables, and a couch that reclines at various angles. My small desk is built into a nook that can barely be seen by clients. My diplomas are on the wall above the desk and can be viewed in the distance should anyone happen to glance in that direction. The ceiling is quite high and slopes upward about 20 feet on one side. It makes a perfect space for very large plants and trees that sometimes share the area with my clients. There is indirect lighting for the afternoons and a ceiling fan for the warm summer days. Now and then a client will choose to sit in a chair, perhaps due to problems with back pain—at those times I sit in one of the other chairs. However, I usually am in a red arm chair facing clients who most often sit on the couch about 3 or 4 feet away from me.

THE THERAPY FOR DONALD GREEN

The referral data in the intake interview for Don Green, contained in chapter 1 of this book, are not what I would have sought had I seen him initially. Since my goal is to empower clients as soon as possible, I avoid interactions that make me appear to be an expert with clients dependent on my expertise. Therefore, I avoid gathering extensive histories because doing so communicates to the client at a certain level a message about dependence rather than mutual involvement. That is, taking a long history communicates that if I have all of the necessary information given to me, the client can take a passive role in the therapy while I, the expert, use all of that great information to administer a cure. Finally, histories typically are oriented toward gathering information that is about what is wrong with the client. They are pathology oriented and not health oriented, and they are intellectual (about pathology) and not experiential (about health).

Instead, I prefer to follow the salient and emerging issues as the client brings them to the foreground (Lankton, & Lankton, 1998b; Lankton, Lankton, & Matthews, 1991). The combination of that strategy and a little common sense about how people live seldom fails to provide the course of action that is appropriate and sufficient for strategic therapy. Were I to have conducted the intake session, I would have involved Don in providing more experiential involvement in fewer topic areas. It also is likely that he would have left that first session with a degree of optimism based on a sense of having more resourceful experiences available and even a slightly different view of himself. Nevertheless, I'll pick up the threads from that first session and proceed as if these strategic errors, from the point of view of Ericksonian therapy, had not occurred and as if the information that was gathered during the intake had still, in fact, been shared with me by Don.

Session 1:

(On the half-hour drive to my office for this first session with Don Green, I was rehashing the things that I already knew about him and letting those pieces of information that in some way congealed or made the most sense to me emerge into the foreground of my mind. As I did, what dawned on me most was the emotional energy that Don had demonstrated in the intake and the sadness he evidenced when he wondered whether or not he would

ever be a normal person who was able to have a sexual partner and a mate.

Thinking about the importance that had for him, now that he was 42, a few other factors fell in line with regard to the motive that created the behavior—the fact that he eagerly sought evaluation such as the executive promotion test and that he asked directly whether or not the interviewer had formed an opinion of him and liked him. Another example is the memory that he reported when he resolved the conflict with both the IRS and the woman who had purchased his rebuilt automobile. In both of these cases, the lack of feedback and understanding about how he was going to be treated or experienced had been responded to with a great deal of negative fantasy in his mind. And he was willing to yield those fantasies to the reality of the interpersonal feedback. It would seem that his desire to learn more about his interpersonal behavior so that he might be able to more appropriately use it for his own purposes seems to be motivating a great deal of his behavior, including the unexpected results that he found on his vocational preference test.

It always seems to me that grasping the direction and energy and motivation of a client is essential to framing the bits and pieces of the client's behavior in an understandable way and then helping him move in harmony with that goal. While that made sense, I could only speculate about why his childhood would have left him with such a paucity of interpersonal skills and little desire to learn them. It certainly made sense that his father withdrew from him a great deal and that the lack of an admired adult male model to follow would leave him with a thirst for that sort of knowledge. But why it was of importance for him at this age and how it connected to his presenting problem of tardiness at work; those connections were so poorly answered that even speculating about them was futile. Most certainly, this would be information I would need to ferret out before I could help him put together resources that he needed in a manner that was relevant for him and solve these concerns in a framework that was relevant to his actual developmental and life stage concerns.

The other thing that plagued me about the first interview was that his tardiness had begun 3 years ago at the age of 38. He never said what the circumstances of his life happened to be 3 years ago. So as I pulled into the parking lot, I had a sense of being able to proceed in a direction of helping him gain focus on his interpersonal skills and I knew that would be relevant for him. But I didn't know how that could yet tie in with his tardiness at work. Perhaps finding out why it began 3 years ago or having a better sense of what else was going on in his life should be how we would use the session.

I arrived at the office 10 minutes before our appointment and was surprised to find him there waiting for me. As I unlocked the door to the office and disengaged the burglar alarm, I complimented Don on not only his lack of tardiness but his enthusiastic ability to be on time.)

LANKTON. I guess you found something about yourself to be valuable from the first session, so much so that you are really motivated to be here today.

GREEN. Yes, I had a lot to think about. I even stayed awake that first night wondering about whether or not I had presented myself properly and whether or not you could have a good understanding of my problem.

LANKTON. Well let's go into the office and sit down and discuss it in there in private, where we can both put our full attention on the resources that we need to move in the direction that is most valuable for you.

We walked silently for a few more moments to the office. Don sat down on the couch facing me, leaning forward with his elbows on his knees. As I sat down in the chair and picked up my notepad, I smiled at him, lifting my head up in a way that indicated I knew he was about to speak and waited for him to begin.

GREEN. Well, I kept wondering if after you thought about what I spoke of in that first session if you felt like you really could help me or, I don't know, wondered if, you know what I mean, can a person like me expect to change?

LANKTON. Don, how would it be possible that you could fail to change?

GREEN. What do you mean?

LANKTON. Well every living organism changes hundreds of thousands of things every single day. You yourself change things every day. Today, you woke up slightly differently from a dream that was slightly different from any you have ever had before. You dressed slightly differently, brushed your teeth differently, perhaps you don't even know how. There was some slight difference in the way you had your breakfast. Sometimes people don't notice these differences. They go on and they notice the similarities and think everything is the same when, in fact, there are hundreds of differences. You arrived here earlier than the scheduled appointment, even earlier than I did and that itself is something different, too. It appears that there is a great capacity for doing things different, and that you have all of those skills and actually have been using them throughout your entire life. I wouldn't be surprised if within a very short period of time you come to think of yourself in a way that's quite different from the way you've been thinking of yourself all along, and that too would be another type of change. Have you thought along those lines at all?

GREEN. I do have sometimes a lot of things I think to do or a lot of ideas, and then sometimes I don't follow through on them and I guess I'm kind of hard on myself, quite negative sometimes really about myself. A lot of times I don't know what to think about myself and I guess I just try not to. I try to avoid it.

LANKTON. Well, what are you thinking about yourself right now? We haven't really talked about that.

GREEN. Right now? I did get here early. I didn't have any trouble waking up this morning as a matter of fact, which was funny. But, um, I hadn't thought about myself really.

LANKTON. Well take a second and do that. Apply what's just occurred in the last few hours to formulating some sense of yourself and tell me what that is.

GREEN. You mean just tell you what I'm thinking about myself?

LANKTON. Yeah, right now, what you're thinking about yourself.

GREEN. Well, I'm kind of excited or happy.

LANKTON. Well, that's good, that's how you feel , but even more than that, how do you feel about feeling that way?

> *(It is valuable to help a client begin to punctuate his experience in a manner that builds desirable feelings. One way to do that is to be certain that Don makes a judgment about his experience. That insures that he has punctuated this chunk of desired experience. Once we accomplish that, Don can use the experience again and again to build both greater amounts of feeling experience and an attitude change about himself.)*

GREEN. How do I feel about feeling that way? That's a funny question to ask. I've never thought about that. I guess I feel optimistic a little bit.

LANKTON. You're optimistic?

> *(I wanted him to repeat himself and dwell on this, so I was careful about what I heard him say.)*

GREEN. Yeah, I feel kind of, um, a little proud of myself for getting up and getting here and you know following through with it because I've tried before and not done so well and so I remember that.

LANKTON. Don't detract from what you think now by telling me what you thought in the past. Stay along the lines of what you're thinking now.

GREEN. Oh, I'm proud of myself, I feel good, I guess that's it, I just feel good.

LANKTON. That's great. Close your eyes for just a second and trace down those bits of body feelings or maybe thoughts or perhaps visual memories or things you're saying to yourself, sensations, urges, the way you feel your breathing, the little smile on your face, the relaxation in your cheeks. Take a little inventory of how you experience yourself that's leading you to experience the pride that you're reporting. What is it about how you're sensing yourself that's informing your conscious mind that you have that experience of pride in yourself? Yeah, close your eyes. That's right.

(When a client is not accustomed to noticing his experience, especially, in view of another person, this first request for him to heighten awareness and increase absorption in an experience by closing his eyes is a bit of a gamble. It can derail him from his expectation about therapy or even turn him off by appearing to be a departure from what he believes ought to happen. However, hesitating to request this as soon as Don was having a novel experience would convey a message that was inappropriate as well. Why should a person wait to discover that he feels good and is confident? As I continued for the next few minutes, I was happy to see that my early attempt to get Don to participate in this way was going successfully.)

LANKTON. Now relax just a little bit more, maybe you notice your breathing, but I want to be silent and let you discover and tell me how you experience yourself, how you feel that sense and where you feel it. And it may be more than just a feeling as well. You may be having some memories. Sooner or later you will have some sense of things that you've done in the past that in some way give rise to how you experience yourself now with pride.

(Don sat quietly in front of me with his eyes closed, not speaking for several minutes. It was a length of silence that didn't seem strained but seemed quite new to Don. I was considering whether I should speak and mention that this too was something new that he was doing. I certainly wanted the silence to be concluded with

something positive and I didn't want to wait until Don possibly shifted into some negative memory to conclude the experience. While I was wondering whether or not to speak or wait a little longer, Don opened his eyes.)

GREEN. I feel like I'm breathing kind of easy and I know that sounds funny.

LANKTON. No, that doesn't sound funny at all. That's a real important thing for people to do. It's very appropriate and wonderful really that you are feeling that way.

GREEN. Yeah, I do, and I don't really ever often feel that I breathe easily I guess around other people.

LANKTON. I tell you what, Don. Something that is of interest to you has been these ideas on how the psychology of people works. I don't know if that's quite the right way to say it for you, but you know that's the impression that at least I've gotten from thinking about how you've scored high on the vocational tests for influencing people as a salesman and other similar things you've mentioned. Do you know what I mean?

GREEN. Yeah, I always have a sense that I don't know what other people are thinking and it has never been anything I understood.

LANKTON. Let me interrupt since we have that common understanding because I want to punctuate this experience that you're having right now by pointing out that there is something you would do if you knew how. And that is to take this experience of feeling good about yourself right now, and you've just memorized it a little bit, just hunted for it and highlighted it and luxuriated in it for a moment, which is something that most people actually don't do, and it's great that this opportunity arose and that you were able to do it. But in addition to that, let's do one other thing with it. And I'll tell you why in a minute.

But close your eyes again for just a second and I want you to think about some experiences that can be expected to occur to you within the next few hours and the next few days, such things as getting up in the morning in fact might come to your mind. And picture and smell and hear some of the sounds, feel some of the feelings in anticipation that you know you will encounter in the next few hours and days while you are having this experience that you enjoy right now. Because as you do make those connections, Don, you're helping your mind realize how to have these positive experiences in those future situations. You told me that you visualize the future very well, well now you can really visualize it well. That is, when you see the future, it is a terrific time to notice how comfortable you can feel. I wonder how difficult it will be for you to visualize the future and feel panic in the future now that you can visualize the future and feel comfort in the present!

(There are different ways of looking at an intervention like this. One is to see this is as a utilization and association intervention. I'm employing a talent Don has for visualizing and I'm asking him to do it while he feels positive rather than negative. If he fails at this, I will have to take a different approach with smaller steps—but if he succeeds, he is using himself rather than me to change. The change I expect him to accomplish is to be able to think about the future and associate to positive feelings rather than what he has been doing by previous habit. As he accomplishes this he begins to associate an important experience of comfort in a context where it is needed. In this way, he also accomplishes what Erickson referred to as a "reassociation of experiential life" or the successful associating of a desired experience into a context in which it has not been available. I have described this process as "self-image thinking" and use it frequently to help clients gain a sense of control over their resource feelings.)

Frequently reemphasizing his pleasant feelings, I listed a few other experiences, perhaps two or three dozen specific items that I was pretty certain Don would encounter such as steering wheels, telephones, the smell of sheets, the sound of alarm clocks, things that he had mentioned and that everyone in general is likely to encounter and reminded him as I did that those anticipated experiences could become a sort of discriminative stimulus to alert him to the fact that he has this ability and has used it and can feel some of it in those situations. When that exercise had passed, I asked Don if he knew why I was having him do that or what the point of that sort of exercise was.)

GREEN. Well you said something about how people don't usually know how to use their ideas very well or something like that, right?

LANKTON. You know you are certainly keeping your attention perfectly focused on the task at hand and on the point, Don, and that is really excellent. A lot of people don't have the wherewithal to keep the context so well in mind as you just did. That's another thing to be rather proud of. And you're quite right about what I'm getting at. A lot of people don't really realize how to use their own mind, experience, and imagination in a manner which is beneficial for them. And they make themselves uncomfortable quite often and don't recognize how they do it. And very often the opportunity to make themselves feel good is right before them and they also overlook that for lack of knowing how.

So here today you have had a perfect opportunity to hold on to the positive experiences of feeling optimistic, proud of yourself, being able to visualize yourself having that good feeling in the future, and keeping focused on the context of your goals. And now you could take a moment to absorb your attention in them and magnify them, and then you could take another moment to imagine other places in the future where you'd like to find yourself having these experiences. Those three things alone are so valuable that if you did nothing more than that for the rest of your waking days, I don't think you would ever be in my office talking to me. Are you disappointed that we've begun in this way or do you feel differently about it?

GREEN. No, I'm not disappointed at all. I kind of feel like I'm, well, kind of changing. I didn't think I'd be changing, but I've never done this before. It feels different, I mean useful and good. And that's some kind of change isn't it? So you think I really can change?

LANKTON. Well, Don, some of the concerns you had when you came in today are what we've been addressing, both explicitly and implicitly by what's unfolding right now in the office and what has been unfolding in the last half hour. I have a question or two that I would like to ask you. When I was reviewing the material that was covered in the first session, it dawned on me that you gave a great deal of detail about a number of topics that were relevant and very helpful. But one specific area that is of great interest is this pattern of sleeping in and getting to work late. It only began, as I recall, about 3 years ago, right?

GREEN. Yeah.

LANKTON. Well, can you characterize for me your best recollection of what the circumstances were surrounding the initial experiences of getting to work late?

GREEN. You mean what was happening 3 years ago?

LANKTON. Yeah, in your best recollection, your own thoughts and feelings, what was happening at work, at home, and so on, anything that might be helpful in giving me a better understanding of what may have motivated that particular change.

GREEN. Well, 3 years ago was 1996, let me think. I don't remember anything specifically. Are you asking if something happened that made me stop wanting to go to work?

LANKTON. Well certainly I want to know that if that's the case. I'm being a bit vague in asking the question the way I am so that anything at all that is relevant that comes to your mind that you haven't shared may be something you can offer.

(Don sat silently for a few moments shaking his head back and forth as if he had no idea of any incident that would be out of the ordinary from that time period. After about 20 seconds of silence, he finally offered that the only thing he could recall from that period was a change in the frequency of visitations between his supervisor and himself.)

GREEN. I do remember, about that time, maybe, there was quite a commotion at work because the supervisor was ill or someone in his family was, but the chief engineer that I reported to was gone for a month and a half, like maybe 41 days, where we didn't see him.

LANKTON. You say 41 days, which is a very specific number. Did it make a big impression on you or why do you remember it so accurately?

GREEN. Well, I just remember, because if it had been 40 days, I just remember that I missed three important reports with him on a project that was due, and we were all hoping he would come back on the 40th day after he had failed to come back on the previous possible times when we had reports due. And on that 40th day, I had one last opportunity to meet with him and get clearance on some technical specifications before the project had to be turned in, a rather big project that we had been working on for some time, and it matured without his ability to see what a good job we felt we had done on it and to give his approval and really participate as the leader of the team that had worked real hard. We had worked hard to do this, and there was kind of an absence that was quite sad I guess you might say. And he came back the following day, one day later than was necessary for the deadline on the drop dead date for that project. So that was 41 days, and it just stuck in my mind. You don't think that has anything to do with it?

LANKTON. Do you feel it's connected in any way? Is that why you brought it up?

GREEN. I don't know why it would be connected.

LANKTON. Don, tell me if you can think back more accurately now since you can remember those time periods so well, did your failure to arrive at work in a timely fashion begin following this absence of your supervisor or prior to the absence of your supervisor?

GREEN. Oh, it wasn't prior to the absence of my supervisor, Don said.

LANKTON. Why do you say that so confidently?

GREEN. Oh, well because we were all working on that project and we were there every day and late every evening . My absence definitely started after that. Yeah. In fact, not too long after that, it seems to me now.

LANKTON. Did your sleep patterns also begin to change at that time?

GREEN. I don't recall. It was sometime later that I began to be kind of alarmed and trying to set up so many ways to be awakened in the morning.

LANKTON. Before I make any other suggestions about the relationship between this incident and your supervisor's absence, could you tell me a little bit more about your relationship with your supervisor as you understood it to be at that time?

GREEN. Well, it's my chief engineer that you're talking about. I always reported to him, and his comments and feedback were always extremely valuable and helpful.

LANKTON. Well you mentioned that there came a period prior to your tardiness where the chief engineer came to be noticeably absent from the customary meetings that you had, and his feedback was something you longed for. Is that something that changed once his illness or difficulty was resolved and he finally came back to work?

GREEN. Well, no, not really. When he came back to work, it was like management had realigned some of the priorities about how supervision and evaluation was going to take place. Actually, his frequent contact with me had been a management strategy that the senior executives were moving away from. They were allowing the old frequent contact to continue as long as it had been established, but they were moving toward more of an e-mail and hands-off approach for more efficiency so that they could eventually have a greater amount of telecommuting and mobile employees. So once he came back, all of the contact that had been a carry over was just never reinstated at all.

(I was now very certain that the connection between his presenting problem of tardiness and his need for approval was related. It appears that Don has learned to be most motivated when an opportunity to be positively evaluated hangs before him like a carrot in front of the proverbial farm animal. His sense of evaluating himself and judging himself has been poorly developed, as if due to his continual desire to allow his parents to provide approval of him. It was as if he was a well-behaved boy who was

so intelligent as a child that he knew how his father ought to behave and set out to give his father the chance to change—perpetually—by continually awaiting for the praise and attention that he hoped one day might come. As a result, he had trained himself to be most sensitive to the attention from other respected male authority figures.)

I quickly balanced this view of his problem-solving style with other facts and problems presented by Don. This previously missing piece of the puzzle seemed to hold the key to interpreting almost all other information. For instance, he was no longer able to be motivated to go to work when his supervisor's continual feedback was removed; he dreamed disturbing dreams about being naked (exposed for having no direction) and having no direction or resources; he can't create a fantasy of the future that is positive if any ambiguity about how another person judges him exists (such as the incidents with the woman and incident with the IRS); his lack of feeling normal and lack of dating, of course; and, perhaps even the rejection of a barking dog has come to trigger a sense of criticism, rejection, or at least nonacceptance!

My intervention plan now became clear. As quickly as possible, Don needed to catch himself being pleased with his own conduct and come to seek his own observation of this fact as a self-reinforcing and positive thing. This actually seemed quite easy to me since he was deliberately motivated to view himself as normal, if at all possible. And too, he could feel comfortable, optimistic, and visualize fairly well. I planned on helping him build this self-reinforcement observation and feedback in as many areas related to his situation and desired change as possible: waking for work, socializing, dating behavior, weight loss, fantasizing the future, and overcoming his phobia of dogs. If Don could at first make only small changes in each of these areas, he could draw a large generalization of himself as normal. Then if he could generalize about his continual successes and feel the joy of his behavior and decisions, he could probably take the next better step and stop using that concept of normal altogether to evaluate himself. At that point he would have a new concept, if you will, to evaluate his conduct—the fact that he enjoys doing what he wishes to do.)

LANKTON. Well how did you feel about that? Was it something that you noticed at the time or only now that I'm bringing it up with you?

GREEN. Yeah, I did feel kind of a vacancy or something like I didn't really know if my work was valuable any more, and I didn't feel like my direction wasn't really on bearing as much as it had been prior to that. I guess I'm somebody who really can shoot for a goal, but I need to make sure I've got the goal in my mind correctly and don't get off course. I mean, I didn't know where I was going and I wasn't sure I had what was necessary, you know, what it took to get where I was supposed to be going, and I didn't know where I was supposed to be going. I just felt vulnerable a little bit.

LANKTON. Well, Don, remember when you spoke of a dream? Do you recall?

GREEN. Are you talking about the dream where I was naked and had no money?

LANKTON. Yeah, that's what was coming to my mind and apparently when you thought about dreams, it came to your mind as well.

GREEN. Yeah, what are you getting at?

LANKTON. Well, it seems as if you are describing a situation that is perfectly congruent with the experience that you symbolized in the dream. You say that you didn't know where you were going, you didn't know if you had the money or the resources to get there and you felt vulnerable or naked.

GREEN. Well, you're right, it certainly does sound like that, doesn't it? I hadn't really made the connection, but now that you mention it, I guess that was kind of the way that I felt at the time and what does that mean?

LANKTON. Well, it means nothing more than what it stands for. It really is kind of your unconscious way of informing you about an experience that you're living through and having or maybe one that is needing to be solved or currently being solved. So you are reporting your conscious understanding of what may have not been so obvious to you until just now.

GREEN. Well, if that's what the dream means, how does it help me to put that together?

LANKTON. Well, Don, you know the relationship between your conscious and your unconscious mind is an interesting one that psychology doesn't have all the answers to by a long shot. I'll tell you what would be interesting though is if you tell me what made sense about it for you. Do you want to try a little experiment?

GREEN. Well, what do you mean?

LANKTON. I mean, let's take this opportunity for you to close your eyes and heighten your awareness for your own sense of how you feel and what you think right now. And when you do—when you have your eyes closed and you begin to breathe comfortably and feel relaxed—you can let your mind relax as well. You can kind of memorize some of the intuitive and creative senses that you have right now so that you recognize that the things you're thinking about are coming to you along with impressions that you're getting from your body, your memory, and other things that impinge upon you, such as the ideas that we are talking about as we have this conversation.

(At this point, Don has closed his eyes and has begun to sit still.)

LANKTON. Now, if we continue along these lines, your sense of concentration for your internal experience will become very heightened and it will be like hypnosis or self-hypnosis where you use my words to put yourself in trance. Now I don't want to do that for very long now because our time is almost up for this session. But let's use this concentration that you have right now, and this awareness of the experiences that are going on in the front and the back of your mind, as a way of making a springboard to using next session for hypnosis and maybe an exploration of those very ideas and the solutions for those ideas.

If that is okay with you, just keep your eyes closed for the time being and for the next 5 minutes, let me help you become absorbed to a greater degree for the experiences you are having now. And help you imagine coming back to them with the same degree of intensity or even more in the next session by having you anticipate sitting here next week and breathing comfortably while you're remembering what we talked about the week before—that's this week—and anticipating the things you might be able to speak about and the connections you might be able to make, and the feelings and associations you may be able to have for your own betterment to better overcome with the help of your own understanding and experiences the impediments you've had to performing the way you want at work and in your social life.

(At this point, I continue to speak to Don about deepening his concentration, how that would allow us to use hypnosis in the next session, and helped him make connections in his imagination to the time that we could spend and the things that we could begin to talk about during the next session. After about another 11 minutes, our allocated time had expired and I asked him to arouse himself gradually and open his eyes. After another few moments, he looked at me and smiled as an indication that he

had completed all of the arousal that he sensed he needed to do.

I then explained to Don that I had a homework assignment that I fully intended for him to complete and spend some time reflecting on before our next visit. That in fact, I would write down in an envelope what the instructions were and that he was to make sure he was rested on Sunday afternoon and then open the envelope, read, and follow the instructions that appeared there.

The instructions were for him to attend a midnight movie, which I knew would challenge his sleeping and awakening routine. I expected several goals to be accomplished. The movie itself was about a pessimistic young man who was poorly socialized and who learned to appreciate living by meeting a vibrant woman. That it is an enjoyable movie makes it a potential place to take a date. That it was a midnight showing makes attending a movie at any other time less difficult—again increasing the ease of attending a movie with a date and having anxiety reduced on this issue. Finally, as I mentioned, the timing would become a challenge to his sleeping. It becomes a paradoxical type intervention. In essence, it says: If you are having trouble trying to get enough sleep, try getting even less sleep. But get less sleep doing so in such a way so as to gain skills that increase self-esteem rather than lower it by having sleep problems.

I told him he should keep careful track of what his reaction was and what he felt he would learn or had learned from the activity after he had completed it. He agreed with some sense of curiosity and watched me as I quickly typed out a note, sealed it in an envelope, and handed it to him. I reminded him again that Sunday afternoon he should be well rested and at that time open the envelope and follow the instructions for the homework assignment that he would find therein. He agreed and took his pen out, and wrote 'open Sunday afternoon' on the outside of the envelope. We shook hands and he departed, setting up his appointment time with the office manager as he left.)

Session 2

Don's second appointment began at the stroke of 2 o'clock 5 days from the previous appointment. He had set the schedule 5 instead of 7 days in the future due to my upcoming travel to conduct a training workshop. Don came in and sat down. He held the envelope that had contained the assignment given to him at the end of the last session. I saw that it had been opened. As I closed the door and sat down, I initiated conversation about this emergent piece of communication.

LANKTON. So I see that you opened the envelope with the assignment in it. Let me inquire of you whether or not you followed the instructions to the letter?

GREEN. Yes, I did, I opened the letter. I had relaxed almost all Sunday afternoon and around supper time I decided I better open the envelope in case what it said pertained to my late evening or my eating or something of that nature. I really didn't know what you meant by homework assignment. I kind of thought that you meant I would have something I was supposed to write down or reflect upon. I was pretty surprised to see what it said.

LANKTON. So did you follow the instructions?

GREEN. Yes. I thought for a minute perhaps that I should call you and ask if you really meant that I was supposed to go to the midnight showing of this movie. But after I read it a couple of times I realized you really did intend for me to do that and you had accurately identified where the movie was playing and apparently you clearly intended for me to see it.

LANKTON. Well, what did you think after you had attended the movie and what do you think the learning was that was supposed to come from this?

GREEN. Well, I didn't know. When I read the movie was "Harold and Maude" I thought it was maybe some kind of comedy or something and I was really surprised to find that it dealt with a sort of obsessively unhappy young lad who, as you know, kind of transformed during the course of the movie. So, when I left the movie, I was thinking that maybe you had sent me to see the movie so that I would think about how someone who was so hopeless and apparently seriously disturbed was able to change as he did simply by meeting such a remarkable person as Maude in the movie. And as I got to thinking, what you might have had in mind was that I should be hopeful.

LANKTON. What about the fact that I had you attend the midnight showing? Anything about that come to your mind?

GREEN. Well, that was curious to me because I noticed there were earlier times that it played and attending the midnight show meant that I would have to go to bed late and I already have trouble waking up in the morning. And that bothered me but I felt that it was really imperative that I do exactly what you said because you had taken such care to mention that you wanted me to attend the midnight showing and no other showing so I figured I would just set an additional alarm clock and I stopped on the way to the movie theatre and bought an additional alarm clock and set it.

LANKTON. And what happened the next morning? Were you, in fact, late?

GREEN. Well, actually, that's the curious thing. I wasn't really late for work. I woke up before my new alarm clock rang and I was kind of bewildered and confused for a moment as to why I had awakened before it rang and I kind of aroused myself from sleep to look at it more carefully and determined that it was, in fact, set for the correct time. I wondered for a minute if I had overslept and set the clock incorrectly because I hadn't heard it. But when I looked at it, it appeared that I had set it correctly and simply had awakened about 4 minutes prior to its ringing. That was on Monday and I did have trouble getting up on Tuesday and Wednesday again. In fact, it was a little worse on Wednesday. So I wasn't cured or anything, if that's what you were wondering. But I don't understand waking up on Monday at all. This doesn't happen very often. Usually, I would expect that I would have just overslept that much more, but maybe you can explain that to me. Am I supposed to stay up later? Is that what you're saying because I don't think that will work.

> (*I considered the best way to answer him. It is likely that all clients will have this question on their minds regarding assignments when the purpose for doing the activity was not clearly stated. As a result, clients will be motivated to consider the meaning of the assignment. Don, however, will be particularly motivated to understand the purpose. The assignment he was given had several purposes. At one level, it is an opportunity to build skill related to dating. At another level, it is intentionally ambiguous, which makes it a projection screen for him to help me understand how he is using therapy. I try to take a posture that will maximize the growth-oriented meaning that clients project into the assignments and have them keep the credit for the discovery.*)

LANKTON. No, Don, I want to be thoughtful about how I impart this to you. The learning that came from this that you got, that struck you, that's what I'm interested in. I want to know how this made sense to you or how you made sense of this. I would rather not say anything about what my expectations were. You know, in the same way that a person who writes a song really ought not tell you what the song or poem is supposed to mean but should let you decide for yourself what that poem means. So you tell me what you think it means and we'll go from there. Because it's your life, and your understandings, and your meanings of things which are really important here, not mine.

GREEN. Well, I'm telling you that I am a little confused about it. My guess is that I would have overslept and I didn't and that's strange.

LANKTON. Did you have any dreams that evening or the next following evenings that you can tell me about?

GREEN. Dreams... I actually forgot to think about whether I was having any dreams. Hold on a minute and let me think. Umm, I do remember dreaming something. I think it was either the night I saw that movie or the next night. It's kind of vague right now though. Let me think for a second. I don't remember the dream very clearly at all. I vaguely remember that I . . . seems like I had a dream in which I...

(Don spoke haltingly for several sentences and finally completed a sentence, saying that he thought he had an encounter or met somebody.)

LANKTON. And how do you remember feeling during the dream? Did you have this encounter that you vaguely recall with feelings that were relatively pleasant or relatively unpleasant? Could you characterize them a bit.

GREEN. I don't remember.

LANKTON. Do you, as you think back on it, remember that the dream was connected to any anxiety or not?

GREEN. Oh, I see what you mean, no I don't remember the dream being unpleasant.

LANKTON. Alright Don, what I would like to inquire about first is if you have any further ideas about what you'd like to use the session for that may be at variance with how we ended the last session.

(Don indicated that there was nothing else on his mind to discuss and that he was interested in where our last session had left off. Therefore, I promptly began an induction of hypnosis:)

LANKTON. Don, as you recall last time, you were comfortably memorizing some experiences that you had with your eyes closed, feelings of a rather positive nature, feelings that you hadn't actually expected to be having. I want you to close your eyes whenever you wish to and begin to recapture those feelings again. Your conscious mind, in trying to do that, may think back to how you sat or breathed last session. Or you may think back to how you felt in your body. Or maybe you were thinking something at the time that can be thought of again now. It may be something that you saw in your mind's eye or something that you said to yourself. It may be some memory from last time or some anticipation from last time that you can have again. There are a number of ways that your conscious mind can aid your unconscious in shifting to those experiences and reestablishing a state of concentration and absorption that you had last time—and even deeper than you did then.

While your conscious mind attempts to do that in various ways, your unconscious stimulates feelings, regulates your breathing, regulates your heart beat, changes your chemical processes and emotional experiences in a manner that you can't understand, have difficulty recognizing. It happens in such a gradual way, so gradual in fact that if I counted backwards from 20 to 1... that's right, go ahead and close your eyes all the way. You don't need to try to analyze your experience, but it would be enjoyable for you to notice it. And if I count backwards from 20 to 1, maybe you could recognize the incremental changes that take place in your experience with each count. Maybe you can't. But you may be able to realize that by the time I reach 1, you've more than accomplished the degree of concentration on those feelings that you had last time. More than accomplished those and begun to apply them in ways that your unconscious mind can calculate and reason to be in a beneficial fashion for your own betterment.

> *(Now I continued counting backwards and helping Don establish a moderate to deep trance state for the next 12 to 15 minutes. He had been quite immobile for the last several minutes and exhibited typical signs of trance activity including involuntary muscle fasciculation, increased skin pallor, muscular lassitude, reduced pulse in the visible arteries of the neck, slowed breathing, and so on. While creating the induction, I had an opportunity to make many comments that directed Don to how the trance would become relevant for his session today and I made several allusions to the fact that there were two important manners in which he would be having personal growth during the trance. One of these was, of course, the presenting problem of reducing and eliminating his tardiness, and the other was more vaguely referred to as his opportunity for developing himself so he could date and have*

a social life. Since Don had discussed both these issues with me consciously and explicitly, there was no reason to disguise the intent of any of the suggestions for the sake of protecting his self-esteem. And no attempt was made to soften the impact of any of the words relating to either of these topics.

These were the things I was thinking I would address in the session and I intended as I got further into the trance of this session to deal with a third topic, which had not been explicitly outlined in our discussion, but rather had only been implicitly discussed, and that is Don's desire to reduce his strong reliance on the approval of other people. This particular item was related to both his social and dating development, as well as his ability to reduce the presenting problem of tardiness. Helping Don understand the logic of the connection behind both of those presenting difficulties to this psychological dynamic was not within the scope of the therapy.

Don had not requested a course in psychology so that he could make the connections. But rather, he realistically wanted to have a solution provided in the shortest possible time and in the most palatable manner. For that reason, I chose to address this particular topic metaphorically and with indirect suggestion until such a time as Don either came to understand consciously this same topic in such a way that we could share openly or I could assess from his reaction the relevance of it and address it openly in the waking state. These were my intentions as I proceeded with the trance.)

LANKTON. I know that your conscious mind is able to experience your own state of excitement about your changing, your comfort, and confidence as you sit there. I know that your conscious mind has an opportunity to reflect upon the surprise that you might have experiencing those feelings. I know that your conscious mind has the ability to even entertain other thoughts for comparison and contrast, for paying attention to the sound of my voice, for anticipating and remembering. And sometimes you have the ability to become so lost in the ideas that you're formulating, or so lost in the meaning that comes to you when I speak, or sometimes so lost in the silence of the space between my words that you don't particularly recall what it is you were thinking about or noticing. And all you can do is rely upon your unconscious sense of security and confidence, and the pride in the fact that change is occurring as you sit there. But change is not occurring without your active participation. And that may be funny—to speak about active participation while you're so immobile on the couch. But you know you are actively experiencing one thing and then the other. And if I told a story about a client that I knew, you would actively experience an understanding of the feelings of the person in the story to the extent that they are relevant for you.

(In the preceding paragraph, I am preparing Don for the introduction of various illustrative stories about other clients and am instructing him as to his response. That is, I am making it clear that there is no one or correct meaning to these stories but that he can make understanding that will be relevant to him. This indirect style of stimulating thinking and focusing awareness, which evokes rather than guides imagery, is referred to as therapeutic or goal-oriented metaphor. It is a style of communicating with clients that was popularized by Erickson. At one level, it is just a story and at another level the client is free to interpret any meaning and develop various experiences as he identifies with characters in the story. Metaphorical communication can often create a "face-saving" learning context in which the client can sort of "eavesdrop" on learnings another client had without ever having to directly acknowledge or admit to similar ignorance or embarrassment.)

LANKTON. So, Don, modify the things that I say so they fit for you as a person, and feel perfectly free to change the meaning of what I say so that you can, Don, discover the lack of need to evaluate yourself in the eyes of others and increasingly become confident that the choices you want to make with respect to sharing joy and confidence is normal and rewarding for you. You recently went to a movie and there were a lot of things you thought about and learned from yourself as you saw the movie.

Recently I saw a client who was not really unlike the young man in that movie. He was a young man who suffered from not having been able to spend intimate time with his parents. Sometimes a person has difficulty appreciating his true value when he has longed for and failed to receive the appreciation of his parents and significant people in his life. This client whom I saw had never really experienced a father. He came to feel that his mother appreciated him, possibly because she spent more time with him or possibly because she was younger than the father. And yet, while clinging to the thought that his mother was without reproach, the young man failed to appreciate how the mother had repeatedly attempted to get him out of the house, send him off with his older brothers.

The client had come to see me due to his fears and his difficulties about dealing with other people. I will refer to him as Frank. When Frank first sat in the chair to see me, he felt that there must be something terribly wrong with him, that he was unable to perform some of the simplest tasks that other people performed. Frank was a carpenter and he envied the way other carpenters performed the simple task of pounding nails straight into the 2 by 4s as they built the houses. He knew that as long as he got the job done, he earned his money. He worked hard and he would even work late if necessary and he would have a job. But he was embarrassed that he couldn't simply pound his nails in straight like everyone else. And he didn't want to tell anyone he worked with because even the youngest of the carpenters was able to do this.

His degree of embarrassment about this was so great that he had had odd dreams about it. He had even begun to do a great deal of avoiding and had gotten quite good over the years at sawing lumber with precision, and he did most of the sawing. He was sad when they had run out of lumber to saw because it generally meant he would have to return to concentrating on pounding in the nails straight. Frank went into trance when we began to work together and in the trance I asked him to think back to times in his life when he could look someone in the eye. Maybe in third grade sitting across the table from a young girl, looking her straight in the eye and beginning to smile and realize the innocence and honesty of childhood. Eight years old, nobody trying to prove anything to anyone else, just two children honestly looking at one another and attempting to be friends.

You look at someone and your pupils dilate. Your unconscious doesn't know how it begins to happen that your sphincters relax, warm blood flow rushes to the surface of the body in the tender organs, salivation begins to occur and you have to swallow and you have to swallow because salivation occurs. And your conscious mind doesn't realize that salivation is simply a way that Frank is beginning to realize his comfort around little girls and eventually his comfort around teenagers and young women. And someday when he grows up, comfort around his wife. But you don't really realize that when you are 8 years old and you're just sitting there relaxed, breathing comfortably, pupils dilated, salivation occurring, blood flowing to the tender organs of the body.

And that rush of warmth makes a relaxation and a pleasure, a pleasure that you need to realize. And how do you memorize your own pleasure? You might notice that your breathing is changed, your heart rate has changed. You might notice that there is a warmth in your muscles. And in that warmth, a certain degree of excitement and comfort. You don't need to do anything with it at all except memorize it and appreciate it and know that it's okay for you to have it. Frank never had closeness with his father or really much closeness with his mother. He never had a situation in which he was able to sit comfortably and have someone explain to him that it was alright to have those experiences and memorize them and apply them in a manner that would bring him a great deal of joy as an adult.

If you don't understand exactly what I mean, Don, picture yourself as a young boy about 8 years old, out in front of us somewhere in the room as if you are detached and seeing him in words and pictures only. And see that young man in words and pictures only standing in front of us while you know that you are sitting on the couch observing from a distance and hearing the sound of my voice in a different year. And in some ways, it might be like you are in two places at once knowing what he knows, even beginning to think more and more like he thinks, having the thoughts that you, he have, has had, but still hearing me and having the thoughts that you have and will have one day. And watching and hearing young Don out in front, focus your attention carefully as the background around him changes. Watch him sitting in a scene that never happened that you might remember now, a scene where he was sitting at the lunch table at school across from a young girl that he had always thought was cute.

> *(The key to using hypnosis to construct an as-if true reality hinges on having an understanding that is suitable to both the conscious and unconscious monitors of experience. The phrase "that never happened that you can remember," is an important suggestion for accomplishing that state. On the one hand, the phrase "that never happened" appeases the mind's sense of truth and reality while the phrase "that you can remember" now provides a sort of permission to pretend and experience despite the understanding that it is not a true memory. Participating in this way Don can maintain the integrity of his personal experience and still play along with a sense of conviction.)*

LANKTON. And watch him in complete comfort in that scene that never happened that you can begin to remember fully now as he interacted with that young girl, laughing, smiling, looking at her, looking at each other eye to eye and breaking into laughter. And listen to them laugh, watching each other, enjoying each other's company with comfort, realizing without hearing their actual words how their conversation reflects their mutual interests, their happiness in each other's company. And watching again, hearing them laugh, as a person might observing two children at play from a distance. And while you watch that scene continue to unfold, with or without sound, and begin to remember how it occurred even though it never happened. From your wise perspective almost 40 years later, it's alright to make some judgments about what you see and maybe even imagine how you could express those judgments to him. You're comfortable, you're enjoying the situation and finding it pleasant. I can tell from the way you're sitting there observing it.

Imagine a conversation between yourself and 8–year-old Don that goes something along the lines of how you've been watching him and you're proud of his comfort and the fun that he has. It's enjoyable to remember and to watch him and you are very pleased to realize what a normal young man he is as he does that. And how you hope that the memory of this event that never happened that you can remember completely now stays with you until you grow up and turn 40 and think back upon this situation with pleasure. And now let the background change again so that you can observe Don again at 11 years of age in a similar scene that never happened that you can begin to remember until you completely remember it, how he was walking in the park on a field trip and managed to change the pace of his walking until he just managed to be walking by purposeful accident next to the young girl that he had always thought was sort of cute in the sixth grade. And notice from your comfortable position of observing him in this scene that never happened that you're beginning to completely remember how Don had a little bit of awkwardness as sometimes the thought occurred to him that he kind of liked her because she was a girl, not just because she was a nice person. And that he would enjoy finding a way to ask her if it would be okay to go to the dance on Friday night.

And while you observe the two of them walking side by side and talking with words that you may not quite hear from your distance, you might notice yourself thinking the thoughts about how you are pleased that Don had the courage to ask her to go to the dance. You're happy when you think back on it that you had these feelings to do these things. And let the scene change to observe that Don in sixth grade going to the school dance. I don't know if they walked there or if they got a ride from his parents or her parents, a friend's parents, whether they took the bus or rode on bicycles. It doesn't matter. Just remember the dance you saw that never happened that you're beginning to completely remember, how he stood around the punch bowl, and how they sat in chairs and looked at the others, and how they listened to the music together, and how time passed until finally Don had his courage about him and he asked her to dance and together they stood up. Notice how he puts his arm around her waist and how he holds her hand in his and begins to move back and forth in rhythm with the music just like you'd expect an 11–year-old to do, trying to act so grown up, so comfortable. And he really wasn't that uncomfortable.

In fact, if you'd like to remember even more how it feels and how it felt, just for a moment hang on to the sound of my voice while you sit here and listen to me, and imagine that you step into that picture. Merge with that Don in the picture and remember how it feels to have that arm around her waist and the little bit of heat that you feel and the fabric of her skirt on your arm and feeling her hand in yours and sometimes feeling her hair brush against your face as you sometimes dance a slow dance a little bit close. And feel the rhythm of that movement and the sound of that music. And try really hard to remember her name. It's been so long but do let yourself have the feeling and the thoughts of your own enjoyment as you relive that scene that never happened that you're beginning to completely remember. And take a few moments to enjoy that dancing.

> *(In a similar fashion, I asked Don to consider his interactions with increasingly older girls and eventually young women so that he spent the majority of 45 minutes in trance being instructed to imagine situations that never occurred but that he could remember. He seemed comfortable with that sort of paradox, and since the material was taken by Don to be relevant to his purposes for growth and learning, he showed no sign of objection to the apparent learning that he was having, even though he may not have been able to explain what relevance and what learning there was specifically, he most certainly had an intuitive sense that he was putting together experiences and understandings that he longed*

for and needed. Finally I concluded this particular section of the hypnosis treatment in the following way:)

LANKTON. And now, Don, let the background change one last time for the Don that you've been observing and move your understanding and memory of events that never happened back to a more recent time in Don's life, a Don who is 40-years old and comfortably watch how Don approaches one of the women that he's seen at work, at the Christmas party, and explains to her that he's happy to have had a chance to get together. And you can continue to remember the situation and have the experiences that you remember though the event never happened so that your unconscious can be satisfied that having the experiences in this manner is perfectly comfortable and fully available to you to have in reality in the future in the proper settings at your own discretion.

And as I was saying, comfortably listen to the manner in which Don approaches the woman and perhaps leans against the table, smiles, makes eye contact, feels the warmth in his body as he acknowledges her eye contact and smiles back. And reaches out and touches her elbow, uses her name, and completes sentences that convey that he's seen her at work and always wanted to have a chance to socialize with her, meet her, and talk to her, that he's glad to be able to be at the party with her like this. Ask her where she's from and how long she's worked at the company, and other bits of information that he couldn't know but would show his genuine interest in her. And watch 10 or 12 minutes of conversation pass, from time to time both of them smiling, laughing, showing interest. And maybe you can't fully hear all of the words he's speaking, but maybe you could have a sense of how you can remember the scene that never happened with comfort and surprise to notice you are happy watching Don do this. And once again, make that judgment from your position here in the future and imagine speaking to that part of your self from the past and saying "I really am proud about the way you comfortably interacted with that woman and the way that you asked for her phone number so that you could contact her and spend some time outside the party on the weekend going to a movie or going to a picnic." And then watch the scene continue to unfold as Don at the party asks for her phone number, asks if it would be alright to call her and set up a time where you could go to a picnic or a movie and dinner. And after you watch that scene unfold completely, watch how they continue to walk around and spend a little bit more time with each other at the party and perhaps eventually say goodnight to each other and each leave. And I doubt that I have to tell someone like you who has already thought about it so much, when a person asks someone for a date, he simply looks her in the eye and smiles.

Feel that warm rush of relaxation and perhaps your unconscious mind doesn't even notice it as you formulate the words "How would you like to see a movie? I just saw a movie that was really enjoyable and entertaining. If you haven't seen it, let's go see it. Maybe the midnight showing would be fun. We could have dinner first and then go see the midnight show." But if that's too late it's always easier to ask someone to go on a date to an earlier showing of a movie. And it's always so appropriate to ask a person to go to dinner before a movie—dinner and a movie. "How about dinner and a movie? I just saw a great movie." But I don't have to tell someone like you that. I'm sure you've thought of that yourself. And right now, you're listening, you're relaxed, comfortable, you're breathing nicely and smoothly, The pausing between my words probably gives you ample time to appreciate how comfortable you are and I'm speaking comfortably. So you know what it's like for someone to be comfortable while someone speaks comfortably. And you know how to speak comfortably when someone says, "how about dinner and a movie? I know a good movie we could see. I'll pick you up at 7:30 and we'll go to dinner." And you're hearing those words right now. The conscious mind may not have realized prior to this how comfortable you could be while you heard those words being said and think about what they mean. But you are comfortable. I wonder if your conscious mind is surprised to realize how comfortable you are imagining those words being said and hearing those words, just being comfortable.

> *(So Don has been able to acquire behavioral and experiential details of socializing that his unique history had failed to map for him. His conscious mind hasn't even been alarmed by any mention of his having to learn these skills for a reason. He has simply been asked to "remember" what it's like even though he has not known. The last segment involving a current age scenario begins to border on more official self-image thinking about how he would like to handle the kinds of situations he has been yearning for but avoiding due to awkwardness and fear.)*

LANKTON. So I'm going to count forward from 1 to 20. And as I do I'd like you to rehearse in your mind all the things we've been speaking about and you've been listening to me talk about. You've been thinking about and you've been feeling. And rehearse them so that you can imagine times in the next few days and in the next few weeks the things that you might happen to notice and say and think or smell or see, can be cues to your conscious mind to recognize how you have all of these experiences and ideas and you're implementing them almost automatically and comfortably. And, of course, it is alright for you to be surprised or for you to be delighted to find out just how comfortable you are and just how clever you've been at the implementation. 1, 2, 3, 4, and you don't really need to remember all of the words that I said, 5. It's enough to remember that you felt your own reaction and heard your own self talk and made pictures of your own, 6, 7, even if you don't remember what that talk was. 8, 9, or what those pictures were, 10.

And halfway back, or even if you have a sense that you've forgotten everything that I said or that you thought or experienced, 11, 12, 13, 14, because those are building blocks and every child learns to walk gradually, one foot at a time, shifting his weight, straightening up his hips, releasing what he's been holding on to until he holds his chest up, moves his feet, shifts his weight, moves his other foot, shifts his weight and moves his other foot. Without even thinking about it, you're beginning to walk and you've learned so very much in the process of learning to walk and button your buttons, and learn the letters of the alphabet and the numbers, and learn how to multiply and to add, 15, 16, 17, but usually we don't think about how much we've learned. But you really should because you've done such a wonderful job of it that it's nice to compliment yourself. And I hope that in the next few, 18, days and even in the next few hours, you compliment yourself in ways that I haven't even begun to discuss with you. Compliment yourself on getting to work on time. Compliment yourself on decreasing the number of alarms you set. Compliment yourself on not alarming yourself any more about being out of time, out of sync, too late in your development, too late in your awakening. Don't be alarmed about being so late. Compliment yourself on how you've closed the gap. Compliment yourself on progress that you're making and the fun that you're having, 19. And compliment yourself in ways that bring a smile to your face and increase the likelihood that you will act, Don, upon the things that you've heard and thought about and experienced and anticipated. And 20, open your eyes. Hi, how are you?

(Don jerked his eyes open as if he'd been in such deep concentration that he was unlikely to remember what had been said to him during the last 20, 30, or 40 minutes.)

GREEN. Wow, I felt really good about that.

LANKTON. About what specifically?

GREEN. About what you were saying.

LANKTON. You felt really good about what I was saying about what specifically?

GREEN. Um, I can't remember exactly what you were saying. I felt good about it, though. You know, I'm not sure what it was that you said specifically, not sure what I felt good about specifically, but I did feel good. And I feel good now, actually.

LANKTON. And you're going to feel good a lot more. And as you are leaving, there's something that I want you to do that I think is a very important piece of homework for you. Here in the city there is a restaurant called 'Magic Moments.' Have you ever been there?

GREEN. No.

LANKTON. Well, here is what I want you to do. On two occasions, I want you to go to Magic Moments Restaurant before I see you again and each time you're there I want you to order two items off of their menu and eat both items. Then I would like you to write me a little bit of an essay so that I can better assess your ability at judgment and writing and expressing yourself about the things that you feel and like. It can be less than a page for each visit on which of the items you liked the best.

GREEN. Just order anything?

LANKTON. That's right, but it must be The Magic Moments Restaurant and it must be two times with two items each.

GREEN. Okay. Sure, I'll do that, just any two nights?

LANKTON. Yes, make it two separate nights. Don't go twice the same night.

GREEN. Alright.

(Don left, totally willing to follow the directions, not knowing that Magic Moments Restaurant features desserts only. I assumed that the trip to the restaurant would accomplish several goals. The slight embarrassment he might feel by ordering two desserts should be very tolerable. But, as a result, he will have still more experience at an activity that could be date-worthy at a later time. Since I'm placing the focus on his writing and expression skills,

Don won't spend his time thinking about how bad a job he would do on a date to this restaurant—rather, he can't really fail at this task. Going to a dessert restaurant will be associated with success (not to mention the pleasure of the food). The assignment will also pertain to the important goal of helping him shift from doing what others judge appropriate to what Don judges to be enjoyable for him! The writing will record this attitude process in time—it will be an indisputable memory for his conscious mind.)

Session 3

Don was sitting in my office when I arrived for our third session. He was dressed more casually than usual. He had gotten a haircut and he eagerly greeted me with eye contact and a smile as I came through the door and greeted him. As we walked to my office, Don spoke.

GREEN. You're never going to believe what happened during the last week.

As we sat down Don began to explain that during the past week there had only been one time when he'd failed to wake up before the alarms rang. He had promptly taken a shower, brushed his teeth, put on his clothes that he had often laid out the night before, and gotten to work on time.

GREEN. This is just amazing. I find it hard to believe that I'm getting to work on time because I'm not exactly sure why I'm doing that.

LANKTON. Don, you might say that you're not being alarmed as much as you had been.

(I was happy to find a manner of reducing the pathological aspect of his tardiness and also introduce this as a problem that was now in the past—it is described with past tense verbs. If he accepts the presupposition that it is past tense, he takes a mental step to dissociate his self-image from it.)

GREEN. Right, I guess I'm not as alarmed as I was before.

LANKTON. Are there any other significant developments that you should be telling me about, because in addition to getting yourself to work in a prompt manner, there is really a much more important and pervasive dilemma that you want to solve and that I want you to solve as well.

GREEN. Dating?

LANKTON. In a word, that would summarize it. Why do you say that?

GREEN. Well, it's just that I feel I have been such a late bloomer and that has been on my mind.

LANKTON. Well, Don, that kind of brings me to something that I wanted to ask you about. Did you complete the homework that I gave you at the end of the last session?

GREEN. Yes, I did and I have the things that you wanted me to write right here. But you know, while I was there I realized that they only have desserts on that menu. Did you know that?

LANKTON. Well actually I did know that, yes.

GREEN. Well, the second time I was there I ordered one of the desserts from the first time I was there, the pecan pie because I really liked it the best, so I only ordered three things out of the two times. Is that okay?

LANKTON. Yes, that is perfectly alright. I wanted to read what you had said and your ability to express yourself about these things. You have written beautifully! Just beautifully! I had no idea. You could teach someone quite a bit with your ability to articulate your feelings so well. I could learn a lot from you in this area. You express yourself and your judgments very convincingly. It appears from this that you enjoyed the apple crêpe the best. You really could recommend that to someone with confidence! Beyond the writing assignment, did you think that I had sent you there for any other purpose? Did you have any idea about that?

> *(I knew that I was reinforcing his judgment and expression of his perceptions—I did it with enthusiasm the way a parent should do with a child many times over the years. Fortunately, he had truly done well and it was easy to lavish praise. The outcome to the assignment allowed me to also switch from that role and express my ability to learn from him, In a symbolic manner in this transaction, the authority figure (me) relinquishes the role allowing the child (Don) to be an equal or superior. It is important to be certain that clients are led to notice these changes so the experiences are chunked and symbolized. Then learning takes place at cognitive as well as experiential levels and conscious as well as unconscious levels. But this learning is not merely listening to an interpretation from an outsider (the therapist) but from within one's own head, so to speak. Don is learning from himself and not from me. Therapy is client centered in a profound way, and the client keeps all the credit for his learning and insights. The insights come from within—they really are insights.)*

GREEN. Well, I thought that maybe you wanted me to be able to talk knowledgeably about desserts because it's the kind of thing that, in a way, a person would do if they were on a date with someone.

LANKTON. Oh, that's an excellent idea, Don. So you've been thinking about dating someone and taking them to this place for desserts. Is that what you're telling me?

GREEN. Well, it did occur to me. Isn't that what you had in mind?

LANKTON. You know, Don, sometimes I don't even appreciate what I have in mind about things, and I think the most important thing is what you've had in mind. Who were you thinking about taking to this dessert bar?

GREEN. Well, why do you think that I was thinking of taking someone?

LANKTON. I wasn't certain that you were at the moment that I said that, but you've taken such a long pause to answer me I'm very convinced that you were thinking about someone. Do you mind telling me who it was?

GREEN. Well, actually, there is a woman named Sherry who I work with who I had thought was kind of attractive and I thought maybe she might date me. She's not been married before and she's 36 years old. I don't know why she hasn't been married.

LANKTON. Why hasn't she been married? (I added humorously) I suppose you could tell her it's because she's been waiting for you to come along.

(Don chuckled and blushed and said he thinks it would be a very long time before he could say something like that to a woman. At that point, Don exhaled very slowly, not deliberately so much as cautiously. He exhaled for several seconds and a sort of reflective look fell across his eyes and forehead. Just as he focused back on me in the chair, I began to offer suggestions.)

LANKTON. Close your eyes, Don. I know that your conscious mind is reflecting upon what you just said and has some doubt. It's always easy for a person to take refuge in an explanation that had once worked for them. It's always easy for a person who's overweight to think that they'll exercise later once they lose weight. It's always easier for a freshman college student to think "I'll continue to attend that class and stop skipping it after I've caught up on my reading in that class." It's always easier for a person who's self-employed to think that they'll keep taking out of their monthly income the amount of taxes that they need to pay once they catch up on their taxes. But you have that doubt, that doubt that maybe what you were thinking in the way of an excuse, really didn't suit you and feel correct to you. It's as if your conscious mind senses a bit of a conflict between the Don Green who intends to stop being so alarmed about arrested development and actually implement the behavior that you will use to solve your problem. And the old concept that you used to have about yourself that explained why you hadn't at that time already begun to change as you have now.

So while you have your eyes closed, I want you to think about how good it feels to realize that you have now begun to change, 20, 19, 18, and just becoming more absorbed in the experience of thinking about how you have begun to change. 17, 16, 15, and becoming more relaxed and more deeply concentrated on the pleasure of knowing that you actually have gotten to work on time, that you actually awoke on time, that you didn't alarm yourself nearly as much this week, 14, 13, 12. That somehow or other, your experience of yourself has been blossoming, and you have been realizing in a conscious way the changes that you've been undertaking unconsciously, 11,10, 9, and while you've been blossoming in these ways, a number of thoughts have occurred to you that normally you try to inhibit, thoughts about Sherry, thoughts about how you know how to go on a date, to a movie, to dinner, to a place where desserts can be purchased, thoughts about the possibility that you misunderstood yourself in the past and that in reassessing yourself now, you're becoming increasingly pleased.

Follow that sense of being pleased with yourself, Don. Being pleased with yourself is a feeling, a concept, a sensation, an anticipation, and a memory. I don't know which way you'll begin to experience it or which way you've already begun to recognize that feeling, Don. I can tell from the relaxation in your body and the smile on your face 8, 7, 6, 5, that there are a number of ways in which you do have that feeling now. 4, 3, 2, 1. While you're having that feeling, take a moment to memorize it. It's a precious gift. You are so fortunate to have it, and some of my clients never have an opportunity to demonstrate to their parents just how fortunate they are. A lot of times children wait until their parent recognizes their own worth before they exude the sense of pride and worth that they have. And in waiting like that, they sometimes manufacture psychological mechanisms of a very subtle type, mechanisms that make it possible for them to arrest their own development and later become alarmed about that.

It's a shame that young Don Green never had an opportunity

to show his father what an amazing young man he was. It's a shame that his father was willing to deprive himself of realizing what an amazing person you are. So extremely quick at learning, that in a single visit to The Magic Moments Restaurant, you applied that situation to something that's been important to you. And you've been thinking about dating. And immediately your unconscious helped you to recognize that you could take a woman there. I had a client one time, and I suggested to him that when he asked a woman for a date, I would not charge him for the next session. Whether he succeeded or failed in securing a date with that woman, I would not charge him for the session as long as he had taken the steps to ask her. And the reason was because the reward that I get from watching a person inspire me with that kind of courage is worth more than the financial gain of the session itself.

I know that you'll have a lot of ideas that you think are your very own when I arouse you from the trance because you don't remember the things that I'm saying right now the way that I intend for you to remember them. It's because you're thinking of so many other things that are relevant to you and important. And that's perfectly okay and wonderful. I think it's enough that you just feel very comfortable and proud of yourself for the effort that you are putting out to change the habitual pattern that you've learned and even realized that in many ways you've learned from childhood. You came to me saying that you wanted to find out how you ticked and the way you ticked and why you ticked, make these changes, and you now have discovered the very things that make you tick. But now you're ticking with a sense of pride and confidence and an understanding that so many clients get that they modify their own conduct to be increasingly pleasing to their parents as a child, only to find that that modification doesn't ever really secure the acceptance of the parents or make the parents happy. So the time was entirely wasted. But wisely.

So appreciate yourself for your own wisdom and begin to stop, continue to stop, anticipate what stopping is like, and stop thinking that eventually you'll please your father and secure the blessings of your father. And tell that young Don that you accept and understand what he is trying to accomplish. Neurons in your own brain, Don, as you sit there on the couch relaxed, solve problems according to the way you understood them in childhood. And they are amenable to change even now while you are in adulthood. And you can change the neural functioning and patterns of brain operation that set you on a course of hesitating and waiting. But let's not talk about that anymore.

(At this point, I begin giving Don very specific suggestions to visualize himself handling upcoming dating challenges in a manner that reflects his comfort, pride, confidence, and relaxation. He has displayed a readiness for therapy to take this turn by relaying an interest in and desire to date a particular woman he has identified. This is a self-image thinking process in which likely scenarios are "directed" in an indirect, speculative manner, detailing possible soundtrack and various occurrences. He is not "remembering" hypothetical scenes from the recent past, he is anticipating possible scenes from the immediate future.)

LANKTON. Visualize Sherry in front of you and visualize Don at work talking to Sherry, maybe at the colloquial water cooler or maybe at the next staff get-together, or maybe something sooner like making certain that you accidentally encounter her as you check in the daytime through security or time clocks or pass as you leave the building. That would be a good idea, passing on the way out as you leave the building so you can say "Hi, Sherry, you know what, I discovered something that I didn't know existed in this city, the Magic Moments Restaurant." And imagine yourself comfortable like you are now, proud of your self confidence as you are now, suggesting to Sherry that the two of you go directly to the Magic Moments Restaurant. Or if she thinks that's the kind of thing that should follow dinner, you'd like to suggest that the two of you go to dinner and then go to The Magic Moments Restaurant. And just listen to that dialogue unfold while you have those feelings now.

(I waited quietly while that conversation unfolded in Don's mind. I said nothing while I observed his behavior, which seemed to be very confident and proud of himself as he proceeded. While I watched Don sit there on this course of thought, I reflected back on the gains that he had made in terms of getting to work on time, going on the assignments to movies and restaurants, voluntarily suggesting to me that he was thinking of Sherry, making and accepting the change in himself that had to do with getting to work on time. I realized that the possibility that Don would be terminating soon might hinge on the singular experience of succeeding in a date with an understanding that he would need to date more, that this date would not be the only date that he would have, and so on. But by terminating at this point with these

successes behind him, the door for returning was always open and the sense of autonomy was greatly increased.

So, I thought through what other experiences Don might need to draw from his past to ask any woman for a date—and follow through for the date, and do so in a way that he evaluated as successful. It would be successful if he could realize his ordinary experiences could be accessed, drawn together, associated with those events of dating. I knew he could do a great job of rehearsing visually and I could help him do so in a fashion that would be like posthypnotic suggestion.

To do that, I tried to place myself in Don's shoes and tried to feel like Don had portrayed himself in the last 4 weeks. And then, once having a sense of those feelings, I drew from that experience the sorts of things that would be necessary for me to continue to feel and do to make the change in the direction of dating. The entire mental exercise only takes a few moments for me. After several moments of Don completing the fantasy exercise that I had casually assigned for him in this state of concentration and trance, I spoke again. I tried to speak of the understanding that I had gained from this final bit of identification of his experience.)

LANKTON. Don, I would like to see you next week and find out how you went about having that date and recognizing your capacity and skill for doing that sort of thing repeatedly until you succeed as fully as you wish. And to cheer you on in that endeavor that you have initiated, I want to suggest to you that I won't charge you for next week's session if you come to me and explain to me how you asked Sherry for a date. If that would be alright with you, you don't need to arouse yourself from the trance. You can just nod your head and as you nod your head, begin to picture yourself with comfort and confidence and hear and see yourself in front of you while you sit there in confidence and comfort, approaching Sherry at work or as you leave work or come in to work or in the parking lot or wherever you might think that could occur. And listen to the things that you'll hear yourself saying to her in the next couple of days to create that situation.

(As Don became increasingly less expressive in the interpersonal field, I observed that he became increasingly more expressive in his imagination. His eyebrows changed. His eye movement altered as if he was focusing on someone in front of him and so on. I gave him about 5 minutes of silence to complete what he was thinking about.

The number of times I had been silent during the hour had created a fairly large gap of time and there was now only about 15 minutes of time remaining before I would have to terminate this session with Don and see my next client. As Don aroused from the trance I reminded him that a thought had occurred to me regarding someone whose fee for a session was completely waived on condition that the client perform a complex homework assignment, and in his case, I thought it would be a good idea if a similar thing was done. As I spoke in this vague general way, referencing the homework assignment of dating which I had already mentioned to Don in the trance, Don nodded his head in an understanding, slow, gradual yes type nod. This gave me confidence to know that Don already anticipated and accepted the offer I was about to make. So I continued with confidence that he was anticipating it with some pleasure.)

LANKTON. So, Don, what I'd like to do is suggest that you have the same sort of arrangement with me as that client did. And in particular, I'd like to offer you the enticement and reward of paying no fee for next session on condition that you ask Sherry for a date. Whether or not she accepts or declines, I'll see you next week without fee. And if you are willing to do that, that's probably a topic that we can discuss when you come. Any questions?

(Don said that he wasn't certain that he was willing to make such an arrangement right at the moment. He'd like to think about it and if he felt confident about it after thinking about it, then he would do so. I suggested he might want to do so based on more than just feelings of confidence because feelings of confidence when you're actually asking somebody for a date are far greater than your imagination of your feelings of confidence prior to asking the person for a date. He said he didn't know that and thought it would have been the other way around. I assured him that the imagination for something that you haven't done before is always potentially misleading and that when he actually stands in front of her, his sense of confidence and his sense of relaxation and joy would be something he would notice and probably be surprised about.

As I said that, I knew perfectly well that I was presupposing that he would accomplish the task and watching his head nods shaking a slow yes led me to believe that he was responding favorably to the presupposition and would in fact carry out the assignment. So with that, I shook his hand and continued.)

LANKTON. You're really doing good work here and I look forward to hearing your report about the date and your further reports about how you're accomplishing getting to work on time. I think that's just wonderful and we're not going to have to have too many more sessions probably before you're fully satisfied with everything you came to accomplish and even more.

GREEN. I hope so. See you next week.

Session 4

Don showed up for our next session on time with a small, brown, thin paper sack with him.

GREEN. I guess I have something to show you.

He reached for the sack and removed the playbill for a local theatre production of a play called "Tommy."

LANKTON. What's the playbill for? Are you planning on attending?

GREEN. No, I did attend. I asked the woman at work if she would be busy on Friday night because I wanted to go see "Tommy" and I would really like the pleasure of her company.

LANKTON. Well, that's amazing. Tell me exactly what you said to her and exactly what she said to you. Don't leave out any details.

GREEN. Well, I planned on asking her and then I planned on not asking her and then I planned on asking her and I went back and forth about 30 times in my head for the 1st hour after leaving the office and then I got involved at work and forgot all about it until I went to the break room to get some coffee. Then it suddenly dawned on me that this was something that I had wanted to do and something you had suggested that I do and that's what I'm trying to do here in therapy. So I knew I should do it and wanted to do it so I started planning on just how I'd meet her at the cafeteria. And I got to thinking over and over about the things that I might say. I was pretty certain I would do it on Tuesday because that was a day people are settled in for the week and have gotten past all their busyness in Monday. But it was so far in advance that I might be able to give her advance notice if she had the possibility of having some other plans. So I rehearsed it over in my head about a hundred times on Monday night.

On Tuesday morning when I saw her go into the coffee room,

and I got so nervous that I waited so long that when I finally went into the coffee room she was in a conversation with someone else and all I had time to do was say "Hi" to them as I passed by. I felt so foolish that I didn't say anything else to her for that whole day. So that was Tuesday night. I had rehearsed what I would say to her over and over and I felt so silly. I felt like I was back in junior high school or something and I got to thinking about our sessions here and somehow I realized that talking to her really wasn't the kind of thing that I should be so nervous about. This was just asking a person to go to the play with me. That was the kind of thing a person could do. But the only problem is that we weren't friends yet so it wasn't easy to just bring up a topic out of the clear blue sky that you haven't talked much before except casually. But I decided that no matter what happened, I would go and see her in the coffee room on Wednesday.

But as I was driving to work I got to thinking there could be other people in the coffee room and if I was going to be embarrassed, I didn't want to be embarrassed publicly so I went up to her cubicle as soon as I got to work. I said "Hi, Sherry. I was meaning to talk to you yesterday in the coffee room but I didn't get a chance to because other people were around and I was kind of embarrassed. So I wanted to get a hold of you as soon as possible this week and ask you if you are busy on Friday night? And, if not, if you'd care to go to see the play 'Tommy' with me. I already bought two tickets and I would really like the opportunity to take you and have some time to socialize." And she said that would be delightful and that she would like to see it as she has been spending too many Friday nights alone as it was.

And at that point I didn't know what to say. I had been spending all my time thinking about how I was going to pop the question to her that I had no further idea about what to say. So I stuttered and stammered for a minute and that was kind of when I got embarrassed. So I said, "That will be great. Let's talk about what time I should pick you up." And we discussed the times of the show, and the drive over there. And we decided that we might want to stop by a coffee shop first. And so it was decided that I would pick her up at a quarter 'till 7 and we would go to the coffee shop and then we would go to the play. And I was thinking that if everything went well during the date at the play, that we would stop at The Magic Moments Restaurant and have dessert. So I was going to bring that topic up while we were at the coffee shop. So, I told here that I better get to my desk and I would see her later.

LANKTON. So what happened during the date?

GREEN. Well, I stopped by her desk before the day was over and got instructions to her house. We both almost simultaneously said, "see you later," and then I left. I picked her up on time and I had bought a new shirt and had my casual suit cleaned. I don't really know how to tell you this I guess. Basically I was a little concerned at first about how close to stand to her and whether I should open the car door for her.

LANKTON. Did you open the door for her?

GREEN. Yes, I did. It didn't seem to be a problem. She just smiled and thanked me. So, we stopped at first at the coffee shop—You know, I figured that if everything went really well we could stop at The Magic Moments Restaurant after the movie but I didn't want to tell her at first in case we didn't enjoy each other or didn't have a good time. I had a little outline I planned on going over. Basically, the surprising thing was… I'm kind of out of breath telling you this. Now I forgot what I was saying.

LANKTON. Something you found surprising, because you had had an outline you were going to go over or read at dinner?

GREEN. Oh, it was only a mental outline. And I had that in mind and I figured that it would be good to ask her how long she lived in the area, and how she liked work, and where she was from, and um, what she was going to do next. But all of a sudden I realized we'd been talking for a few minutes and I'd totally forgotten my outline and whatever it was I was gonna cover in the outline. I was surprised at how comfortable I was talking to her. The waitress came and took our order. I was expecting to be nervous about trying to not look stupid about how to order for her. I figured she probably knew how dates should go. Which is funny to say, because I'm being nervous while telling you that I was not nervous.

(That Don had discovered unexpected comfort and success on this pivotal date was important. His risk-taking behavior had been positively reinforced and he had accomplished many experiences worthy of indepth elaborating, detailing, memorizing, and associating to logically upcoming additional events. He was "on a roll" and I wanted him to apply this success experience to more success in the delicate matters of his long overdue sexual and interpersonal development. I planned to use this trance session to focus his awareness on details of small but essential aspects of normal

development involving connecting with other life forms in a mutually respectful manner.)

LANKTON. Don, I really do want to hear the rest of the details of this date. But I fear that the entirety of them would fill this entire time we have for this session. I wouldn't want to lose an important opportunity that we have at this very second. Do you mind if I interrupt under the circumstances? Okay, close you eyes for a few minutes, Don. You are feeling quite proud of yourself and excited. A lot of people fail to take advantage of the opportunities they have, that's one breath, to memorize the way they feel when they feel good. Usually parents forget, that's two breaths, to instruct their children to pay attention to what they feel in their body, feel comfortable, and notice whether or not it's because you like the way air comes in through your nose or the way your lungs feel as they fill up, that's three breaths. But it's good you've taken the opportunity right now to memorize how good you're feeling and how proud of yourself you are.

And the reason you're taking this pause to concentrate on this experience, and that's four breaths, is because you've been thinking about something that usually would make a person uncomfortable in your situation, five breaths. But you're comfortable. You're actually excited and comfortable and happy, sitting there telling me in detail, about a risk-taking adventure you had, seven breaths. And still more absorbed, comfortable, listening to the things I'm saying, an adventure you had with a whole new area of development that you're going to do for a long time: dating, meeting people, being with women enjoying your company, and another breath, and still more relaxed and comfortable while you're thinking about and evaluating the fact that you've taken risks and been comfortable, that you've been on a date. And you're thinking about the things on the date now and you're still comfortable and relaxed and excited, smiling and proud of yourself. And another breath.

And it's very important in the development of a person, and there's another breath and still just as comfortable as you can be, when they have significant changes in their behavior and they have significant gains in their life, significant feelings of comfort and pride in their performance, it's important for them to sit down and appreciate themselves, refine their ability to feel proud of themselves and polish their ability to recognize that feeling and have it whenever they wish. Because it is a valuable and beautiful feeling. You're entitled to it and, so often, life doesn't give us the opportunity to either feel the feeling like that or to take the time to know that we are entitled to feel good about it.

And speaking of the time you take polishing and feeling proud, you know that there is quite a feeling of control about how you restore the luster to a car. Perhaps more than most people, you have a head start on having learned the necessity to carefully apply the right amount of paint in the right amount of time, the right amount of primer, the right amount of polishing, the right amount of pressure as you restore the luster to an old automobile. Polishing your car is an easy thing. You've done it thousands of times, just sitting comfortably and without knowing it, your unconscious gains a sense of mastery and a sense of control over your environment. Without thinking about it, your unconscious keeps track of how you believe you're doing according to your own guidelines and your own judgment. And your conscious mind couldn't possibly understand the intricacies of the brain that your unconscious does for you automatically. Without thinking about it, your unconscious uses your own judgment about your performance as you polish the car. And you do it comfortably and with a sense of control over your environment. Where do you feel the sense of control? How do you know when you have it? It's something you seldom think about. It's something you seldom have reason to speak about. Think about it now and I'll speak about it now as you sit there feeling quite proud about what you have done to increase your own sense of mastery and control.

In the back of your mind, the knowledge of how you increase your control by polishing and restoring the luster to an old automobile is something you've come to have great pride in as well. If your conscious mind thinks about how you move the polishing cloth back and forth, back and forth across the surface, gently rubbing it like a child would, gently rubbing it back and forth with the care that you would give to a living being. Gently rubbing back and forth restoring the luster to an automobile, perhaps you recall how you feel proud and comfortable and in control as you do that. Maybe you don't actually recall it consciously so much as you recall it unconsciously. It changes the way you hold your shoulders and your chest and your head. It changes the way you breathe. Maybe it's a memory of how you polish or maybe it's a memory of the cars you've satisfied other people with. Or maybe it's a sense of satisfaction that you get knowing that you can do such a good job so well. Maybe you do it by speaking to yourself or having the feeling somewhere. Maybe it's much more subtle than the way you breathe in and out like you're doing now. And while you have the experience unconsciously, Don, it would be interesting to note that you can hold on to it no matter what you think or I say.

One of the things I was thinking about saying was that as you hold on to that experience of confidence and comfort and pride, it's really very much like the way a small child would go across the surface and pet a living animal, a small puppy. You've learned a great deal about petting small puppies. You've learned a great deal about petting that you didn't know you knew. And you feel comfortable as you do that. Bringing comfort and joy to a living creature that gently allows you to pet, gently allows you to rub and caress the surface. It's something your unconscious has known how to do for a long time and you really ought to be rather proud of how your unconscious knew it and developed it outside your own awareness. I know you've never thought about the possibility of how you would be able to comfortably pet puppies, bringing joy to other living creatures as you gently caress and rub them as you're polishing the imperfections and bringing the luster to those automobiles. But it is something you do and something you can do very well. You're thinking about how you do it now, in fact.

And I know you've spoken to me about how you thought you would be frightened by dogs because you'd been frightened in the past. But often people forget that being frightened in the past is not the same as being frightened in the future. And so often people will say, like a client I saw the other day who said "there's nothing about exercise that I enjoy." I had to point out that she was quite wrong. The truth of the matter was not being spoken by her when she said that. When she said "there's nothing about exercise that I enjoy," she wasn't telling the truth. The truth was that there was nothing about exercise that she had found enjoyable in the past. But she wasn't exercising right at the moment. The truth was she might find something about exercising that she could enjoy in the future that she hadn't in the past. And the same thing is true for you. You thought you were afraid of dogs. But the truth of the matter is you had been afraid of dogs. And there are things about petting puppies that you could enjoy just like you're feeling a feeling of comfort now while your mind is thinking about it as I speak. You just put the polish on to restore the luster and you rub your hand smoothly, effortlessly almost back and forth across the surface, with just a small amount of pressure, enough so that your unconscious can allow you to know that you have control and you are bringing a sense of pride to yourself with that control even if your conscious mind doesn't know it.

And it's nice to know that you have the ability to pet and that your petting skills are just as capable of doing a good job petting as any other young man who finds himself holding a small, gentle, tender animal. So enjoy that for just a moment and don't even think about the fact that you could have anything older than a puppy. Just think about that puppy. No need to think about petting a dog. Puppies are a lot of fun to pet. So enjoy it for a little bit more before you think of something else. But I don't know what else you'll think of. I have talked to a lot of clients and words mean different things to different people. You're feeling comfortable and that's a nice thing to know. You can depend upon that remaining. You especially might appreciate letting the feeling of comfort remain while you make a picture of Don out in front of you, polishing a car, watching him restore the car by carefully removing old paint, old parts, cleaning out engine blocks, grinding cylinders, customizing gaskets, piecing in windshields and grommets, machining certain parts that are difficult to obtain, dipping and stripping various parts that are found in junk yards, hammering out problems in the body. Until finally, at long last, there you are buffing and restoring the finish on an old car, making it look like a new, proud item.

And while you do that, it would be nice to notice in the background a younger Don petting a puppy comfortably, while you sit here on the couch and realize that you're feeling proud of what you've accomplished over the last few days of growth. And perhaps wondering too, could it be that you would actually be comfortable around dogs? One of my clients wasn't comfortable with the concept of petting because he had heard that it was what boys and girls did together when they were alone. Sometimes you never know where a person gets a wild idea or how they make a connection. You didn't relate to me any reason why you would have a problem or a difficulty with an actual dog. But you didn't relate any reason that petting would be a difficulty. And what does petting actually mean in the context of dating?

I had a client that wondered one time and asked me out loud: 'Could you explain to me what it means when a boy says to me that he wants me to go petting with him or he wants to go somewhere where we can pet.' She really wanted to know what it meant. Everyone has their own idea. I sort of thought it meant kissing. And kissing in such a way that you're showering affection on the other person just like a little boy showers affection on the puppy. Just like you've seen yourself shower affection on an automobile that you've restored. The key element in each case involves an awareness and a respect, both with your eyes and your hands, for the fine quality of workmanship. And the respect you have for the thing before you, whether it's a living thing or an inanimate object. And it's nice to know you can feel that sort of respect for a living thing, for a human being. Some people, as children, missed the opportunity to learn what a sense of respect was like when it was shared. If you can imagine that little boy showing respect to that puppy, I wonder if you can imagine how it would be for you to approach that young Don. Perhaps having the Don from the visualization of the automobile restoration somehow move into the picture of the Don that was sitting comfortably petting the puppy.

And I can see from your face that you have a mixture of awe and surprise and comfort when you think about both of those things. Let the imagination unfold so that you can see yourself walking to that Don in the past and telling him that you really respect him as a person, that you have such a respect for the way he's been able to contain his needs over the years and try to accomplish everything he could without bothering other people. And you really respect the way he admired the opinions of other people and wished for them to explain to him how they saw him, explain to him how they wanted him to perform. You really respect his consistent desire to keep that foremost in his mind over the years and you respect the fact that he intended to be a kind, honest person. And tell him that you've learned a great deal by thinking about him and what he stands for and stood for. And after you complete imagining that kind of conversation, just imagine how it must feel for that young Don to realize that someone from the grownup world would so honestly and comfortably have that respect for him.

And just imagine the chain of petting going from that little boy to the puppy, from that grown Don to that little boy, rubbing your hand down the back of his shirt, patting him on the shoulder, rubbing around his shoulder blades in a small, circular motion, patting him gently on the neck. Standing up beside him, your hands on his shoulders, tapping him gently on the top of the head as you walk away to show that your ability to express respect for him as a living being can be conveyed through a touch. And then observe whether or not his ability to touch the puppy in a gentle way has changed at all. Because you learn from the teachings of your adults how to express yourself and how to behave.

I don't know how many breaths have gone by since we began. You have a number of ideas about the date. I wanted to hear them and you wanted to share them. I don't even know whether or not you've gone to the dessert restaurant yet. But at some point my client wanted to visualize how she could be comfortable if she was engaged in the same kind of conduct her boyfriend described as petting. I asked that in sitting there and listening to my voice, that my client make an image of herself and their date, sitting under the stars, looking up through the windshield of the car. And imagine how it would be if they took the first step to scoot across the seat and put their arm around the other person and say: 'it's been a beautiful night. I've had a wonderful time. I'd really like to kiss you.' And watch as the other person smiles, responds in kind, or possibly says, 'it has been a beautiful night, but I don't think we should move to the stage of kissing just yet.' In either case, the entire incident is about respect.

You need to be able to respect the other person and accept the respect that is given and have enjoyment in the process. And I used it as an opportunity to point out that if they were to ever engage in sexual relations, that they needed to take precaution with respect to hygiene and sexual contact, both for the sake of protecting themselves from bodily fluids and unwanted pregnancies. And the two people could speak about that as mature adults, just what methods they would use and employ. But they needed to be comfortable speaking about it. And my client was happy that they had considered and thought about these things in the context of petting.

Finally, time passed, and my client and I spoke about a number of things, making certain that various ramifications of dating and courtship and respect for the other person, adherence to their own beliefs about personal conduct and morals, and religious guidelines were all balanced together in their understanding of whether or not their sexual contact prior to marriage was one of consummation of sexual intercourse or if it was constrained to petting. There are so many different ways that it is done by different people, and done by the same person over time. But we can't go into that now. It's actually the kind of thing that is a pleasure to discover for oneself. And Don, while you discover what it is that you discover in your life, I can't think of a more wonderful problem for a person to get to solve over the years. I don't think that there could be a better problem to solve than figuring out how comfortable one is going to be dating and how they would like to conduct themselves under the circumstances of dating a person who they enjoy and who enjoys them. It's so much nicer to have that problem than to have the kinds of problems that a lot of people have. So I'd like to congratulate you on that problem. And it's just something else that you can feel proud about, knowing that the kinds of things you do to solve that problem are among the most enjoyable things that can happen.

And I hope that, as you sit there thinking about that, the pictures you make of the future reflect the degree of comfort I can see on your face right now while you're breathing comfortably. I couldn't tell you how many breaths you've had now. You've been breathing comfortably for some time. So I'd like to ask you to continue to memorize the comfort and think about the several different ways you've expanded your sense of comfort and pride in your conduct and in yourself to other things while I've been talking and you've been listening to my words and making them into things that fit for you and your own future.

So that I can count back to 20 from 1 and, as I do, you can arouse yourself from this concentration and memorization of your experience, and after you arise from the trance, tell me what else happened on the date because I am very interested in knowing just what happened and what you're going to do in the future. 1, 2, 3, 4, 5. Keeping in mind that the things you've been doing unconsciously and the things that you're doing consciously 6, 7, 8, 9, 10 while you were in the trance just now, 11, 12, 13, are not just thinking about certain areas but learning to think about lots of areas, not just getting a fish but learning to fish, not just memorizing your experience but expanding your experience in a number of different areas, and not just expanding your experience in different areas in the future but learning the process of expanding your pride and your comfort to any area you wish any time for the rest of your life.

And I hope your conscious mind has really noticed that you're learning that process because that's really something that will give you an ongoing sense of pride more than anything else can do. And no one could deserve it more than you because you've worked really hard to build that experience. And I'm proud to know that you've worked with me and I'm proud to have worked with you on such an important item. Because it's wonderful to do good work and to do good work with good material. And I know you know that from all of the automobiles that you've restored, it's a pleasure to do good work with good material. And I've had the honor of working with you. 15, 16, 17, 18, 19, and 20 and open your eyes. Hi, how do you feel?

GREEN. Whew, I feel fine. I was doing a lot of thinking while you were talking and I think I have come to some conclusions.

LANKTON. Fine, I'd like to hear your conclusions, but I'd definitely like to hear what else happened on this date before our time is up. Could you tell me the rest as succinctly as possible? I'm just really eager to hear how well everything went and whether there were any difficulties whatsoever for you.

GREEN. There's really not much more to say about the date. We went to the play and really enjoyed it. She seemed to be happy and I was feeling like I had come such a long way in my development as a person. After the play I asked her if she'd like to go to dessert and coffee somewhere and we ended up at the dessert restaurant. I recalled how you really liked my judgment about the apple crepe and I suggested she order it and told her why it was delicious. And you know what? She ordered it! I had a great time. You'd never have known how much of an amateur I was at all of this stuff.

LANKTON. You really are moving along, that's for sure. And speaking of moving, I have another suggestion for you: keep moving along on this course even when you are alone. You probably don't know what I mean. But what I do mean is that, either at sunrise or sunset, either one—you decide—I'd like for you to walk a couple of miles per day. I know you enjoy walking on vacations but I'd like you to move that pleasure into your daily life. Why not? You don't need to wait until you go on vacation to have that pleasure and besides, you want to look as good as you are acting, right?

GREEN. Do you mean I should begin exercising regularly?

LANKTON. I don't know if you would call walking a couple of miles exercising or not—but that is all I have in mind. I think it will help you hold your posture better, breathe better, and improve your circulation. What do you think?

GREEN. I think it sounds like exercising! But, it's a good idea. Do you think I could get up in time to do that in the morning?

LANKTON. How has your awakening been going, Don?

GREEN. I haven't had to have more than one alarm set in over a week. I get up and shut it off and I am usually about half-way done with my shower before I realize that I have not had a problem. Then I get sort of a proud feeling when I notice that. And, I guess this is sort of superstitious, but I don't want to keep thinking about it too much for fear I will jinx it—so, I put it out of my mind and keep getting ready for work. Is that silly?

LANKTON. It isn't silly to feel proud, that's for sure. But it's fine to put this matter behind you and not concern yourself with it anymore. So how about getting up an hour earlier and walking? If you don't want to agree now, at least agree to think about it, okay?

GREEN. Well, I'll tell you what. I'm pretty satisfied with what I have been accomplishing so far, so I will agree to get up and walk—at least I'll try —fair enough?

LANKTON. That's terrific, Don. It is time to end our session for this week. As I promised, I won't charge you a dime.

Session 5

Don arrived on time for his session as usual. We greeted each other in the waiting room and Don was silent until we reached my office and were seated. He faced me, holding his mouth in an expressive way—somewhat like he was preparing to speak.

GREEN. I've had another atypical week.

LANKTON. Let me guess: You've been on time for work each day, you've been walking almost daily and enjoying it, and better still, you've been on another date with Sherry. How'd I do?

GREEN. How'd you know?! I was preparing to surprise you with all that. Did you hypnotize me into it or something?

LANKTON. No, not at all. You did it all yourself—I only recommended the walking as I recall it. But, Don, you made one important mistake, I'd say.

GREEN. What's that?

LANKTON. It was something you said about your week being unusual. I'd say you better rethink what is usual for you.

GREEN. Why do you say that?

LANKTON. Well, because, if I can pinpoint what you did to the T, you didn't actually do anything unexpected. You might think that your previous conduct was out of the ordinary and that you are back to your real self—or back to your normal self—now. Do you know what I mean?

GREEN. I sure hadn't looked at it like that. I was thinking my normal self was someone who was, I don't know how to characterize it, I guess, sort of getting more and more behind in life.

LANKTON. Yes, you were getting more behind and you were very alarmed. That is why I think this is your normal self. You were alarmed because what you were doing didn't suit the real you. It disturbed you. You were trying to awaken yourself from that lifestyle you were developing. Somewhere inside you knew that was not you. And this recent turn of events—it seems like the normal you. You are not alarmed. You are proud and happy. You might even say you are excited being alive. And believe me—that's how it should be!

GREEN. You think this is how I was meant to live?

LANKTON. Yes. If it suits you and seems to be in step with your values, your desires, and your common sense—I'm all for it. You've done great work in a short time. Where did you go on your date?

GREEN. After work on both Tuesday and Friday, Sherry and I went to the dessert restaurant. We just met there and talked and then went home in our own cars. But it was like a date!

LANKTON. Wow. It sounds perfect. What's next?

GREEN. That I don't know. I had a dream in which she and I were in my garage and I was showing her the car I recently refurbished. Only, it wasn't a car I really worked on. I mean, I was working on a blue 1973 Chevy Impala and the car in the dream was a silver 75 Corvette. I was showing her the headlights. I remember showing her the way headlights swing out from the fender. And then—well this is the part that is pretty embarrassing—we were in the back seat, and I was trying to kiss her. In the dream it seemed okay—but when I thought about it, after I woke up, it seemed like—well, I would just never do that. It was just a dream. I'd never do that! I don't want to do that.

LANKTON. Well, of course you don't want to kiss her yet. You don't know her very well—you've only just begun to spend time together. Maybe your unconscious knows something you don't know—but you don't want to kiss her yet. Do you think you ever might?

GREEN. I'm not sure about that. I did think about it once. But that whole topic area sort of frightens me.

LANKTON. It's reasonable that you would consider kissing, and not just her, but various women. But enjoying thinking about it and actually doing it are two very different things, you know. Since you thought of yourself as someone who was hopelessly behind in the area of social development, you most certainly would think about kissing—and probably having sexual intercourse as well. Think about it. That's a part of developing the skill and desire. Dr. Erickson once said to me, "you can pretend anything and master it." I learned a lot from that idea. But you don't wish to kiss Sherry yet in real life—or you would have asked her if you could kiss her. You probably sense that she is not comfortable with that and you are not comfortable with that—and the time is not right. When the time is right, you will know it. I'm certain of that. When it comes to refurbishing an automobile, you know when the time is right to paint it and polish it and when the time is right to take it on a test drive. Right?

GREEN. Yeah.

LANKTON. So, see—you'll know. Now tell me how your walks have been.

GREEN. Okay, so here's what happened on my walking. Yes, I've been walking. You had sort of suggested that I should walk in the morning before work. I haven't done that yet. I think I might actually. I might give it a try. But I haven't done that yet because that seems like an awfully hard thing to do. I mean, I only have walked on vacation when I didn't have to get back in time for any thing. And it takes a pretty long time for me to figure out what I'm going to wear. And of course I can't wear normal shoes like I wear to work. So I went down and bought some new tennis shoes to wear on this regular exercise walking and they've got 50 different kinds of tennis shoes. It was kind of a project to figure out which kinds of shoes to buy. But I bought the shoes that cost me about $65 and they're comfortable. And then, depending on whether it's a little chilly out or not you have to select carefully a windbreaker and blue jeans and anyway, I don't even know what route to walk. I've been going around a few blocks and I kind of got to thinking that it was enjoyable. And that maybe I'd try to walk early in the morning on the weekend once I got used to where I was walking and what I was wearing. So I had that kind of plan about it.

LANKTON. Well, when was your first time walking? How did that begin for you?

GREEN. Well, the first time I walked, it was kind of funny, because I met with Sherry at the restaurant and had dessert. We went right after work. And we had dessert and coffee and then I drove home. And I got to thinking that it was just about sunset and you had mentioned that I could walk at sunset or sunrise, and it was sunset and I had these extra calories from eating dessert. And I wanted to lose weight so I would be more physically fit. So I thought this would be the perfect time to walk off the calories I had gained by eating the dessert, which was kind of extra. So, I went home and I was in a good mood. So I got my clothes on, took off my tie and coat and stuff and I walked. That was the first day I walked, and my work shoes were pretty uncomfortable. So the next day I went out and bought the walking shoes. I wasn't going to walk that day because I thought it was going to rain. But I got home from work and I didn't really have anything planned right at that moment so I went ahead and walked then before dinner. And that was more comfortable with the new shoes. So the next day when I met with Sherry again for dessert, I thought it would be a perfect idea to go out and walk off the calories that I got from eating the dessert. So I walked again that day, and it turns out now that I've walked every day. I haven't walked in the morning though on weekends. I just walked in the afternoon every day.

LANKTON. Well, have you noticed that you've lost any weight or begun to feel better because of the walking?

GREEN. Well, I wish I had gotten on the scale to weigh myself before I started walking because I think maybe I have begun to lose a little weight. But I'm not sure. It does feel good to be walking. I feel like I'm doing the right thing to be exercising. It just sort of adds another piece of the overall picture of me doing things that are really good for me. And it just makes me feel normal or something. I like it.

LANKTON. Well, Don, you're not actually normal by doing what you're doing. You're above normal. Because most people by your age have no more wisdom than you have. They just have different experiences that they kind of wish they didn't have. They don't exercise, most of them. Many of them may have begun smoking and drinking, gotten involved with people they didn't really want to be married to and ended up with divorce, families and children they are not really seeing the way they should see. And it's a very small percentage of people who are happily married and raising families and keeping themselves healthy. And you are not far from being in some sort of superior category here, being a person who is dating and working on being healthy, gotten a college degree, held down a job that is difficult and requires dedication. You maybe need to reassess yourself and up your self-esteem a few notches as you think about who you have become. Have you thought about that?

GREEN. You paint a really good picture of me whenever I come here. I hadn't looked at it that way, no.

LANKTON. I'm not trying to paint an unrealistic picture of you because that wouldn't help anybody. But I think that a realistic picture is far more optimistic than the picture you've been calling realistic all these days and months and years before we met. So I'm really glad you came. I know you're going to stop coming pretty soon. In fact, this may be your last session since you are feeling as good about yourself as you're reporting.

GREEN. Well, I was thinking about that. It is kind of costing me some money to come here and I've accomplished what I wanted to accomplish. I've been going to work on time and I'm not really sure why but I've been doing it without fail for several weeks now. And I'm on sort of a little path of beginning to get healthier. And I've started dating, and I suppose I will continue, maybe not always dating Sherry. I can't really handle much more social life than I've gained and I think maybe, um, I would like to stop coming as long as I could always come back some time.

LANKTON. Oh, certainly, the door is always open for someone who works as hard and is as much fun to be with as you. And like I said, it is a pleasure to do good work—and to do good work with good material. And of course you know that yourself. It's been a real pleasure meeting you. There are a couple of things you may want to think about before you leave today though. One of the things you mentioned to me in the past was anxiety attacks and I wanted to know if you have discovered that your anxiety attacks have diminished in any way.

GREEN. Well, that's hard to say. I haven't had any anxiety attacks. I forgot to think about things being bad in the future. That's kind of a funny way to put it but I haven't been thinking about negative things in the future. In fact, I guess I've been thinking the future is pretty positive. So I feel good about that and I haven't had any anxiety attacks, no.

LANKTON. Another thing you mentioned was that you had a fear of dogs. Do you have any sense of whether or not this is important to continue discussing or whether that's changed in any way?

GREEN. Um, no, I haven't thought about having any contact with dogs or fear of dogs I guess. Maybe I should go to a pet store and see how I feel or something.

LANKTON. Is that something you're willing to do to test your experience around dogs?

GREEN. Um, yeah, maybe in a week or two I think maybe I might do that just to find out. I mean it's not really important to me to change it so much because I don't have any need to avoid dogs or be around dogs either way.

LANKTON. Well, you never know when a cute puppy might be a really nice roommate, and boy, you sure can meet a lot of people walking your dog. A lot of them will be women, you know. But that's something to think about in the future. But I know that the Christmas present that a granddaughter bought for her grandfather last Christmas was a little Schnauzer puppy because he lived alone. He at first thought he couldn't handle the puppy, that it would be too much work for him, and that maybe he was too old and too inactive, and he wouldn't be able to take care of the dog in the way the dog should have. But it's October and it's been 10 months and this particular fellow talks about that dog every time you talk to him. And it's really given him a lot of companionship. And he's even said that. And he's not a particularly expressive man about his emotions but he's actually said to that little girl that he really appreciated the thoughtfulness of that gift because that dog has really brought him a lot of comfort. Now when you think about that it makes you wonder. It would be nice to know that another avenue of your life has opened up for you and another option is available for you. It's just something to think about. I don't know what your desires and plans are in those areas at all. So, your anxiety is reduced, your willingness to investigate your dog phobia is changed, your dating is changed, your exercising is changed, your weight loss may be beginning and continuing as you exercise, you're getting to work on time, which was really the major difficulty you were having. And your work, has it improved, stayed the same, or what?

GREEN. Oh, well I think work has improved actually. I feel better about going to work and doing my work. I don't have an evaluation yet. It will be a couple of weeks before I get another evaluation, but I'm certain I'll get a good one.

LANKTON. Well, then I would say it is time for us to bid farewell to these sessions and I recommend you continue along the course you're following right now. And if any confusions come your way that you want to run by me, call my secretary and make an appointment and I'll see you right away. How does that sound?

GREEN. That sounds wonderful. Thank you very much for helping me. It just seems like I needed a teeny little nudge in the right direction, and I really appreciate that you helped me get it. I kind of thought that coming to therapy was gonna make me feel like a real hopeless case or something but I just needed a little nudge. So thanks a lot. I'll keep in touch from time to time. And even if I don't come back to see you, it's nice to know that I can. And, again, thanks a lot.

Don shook my hand and left without looking back. I haven't heard from him since that day, but expect that I might hear from him from time to time over the next few years. I would imagine that he might show up with questions about fine tuning his late-blooming sexual involvement. He may possibly need to overcome fear that that situation may have stimulated. But that's just a guess—Don might surprise me as other clients have and not stumble at that step at all. If that is the case, he will have made all the changes on his own and only used me to help turn his attention in the direction of noticing. Brief therapy often initiates strategic changes that continue after therapy sessions have ceased. It is like a snowball being thrown onto the side of a hill such that it begins to roll and gather more snow as it proceeds. One change stimulates another which becomes the foundation for another, which leads to another, and so forth in classic domino style.

Healthy development is a predictable process except that it is subject to all kinds of unexpected snags. Logs floating downstream will proceed smoothly unless there is a tricky turn that one log or another fails to negotiate successfully and before you know it, a big jam has occurred with all the logs just backing up on themselves and blocking any new ones from moving by. We can think of brief therapy as an untangling agent that gets the blockage removed so the logs get moving again and then nature will take its normal course.

While Don still has lots of developing to do before he accomplishes mature dating, mating, and other aspects of being "normal;" he has put together experiences of success that can become the foundation on which he continues to build the additional success with confidence, pride, and excitement. He can do this with or without additional therapy. The current therapy has been a success by his definition in that it helped him create satisfactory new arrangements with all of his presenting problems, and at this time he is anticipating himself able to successfully project these learnings into his ongoing future. ■

CRITIQUE OF DONALD GREEN'S TREATMENT BY ERICKSONIAN PSYCHOTHERAPY

by Betty Alice Erickson

Stephen Lankton treated Donald Green in a typically Ericksonian fashion, providing therapy that expanded the client's abilities and perceptions rather than removing dysfunctional thinking or behaviors. He assumed that Don had the abilities to solve his own problems and built much of the therapy on the resources that Don had neither used nor even realized that he had.

The capabilities that reside within each person's unconscious can be accessed using hypnosis (Zeig, 1980, p.179). With hypnosis, Lankton bypassed the conscious defense mechanisms Don had constructed over the years and had expanded into dysfunctional behavior patterns. Don was an excellent subject, and Lankton was therefore able to use trance extensively.

Lankton provided multiple examples of utilization, that is, he used whatever the client presented as building blocks for productive change. Positive and growth-oriented behaviors became stepping stones for further options and ideas. Further, he engaged the human element of curiosity about what, how, and when further changes would occur. Not only did this presuppose changes would occur, but the definition of change was expanded to include the pleasant sensation of curiosity. Eminently Ericksonian.

Construction and Development of Therapy

Lankton's focus is on what is important to the client and on the utilization of that reality as raw material. Don was an engineer. In that world of concrete issues, everything is based on logic. Problems are solved in specific and linear ways, and there are only a small number of "right" answers. When Don wondered if he could really change, Lankton addressed that fundamental fear logically and with the weight of indisputable truths. Change is a constant; it always occurs. Therefore, of course, Don would change. The acceptance of that reality opened the therapeutic door; now the task became figuring out how best to direct the process.

Lankton insisted Don stay in the present and did not dwell on Don's thoughts in the past. This is a simple enough orientation, but important because it stopped the repetitious negativity of Don's circular thinking patterns. The memorization and practice of fledgling feelings of pride and connecting these to physical sensations enabled Don to expand perception of his own behaviors and gave anchors with which to reaccess these feelings and practice new behaviors.

Ericksonian Psychotherapy builds on success, and Lankton provided multiple opportunities for that. Don was taught to see himself comfortably in the future, and perspectives on new successes were created for him. Learning is based on new internal experiences (Erickson, 1980. Vol. I, p. 148). As Don's feelings of pride and competency grew, the internal experiences on which he built behavior began to change. He learned a way to strengthen his independence, and he realized more of his competencies.

Oversleeping was addressed in a way that made it clear that it was a symptom of more troubling realities of his life situation. Lankton did not overtly draw a connection between the sparseness of parental validation in Don's childhood (as well as the lack of validation by his superior in the workplace) as a reason that he was unable to wake up on time. He also talked about Don's dream, where he was naked and penniless, putting that dream into a logical and nonpathologic framework and context without tying it directly to Don's upbringing. The indirectness of this approach obviated defensiveness on Don's part. Further, he did not have to confront more about his childhood than was necessary. Energy was not spent examining the unchangeable past because the focus was on changing the future (Erickson & Rossi, 1979, p. 358).

Homework assignments serve many purposes. Don's assignments introduced elements of anticipatory and pleasurable curiosity and provided clear building blocks for his future. How he interpreted the meanings of the assignments was left up to him. Recognition that he could take charge of exactly how he understood, and then implement his assignments, empowered him. Don's independence and sense of self were fostered in this process (Haley, 1986, pp. 26–30).

An underlying issue for Don was his social and sexual isolation. Again, Lankton used the indirect Ericksonian approach of telling meaningful stories. This respectful method of influencing and modifying the client's construction of his world allowed Don to keep and build dignity. Further, it normalized feelings and gave him information in nonthreatening ways. Don will probably remember these stories and use them in other instances; storytelling permits people to use the information at different times and on different levels (Zeig, 1980, p. 25).

Storytelling is also a fine way to induce a trance. The concentration required to listen and decipher the story, the vividness of the pictures that can be drawn, and the intensity that people develop as they connect to the story develops a trance state in a natural informal way. This creates opportunities for new internal experiences for the listener, which then provide new learning. Because the client is producing the new learning from material offered in the story, resistance is more easily bypassed.

During hypnotic age-regression, Lankton reminded Don that he could now see things from a different and wiser perspective. He constructed an imaginary future, a rehearsal for the rest of Don's life. The posthypnotic suggestions interspersed at the end of this trance built on Don's need to be nurtured. We "don't think about how much we've learned. But you really should, " Lankton said as he then listed some of the ways Don could compliment himself. Don can incorporate into his understanding the sad fact that he can never get the nurturing he needed from his parents; and that the only person who can now fulfill the role of providing loving nurturance is Don himself. Compliments are compliments, even if they are from ourselves, and as Don gives praise to himself, he will discover how satisfying self-nurturance can be.

Lankton continued to build on these interventions. Each trance expanded Don's internal experience of reality. Don was reminded of his regret that he could not show his father what a fine man he had become. The responsibility for this sad event was placed on the shoulders of the father by telling Don it was a shame that "his father was willing to deprive himself of realizing what an amazing person you are." The wording of this was careful. The logic, important to Don, was flawless, the compliment woven and intertwined within factual statement. Acceptance of the logic will tend to bring acceptance of the compliment.

Telling Don the therapy fee had been waived for another client who achieved a goal similar to Don's opened a new vista. Asking for a date became part of an enjoyable game. The mere act of asking became the success. Even with a refusal, the next session would have been wrapped in a tangible measure of success—money.

Lankton rejoiced in the sharing of Don's triumphs, while continuing to cement progress. Don's hobby of refurbishing old cars was tied to the continuation of growth, using the metaphor of restoring an old damaged car to something new and proud (see Close, 1998). In the last session, Don and Lankton assessed what they had done. Alert to the power of words, Lankton truthfully redefined Don's "atypical" week as a week that was typical. Tying the end results to the original reason for therapy, Lankton pointed out that Don was trying to awaken himself from a life style that didn't fit anymore. In an Ericksonian fashion, Lankton here normalized instead of pathologized Don's behavior. And he gave the credit for the changes to Don, praising him for the work he'd done. He pointed Don to a brighter future with concrete suggestions of how to reach that goal. Last, he wrapped it all in humor, an authentic microcosm of the best of Ericksonian Psychotherapy.

Overview

Ericksonian Psychotherapy has no formal theory as such. Therapy is crafted specifically for that unique individual that each client is, so there is an enormous range of treatment options and interventions. Don presented with a multiplicity of complaints within the symptom of oversleeping. Some of these complaints were apparent to him. He was lonely, depressed, knew he lacked a social life, and felt trapped in his way of living. Some of the dysfunctions were not as clear to him. The effects in his adult life of his loneliness as a child and of its possible residual anger seemed to be only partially understood. His dependence on authority for self validation was playing out in his work-related problems. Each one of these issues could have served as a beginning point for effective therapy.

Almost anything can be used for a therapeutic end. The workplace environment, reading, television, hobbies, pets, interactions with other people, all can provide opportunities for growth. Weaving ordinary life into therapy gives clients tools for the future. As Lankton met Don in his world, he found a wealth of possibilities for choosing an area on which to focus. Beginning with a "minor" symptom is not only respectful for the client, it instills hope for change and builds a platform of success for other changes.

Trance states are an integral part of Ericksonian Psychotherapy.

Lankton relied on formal hypnosis. Naturalistic, or conversational, trance states, which incorporate the phenomena of a formal trance, but which are developed in ordinary focused interaction, are also used extensively. The multilevel communication possible with trance allows the therapist to "speak to the unconscious," and to access more readily the resources of which the client is not fully aware.

The quality of the relationship between the therapist and the client is of utmost importance. Almost two decades after the death of Erickson, people still speak movingly about the atmosphere of acceptance and good will and playful humor in his office. Creating this atmosphere not only adds to the therapist-client relationship, but effectively conveys a message—whatever the client has brought is a solvable problem and the therapist can help. It is easy to recognize that Lankton is skilled at creating opportunities for change, and that he just plain likes his clients and thoroughly enjoys doing therapy. His overall approach to this client incorporates the powerful therapeutic tools of friendly acceptance and enjoyment of life. And his effective, brief, and respectful therapy was well-grounded in the premises of Ericksonian Psychotherapy.

Alternative Treatment Strategies

Therapists approach clients with different perspectives. Lankton's reliance on formal trance served him and Don well. Another therapist less skilled in hypnosis or with a client less able to be a good hypnotic subject would have had to use different ways of working. Storytelling and use of metaphors create naturalistic hypnotic trances for the listener but do not require expertise in the use of hypnosis. Joint construction of scenarios of the future also create hypnotic phenomena, but in a way manageable for those not comfortable with formal trances. There might have been a heavier reliance on helping Don understand issues cognitively. Then, recognizing and even being fondly amused at how illogical it was to maintain behaviors that were no longer useful could have enabled him to see himself differently.

Normal psychosocial developmental stages, important in an Ericksonian framework, were not addressed. Another approach might have been to redefine Don's isolation and dating reluctance as merely a lack of usual development in this arena. A programmed plan of action for a client who valued logical understanding and could see life as a series of skill-building exercises would also have been valuable.

Another therapist might have focused more on remedying the lacks caused by the apparent inadequacy of parental validation and the remoteness and anger the client felt surrounding his sister. Lankton did touch meaningfully on the loss that the father created for himself by not engaging more fully with Don. However, the pain created by a mother who was "saintly" but did not insure a fully loving and protected childhood for Don and by a sister who was "mean" to him might well be related to his inability to socialize and date. The same types of healing interventions that Lankton used so masterfully in creating senses of competence in Don might have been used to heal those tender areas of his memories. Healing the pain created by a neglectful or abusive past can be the basis of multiple changes in the present and future.

Don had already been identified by coworkers as rather odd. Another therapist might have thought it wise to prepare for a potential rebuff by the girl he was asking out. Lankton had skillfully redefined asking for a date as the goal, rather than the date itself. And his obvious faith in Don's worthiness and success may well have been an integral part of Don's success.

When therapy was being terminated, a nice summary of progress was given. Never missing an opportunity to reinforce a positive step, Lankton combined praise with suggestions for even further growth and change. Even though Don seemed content therapy was over, another therapist might have emphasized a desire to hear from Don again. A carefully worded invitation could convey warm optimism that the contact would be filled with further good news as well as serving as a metaphor for the involvement and caring that Don missed during his growing up.

It's always easy to say that this way might have been more productive or that way could have achieved more. But the reality of this is that Lankton guided Don to successful resolutions for problems that both were and weren't addressed directly, and he made sure Don knew he had those tools for future use. There is no better ending to a case than that.

REFERENCES

Close, H. T. (1998). *Metaphor in psychotherapy: Clinical applications of stories and allegories.* San Luis Obispo, CA: Impact Publishers.

Erickson, M. H. (1980). *The collected papers of Milton H. Erickson.* (Vol. I) E. L. Rossi (Ed.). New York: Irvington.

Erickson, M., & Rossi, E. (1979). *Hypnotherapy: An exploratory casebook.* New York: Irvington.

Haley, J. (1986). *Uncommon therapy: The psychiatric techniques of Milton H. Erickson, M.D.* New York: W. W. Norton.

Lankton, S., & Lankton, C. (1998a). Ericksonian emergent epistemologies: Embracing a new paradigm. In M. F. Hoyt (Ed.), *The handbook of constructive therapies* (pp. 116–136). San Francisco: Jossey-Bass.

Lankton, S., & Lankton, C. (1998b). Erickson approaches in social work. In R. Dorfman (Ed.), *Paradigms in clinical social work* (Vol. 2). New York: Brunner/Mazel.

Lankton, S., Lankton, C., & Matthews, W. (1991). Ericksonian family therapy. In A. Gurman & D. Kniskern (Eds.), *The handbook of family therapy* (Vol. 2). New York: Brunner/Mazel.

Lankton, S., Lankton, C., & Matthews, W. (1994). Ericksonian approach to hypnotherapy. In E. Kirsch, S. Lynn, & J. Rhue (Eds.), *The handbook of clinical hypnosis* (Vol. 2). Washington, DC: American Psychological Association.

Zeig, J. (1980). Teaching seminar with Dr. Milton H. Erickson. New York: Brunner/Mazel.

Rational Emotive Behavior Therapy (REBT) is a pioneering form of cognitive behavioral therapy (CBT), which holds that people do not *just* get disturbed by the unfortunate things (Adversities) that happen to them; they often largely upset themselves *about* these things. When their goals and desires are thwarted at point A (Adversity or Activating Event), and they feel anxious, depressed, or enraged and act self-defeatingly at point C (emotional and behavioral Consequences), they have largely upset themselves at point B (by holding irrational Beliefs). So A x B = C. Their environment significantly contributes to their agitated state, but their Belief system—what they tell themselves about their unfortunate environment—is also crucial to their disturbances.

People first have a set of rational Beliefs (rB's), which consist of preferences or wishes—such as, "I don't like these Adversities I experience, but they're not *too* bad and I can *stand* them and still lead a reasonably happy life." If they only have such preferences when they are frustrated, they produce healthy negative feelings, such as sorrow, regret, and disappointment. But often they also have a set of irrational Beliefs (iB's), which consist of absolutist, grandiose *demands* or *commands*—such as, "I *must* not experience these Adversities! It's *awful* when I do! I *can't bear* it! I'm a *bad person* for letting them occur, and the world is a *rotten place* for presenting them to me!" Therefore they have unhealthy Consequences (C), such as feelings of panic and despair.

REBT contends that people can minimize their unhealthy and self-defeating feelings and behaviors if they: (a) clearly see and acknowledge their irrational Beliefs; (b) scientifically and realistically Dispute them (at point D) until they change them back to simple preferences; (c) strongly work at *feeling* differently; and (d) *act* against them in a determined and persistent manner. They then arrive at an Effective New Philosophy (E), which enables them to retain their healthy feelings and actions and minimize their self-defeating behaviors.

Albert Ellis

3

Rational Emotive Behavior Therapy

SOMETHING ABOUT THE THERAPIST • *Albert Ellis*

I started out as a writer, not a psychotherapist. At the age of 12, partly because I was encouraged by my junior high school English teacher, I decided to write the Great American Novel—not to mention become the Great American Playwright, Poet, and Essayist. Realizing, however, that truly good writers did not necessarily make much money—while the authors of potboilers often did—I picked the goals of first becoming an accountant and business man, then presumably retiring at the age of 30 with a million or two dollars. I could then be free to devote myself to what I personally wanted to write and not mainly what the reading public wanted to buy.

Unfortunately, the Great Depression hit the world in 1929, when I was 16, and destroyed my dream of early retirement and devoting myself to writing without great economic gain. Being bored by accounting—though I was very good at it—I deliberately worked at part-time jobs for 8 years after I finished college in 1934 so that I could still keep part of my dream and write anything I wanted. Between the ages of 19 and 28, I actually wrote hundreds of stories, articles, poems, and song lyrics, as well as 20 book-length manuscripts—none of which got published. These novels were very good, said several editors and publishers, but not exactly saleable.

Undiscouraged, I turned to writing nonfiction books, especially on sex, love, marriage, and human happiness. To do this I read hundreds—yes, hundreds—of articles and books on these subjects and made myself into a pioneering sexologist. No, I still wasn't really published, except for some comic verse in newspapers, up to the age of 28. But my friends and relatives, seeing that I was something of an authority on human problems, came to see me with their personal difficulties. To my surprise, I found that I was able to help them appreciably in a few short sessions and that I also greatly enjoyed doing therapy with them. So I went for a degree in clinical psychology at Teachers College, Columbia University in 1942. I received my M. A. a year later, and began to practice therapy (there were no licensing requirements at that time) while I finished my Ph.D. I've been at it ever since.

That I had two serious phobias of my own gave me a personal interest in psychotherapy. I had an extreme fear of public speaking. I also had a fear of encountering young women to try dating them. I read all the prominent therapists, especially leading psychoanalysts, to try to help myself overcome these phobias. I got little help from them. So I resorted to the philosophic writings of the ancients—particularly Epicurus and Epictetus— and some of the moderns—especially Bertrand Russell and John Dewey. I soon realized that I got more help from them than from psychologists and psychiatrists. Additionally, I read about the in vivo desensitization experiments of John Broadus Watson and his coworkers. Using this material, I forced myself, uncomfortably, to speak in public and to approach women I was attracted to. I completely overcame my phobias. Within a few weeks of self-therapy I became an adept public speaker and something of a womanizer!

Because I had successfully used it on myself, I began to do therapy in an active-directive, cognitive-behavior manner. Unfortunately, however, I let myself get sidetracked. Between 1947 and 1953 I was trained in psychoanalysis and used it with practically all of my clients. When I found after awhile that the psychoanalytic method produced highly inefficient results, I returned in 1953 to calling myself a psychotherapist instead of a psychoanalyst, and I resumed using cognitive-behavioral methods, which proved to be far more effective. I still sought a theory to go with my eclectic practice, and I developed it between 1953 and 1955 by welding philosophy to behavior therapy.

I first called my new theory and practice rational therapy, or RT, to emphasize its highly cognitive aspects. But it was also from the start quite emotive and behavioral. So in 1961 I changed the name to rational-emotive therapy (RET); and then, urged by Ray Corsini to give it its full descriptive title, I have called it rational emotive behavior therapy (REBT) since 1993.

For a full decade from 1955 to 1965, I and REBT were viciously vilified by many other therapists for being so active-directive and heavily cognitive. But in the late 1960s, several other therapies started following many of my procedures, particularly those of Aaron Beck, William Glasser, Donald Meichenbaum, and Albert Bandura. I was delighted to see how popular this form of therapy was becoming.

If I had not practiced REBT on myself during the first decade of its existence, I would have become discouraged with so much opposition and perhaps abandoned it. Almost all other therapists, with persistent anger, violently opposed it—the one notable exception being the leading Adlerian therapist, Rudolf Dreikurs. He favorably corresponded with me about my first paper on REBT, which I presented at the American Psychological Association's annual convention in Chicago in August 1966. I was disappointed with the vast amount of criticism I received. But I convinced myself, true to the teachings of REBT, that I didn't need the approval of my critics, though it would have been very nice to have it. So I thereby survived all the lambasting and persisted with my revolutionary theory and practice.

Because of my firm persistence in promulgating REBT, and because it and other forms of cognitive-behavior therapy have produced hundreds of research articles that support its main procedures, this form of therapy has forged ahead during the past 30 years to become one of the most popular forms of psychological treatment in the world. That, of course, has pleased me immensely and encouraged me to apply REBT to many fields other than therapy—such as business, education, religion, and even politics. My personal and professional interest in psychotherapy and related areas has, I think, been notable. I am delighted that REBT and cognitive-behavior therapy, through my efforts, have spread so widely and helped create profound changes in the psychotherapy and self-help field. As Frank Dumont has noted in the introduction to this book, psychotherapy today is much different than when I began to do it in the 1940s. Much of this difference has stemmed from the influence of REBT.

People sometimes ask me why, as a therapist, I picked the career track that I have. I first picked private practice and then founded the nonprofit Albert Ellis Institute that I direct, which trains therapists, runs a full-time psychological clinic for clients, and provides numerous popular talks and workshops for the public. Why did I not pick an academic career, as Rogers, Beck, and many other well-known therapists have done?

Frankly, I had little choice. I like academe. I've been a visiting Associate Professor at Rutgers University, United States International University, and Kansas State University, among several others. But after I left my position as Chief Psychologist in the Department of Institutions and Agencies (now the Department of Human Resources) of the State of New Jersey in 1952 and applied for full-time academic positions in New York and elsewhere, I was rudely rebuffed. By that time I had already become a renowned sexologist-practitioner, as well as a writer, in a liberal vein, of sex articles and books. I was therefore considered "too controversial" by the academic community. Today you can get a Ph.D. in sex therapy and in marriage and family therapy in a good many universities; but, not at the time that I applied to teach at these institutions! So my academic aspirations were clearly thwarted. Again, I used the theory and practice of REBT to convince myself that this was unfortunate and disappointing—but not awful and terrible.

REBT theory states that when humans have strong desires and goals (G) and encounter Adversities (A) that block these goals, they have the choice of making themselves experience Consequences (C) that consist of healthy negative feelings, such as sorrow, disappointment, or regret, and of experiencing unhealthy negative feelings, such as anxiety, depression, rage, and self-pity. They consciously or unconsciously make these choices by having strong beliefs (B) about their Adversities(A) by which they largely construct their consequent feelings and behaviors. They are born and reared as constructivists—creative problem solvers—and have considerable choice at point B as to how they react to the adversities of their lives.

However, REBT theory holds that people's thoughts, feelings, and actions are integrally related and inevitably and importantly influence one another. They feel how they think and behave; they behave as they think and feel; and they think as they feel and behave. When they bring on emotional disturbances—such as, again, feelings of depression and rage and dysfunctional actions of withdrawal or compulsive action—they largely do so by their Beliefs. But these Beliefs include powerful emotional and behavioral, as well as cognitive, elements. It is really, therefore, their Belief-Behavioral system (B) that responds to

Adversities (A) to produce dysfunctional Consequences (C). Thought, itself, invariably includes cognitive, emotional, and behavioral aspects. As I noted in my first paper on REBT in 1956—and as Alfred Adler noted years before that—human thoughts, feelings, and behaviors are integrated and holistic. They rarely if ever, exist by themselves, in pure discrete forms.

REBT is unusually philosophic but always, as my case presentation with Don Green shows, includes a number of cognitive, emotive, and behavioral methods. In Arnold Lazarus's terms, it is heavily multimodal. It follows the constructivist position that people faced with Adversities largely upset themselves, have the ability to refuse to do so, and the power to change their unhealthy negative feelings to healthy, self-helping ones. They can do this by forcefully and persistently giving up their unrealistic and illogical demands to perform well, to win others' approval, and to experience good conditions and receive fair treatment. They can change these demands to realistic preferences. But again, they had better do so cognitively, emotively, and behaviorally—as REBT urges them and teaches them to do.

The Setting for Therapy

I am now the president of the Albert Ellis Institute for Rational Emotive Behavior Therapy in New York City, a nonprofit training institute and clinic that was established in 1959. I see about 80 individual and group therapy clients at the Institute every week. I also give many talks and workshops in New York and around the world for both professionals and the public. I actively participate in the certificate programs that the Institute gives in New York and other cities. And I regularly supervise a dozen members of our therapy staff in individual and group therapy every week. I am rather famous for the live demonstrations I give with volunteer clients at my regular Friday Night Problems of Daily Living Workshop in New York and at many other worldwide workshops. I have written over 65 books, over 800 articles, and made more than 200 audio and video cassettes, mainly on REBT and its applications to group therapy, relationship therapy, sex therapy, workplace therapy, and other forms of psychotherapy. As you see, I hardly dawdle!

I do my individual psychotherapy sessions in my large office at the Albert Ellis Institute, including phone sessions with clients in many cities other than New York. I also see some clients during my visits for talks and workshops in other communities. The Institute also has 25 other therapists who see about 350 clients a week in individual and group therapy sessions. Its therapists have reached as many as 200,000 people in professional and public workshops during the last 35 years. It also publishes and distributes many books, pamphlets, audio and video cassettes, and other psychoeducational materials on REBT. Its main building, which it purchased in 1964 with funds from royalties on some of my books, has six floors, two basements, and a large auditorium.

Clients come from a wide variety of sources, but the majority of mine come from referrals from previous clients. Prior to the first interview, clients are asked to fill out an intake package, including a biographical information form and several tests and inventories. Some of these are readministered every month to monitor client progress.

I normally see my individual therapy clients for 30–or 60–minute sessions, at first, once a week, and then once every other week. Most clients, such as those I diagnose as "nice neurotics," I see briefly—for from 1 to 12 sessions. Those with severe personality disorders or psychosis may be seen for a year or more—but less than once a week during this time. Research studies are continually done by our therapists and supervisors to check client progress and the efficiency of REBT methods.

REBT training institutes are organized in 21 cities, including several in the United States, Canada, and South America, as well as in a number of European, Asian, and Australian communities. They keep growing and expanding in many ways.

I have always enjoyed doing psychotherapy, not only because I like to help people solve their emotional problems, but also because, with the help of my clients, I keep developing REBT theory and practice. I expect, at my present age of 85, to keep doing so until I die in the saddle.

THE THERAPY FOR DONALD GREEN

In my early days as a psychotherapist, from 1943 to 1953, I probably would have considered Donald Green a seriously neurotic individual, who was largely a victim of poor family relationships. Obviously, his father was mainly into himself, his mother was superficially nice but unaffectionate, and he perceived his sister as jealous and hostile. His family environment was almost as bad as it could be; and according to psychoanalytic theory, which I largely subscribed to at that time, he was clearly a victim of his upbringing and could therefore be expected to have many of the disturbed traits that he actually exhibited.

When I stopped doing psychoanalysis in 1953 and started to create Rational Emotive Behavior Therapy (REBT), I still largely believed that people were made disturbed by the Adversities (A) of their early or later environments *times* the Beliefs they told themselves *about* A. Therefore A x B equaled C, their disturbed Consequences or neurotic symptoms. This was a radically different, and much more constructivist, position than that held by almost all analysts, and also significantly different from that of most other therapists. For if people's Beliefs (B) about their Adversities (A) help bring them disturbed Consequences (C), and if their past Adversities cannot (obviously) be changed, and their recent Adversities (such as disease, poverty, and unfair treatment by others) can often not be ameliorated either, they are nevertheless usually in control of their own Beliefs and have considerable power to change them. So they can be fairly optimistic about modifying their Beliefs. This can help them feel considerably less distraught about both past and present Adversities.

This, of course, has been noted by many philosophers and other observers of human behavior over the centuries. Some people take a serious Adversity (such as the loss of a limb or a desirable job) with unusual equanimity, some take this same misfortune with healthy negative feelings of sadness and regret, and some take it devastatingly hard and make themselves seriously panicked and depressed about it. Quite a difference!—largely because of their different *view* or *attitude* about a similar misfortune. This is why REBT holds, and teaches, that some Beliefs about Adversity are rational and self-helping and will usually lead to healthy negative feelings (such as sorrow, disappointment, or frustration); while other Beliefs about similar Adversities are irrational and self-defeating and will often lead to unhealthy negative feelings (such as panic, depression, rage and self-pity).

More specifically, REBT theorizes that Rational Beliefs (RB's) about Adversities usually take the form of preferences and wishes and tend to be flexible and to include a realistic and logical *but*. For example, "I really wish this job loss had not occurred, *but* it's not the worst thing that could happen to me, and I certainly can stand it and not be devastated by it." On the other hand, Irrational Beliefs (IB's) tend to be absolutistic, dogmatic, and overgeneralized. For example, "This job loss *absolutely should not* have occurred, and because it did come about, my career path and my life are totally ruined, I'll *never* get a decent job again, and I can't be happy *at all!*" (Ellis, 1994b, 1996; Ellis & Blau, 1998; Ellis & Dryden, 1997; Ellis & MacLaren, 1998).

For awhile, I thought that people's RB's and IB's were largely learned or conditioned. Therefore, their disturbed feelings and behaviors that they helped create about Adversities had to be unlearned or reconditioned. I still partly believe this, and therefore I show my psychotherapy clients how to actively Dispute (D) their IB's, to thereby arrive at an Effective New Philosophy (E). I also show them how to use many emotive-evocative and behavioral techniques that significantly help them to give up their IB's and change them to RB's or flexible preferences. This combined psychoeducational disputing of disturbed people's IB's often works quite well — as many studies of the effectiveness of Rational Emotive Behavior Therapy (REBT) and Cognitive Behavior Therapy (CBT) have shown (DiGiuseppe, Terjesen, Rose, Doyle, & Vidalkis, 1988; Lyons & Woods, 1991; McGovern & Silverman, 1984; Meichenbaum, 1993; Silverman, McCarthy, & McGovern, 1992).

Fine. There is now considerable research evidence that people who hold many IB's and hold them strongly and rigidly are more disturbed than those who hold fewer IB's and hold them lightly.

So far, so good. But as I used REBT with more and more clients, I importantly modified my views on the environmental aspects of human disturbance. I still believe that external Adversities — such as injustice, incest, rape, child abuse, and wars — contribute mightily to disturbed emotions and behaviors at point C. But in the 1960s I began to see more than ever the great importance of biological components to disturbance.

Thus, some people more often than others raise their *strong* preferences (e.g., "I *greatly* want you to love me") to absolutistic musts (e.g., "Therefore, I *must* satisfy my great wish for your love!") And some people more often take their *strong* dislikes (e.g., "I *really* hate lying") and raise them to absolutistic musts ("Therefore, you *must* not lie and I hate you when you do!") Whether people have strong or weak preferences — for love, truth-telling, or anything else — partly depends on their temperament, which is biological as well as learned. And whether they also raise their preferences into absolutistic demands also somewhat depends on their innate temperaments as well as their upbringing and their history of experiences.

I am hypothesizing, in other words, that people are constructivists, and learn and create their RB's and IB's about the Adversities (A's) they encounter in their lives, and that their tendencies to do so are *both* innate and acquired. Moreover, their dispositions to change their

IB's and to act more self-helpingly and less self-defeatingly about Adversities are also partly learned and partly innate.

My observations of thousands of REBT clients since the 1950s has encouraged me to place them in three main categories, each of which has several subheadings. In the first and most disturbed category, I place psychotic or neurologically dysfunctional individuals, practically all of whom seem to have physiologic deficits and dysfunctions. In the second category, I place the severe personality disordered individual, who also usually has some physiologic deficits and dysfunctions. These are more often remediable and less severe or complicated than the problems of individuals with psychosis. In the third category, I place what I call the "nice neurotics," who have little or no neurologic deficits and disabilities, but are nonetheless prone to experience dysfunctional beliefs, feelings, and behaviors that partly accompany and reflect their IB's.

A main point that I shall make in this chapter is that I do not see Donald Green as having one of the major psychoses, but I do definitely see him as having several traits that are common in those who have severe personality disorders. Although I would have treated him early in my psychoanalytic career as a "nice neurotic," albeit a serious one, I would treat him today as personality disordered.

Let me be more specific. People who have a severe personality disorder have many of the common IB's of the neurotics. But, in significant respects they usually also have distinct cognitive, emotional, and behavioral deficits or neurological deficits — with which they were born or resulted from early physical trauma—that nice neurotics do not have.

Thus, I would tentatively diagnose Donald Green, after Ray Corsini's intake session with him, and my subsequent sessions with him, as having a schizoid personality disorder. He has a severely restricted social and sexual life, knows that he is a "loner," but feels fairly comfortable remaining that way. He is shy — and makes little effort to overcome his shyness. As a child he played a lot by himself, avoided summer camp, and was mainly preoccupied with reading and almost compulsively did his chores and his homework. He sometimes felt lonely and depressed but made little effort to befriend others and intimately reveal his feelings to them. As a result of his self-chosen isolation, he said, "Sometimes I felt desperate. I even had thoughts of suicide."

Typical of individuals of a schizoid disposition, Donald, in spite of his competencies as a child and as an adult, has severe feelings of inadequacy and lack of identity. He feels "worthless" and "deep down [has] a fear of other people." He is apparently afraid that if he gets close to them, they will get to know how insecure and worthless he is. Over and over, as many self-doubting people do, he dreams that he has failed a crucial examination, and that he is naked and lost.

In a typical schizoid manner, Donald sums up: "I feel I have been a failure in life—living like a hermit—no real friends—no women—no possibility of settling down, getting married, having children—being scared of dogs barking—the fantasies that become so real."

No, truly Donald is no "nice neurotic," even a serious one. He is an intrinsically deficient person—a schizoid lost soul. He indeed has several profound IB's, such as, "I must not get close to others, lest they see my fundamental inadequacies." "I must do the right things, such as file my income tax on time, or else I will be incredibly punished." "I must always control myself, or else I will panic and get completely out of hand."

However, if I am correct about Donald's having a schizoid personality disorder—of which I am about 85% convinced on the basis of the relatively little information I have about him—I think that he has cognitive, emotive, and behavioral deficits, and that he was probably born with these deficits or neurological deficiencies. Just about all the individuals with severe personality disorders whom I have seen over the last 55 years seem to have several neurologic deficits as well as to have strong IB's.

Cognitively, Donald greatly exaggerates possible penalties and dangers—like being jailed for sending in his income tax late. He is competent but sees himself as utterly worthless. He has many crazy fantasies. He constantly dreams about failing a crucial examination and not getting his degree. He also steadily dreams about being lost without money and being naked and lost. He ruminates about a lot of things that bother him. He sees himself as a total failure though he has considerable achievements. He paranoiacally sees a woman whose car he fixed as being very angry at him when actually she is very satisfied with the car.

Emotionally, Donald does little socially and engages in no intimate relating with people. He is exceptionally shy with women. He feels lonely and depressed. He feels trapped in his restricted existence and has suicidal thoughts. He very much wants to be liked, but is afraid to risk opening up to people. He has no close associates where he has worked for many years. He not only has severe anxiety, as do many neurotics, but crazily becomes panicked and desperate, as do a good many individuals with personality disorders.

Behaviorally, Donald is compulsively late to work in spite of making efforts to be awakened on time. He avoids women and sex though he is not homosexual. He played a lot by himself as a child and is still a loner. He is unassertive and doesn't stand up to people at work or in his personal life. He has a phobia of the harmless barking of dogs. He avoids person-centered activities, although a test of vocational interests shows a preference for them.

These cognitive, emotional, and behavioral deficits are fairly extreme and have been part and parcel of Donald's character practically all his life. His father and mother, moreover, were both socially and intimately avoidant, and his mother was not really affectionate. I suspect that, like Donald, they were competent but withdrawn people; and I would have preferred to get more details from Donald about the withdrawn tendencies of some of his other close relatives. I suspect that his schizoid character is at least in part inherited from both sides of his parents' families.

Because of Donald's (as well as his father's) extremely withdrawn and obsessive-compulsive character traits, and because he has so many bizarre reactions, I would definitely diagnose him as a serious personality disorder. He is mainly schizoid, but could be given a dual diagnosis, as he is avoidant and obsessive-compulsive. So he is hardly purely schizoid.

Because I tentatively see Donald as having a severe personality disorder, I would try the usual REBT cognitive, emotive, and behavioral techniques with him, to test this hypothesis. I believe that how a client reacts to REBT provides clearer and more accurate diagnoses than the usual kind of psychological assessment, which stresses paper-and-pencil and projective techniques. I find both these kinds of test deficient, because the former tests can easily be defensively, and therefore untruthfully, answered; and the projective techniques often show more about the person who interprets them than the client who takes them.

Typically, Donald was given a series of vocational and paper-and-pencil questionnaires by an industrial psychology assessment firm and was found "to fall well within the limits of normality." He was also found to be "content on his job and...well suited for his work." I suspect that both these statements about him are quite wrong. They largely tend to show that when in contact with the outside world, he defensively holds up pretty well and doesn't show his severe personality problems to others. But in his inner life, which he deliberately fails to reveal to others, it is quite a different story!

REBT is a comprehensive form of therapy that teaches clients how to use cognitive, emotive, and behavioral methods that are more efficient for the achievement of their desires, purposes, and goals than the ineffectual ones they have been using for a long time—sometimes for their whole lives. Consequently, its therapy presents clients with various kinds of problems to solve, to help themselves; and the REBT therapist closely watches the reactions of the client in the relationship with himself or herself, and also attends to how the client understands, uses, and does the homework that he or she agrees to do.

In other words, REBT is an important set of conditions and relationships that the client—in this case, Donald—has voluntarily entered to help himself overcome some of his difficulties. So closely observing him in this kind of setting is usually more indicative of his basic personality and his reactions to life than his response to artificial test conditions. I therefore often find, by using a few sessions of REBT, that clients whom I initially regard as "normal neurotics" have, I realize after several sessions, severe personality disorders; but I also find that some clients who exhibit bizarre symptoms, and whom I therefore tentatively diagnose as personality disordered, actually turn out to be, after reacting very well to a few REBT sessions, rather "nice neurotics." This does not mean that I see all difficult clients as having personality disorders. But I must note that clients who are diagnosed by me, as well as by other professionals who have seen them, and who are seen as having a personality disorder, do on the whole take longer in therapy. Even after a large number of sessions, they make fewer therapeutic gains, and much more frequently fall in the personality disordered classification than do less difficult clients. Parenthetically, I may also note that clients who are diagnosed as psychotic—such as schizophrenics —also require prolonged psychotherapy (plus medication), and even when they have it achieve relatively poor results.

In any event, I suspected from the start, on the basis of the information gathered by Ray Corsini during his intake session, that Donald Green had a severe personality disorder; and, as you will see in my subsequent sessions with him, this was pretty much confirmed. As I usually do, I used active-directive REBT with him immediately, pretty much as I would use it with my neurotic clients, to see how effective it would be and to check on my tentative diagnosis. Hopefully, he might have no trouble in quickly learning and using some of the main REBT techniques, especially the cognitive methods. If so, this would be (inconclusive) evidence that my first impression was wrong and that he really was a "nice neurotic." So I immediately tried to determine the main emotional-behavioral symptom that Donald wanted to work on to help himself.

Session 1

ELLIS. Make yourself comfortable, Donald. I'll call you by your first name, if you don't mind.

GREEN. That's fine. Shall I call you Dr. Ellis?

ELLIS. Anything you like. Most of my clients call me Albert or Al. But if you are more comfortable with Dr. Ellis, or Doc, or anything else, that's fine with me. Just be yourself. That's what we're here for—to help you with any problems you have.

GREEN. That's fine. That's what I want.

ELLIS. In your intake session with Ray Corsini he mainly got a lot of information from you but really didn't do any therapy. In this and my subsequent sessions with you, I would really like to get to the point of one or two things that are bothering you most and see if I can help you with them.

GREEN. Good. Well, uh, I guess I'm an anxious person. And one thing I'm most anxious about right now is this therapy itself. I've never had any therapy before. Since it's the first time, well, uh, I guess it's making me anxious.

ELLIS. I like the fact that you honestly said that at the start. Many people are anxious about therapy, especially when they first have it. Let's try to explain your anxiety right away and see if we can lessen it.

GREEN. I'd appreciate that.

ELLIS. First, to help you be less anxious, let me explain what particular kind of therapy I do and how it can most probably help you. It's called Rational Emotive Behavior Therapy, REBT for short, and it's different from most other therapies.

GREEN. You mean it's not like psychoanalysis or anything like that. I wouldn't want psychoanalysis or any long-winded treatment like that. It's too intense for me, and might take several years.

ELLIS. Yes, that's right. That's why Ray Corsini thought that REBT might be suitable for you and why he referred you to me. REBT tries to be as simple and quick as possible. But also deep and intense—as I'll soon try to show you.

GREEN. Can it really be both short and intense? I would really like that.

ELLIS. Yes, providing you really work at it. I invented it in 1955, after I'd been trained in psychoanalysis, had used it for 6 years, and then had to admit that it was prolonged, all right, but not really deep. As I say to my professional audiences, it intensively goes into every irrelevancy under the sun—and misses just about all the philosophic relevancies: the ideas that *really* make people disturbed.

GREEN. It does? That sounds interesting.

ELLIS. Yes. Let me quickly show you one of the main ideas of REBT, which I hope will be helpful to you. When you are feeling anxious, as you have said, about having therapy for the first time, you think, like most people seem to do, that the therapy makes you anxious. But actually, by itself it can't.

GREEN. It can't? But it does. In fact it makes me very anxious.

ELLIS. No it doesn't. I'll show you why it doesn't. Suppose a hundred people, just like you, went for therapy sessions with me as the therapist. Would they all, like you, be anxious about the therapy?

GREEN. Well, no, not all of them would be. But many would.

ELLIS. Yes, many, of course, would be. And some of the many, even worse than you, might be positively terrified and panicked.

GREEN. See!—even worse than I am.

ELLIS. Right. But if it were really the therapy alone that created anxiety in people, all the people who took it, especially with me, would be anxious. Their therapy would *make* them anxious if *it* were truly, and always, anxiety-provoking.

GREEN. Yes, I see that.

ELLIS. But, as we just said, we know that all therapy clients are *not* anxious. In fact, some of my own clients, from the very first session onward, are calmer than they've been in years. Because they expect that I—or some other therapist—will quickly help them, they're happy.

GREEN. Yes, I can see that. Their *expectations* about their therapy, not the therapy itself, make them calm.

ELLIS. Exactly! Things and events *contribute* to your feelings of anxiety or calmness but they do not, by themselves, give you *feelings* about these events. *You* give yourself feelings about things and events by first having goals and purposes about them and then by having demands and expectations about the fulfillment of your goals.

GREEN. I guess I can see that's so. If I had no goals about therapy, which I definitely do have, I suppose I would have no feelings about it.

ELLIS. No, you probably wouldn't.

GREEN. But I do have the goal of being helped by you and your therapy..

ELLIS. Yes. Otherwise you wouldn't be here. But you also have thoughts and expectations about that goal. You *think* the therapy may be good for you—but you also think it might not be. So you have conflicting thoughts *about* your goal. If you weren't in doubt and were *sure* that the therapy would be beneficial, you would be calm, happy, and not anxious.

GREEN. Yes, I would be. I do think it will probably benefit me and that you specifically will help me. But I also think it may cost me a good deal of time and money—and that it will not be worth it. Also, that it might possibly harm me.

ELLIS. Right. So you are conflicted. But that's not exactly why you're anxious.

GREEN. It's not? I thought that conflict usually causes anxiety.

ELLIS. No, not exactly. It usually causes concern—which is a light form of anxiety—but not *over*concern—which is a serious form of anxiety.

GREEN. How is that?

ELLIS. Well, your goal is to be helped by therapy and you are not sure, right at the start, that you will be. So you are concerned about what you will find it to be—beneficial, nonbeneficial, or even harmful. Your feeling of concern is a healthy negative feeling, because it spurs you on to investigate—to be open minded and to experiment and find out whether it will really work for you. With concern, you talk to yourself and say something like, "I hope therapy works out but if it doesn't, that's bad, since I will be spending valuable time, effort, and money at it. But if it doesn't, too bad. I will at least have discovered if it works for me and it's not the end of the world if it doesn't."

GREEN. So concern is healthy for me. It goes along with my goal of being helped by therapy and lets me investigate if I will be helped. As you say, it encourages me to experiment.

ELLIS. Yes. Concern—or caution or vigilance—lets you try new things and experimentally find out whether they work. As long as you keep your *preferences* to benefit from therapy, and don't turn them into rigid *demands,* or insistences that your preferences must be fulfilled. Demands just won't work. They lend to overconcern or anxiety.

GREEN. So I'd better not *demand* that my therapy with you be helpful even though I strongly *prefer* it to be.

ELLIS. Yes, that's why you're anxious about your therapy with me. You are consciously, or perhaps unconsciously, *demanding* that it work out well.

GREEN. I am? Maybe. But I don't *feel* it as a demand.

ELLIS. No, but I'll show you. If you were *only* telling yourself, "I'd very much *wish* that I get a lot out of therapy, but I don't *have* to do so. At least I'll learn something valuable about myself even if it fails." If you were *only* telling yourself that, how would you feel if you then failed to get much at therapy?

GREEN. Anxious.

ELLIS. No, guess again. You would most probably feel—what?

GREEN. Oh, I see. Not anxious, but quite disappointed I guess. Really sorry. But not very anxious.

ELLIS. Yes, *healthfully* disappointed and sorry. Because you would then not be getting what you wanted. Your feeling sorry and disappointed would show you that fact—and perhaps motivate you to try another therapist, instead of me, or perhaps to try some other path, such as medication for anxiety, or various kinds of relaxation methods. But disappointment and sorrow would not stop you from looking for other solutions for your anxiety.

GREEN. But anxiety would stop me from doing so?

ELLIS. Yes, it probably would. If, for example, you strongly told yourself, "I absolutely *must* not be anxious! What a dunce I am for making myself anxious! How terrible for me to be anxious!" you would then be anxious about your anxiety—and probably make it much worse.

GREEN. So, again, I would be harming myself by turning my *preference* into a *demand*. I'd better watch that!

ELLIS. You really catch on fast! I can see that REBT is going to be very helpful to you. For it very simply—and I think accurately—says that when you or other people take their legitimate desires for anything and make them into grandiose demands—like, "I *must* perform well!" or "People absolutely have to treat me nicely and fairly!" they get into emotional trouble and usually act more inefficiently than they would, otherwise. As I said in *A Guide to Rational Living* a quarter of a century ago, "Masturbation is good and delicious, but musturbation is evil and pernicious!" I still say so.

Donald Green laughs.

Notice how I jump in immediately with the theory and practice of REBT. Instead of gaining rapport, as most therapists seem to do, by spending several sessions being very nice to Donald, (and thereby getting him to like me and listen to me), I take a risk: I try to show him how REBT can quickly help him to solve one of his emotional problems—anxiety about starting therapy—and thereby get him to favor therapy. REBT, as I shall show Donald a little later, is heavily into relationship therapy, as it strongly encourages therapists to have unconditional acceptance for all their clients and to show them also how to have unconditional other-acceptance (UOA) for all other people. The REBT practitioner shows clients how to have unconditional self-acceptance (USA) whether they achieve outstandingly and whether they are approved by significant others. But, unlike the theory of Carl Rogers, it actively teaches the virtues of USA. For Rogers believed, quite mistakenly, that if the therapist gives clients unconditional acceptance (that is, models it) they will then feel good and automatically give it to themselves. How superoptimistic of Rogers!

Actually, if a therapist unconditionally accepts clients, they may still not accept themselves at all—because their self-downing for their inept and immoral behavior is quite strong and habitual. Moreover, they almost always accept themselves, when they do, because the therapist accepted them with their feelings. But this, of course, is conditional *acceptance, which humans often have when somebody else accepts them. That is their nature—and their disturbance—to accept themselves when they do well and when others accept them. Highly conditional and dangerous!—because only very few individuals, such as their therapists, thoroughly accept them, and many people, of course, severely criticize them. So they will almost certainly, if they go by conditional acceptance, go back to flagellating themselves again.*

I jump right in, to teach Donald the basics of REBT, so that he can quickly help himself, *and not need my help. I give him an unusual degree of teaching help at the start, just as a math teacher would do, so that he can teach* himself math *(or anything else) in the future.*

GREEN. So I must not musturbate, if I am to stay emotionally healthy. Quite a thought.

ELLIS. Yes. Let me give you a story that I give most of my clients during their first session. I'm sure you'll find it instructive.

GREEN. Story?

ELLIS. Yes it's just a story—an analogy—but it quickly shows the basic theory of REBT. Suppose you're out in the streets of New York and you don't know how much money you have in your pocket to spend. But before you look, you say one thing to yourself: "I wish,

I prefer to find a minimum of 10 dollars. That would let me take a taxi or go to a movie. So I hope I have at least 10." How would you feel if you preferred to find 10 dollars in your pocket and only found 9?

GREEN. Well, if it were just a preference, a wish, I'd probably feel, uh, disappointed. "I don't have 10. But I'll make do with 9."

ELLIS. Right. With a preference, it won't bother you that much, so you'd feel slightly disappointed to find one less. Now the next day you again don't know how much money you have in your pocket when you leave the house, and again you're going to look to find out. But this time you foolishly say to yourself before looking, "When I look in my pocket I must, at all times, find a minimum quantity of 10 dollars. I have to, I must find it, at all times!" Again, you actually look in your pocket and again you find 9—one less than 10. And there's no way you can get more. Just 9. *Now* how do you feel?

GREEN. Oh, I see. I *must* find 10 and I only find 9. Hmmm. Very upset, I guess? Quite angry, I'd say.

ELLIS. Yes, but it's the *same* 9. The only thing that has changed is your *must.* It's that *must,* not the 9 dollars, that upsets you, makes you angry. See?

GREEN. Yes, I do see. My *must* makes all the difference.

ELLIS. You, and all the rest of the people in the world, rarely become upset—such as angry, depressed, or anxious about *anything*—without a must. Is that clear? Do you really see it?

GREEN. Yes, I think I do. *Musts* lead to trouble.

ELLIS. Right. Now for the first part of the REBT model. The next day, you once again don't know how much money you have in your pocket and before you look, you tell yourself the same things as the second day: "When I look in my pocket I have to find a minimum guarantee of 10 dollars at all times." Then you look and this time you find 15 dollars. Do you know how you would feel?

GREEN. Happy. Very happy.

ELLIS. Fine. You probably would feel happy. But a minute later, with the 15 dollars still in your pocket—you haven't lost it and you haven't said, "I really must have 20 or 30 dollars,"—a thought would occur to you to make you panic. What would that thought be, to make you anxious?

GREEN. I'd panic? I don't think I would if I still had 15 dollars.

ELLIS. Yes, a thought would make you panic. What thought?

GREEN. Oh, yes. I see. "I now have 15 dollars. But what if I spend 6? What if I lose 6?"

ELLIS. Right! Or, "What if I get robbed?" You must have 10 *at all times.* You have it *now.* But what about the future?

GREEN. Right. I'm demanding that I have 10 *at all times.* I see.

ELLIS. You see the tyranny of musts—as Karen Horney called it. Once you demand that you must, absolutely must, at all times, have 10 dollars—or *anything*—you're upset when you don't have it and you're upset when you do. For you could always lose it. So you're perennially anxious. See?

GREEN. Yes, that's really remarkable. I never thought of that before. Those musts are ridiculous!

ELLIS. Yes, and you see how they make you anxious about even a safe and helpful thing like therapy.

GREEN. Yes. "I must have a guarantee that it will work!" That's my must.

ELLIS. Yes, and of course that's exactly what you can't have in this world—any guarantees. A high degree of probability, to be sure, that therapy will be helpful, or that you will pass a test if you will study for it, or that you will keep your job if you are a good worker. But no damned guarantees. None.

GREEN. I'm beginning to see that. No guarantees.

ELLIS. No, no certainties. Just varying degrees of probability.

GREEN. Such as a probability that people will like me, accept me.

ELLIS. Yes. I'm glad you brought that up. You mentioned in your intake interview that you were shy with women. Let's talk about that for a moment. Your shyness is probably created by one of your big musts. You must what? What would you guess that your must is that's helping to create your shyness?

GREEN. I never thought about that. Let me see. *(Pauses a minute.)* Oh, yes. "I must be approved by them! They must like me!"

ELLIS. Right! If you have it even with me—"My therapist must like me and help me!"—I'll bet you have it even stronger with them. "Because I like women and sometimes think of them sexually, they must like me. They *must* not disapprove of me!"

GREEN. Yes, I'm beginning to see that.

ELLIS. And, "If I like a woman, am quite attracted to her, and she dislikes me, is repulsed by me"—what? What do you then think?

GREEN. Oh, it's pretty awful! I couldn't stand her rejection. That would make me even shyer.

ELLIS. See! I know you a short while. But with my REBT theory of musturbation, I've helped you get to the bottom of one of your main problems, shyness. You *must* succeed in getting the approval of certain women. Therefore, you won't take the risk of approaching them. So you call your fear of rejection, *shyness*.

GREEN. That really hits home, rings true. I prefer some women and would want them to like me. But I don't try because of my must.

ELLIS. Yes. "I must succeed with them! I must, I must! And suppose I don't? That would be awful! I'd be an inadequate person." Does that ring a bell?

GREEN. Indeed it does. Amazing how you know me so much already. In such a short period of time!

ELLIS. That's because you have so much in common with practically all people: the tyranny of the musts. REBT says that just about all the 6 billion people on this earth have it, about one thing or another. They all, at times, are great musturbators!

GREEN. So I may be one, too, when I am afraid to approach women. I'd better clearly see my musts.

ELLIS. Yes, and then dispute them and change them to preferences. Let me show you how to do this with the ABCs of REBT. We'll start with G, your goals and values. One of these Goals is to be approved by women you find attractive.

GREEN. Yes. That's my Goal, but I don't act on it.

ELLIS. Because at A, in the ABCs of REBT, you meet with Adversity or possible Adversity—namely, rejection.

GREEN. Yes, I may get rejected—especially by a few women I find attractive.

ELLIS. Yes, so at C, Consequence, you feel anxious and withdrawn—you are shy.

GREEN. Very! I never approach women. Never have done so. It's not my nature.

ELLIS. Now you, like most people, wrongly believe that A, the Adversity of rejection, causes C, your shyness. Well, it contributes to it but it doesn't actually cause C. Because not everyone, by any means, is afraid of rejection. Isn't that so?

GREEN. Yes. My friend Jim isn't the least afraid. He tried with many women and got rejected by them before he won Mary. Rejection didn't stop him.

ELLIS. Because of his B, his Belief about rejection. "I don't like it, but it's not horrible. I don't *have* to be accepted, and it doesn't make me a bad person if I am. So I'll keep trying, till I get accepted."

GREEN. That's it! Even Mary rejected Jim several times, but he kept trying and finally won her approval.

ELLIS. Right. But in your case, what? What's your B, your Belief, that makes you anxious and shy of rejection by women?

GREEN. I guess it's, "I *must* be accepted. I'm no good if I'm rejected."

ELLIS. Yes. "And since it's terrible if I'm rejected, and since it makes me a nogoodnik, I can't really try. It's too dangerous." Your belief, at B, about the horror of rejection, and not merely the possibility, at A, that you *may* be rejected, leads to the Consequence, C, your anxiety and shyness.

GREEN. That's becoming clearer and clearer to me.

ELLIS. Great! If we can really get you to Believe, at point B, that any Adversities (A) in your life are bad and unfortunate—that is, unpreferential—but that they are *only* that, happenings you don't like but can accept and live with, you will then be less disturbable than you have been for years.

GREEN. Can you really make me do that—see the Adversities I don't like, such as being rejected by a woman I favor, as *unfortunate* and *bad* but not terrible? Is that possible?

ELLIS. Very possible. You were born and raised with strong tendencies—to be both constructive and problem-solving and to be, at many times, destructive and self-defeating. REBT shows you how to keep using your constructive, self-helping tendencies to minimize your self-destructive propensities and teachings.

GREEN. If it really shows me how to do that, it will be great. I know I have some real self-defeating ideas and actions. I hope your REBT shows me how to lick them.

ELLIS. We shall certainly try to do so!

So far, Donald has been an almost perfect client. He really seems to understand the ABCs of REBT and is willing to use them experimentally. Because he does so, I am beginning to suspect that he is only a "Nice Neurotic" and that he may not have a severe personality disorder. But we shall see!

To see if he not only understands some of the principles of REBT but is ready to implement them, at the end of the second session I get him to agree to several homework assignments:

1. Fill out the information forms we give to all new clients, including a questionnaire of Irrational Beliefs (IBs) that he acknowledges holding and the Millon Clinical Multiaxial Inventory.

2. Read some of the REBT pamphlets that we give all new clients. These pamphlets briefly explain some of the main REBT theory and therapy methods and give more details than I have already given Donald in my first session with him.

> *3. Get a copy of A Guide to Rational Living (Ellis & Harper, 1997) and How to Control Your Anxiety Before It Controls You (Ellis, 1998) and start reading them. They both include more details of REBT theory and practice, which will save him time and expensive therapy if he understands and uses them.*
>
> *4. Fill out at least one of the REBT Self-Help Forms (see Figure 3.1) when he is anxious, depressed, or enraged about anything that happens during the week. Get some free forms at the reception desk downstairs, and try to fill out one or two of them.*
>
> *5. Preferably try to do something risky during the week, such as argue with a foreman or mechanic at work instead of cowering before such an argument. See if he can do this risky thing and see how he feels about doing it.*

Donald said that this was a good deal of homework to do. But I explained that REBT involves actively and forcibly changing one's musturbation Beliefs (Bs) but also very much involves acting against these IB's. Donald said that, as an engineer, he could well understand that. So he said he would really try to do some of the homework. We ended the session on that note.

Session 2

Session 2 with Donald began 4 weeks after Session 1, although it was originally scheduled by him 2 weeks after Session 1, then postponed for a week, and then postponed again. He explained at the start of the session that he had been busy with important projects at work and on his paid hobby of fixing up cars, but as far as I could see this was not exactly true. I questioned him about this.

ELLIS. Are you sure you weren't anxious about resuming therapy, and put it off for a couple of weeks because of your anxiety?

GREEN. Well to tell you the truth I think I was somewhat anxious.

ELLIS. What did you tell yourself to make yourself anxious?

GREEN. Well, first of all I didn't do much of the homework we agreed upon. I knew it would help me—certainly help my therapy with you—to do it. But I kept putting it off.

ELLIS. Because?

GREEN. I guess I was afraid that I wouldn't do it well enough—and

REBT Self-Help Form

A (ACTIVATING EVENTS OR ADVERSITIES)

- Briefly summarize the situation you are disturbed about (what would a camera see?)
- An *A* can be *internal* or *external*, *real* or *imagined.*
- An *A* can be an event in the *past*, *present*, or *future.*

C (CONSEQUENCES)

Major unhealthy negative **emotions:**

Major self-defeating **behaviors:**

Unhealthy negative emotions include:

- Anxiety
- Depression
- Rage
- Low Frustration Tolerance
- Shame/Embarassment
- Hurt
- Jealousy
- Guilt

IB's (IRRATIONAL BELIEFS)

To identify IB's, look for:

- DOGMATIC DEMANDS (musts, absolutes, shoulds)
- AWFULIZING (It's awful, terrible, horrible)
- LOW FRUSTRATION TOLERANCE (I can't stand it)
- SELF/OTHER RATING (I'm / he / she is bad, worthless)

D (DISPUTING IB'S)

To dispute ask yourself:

- Where is holding this belief getting me? Is it *helpful* or *self-defeating*?
- Where is the evidence to support the existence of my irrational belief? Is it *consistent with social reality*?
- Is my belief *logical*? Does it follow from my preferences?
- Is it really *awful* (as bad as it could be?)
- Can I really not *stand* it?

E (EFFECTIVE NEW PHILOSOPHIES)

To think more rationally, strive for:

- NON-DOGMATIC PREFERENCES (wishes, wants, desires)
- EVALUATING BADNESS (it's bad, unfortunate)
- HIGH FRUSTRATION TOLERANCE (I don't like it, but I can stand it)
- NOT GLOBALLY RATING SELF OR OTHERS (I—and others—are fallible human beings)

E (EFFECTIVE EMOTIONS & BEHAVIORS)

New healthy **negative emotions:**

New constructive **behaviors:**

Healthy negative emotions include:

- Disappointment
- Concern
- Annoyance
- Sadness
- Regret
- Frustration

FIGURE 3.1

that you wouldn't like me if it were imperfect. Yes, I guess that's really a big thing with me. I hate to do any important thing imperfectly.

ELLIS. Because if you don't—what?

GREEN. Well, I guess, yes, I'm sure I would see myself as pretty worthless if I did things imperfectly.

ELLIS. And if I *saw* you do your homework imperfectly, not to mention badly? What then?

GREEN. Uh, that would make it even worse. I would know it—and you would know it. And we both would look down on me. I couldn't stand that.

ELLIS. You mean you'd be a double shit. In your own eyes, for doing badly, and in my eyes, as the observer of your unforgivable bad behavior. We'd both think you're a worm—and we'd be right. You would be.

GREEN. Yes, definitely yes. I would despise myself for doing badly, and I would despise myself for your despising me for doing badly.

ELLIS. Double shithood! But you're wrong about one thing at least. Not your doing badly, for you really might, by normal standards, do badly in your own and my eyes. You really might.

GREEN. Yes, there are some reasonably objective standards of my doing badly.

ELLIS. Yes, as one of the AA sayings goes, "If ten people say you're drunk, you'd better lie down."

GREEN. So we can agree on standards of conduct.

ELLIS. Well, not completely, as the postmodernists say, for we all see things and events somewhat differently. There is no absolute or completely objective standard. Just some degree of agreement.

GREEN. What am I wrong about, then?

ELLIS. You are right about my agreeing with you about your poor behavior—such as your not doing your homework when we agreed that you'd do it. So we both can see that as wrong, mistaken, or foolish.

GREEN. You see!

ELLIS. No, but I wouldn't despise *you* for your wrong acts. Only the acts themselves, not the *person* who performed them. I and Alfred Korzybski would probably see your behavior as wrong or stupid, but refuse to see you, the doer of this behavior, as a stupid or *wrong person*. We would rate *it*, but never *you*, as inept or wrong.

GREEN. Oh, I see! You mentioned that last time. I *am* not what I *do*.

ELLIS. Yes, that is what Korzybski, an engineer and a philosopher, said in *Science and Sanity* in 1933. You never *are* what you *do*. For you do thousands of things—good, bad, and indifferent. And you do them often well—and often badly. Even if you did them all badly—which is almost impossible—you will still be able to redo them in the future, and perhaps do them very well. So although virtually all humans think that they *are* bad when they *act* bad, and that they *are* good when they *act* well, they are quite inaccurate and they greatly, and falsely, overgeneralize. They are merely *persons who* (at times) act nicely and *persons who* (at other times) act badly. They are not *good persons* or *bad persons*. No matter how foolishly convinced that they are.

GREEN. Yes, I see that.

ELLIS. You *say* you see that. But do you *really* see it? If you did, would you have been so afraid of doing the homework we agreed upon, or afraid of coming to our scheduled second session and telling me that you didn't do it? Think now! If you believed, really believed, you were never a bad person even when you did the bad act—like failed to do your homework—would you then be so anxious?

GREEN. No. I'm glad you caught me on that. You're right. If I didn't think I *must* do well, and *must* please you, or otherwise…or otherwise I'm something of a worm, I would hardly be afraid.

ELLIS. No, you probably wouldn't be. You have a *light* Rational Belief—"I'm okay even if I fail at an important assignment." But you also have a strong—*very* strong—Irrational Belief—"I truly *must not* goof on the homework and be disapproved of by Al Ellis. Or else I really am worthless."

GREEN. And my stronger Irrational Belief makes me anxious, even when I weakly believe, "I'm okay."

ELLIS. You got it. Now our problem is: How to get you fully to admit your strong Irrational Belief—and then, even more importantly, strongly give it up.

GREEN. *Strongly* give it up?

ELLIS. Yes. When you strongly hold an irrational, self-defeating belief, you first have to bring it to your consciousness—and then *strongly* beat it over the head till you surrender it. Like in baseball. When you are weakly hitting the ball into the infield and getting caught at first base, you have to hit it more strongly into the outfield. The fact that you know how to hit isn't enough. Your hits better have power—and also your rational beliefs. Such as, "I see that I am not a worm and see that I can accept myself even if I do screw up on my homework. I can refuse to put myself down, no matter how many times I fail. I *can*, I *can*, I *can*."

GREEN. You say, "I can accept myself" with real power.

ELLIS. *You'd* better say it with power—till you really believe it.

I have now partly confirmed my assessment of Donald as having a severe personality disorder. First, he has postponed his second session with me twice. Second, he seemingly had good rapport with me the first time, he has fallen back to being afraid of my disapproval again and is anxious about failing to get it. Third, he is quite prone—almost eager—to put himself down for his own failings and for my possible disapproval. He easily *resorts to self-downing, as many do who are schizoid personality disordered. Fourth, he only* lightly *sees that I might put his* behavior, *not his* self, *down, even though he says he sees it. Fifth, he shows that he* lightly *and quickly understands several REBT points, but that he really doesn't* believe *them. He gives them lip service, but underneath (deeply and unconsciously) he still subscribes to and acts on his self-disturbing philosophy.*

These observations of mine do not thereby confirm my hypothesis of Donald's having a personality disorder. But they are common among those who do have such a disorder, so they lead to my greater suspicion that he may well be in that category.

Although I would use certain REBT methods with nearly all my clients I choose to use two definite ones with Donald—again partly to test out my speculative assessment of him. The first one is unconditional acceptance. If I can get people like Donald to accept themselves unconditionally—that is, again, whether *they perform certain tasks well and* whether *I and other people approve of them—I can help him accept himself with the severe limitations, physiological and psychological, that usually go with this disorder. If he turns out to be merely a "nice neurotic," he can still—like all of us—put unconditional self-acceptance (USA) to good use.*

Second, I use with Donald the REBT method of learning how to strongly dispute and challenge his Irrational Beliefs and how to rigorously *and* convincingly *replace them with effective, rational beliefs. For in using REBT, I and my associates frequently find that "normal neurotics" have a hard enough time convincing themselves that Irrational Beliefs (IBs) are self-defeating and simply won't work very well. People with personality disorders—like perhaps Donald—have an even harder time giving up some of their IBs, because they tend (biologically and experientially) to easily create and then rigidly stick to them. That is often their nature—just as it is the nature of paranoid schizophrenics to invent persecutory beliefs and, despite all contradictory evidence, to stick to them.*

To help Donald accept himself unconditionally, I taught him how to vigorously dispute his Irrational Belief that his worth as a person depended on his acceptance by me and other people. One REBT method of doing this was to record one of his beliefs—specifically, that he absolutely needed the love and approval of others to accept himself—and then to vigorously dispute it on the same tape, and let me and others listen to his disputing and critique it to see how strong it was.

At first, Donald fizzled out almost completely on this REBT exercise. His disputing was accurate enough in content, but delivered in a namby-pamby manner. It wouldn't convince anyone, including himself. Moreover, when my other clients get several of their friends or relatives to listen to their tape and to critique how vigorous their disputing was, Donald said he could find no suitable critics. He was ashamed to play the tape and thereby to reveal himself to his only close friends, Jim and Mary; and he couldn't come up with a single other person to critique the tape. He only somewhat reluctantly allowed me to listen to it, and I kept seeing his disputing as much too mild and had him do the tape several times over before I found it reasonably convincing.

Finally, with great effort he made a suitable recording of his irrational belief, which went like this:

"I very much would like the approval of other people, including my therapist, but I NEVER, NEVER NEED it! Why? Because I just DON'T! Their approval can give me many rewards, such as money, love, and sex. But it can't make me a good or a bad person. *Only I can decide that. My* personhood *is only in MY hands, and not at all dependent on external things. Unless I, damned foolishly, MAKE it dependent."*

Even this forceful dispute only worked for a while. No self-statement about his personal worth seemed to work permanently for Donald, as he kept reverting, especially under the stress of a few failures, to thinking that people looked down on him—and that, of course, they were right.

Sessions 3 to 6

In the third to sixth sessions of REBT with Donald I kept trying out several emotive and behavioral techniques with him, as I became increasingly convinced that he had a severe personality disorder. Even had this not been the case, I might have used most of these same methods because they are part of the REBT armamentarium of more than 20 cognitive, more than 20 emotive, and more than 20 behavioral techniques that we use with our clients at the Institute. We select them to fit particular clients, but we use several of them with almost all clients because REBT emphasizes the importance of cognitive, emotive, and behavioral *integrated* processes for just about all disturbed people.

In Donald's case, however, I used some of our emotive and behavioral methods both therapeutically and diagnostically—since determining how well clients *act* on them frequently reveals how rigidly they stick with their disturbed ideas and habits and consequently how likely they are to resist changing them. REBT stresses diagnosis through therapy rather than through testing alone to see how clients *actively* react to therapeutic procedures.

Then I gave Donald the REBT version of Maxie Maultsby Jr.'s (1986) rational emotive imagery, which is a technique that gets clients in touch with their feelings and trains them to replace unhealthy negative feelings with healthy negative ones. I explained this to Donald as follows.

ELLIS. To help you train yourself, to become less anxious and panicked, I'm going to teach you how to do rational emotive imagery. We want you to feel quite concerned about some of the things you do—or don't do—because you want to do them well and be approved by other people. But if you become panicked about performing well with me or with others, your panic is overconcern and won't help you do well. In fact, it will often make you withdrawn, too shy, and inhibited. Then you'll get little practice in doing what you want to do. Like, for example, being close and open with others.

GREEN. Yes, it stops me from approaching people and opening up to them. I practically never do so.

ELLIS. And you would like to, wouldn't you?

GREEN. Yes, sometimes I think I really would. Though I'm not miserable when I'm by myself.

ELLIS. Yes, you act constructively when you're on your own. You're rather good at that. But it doesn't get you over your fear of relating to others.

GREEN. No, it doesn't.

ELLIS. Alright. Let me show you how to get over some of this fear. First, close your eyes.

GREEN. *(Closes eyes.)*

ELLIS. Now imagine, vividly imagine one of the worst scenes. Imagine that you are at your company's Christmas party and everyone is having a good time talking, joking, and dancing and that no one is talking to you, everyone is ignoring you, and some people, in fact, are looking strangely at you since you are just about the only one by yourself, the only one alone. And they are wondering about that, and looking oddly and critically at you. Now can you vividly, vividly imagine that?

GREEN. Uh, yes. It practically happened at our last Christmas party. Everyone was involved, talking animatedly to each other, and for a while I was the only one alone. I was quite conspicuous—at least I thought I was.

ELLIS. Good. Vividly imagine that. You are conspicuously alone, alone, alone. Everyone else is actively chatting and dancing—and you're really alone. And they see it, see you alone, and think you are very strange. Imagine it clearly. Really get that picture in your mind. Do you really see it?

GREEN. Oh, I do. I see it!

ELLIS. Okay, fine. How do you *feel* as you imagine your aloneness and people putting you down for being so different?

GREEN. Oh, I feel depressed, ashamed. And anxious. Down on myself. Hopeless.

ELLIS. Good! Let yourself really feel it. Feel as anxious and depressed as you can feel. Get in touch with your feelings. Feel it, feel it, feel it.

GREEN. Oh, I really feel very anxious.

ELLIS. Good. Now, keep the exact same image of your being alone and looked down upon. Don't change it at all. Keep imagining it. Now make yourself, with this image, feel the healthy negative emotions of disappointment and regret, only disappointment and regret—but not anxiety. Only disappointment and regret about what's happening. No anxiety. Feel only disappointment and regret—and tell me when you no longer feel anxiety but only feel disappointment and regret.

At this point, to my surprise, Donald stopped, showed even greater agitation than he had been feeling, and said, "No, it's too dreadful. It's awful!! I can't go on. I'm feeling very panicked. I have to stop!"

I was quite surprised, because I have used rational emotive imagery with hundreds of my clients and with hundreds of other people who volunteer to present emotional and behavioral problems at my many workshops. I very rarely encounter anyone who is so frightened by the images that I present to them that they withdraw in terror, as Donald appeared to be doing. Quite the contrary: when I deliberately get them to try to imagine a gruesome image and react to it, they frequently say, "I can easily imagine that. In fact, I always do!" So they are used to imagining really bad things happening to them. In fact, this is one of the most common things that disturbed people do. Donald, apparently, kept thinking of himself being isolated and despised, suddenly panicked, and then ran away from this "horrible" image. He couldn't even think about it without terror, so he somehow blocked out the thought. This showed that the very thought of becoming intimate with others or, worse, being rejected by them severely upset him; and he immediately put it out of his mind. Anyway, I didn't give up. I usually find that even my most terrified clients are able to use rational emotive imagery if I persist with it. So I persisted with Donald:

ELLIS. Don't worry. You can do it. Your panic will go away if you keep trying to do it. Focus now on this image that I am presenting to you. Don't be afraid. You can keep focusing on it without getting panicked. It will be good for you to do so. Then you will be able to face your worst fears without being panicked. Normally, you run away from them and thereby keep them alive. Now is your chance to face your fear of isolation and see that you are not destroyed in the process. So go back to this image. See yourself at the Christmas party as being alone, isolated, and looked down upon as a strange and pitiful creature. Focus on this image. Don't run away from it. I'll show you how to cope with it. But first let yourself focus on it and react to it. Go ahead. You can do it.

GREEN. Alright, I'll try. But it's really dreadful! And I feel very very anxious.

ELLIS. Don't be afraid to concentrate on this image, no matter how bad you find it. Steady, now. Focus on it, focus on it.

GREEN. Alright, I'll try. (*He kept grimacing, as if he were in pain. But he kept at it.*)

ELLIS. Good. You can do it. It's difficult but you can do it. And it will help you if you do it. I'll show you how to handle your worst fears, including this one. So keep focusing. Focus on this image of your being isolated.

GREEN. I'll try. (Pause). Okay, I can do it.

ELLIS. I told you you could do it! Fine! Focus on it, focus on it.

GREEN. I'm doing it. I can see it.

ELLIS. Fine. Now, how do you feel? What is your honest feeling. Let yourself feel and tell me what your real feeling is.

GREEN. I feel—uh—anxious. Uh, panicked. Quite panicked!

ELLIS. Good. Get in touch with your feeling of anxiety and panic. Feel it, feel it! Let yourself really feel it. Feel as anxious and panicked as you possibly can feel. Let yourself go and feel it.

GREEN. Oh I really feel it. Really feel panicked.

ELLIS. Good. I told you could do it. Keep feeling it. Feel it. Feel it.

(Donald is having a hard time, but obviously feels panic as he imagines himself alone and despised.)

ELLIS. Very good. You are doing very well. Now, keep the same image in your head—that you are being very alone, isolated, and despised for being strange, and work on your feeling to change it to a healthy feeling. Keep the same image, and make yourself feel healthily sorry and disappointed, *only* sorry and disappointed, but not anxious and panicked. Feel only disappointed and sorry, now, not panicked. You can do it. You control your feelings. With the same image, you can make yourself feel *only* sorry and disappointed with what is happening to you. Not panicked, not anxious. *Only* sorry and disappointed. You can change your feelings. Now, change them. Make yourself only feel sorry and disappointed.

GREEN. I don't think I can. I don't think I can do it. I really can't do it.

ELLIS. Yes, you can! You definitely can! You can change your feeling. You control your feeling. Change it. Work at changing it. You can do it!

GREEN. (Struggles to do it.) Um. Maybe I can. Yes, I think I can.

ELLIS. Yes, you definitely can! Do it, do it!

GREEN. Alright. I'm doing it. Yes, I'm doing it.

ELLIS. Fine. Great. Now, how did you do it? What did you do to change your feelings of panic to those healthy feelings of "sorryness" and disappointment? What exactly did you do?

GREEN. Well, I, I told myself that I really was strange, and that I wasn't relating to the other people at the party or acting the way that they did. And they were looking at me and criticizing me for acting so strangely. But that it isn't so terrible. I was merely a lot different from them, and that was all there was to it. It wasn't horrible. I was just different. And for the time being I could accept myself with this difference. Yes, I could accept myself and not put myself down the way they were doing.

ELLIS. That was really fine. That would do it. That would really change your unhealthy feelings of anxiety and panic to the healthy feelings of sorrow and disappointment. You really did it. See, I told you you could do it.

GREEN. Is that all there is to it? Is it really as easy as that?

ELLIS. Yes, essentially. When you tell yourself the right things—such as that you are different but it isn't awful to be different and to be criticized for being different, you change your feelings remarkably. It really is that simple and easy—though, as I shall show you, it has its complications. Now to make sure your new feelings of sorrow and disappointment are solid, do this same thing, rational emotive imagery, every day, for a few minutes a day, and train yourself to become automatically sorry, regretful, and disappointed in your behavior, but not panicked and self-downing about you, the doer of that behavior.

GREEN. You mean I can train myself to keep feeling this healthy way instead of my usual unhealthy way?

ELLIS. Yes, exactly. And to do this, all you have to do, for the next 30 days or so, is to imagine the same gruesome image that you just imagined—that you are isolated at the Christmas party and being frowned upon by others. Let yourself, as you did at first, feel very anxious and panicked about this state of affairs. Feel as panicked as you can feel for a short while. Then change your feeling of panic, as you just did, to feeling sorry and disappointed, but not at all panicked, about what you're imagining is happening to you.

GREEN. Once a day for 30 days?

ELLIS. Yes, once a day for 30 days. Until you will find, almost certainly, that you automatically start feeling sorry and disappointed, which are healthy negative feelings, instead of anxious and panicked, which are disruptive and unhealthy feelings, when you imagine being isolated and criticized. Or, actually, if this same event actually does occur, and not just in your imagination, you will tend to feel just sorry and disappointed, and not panicked.

GREEN. I will?

ELLIS. Yes, you will. If you keep doing it once a day for a good many days. What is more, you can use the same rational statement you used today to change your feeling. Or you can use other coping statements, such as: "Too bad that I have such trouble socializing like others do at this party. But it's not the end of the world!" Or, "I wish I were more comfortable socially, and some day I may be. But right now I have difficulty doing so. Tough! But that will change if I keep trying to socialize and learn the knack of doing so."

GREEN. I see. I can use other coping statements too. I can come up with an Effective New Philosophy, as you call it in REBT.

ELLIS. Exactly! That is what this technique of rational emotive imagery enables you to do. You keep imaging one of the worst things that can happen to you, let yourself feel quite upset about it, and then change your agitation to healthy negative feelings. Will you therefore practice this technique once a day for the next 30 days?

GREEN. Yes, I will.

ELLIS. Well, just to make more sure that you will, let me give you some operant conditioning or reinforcement. What do you like to do that you do almost every day of the week, just because you enjoy it and get pleasure from it? What sort of activity?

GREEN. Let me see. Well, fixing up old cars for people and getting paid for doing so.

ELLIS. Okay, for the next 30 days that you are doing rational emotive imagery, you only fix up the cars *after* you do it and change your feeling of panic to one of feeling sorry and disappointed. If you don't do the imagery and change your feeling, no fixing up of cars. Is that okay?

GREEN. I only allow myself to work on the cars after I do the rational emotive imagery and change my feeling?

ELLIS. Agreed. And what chore or task do you hate to do, that you usually avoid doing because you hate it?

GREEN. Well, let's see. Oh, yes. Cleaning the toilet.

ELLIS. Fine. If you don't do the rational emotive imagery on any one of the next 30 days, you stay up for an hour past your regular bedtime and clean the toilet. If it gets too clean, by all means clean your neighbors' toilets!

GREEN. (Laughs). All right. Agreed.

By persisting, I finally induced Donald to work at using the rational emotive imagery exercise, in spite of his original panic at using it. But his panic and resistance to using it was still unusual. He did it for the first week after I taught him how to do it. But then he did it quite irregularly, saying that he had forgotten to do so. And he didn't use the reinforcement or the penalty we had agreed on if he failed to do the rational emotive imagery any day. This resistance of his, since he was usually a dedicated person when he had a job to do, was again suspicious. Also, a few of the times he did do rational emotive imagery, he really panicked on doing so and soon abandoned his attempt to do so. This falling back to his panic state and not persisting in stopping it was again a sign of possible severe personality disorder.

I had similar trouble in inducing Donald to do his activity homework assignments. When anyone is as inhibited and fearful as he, they not only have to change their Irrational Beliefs that are leading to their irrational fears—such as the Belief, "If I were to attempt to socialize and were rejected by people, that would prove that I am an unworthy, unlovable person who will never be able to succeed at socializing!"—but they also have to do, and keep doing, the acts they are terrified about doing. Risking exposure or in vivo desensitization is one of the main REBT techniques. And we probably use it more than other kinds of cognitive behavior therapy. For unless phobics actually act against their phobias and experientially see that they can do so and become comfortable about doing so, their telling themselves that the activity they irrationally fear is really not that frightening falls on deaf ears—their own deaf ears. So we emphasize exposure to feared situations in REBT, and I kept giving Donald homework assignments of socializing with people at the office, asking some of them to go to lunch with him, and talking with one young woman at work who seemed to be very friendly and to whom he was quite physically and mentally attracted.

No go. Donald kept avoiding these kinds of assignments, forgetting to do them. Or he was actually about to do one—to ask someone to have lunch with him, for example—and then froze up completely and was not able to get out the invitation. With one man at the office with whom he seemingly got along quite well and wanted to get closer, he tried to ask him to lunch several times, but never was able to get the words out of his mouth. Then, as he usually did, he beat himself for being so afraid and for not going through with the assignment. I showed him several times that his going dumb when he was about to try to arrange a lunch date was inept and "bad" behavior *but that he, Donald, was never a "bad person" nor an "inept person" for failing. He agreed with the concept I was trying to get him to accept—but not for himself. Other people were okay if they failed at this kind of a task; but he, Donald, was so inept at it that he really was thoroughly rotten and incompetent. He "saw" that this was not so, but still strongly felt that it was. In very important projects like this, he definitely refused to forgive himself for failing. He clung to his self-castigation vociferously—as many of the people with severe personality disorders do. They seem to be innately, biologically predisposed to damning themselves and not merely their poor behavior, and they often have great difficulty giving up this self-flagellation. Donald certainly did have trouble unconditionally accepting himself.*

I found the same thing with Donald's feelings of hostility and rebelliousness. On the surface, he was a "nice guy." He treated people considerately and, unlike his sister, didn't get in any trouble with them. But underneath, he had an enormous, rigid sense of "rightness" and didn't tolerate people's being indubitably wrong, and especially wrong with him. This particularly came out when we explored the possible reasons for his lateness at work. On the surface, there was no good reason for his persistent lateness, especially when he went out of his way, with several alarm clocks, to be on time. Also, he was a well-ordered individual, did his various jobs well, and was not at all a shirker and a procrastinator. Why, then, the persistent lateness?

I suspected that Donald's thoughts and feelings about "rightness" and the consequent hostility they led him to at times had something to do with his lateness. So I questioned him about this:

ELLIS. Don't you sometimes feel upset about how they keep after you at work for being late? After all, you make up for the time you lose by staying after hours without pay and by working on weekends. Don't you think that makes up for it and that they should largely forget about it?

GREEN. Well, now that you mention it, I do think that. After all, I do my work very well and have consistently done so for many years. And I do make up the time I lose. So I think they're unfair in keeping after me like they do. It's really not right! They *should* consider all the work I do and not merely this small part of it. Yes, it's very unfair!

ELLIS. And how do you really feel about their unfairness?

GREEN. Well, to be quite honest about it, I hate it. It's very unfair—and people *shouldn't* be that unfair. Especially when I do so much for them.

ELLIS. Well, let's agree that it really is unfair. After all, you have a fine record with them, and they have no complaints about you other than your lateness. So it's unfair. But where is it written that people *must* be fair?

GREEN. What do you mean? Of course, they should be fair.

ELLIS. Why? It would be nice if they *were*—in fact, it would be fair. But, again, why must they be fair? Is there a law of the universe that says that "people must at all times be absolutely fair"? If so, I haven't noticed it.

GREEN. But if people are unfair, we'll have chaos. Everyone would do what he wanted. We could not exist.

ELLIS. But we do. There's an incredible amount of unfairness in the world. Just read the New York Times every day and see. But the world nonetheless staggers on. Unfairly!

GREEN. Yes, I suppose it does. *(Donald seemed stymied, almost at a loss for words).* But it shouldn't be that way!

ELLIS. Granted that it's undesirable and leads to great harm—as unfairness almost always does. But still, *must* it not exist? Why should it absolutely not be that way? Why *must* everyone be fair?

GREEN. Well, I guess that they don't have to be. But—*(he was stymied again).*

ELLIS. No, it definitely does not have to be. But it *is.* And if you don't accept the fact that it is—not like it, but placidly *accept* it—what will be your result? How will you feel?

GREEN. Angry, I guess.

ELLIS. Damned angry! So angry, in fact, that when your firm acts unfairly and doesn't let you make up for your lateness with the extra work that you do, don't you think that you're very often angry at them, and that your anger itself might help you, consciously or unconsciously, to keep being late. Is that possible?

GREEN. Well, yes. I never thought about that before. Maybe I am often angry at them. And maybe that has something to do with my continued lateness. I never really thought about that.

ELLIS. Well, I'm just suggesting it as a possible hypothesis. Perhaps you'd better give it some more thought.

Donald did give it more thought, and by the time we had our fifth session he was able to see pretty clearly that he was quite angry at his firm and that his lateness most probably stemmed from this anger. This insight, however, didn't help him give up his anger. He still thought it was absolutely "right" that special allowances should be made for him in regard to his lateness, that it was most unfair that they weren't made, and that the firm definitely shouldn't be that unfair. Why? Because fairness was right and should not be abrogated. So he saw his anger, and saw that it was doing some harm; but he refused to give it up and go along with the firm's unfairness. His lateness abated a little—but only a little.

Secondly, I suspected that Donald's lateness was the result of his low frustration tolerance. When he was really uncomfortable—notably in socializing and in trying to get into a relationship with a woman—he immediately retreated and "comfortably" withdrew. Since he got along well by himself and occupied himself with enjoyable things to do, he stayed "comfortably" withdrawn—and became more and more afraid of the "dangers" of socializing. This behavior is native to practically all phobics. They define some activity such as being in elevators or trains as "very dangerous." They then experience panic at doing, or even thinking about doing, this activity. Then, to avoid the very uncomfortable feelings of panic, they "comfortably" continue their avoidance. Result: They become more and more phobic. So I questioned Donald about this to check my hypothesis of his having low frustration tolerance (LFT) about getting to work on time.

ELLIS. Don't you really find getting to work on time, in addition to the unfairness you think is involved in their making you do it, a royal pain in the ass? Isn't it a bit too regimented for you?

GREEN. Yes, I guess it is. I don't mind working—since when I do that I enjoy it and when I work on fixing up cars in my spare time I also enjoy that. But getting to work on time means that I have to carefully watch everything I do before I get to work. I have to watch the time I take to shave and shower, to eat breakfast, to get to the train, and so forth. I'm not really free to vary things in any way and am forced to keep a strict schedule. I don't like that. And I resent having to do it.

ELLIS. Okay, so you don't like scheduling yourself so stringently. That's understandable. And you like doing the actual work you do, which maybe doesn't require so much scheduling. Fine. But you just can't get to work on time, like all of us can't, without watching the time and scheduling things. That's necessary for time-keeping. So why don't you put up with the schedule even though you don't like it?

GREEN. I guess I think that I shouldn't have to do it. It's such a restriction that it shouldn't be that way?

ELLIS. Why shouldn't it be? Why shouldn't you be restricted, first, because you don't like to be and, second, because they could withdraw the restriction and let you come as late as you want? Why *must* things be the way you want them to be?

GREEN. Oh, I see again. You're starting to show me that there is no reason why bad things must not exist just because I don't want them to. I guess you're right there. Yes, there's no reason why they must not exist because I find them so repugnant.

Again, however, Donald saw his demand—when I pointed it out to him—and saw that it was silly—because he hardly ran the universe. But he still only saw this very lightly and refused to give up his demandingness. In some ways, as I have indicated, he had unusually high frustration tolerance. But when he disliked something, really disliked it, he vigorously rebelled against doing it—even though he seriously defeated himself in the process. This is a characteristic of just about all humans. When they seriously object to doing something, they often refuse to do it, even when they seriously defeat themselves by this refusal. People with severe personality disorders can intelligently see their low frustration tolerance and its concomitantly getting them to refuse to do things for which they would get desirable results if they did them. But they still stubbornly rebel against many uncomfortable performances. The world absolutely should *not,* must *not make them do what it is making them do. They'll be damned if they do it. So they create needless criticism of themselves by not doing it. Donald had more LFT in this respect than I would expect a "nice neurotic" to have. So again I suspected him of having a severe personality disorder.*

After several sessions with Donald, I was fairly convinced that he suffered from several typical neurotic traits and behaviors, but that he rigidly resisted the most concerted efforts to change them. He saw how disturbed he was, and saw many of the irrational beliefs that he was telling himself were creating his own disturbances. But he only lightly disputed these beliefs and intermittently did the activity homework that seemed to be required to change them. I thought about the possibility of discussing with him his conscious and unconscious resistances and informing him about his having personality disorders, so that he would be fully aware of them and realize that he well might have to work harder than most people to help overcome them.

This is a tricky business, informing people that they have a personality disorder, and that it most probably has biological as well as environmental sources. Even if we could be sure, in a particular case, that an individual is schizoid or a depressive, is it wise to tell him or her about this? Many clients, when so informed, think that because their difficulties are partly biological, they can do nothing about them—that they are hopeless. Other clients, who have low frustration tolerance to begin with, think that they may not be hopeless, but that they will have to work unusually hard to overcome their disturbed state—and they don't want to work that hard. Other clients, when informed of the depth of their disturbance, either rush for psychotropic medication instead of psychotherapy, or they are terrified of medication and completely avoid it. Still other clients think it disgraceful to have a severe personality disorder, therefore put themselves down for it, and thereby increase their disturbances.

For reasons like these, telling a client that he or she has a severe personality disorder is risky. But it is also risky not to inform them of this possibility. First, it gives the client an explanation of why they are resisting so much when they are doing their best to change and not succeeding. Second, it may give them an incentive to work harder at therapy because that is what is usually required of them if they are to make progress with a personality disorder. Third, it may give them important directives on what they had better change in themselves and how this is to be accomplished.

For reasons such as these, and because I thought he could accept it—especially since he was an engineer and did work very well in many aspects of his life—I decided to tell Donald about my diagnosis. I explained to him that he had definite schizoid tendencies; that in all probability they were partly innate; that his parents did not necessarily create them by the way they raised him; and that he had better realistically face his personality disorder and do his best to change some aspects of it and to live with other aspects that he might not change. One of the conversations I had with him went along these lines:

GREEN. I'm certainly trying hard to change some of my thinking and actions, but I'm getting discouraged. At times I just can't seem to do it, though I understand what you're telling me and really am doing my best to use it.

ELLIS. I think that's partly because you not only adopted some of your dysfunctional ways of thinking, feeling, and behaving, but that you were probably born with strong tendencies to have them.

Also, you have also practiced them for so many years. So you easily act in a somewhat avoidant and withdrawn way and you are habituated to doing so.

GREEN. So you think that I was really born this way and that is why I am having so much trouble changing?

ELLIS. Well, it's a little more complicated than that. But a good deal of research has shown that people who are somewhat like you have strong innate tendencies to act the way they do. They easily are shy and withdrawn, because their brain chemistry is somewhat different than that of other people. Their neurotransmitters are somewhat defective, and often their serotonin level is low. Because of this, they act poorly in some respects from early childhood onward; and they are also treated differently by their parents, peers, and other people. They are wrongly blamed for some of their behavior and put down for it. Also, because they easily withdraw from social affairs, they get less practice dealing with social situations; and then they sometimes become even more withdrawn. So it's rather complicated.

GREEN. But it does have a biological or neurological element? Their brain chemistry is off?

ELLIS. Yes, to some extent. And sometimes it can be remedied by proper medication, such as Prozac or Xanax. But sometimes no medications work well. So they have to handle it themselves.

GREEN. And how can they do it? What can I do if I am in that category?

ELLIS. There are several things you can do and I will explain them to you. But the main thing is for you to first accept the fact that you may have a biological difference from some other people—just as I do. I am diabetic, and have been for many years, because my pancreas doesn't function as well as other people's do. Therefore I have to take insulin every day, test my blood several times each day, avoid foods like sugar, and follow a diabetic regimen. Fortunately, I have done so for many years and I have therefore outlived my brother, who did not have diabetes.

GREEN. So that there are things I can do to help myself if I am innately predisposed to being shy and withdrawn?

ELLIS. Oh, yes. Just as people with weak muscles can work to improve them. Some people are born with muscular deficiency; and some have an ailment like polio during their lifetime and develop poor muscles. But despite this handicap, some of them do an unusual amount of exercise, develop their muscles, and actually become champions in swimming or some other sport. See?

GREEN. Yes, I see. There is something I can do.

ELLIS. Yes, definitely. But mainly you can accept yourself with your disability and not put yourself down for it. People who have personality disorder, such as the one you may have, frequently notice it at an early age and put themselves down for having it. They see that they have certain deficiencies and then tell themselves, "I shouldn't be deficient! It's awful to be handicapped!" They then almost always become much more handicapped than they otherwise would be.

GREEN. And they are criticized more by others? Like I think I was when, as a child, I wasn't too social. People noticed it and put me down for it.

ELLIS. Yes, as I said before. They get greatly criticized by others who think they are not really trying: they then internalize this criticism. Then they are more handicapped by their self-blaming than they are by their handicaps.

GREEN. I think that definitely happened to me.

ELLIS. Yes, I think it did. Now we have to counteract it and get you to the point where you practically never criticize or blame yourself for anything. You acknowledge your human failings, and perhaps some of your special failings. But you achieve what I've been trying to help you work on—USA, unconditional self-acceptance—in spite of your distinct limitations and failings.

This and several other conversations with Donald went over well. He seemed to accept the fact that in some ways he was quite different from other people, that in all probability he inherited some of his tendencies for withdrawal and isolation, and that he also had innate tendencies to be panicked and depressed. He looked up some psychology books, recognized that he was probably a schizoid personality, and dealt with this possibility well. I saw that I was right in bringing his personality disorder to his conscious attention.

My therapeutic plan was to keep working, though at a somewhat slower pace, to help Donald to overcome his relationship problems, his panic states, and his underlying anger and rebelliousness; but to do so within the framework of helping him, like all my clients, to achieve unconditional self-acceptance and high frustration tolerance (HFT). These traits are exceptionally important, I think, for practically all people, including neurotics, to achieve. But they are especially important—almost necessary—for individuals suffering from severe personality disorders. With-

out acquiring them, little progress in changing their disturbed feelings and behaviors is likely to be achieved. I directly showed Donald how desirable this process of change would be and asked him if he would be willing to work very hard to achieve it. He said that he would.

Sessions 7 to 12

I was by now reasonably convinced—though not certain—that Donald had a severe personality disorder—including a pronounced tendency toward schizoid shyness and withdrawal as well as a strong predisposition to anxiety and depression—so I realistically decided to go more slowly with him than I would have gone with a "nice neurotic." I would work more concertedly on his three major problems—self-downing, rebellious hostility, and low frustration tolerance. But I would also significantly work on social inhibitions and his compulsive lateness to work, his panicky dreams and fantasies, and his phobia of dogs barking. Whether we succeeded in alleviating these presenting problems—and their interference with his life—we would try for a profound philosophical change, which would then enable him to live with any disabilities and limitations that he did not ameliorate within the course of therapy.

This is usually my general plan with people who have severe personality disorders. I try to help them relieve themselves of their specific phobias, compulsions, and panic states, which tend to interfere with their lives. But in case we have limited gains in this respect, especially in certain areas, I hope that they acquire during therapy a strong philosophic outlook that enables them to live successfully, though still restrictedly, with their remaining limitations. Therapy relieves them of some of their main presenting burdens; but to the extent that it does not do so, it allows them to live more peacefully—and especially less self-damningly—with the handicaps that they do not reduce. This plan is somewhat similar to that I used with people who have serious physical limitations, such as blindness or loss of a limb. I try to help them overcome their physical handicap to some extent—to do productive work, for example, in spite of their blindness. But I also help them to accept the limitations that they cannot overcome and to lead fulfilling lives in spite of these restrictions. So what I call general REBT—achieving unconditional self-acceptance, unconditional other-acceptance, and high frustration tolerance—helps handicapped people conquer some of their limitations. But it also appreciably helps them to live successfully and uncomplainingly with those that they cannot remove.

Because schizoid individuals, such as I thought Donald to be, have enormous propensities for conditional instead of unconditional acceptance and consequently wind up with considerable conscious or unconscious self-deprecation, I kept working with him on USA. He, you might say unfortunately, had a great deal of conditional self-acceptance—or what is normally called self-esteem. He knew that he was good at engineering, at fixing up old cars, and at being generally reliable and trustworthy; and he therefore considered himself a "good person" with "good character." But this was an exceptionally shaky concept, because when he acted "badly" or "immorally" he felt supremely guilty, worthless, and deserving of great punishment. That is why, we figured out together, he was so easily terrified of not living up to his virtues, of being found wanting by others, and of being greatly penalized. Thus, he didn't get too close to even his best friends, Jim and Mary, because they might discover his hidden failing. He was afraid that the woman whose car he fixed would find it defective and would sue him. He was sure that the FBI would arrest him for tax evasion and put him in prison. He was afraid to correct his supervisors at work, and therefore fixed the errors himself. And he dreamed constantly of failing a crucial examination and not getting his degree. If he did any of these "wrong" or "bad" things—which he took care to work hard at not doing—he lost his very tentative self-esteem and considered himself an unworthy person who deserved to be punished severely for his "terrible sins."

Because Donald's gaining unconditional, unassailable self-acceptance was so crucial, I kept using the "elegant" REBT form of disputing with him. When, for example, he beat himself for not fixing up the woman's car perfectly and therefore warding off her anger, I could have shown him that her rage was highly improbable for several reasons. (1) He was a very good car fixer and normally did a fine job. (2) The fact that he saw the car in front of a garage most probably didn't mean that she had to get it fixed. (3) If there was really something a little wrong with it and she had to get it fixed, that probably didn't mean that he had done a poor job with it. (4) Even if she didn't like the way he had fixed the car she might not be too angry with him. (5) She would, if she were angry, most probably decide not to sue him because it would be too expensive to do so. (6) If she did sue him, she would most probably not win the suit. And so forth. I could have used these arguments to show Donald that he really was in no danger of the woman's anger or of her suing him.

Instead, I used "the worst that could possibly happen" argument, as follows:

ELLIS. Actually, there is very little chance that you did not fix her car properly—as you finally found out from her. But let us suppose the worst. Let's suppose that you really did a very bad job on the car and she got very angry at you, vowed vengeance, and kept harassing you in many ways, calling you and telling you what a louse you were, suing you in court, telling the judge and jury how you couldn't fix any car well, and actually winning the lawsuit for a tidy sum. Let's even suppose that as a result of your fixing her car badly she got in a serious accident, was crippled for life, and sued you for several million dollars, and won the suit.

GREEN. Oh, I really thought that some of those things would happen. I was sure that I had fixed her car very badly and that my doing so would have very serious consequences, somewhat like you said. That's why I was so terrified and kept being panicked.

ELLIS. Yes, I realize that. But there's something worse there than your just ruining her car and being penalized by a malpractice suit and losing money. Something much worse than that. What do you think it is?

GREEN. Something worse? I can't see what it is. What is it?

ELLIS. How about your opinion of *yourself*—if all those bad things occurred. What would you think of *you?*

GREEN. Oh yes, you're right! I would think terrible thoughts about me. I would think I was an utter worm, an incompetent person.

ELLIS. See! That's the real issue. You would put *yourself* down and see yourself as an utter no-goodnik.

GREEN. I certainly would. And wouldn't I be right about that? Wouldn't I be a really rotten, hopeless person?

ELLIS. No, you definitely wouldn't be. Let's suppose all those vile things happened—the woman got in an accident because of the bad way you fixed her car; she got very angry and sued you; and she easily won the suit because the judge and jury all agreed that you were incompetent and had harmed her. Why would you still not be a worthless, bad person? Why?

GREEN. Why would I not be?

ELLIS. Yes, why would you definitely *not* be worthless, no good?

GREEN. Well...Oh, yes, you're trying to get me to see that my bad deeds, my incompetence in regard to her car, and my doing the bad deed of hurting the woman would be wrong and destructive. But that would merely be some of my traits or doings and these traits would not make *me* bad, make me a *bad person.*

ELLIS. Right! That's what I'm trying to get you to see—that no matter how badly you do and what rotten results you get, it is very bad, it is sad and deplorable. But you, the entire person, are never bad—no matter how poorly you do. That is the point. Can you see that?

GREEN. Yes. I see it partly. But I'm really having difficulty getting that idea. If I really do that badly, hurt the woman, and get sued for a million dollars...that's doing *so* badly, *so* many bad things, that I can't help thinking that *I* am bad, *I* am a very rotten person.

ELLIS. You can't help thinking that because that's your basic, self-defeating philosophy. You only accept yourself when you do well—quite conditionally. And as soon as you do poorly again—which of course as a fallible human being you will—you sink back to self-deprecation. You stupidly think, "I am no good," instead of, "What I did is not good." But you are a fallible person who did a bad thing. You are never, never a worm, a louse, or a "no-goodnik." Can you see that?

GREEN. Very shakily.

ELLIS. Yes, very lightly. Now we'd better help you see that very *strongly* and *consistently.* Until you really believe it. Until you accept yourself unconditionally—whether you do well or badly, whether people love or hate you.

So I used the elegant disputing solution many times with Donald, to show him that even if he did very badly with the car and the woman, or with anything else in his life, he was at most a person who acted incompetently and never an incompetent, rotten person. Gradually, and without some temporary real setbacks, I helped him see this.

Similarly, I used the elegant disputing solution to help Donald gain increased unconditional other-acceptance. Thus, I could have shown him that the people at work were really not that unfair in keeping after him about his lateness. For even though he was a good and steady worker, and even though he made up the time he lost by being late to work, they had good reasons for getting after him. After all, he was a bad example to other workers; he was rebelliously defiant of their rules; he interfered with the work of others when he came late and when they couldn't rely on him. So he was harming the firm and he was harming his coworkers. Therefore they had some good reasons for blaming his lateness, and he'd better not just think that they were unfair.

I at times used these arguments with Donald to show him that he had better not be so hostile to the firm and to his coworkers for insisting that he be on time. But I also used more elegant REBT disputing arguments:

ELLIS. Let's suppose that people are really unfair to you at your work. You treat them pretty fairly by doing extra work, but they ignore this and are really unfair to you. If so, how can you accept them with their unfair behavior?

GREEN. Well, I could tell myself that they're really not that unfair. After all, those are the rules of the game: you are given certain hours to come in, and you agree to those hours. Therefore it's not really that unfair that they ask you to keep those hours.

ELLIS. Yes, you could tell yourself that and then you would not tend to be so hostile. But even if you were thoroughly convinced, and other people were, too, that your firm treats you unfairly in forcing you to come in early, when you really are doing more work than the others and staying overtime without pay, how could you still accept them with their unfairness?

GREEN. I suppose I could say, "So what? So they're unfair! Unfairness just exists, and that's the way it is. If I want to work for them, I just better put up with their unfairness. I don't have to make a federal case of it."

ELLIS. That's much better. That accepts grim social reality. But you went a little too far in saying, "So what?" It is important if people treat you unfairly and you'd better not ignore it. If you do, you won't even try to do anything about it—to change what you possibly can change. A "so what" attitude isn't very accurate or rational.

GREEN. Yes, I'd better not say, "So what if the bridge falls down. It's not the end of the world." I'd better build it so it doesn't fall down. I see what you mean. Well, I could say, "It's bad, really bad, if they continue to treat me unfairly. Unfairness is wrong. But it's not awful. And it's not totally unfair, since they treat me fairly in other respects." So I can accept the unfairness, even if it's rotten, as just one element in my job. And maybe I'll give up my hostility, my rage about it, and then get myself to come to work on time.

ELLIS. That's really excellent! Good thinking! You can accept the fact that it's not unfair, without making a total disaster of it. You can put it in its place, along with all the unfairness that your firm gives you. Then you can see things in perspective.

GREEN. Yes, as you keep showing me, I can accept the sinner but not accept, or at least like, the sin.

ELLIS. Beautiful. And you can do that in various other ways. Accept the fact that people don't go out of their way to be too social with you, and actually criticize you for being stand-offish. Maybe they're wrong, even though they're the majority, and maybe they're unkind and unfair. But that's the way people often are—negative and hostile. You, of course, are in some ways like that yourself. But that doesn't necessarily excuse them. If they're wrong, they're wrong. And they don't *have to be* right, as you often keep insisting that they have to be. Wrong is wrong, in many ways. But wrongdoers are not lice or vermin for being wrong. Just fallible, screwed-up humans!

Again and again, I went over this point with Donald. I also gave him homework assignments of deliberately cultivating some of the people he believed to be most wrong. Instead of avoiding them, as he easily did, he was to stay with them and have more contact with them. Let them be as wrong and bigoted as they could be—and still accept them *though not their* wrongdoings. *As he did some of these homework assignments, particularly with one woman at work who was very bigoted against foreigners and Catholics—and Donald's grandparents on his mother's side had been both Polish and Catholic—he was able to accept her unconditionally, while deploring her bigotry, and give up his anger toward her. He concluded, "She is definitely bigoted but that doesn't make her a thorough bigot and a rotten person. She is otherwise kind and considerate—and good to her goddam mother!"*

I kept after Donald on many different occasions, especially in regard to his self-righteousness and the indignation it frequently produced. I didn't object to his beliefs of what was "right" and "wrong," but to his rigidity in holding these beliefs and condemning other people when they were "wrong." I even encouraged him to volunteer to help an antiracist group while working on his problem, not despising racists as people.

In regard to his low frustration tolerance, I especially focused in on Donald's horror of dogs barking. He was sensitive to sudden noises and felt that at all costs people should prevent them. Dog owners could, obviously, not completely stop their dogs from barking, but they could arrange for the dogs not to be in an apartment alone and they could even get dogs that didn't bark too much or didn't bark loudly. They were completely inconsiderate of other people, especially himself, when they went away for several hours and left their dogs alone to bark. Of course, the more that Donald saw and felt how awful it was for people not to take care of their barking dogs, the more upset he became whenever he heard dogs barking. He also realized that other people were less upset about barking dogs than he was. So he had a secondary symptom of putting himself down for being so sensitive to barking dogs; and he was intolerant of his low frustration tolerance about them.

I first worked with Donald on his secondary symptoms about his sensitivity to barking dogs. I helped him see that this was a poor trait—since the mere barking of dogs wasn't dangerous to him and many of the barking dogs were actually confined to their own apartments while barking. But he was allowed to have foolish fears and never had to put himself down for them. Also, he exaggerated how noisy and "horrible" was the barking of dogs, and his low frustration tolerance in this respect was indeed silly and self-defeating—but he didn't have to have LFT about his LFT. He could bear it, work to reduce it, but accept it as a mere handicapping trait.

Then I helped Donald see that his demanding that owners of dogs be more considerate about their barking and do more than they were doing to curb it was only creating more frustration for him. It was bad enough that he did not like noisy dogs. But his defining the noise and the dog owners' refusal to curb it as "terrible" and "awful" and his continually telling himself, "I can't bear it! I can't stand it!" was only making conditions worse—was increasing his frustration. Therefore, he'd better keep his distaste of noise and of dogs' barking without whining and screaming about it.

Donald did work on his LFT in this respect. He even used his accepting of the inconvenience of barking dogs as much less than a "horror" to modify his other aspect of LFT—such as his "horror" of having to regiment himself to get to work on time in the morning. He made it a challenge to dislike but not to horrify himself about barking dogs and by doing so raised his general low frustration tolerance to a small degree.

I thought it strange that during his sessions with me Donald was rarely depressed. I had tentatively diagnosed him as schizoid and depressive, with perhaps some degree of obsessive compulsive disorder (OCD). I considered OCD because he compulsively kept up at his regular work and his extra work of fixing up old cars, and he was compulsive in the sense that he kept being late to work despite some real efforts to set various alarms and to get a special telephone call in the morning to wake him. People who are schizoid and who have OCD are frequently depressives and tend to have a serotonin deficiency. So I suspected that Donald was in this category and had an inherited tendency toward depression, particularly from his reclusive father. As was noted in the intake session, Donald was sometimes lonely and depressed, felt trapped in his style of life, sometimes felt like screaming, and had even thought of suicide. "Very suspicious!" I thought. So I kept looking for severely depressed symptoms.

Then I figured out the possible solution to this problem. Like his father, Donald kept compulsively busy; and during the sessions with me he was typically busy, figuring out what to do and how to answer me during the sessions and also figuring out how to do the homework—or not avoid doing it—and sticking to intense problem-solving. Therefore he—like his father—was not overtly depressed, but lived a self-trapped, exceptionally busy life that enabled him to avoid, for the most part, overt feelings of depression. However, I still tentatively diagnosed a severe depression that underlay this. I therefore brought up with him his feelings about being trapped in his life style, his loneliness, and his occasional thoughts about suicide. He seemed to feel glad that I remembered these manifestations and was quite ready to discuss them.

We spent several sessions discussing his depressive tendencies and also that of his father and his father's two brothers. All three of them functioned well in their professional lives, but little more than that. The father's two brothers never married and never seemed to have dated. They both worked well—one as an attorney and one as an accountant—and that was it. They lived together and came home to a life of television watching and a mutual obsession with stamp collecting. They had no male or female intimates, got in no trouble, and were not overtly miserable. But, like Donald and his father, they led very restricted lives. Nothing ventured, nothing gained! As far as I could see, they were closet depressives.

As for Donald, he kept busy at work, at his hobby of car

fixing, and at his therapy, so he too was not overtly depressed. But from time to time his life seemed completely boxed in and hopeless, and his underlying purpose of having a close relationship was never consistently worked at. As soon as he got even reasonably close to establishing one, he retreated into his superficial problem-solving activity and managed to get nowhere with his "goal."

Donald himself, with some help from me, put two and two together and came up with what seemed to be a viable hypothesis about his depressed condition.

GREEN. I've been thinking things over during the last 2 weeks that I haven't seen you and I realize now that I really am often more depressed than I seem to feel. I keep so busy, as you've pointed out, that I don't usually give myself time to feel depressed. But a sense of hopelessness and purposelessness is always there.

ELLIS. Yes, I'm glad you've been thinking about that. And what do you think are some of the basic causes of your depression?

GREEN. Well, putting several things together, I think my depression is caused by the three main things we've been talking about: self-downing, anger, and low frustration tolerance. I keep almost frantically looking for things about me—imperfect things—to put myself down for. I am really very angry at other people for not appreciating me and balking me, and my righteousness against them makes me feel good temporarily and covers up my incessant self-downing. Then, thirdly, I have, as you keep noting, strong LFT and keep at times whining and screaming about the "terrible" restrictions that my own state and the rules of others put upon me. So in several basic ways I react with depression to the common restrictions and frustrations of life.

ELLIS. That's very good. I think you've come up with an accurate diagnosis and several basic reasons for it. This sort of confirms my own view and shows that we have been on the right track. If your depressive tendencies are largely created by your self-denigration, your anger at others, and your LFT, then you had better keep working on these three processes, as I think you have been doing already. Let me congratulate you on seeing things so clearly.

GREEN. You can congratulate me more if I keep working to change these things.

At this point, we discussed the possibility of Donald being assessed by a psychopharmacologist and his taking some antidepressive medication. He thought about doing so, but was somewhat opposed to taking almost any "artificial" medication—he even avoided taking aspirin when he had a headache. So he decided against trying psychotropic drugs for the time being and said that, instead, he would work harder at changing his basic depression-creating philosophies. I agreed that this would be a good idea.

Normally, when I bring my clients' attention to the possibility of their having a severe personality disorder, I tell them about recent neurological research and give them the option of being assessed for psychopharmacological medication. I especially do this when they seem to be working very hard at REBT and are still having quite limited results. But even then I inform them that medication is to be tried experimentally, since sometimes it helps greatly and sometimes it hardly helps at all, and may even lead to worse results than they are getting. Moreover, various medications have side effects—such as interference with people's sex life—and may not be worth it. So they have a choice about being psychiatrically evaluated and, even then, about using or not using medication. Sometimes, it helps them to think much straighter and to feel much better, and therefore is well worth it. But sometimes they try one of several medications—such as Prozac, Zoloft, Wellbutrin—and get temporary improvement or no improvement at all. So the choice is up to them and I merely urge them to work harder at the REBT if they decide not to take medication.

Sessions 13 to 20

By the end of the 12th session Donald had considerably improved in several important respects. He came to work regularly on time and only occasionally was late. He accomplished this by working on his anger at his firm and his low frustration tolerance and also by penalizing himself by making himself talk to some boring and stupid people for a solid hour every time he was late. He opened up with his friends, Jim and Mary, and told them a good deal about his shortcomings and his problems that he had previously kept from them. He first did this as a homework assignment, at my suggestion, but his closeness with them began to go so well that he spontaneously continued it on his own. He continued to confide in me, but he had much less need of my approval for him and began to do things primarily to please himself and not mainly to please me and win my favor.

Donald stopped fantasizing catastrophes and had few panic states. When he did something that he considered wrong, he convinced himself that nothing serious would happen to him and that even if it did, he could handle it. He became much more assertive with the men at work whom he supervised and when they didn't like his new assertiveness, he held his ground and was strict but not hostile with them. He had few dreams about the horror of failing an exam or of being lost somewhere without any money resources.

Because of this progress, I started seeing Donald every 2 or 3 weeks and then every month. He was very happy with his progress and looked forward to telling me new risks he had taken, especially social risks, and what great strides he was making. Actually, however, his progress in social relationships was rather superficial. I got him to take one of the social skills training courses we give at the Institute, and he actually took it twice, for 8 weeks at a time. He also, at my suggestion, took several lessons in social dancing and soon was able to dance quite well and to be able to go to a dance at a Y or some other place and easily ask appealing women to dance with him. When he was in a social group, he felt reasonably comfortable and was able to carry on with suitable conversation.

Getting him into an intimate relationship with a suitable woman, however, was quite another matter. Most of the women he dated found him distinctly eligible, since he had a good job, was financially secure, and he treated them nicely. They found him, however, too stiff, formal, and self-conscious. They were looking for someone who was more relaxed and could more easily "have fun" and he didn't fit that bill. His affection didn't go very deep and sexually he was able to go through the motions and to satisfy his partner and come to orgasm himself. But as one of the women described it after dating him several times, he had no real sensual or sexual enthusiasm.

The one woman, moreover, that he was quite attracted to and was inwardly enthusiastic about, he was still anxious and inhibited with. She worked in his office and showed some interest in him. But it took him many weeks before he could ask her to lunch and attempt to date her; and he always remained stiff and anxious with her on their dates. He tried a problem-solving approach to their relationship and was able to keep steadily dating her for several months. He did everything that regular boyfriends were supposed to do, including becoming friendly with her close relatives and getting them to like him. He even became her brother's regular tennis partner and got along with him as well. But though everyone seemed to like him and think that he was a suitable partner for the woman, Marcia, she found him "nice, but too absorbed in his work and his problems. Not really with it."

After seeing him for a year and having him really appreciate "the great progress we've made together," I stopped seeing Donald for regular sessions and now only see him once or twice a year for booster shots. He still feels grateful for the therapy he has had and is not depressed about his failing to mate with a partner whom he finds attractive and really intelligent. He sometimes thinks of compromising and settling for a very bright and nice woman who is not too attractive and thinks that he may do so in the future. But he is not upset about this and is willing to go on with his pleasant and little-disturbed life if he never marries and has children. In fact, he sometimes thinks that being a responsible father would be a great idea, but that it would also lead to hassles and complications that he wouldn't thoroughly enjoy. So he keeps his mind open about this but is not desperate and is willing to face the rest of his life alone if that is to be.

I think that the case of Donald is one of my most successful ones, in that he was quite disturbed in several ways when I first saw him, and now he has improved appreciably in his work and social life and is practically free from panic, depression, and underlying hostility. In fact, he is doing much better in these respects than some of my "nice neurotic" clients are doing. I still think that Donald has a severe personality disorder, and that he is improved but not exactly cured. It still limits him to some extent and may never be completely gone. This is typical of people who suffer from personality disorders. They not only have irrational beliefs and tend to hold them very strongly, but they also—as I have pointed out in several papers on this subject (Ellis, 1994a, 1994b, 1994c) have cognitive, emotional, and behavioral deficits, which can be ameliorated to some extent but which are rarely eliminated completely. Hence, they are less effective at work and play, and especially at relating, than they would otherwise tend to be.

Many people with severe personality disorders make many fewer gains than Donald made. They stay for years in therapy and frequently return for renewed sessions again, and they more or less act inadequately all their lives. Why were my sessions with Donald relatively successful? For several reasons, I think. (1) He was quite intelligent and capable in several aspects of his life before therapy. (2) He was especially willing to work hard at changing himself—which many "nice neurotics" are not willing to do. (3) Although his social life was seriously deficient and he was quite anxious and panicked, he had already made some adjustments himself and was by no means living a completely miserable life. (4) I think it was good that I recognized his basic personality disorder, and from the start kept emphasizing with him the desirability of unconditionally accepting himself, accepting other people, and accepting unfortunate environmental conditions. (5) Following my lead, he worked exceptionally hard, against odds, to do this kind of triple unconditional acceptance. As he did so, he was able to perform practical homework assignments and to gain several useful experiences that reinforced his changing his anxious and depressive character structure. (6) He was able to face the fact that he suffered from severe personality disorders and to work unusually hard at dealing with his self-sabotaging innate and acquired tendencies.

I want to stress again what I said at the beginning of this chapter. Practically everyone of the 6 billion inhabitants of this world have their neurotic tendencies and tend to often think crookedly, emote in disturbed fashion, and behave dysfunctionally. The human condition for almost all of us is constructive, problemsolving, and creative. But we also tend to construct poor solutions to the difficult human condition. Therefore, there are relatively few individuals who could not use psychotherapy—or at least considerable therapeutic education. And we had better arrange this, preferably starting in our school system, as we teach youngsters how to cope with life problems.

At the same time, we had better face the fact that a large minority of individuals—at times, I think as many as 30% of them—are born and reared with distinct cognitive, emotional, and other limitations. A small percentage of them are psychotic but most of them suffer from one or more severe personality disorders. We had better suspect many of our psychotherapy clients of being in this category, be unusually alert to accepting them with their limitations and resistances, and teach them—as well as the "nice neurotic" clients—to give themselves unconditional self-acceptance, other-acceptance, and high frustration tolerance.

If we do so, we will be able to help these difficult customers more than we often do by ignoring their unfortunate psychophysiological condition. ■

CRITIQUE OF DONALD GREEN'S TREATMENT BY RATIONAL EMOTIVE BEHAVIOR THERAPY

by Shawn F. Blau

Albert Ellis's illustration of his own creation—rational emotive behavior therapy—nicely demonstrates many of its therapeutic strategies, tactics, and methods. Ellis's distinctive theory of treatment has been reviewed at length by Ellis himself and by others (see bibliography). But this chapter's main strength is that it sheds **new** light on REBT's original and iconoclastic theory of psychological *assessment.*

Clinical Assessment

1. The great strength of Albert Ellis's presentation is that it gives us an unusual degree of insight into REBT's philosophy of assessment and diagnosis. Ellis's philosophy of assessment stems from REBT's view of human nature, which hypothesizes that human beings respond to adversities with their own personal repertoires of evaluative beliefs (**B**'s). All humans have an unfortunate tendency to respond with irrational evaluations (**IB**'s), along with rational evaluative beliefs (**RB**'s). The goal of assessment in REBT is to identify the client's own unique mix of rational evaluative beliefs (**RB**'s) and irrational evaluative beliefs (**IB**'s). REBT hypothesizes that the clients *bring* this repertoire of **RB**'s and **IB**'s to the practical problems they confront.
2. REBT doesn't depend on standard paper-and-pencil instruments, nor does it devote a great deal of time specifically to diagnostic procedures. Rather, Ellis uses the therapeutic experience itself, and Green's various reactions to therapy, to come closer and closer to an accurate diagnosis. Ellis looks for evidence that Green may have one or more long-term personality disorders. REBT hypothesizes that biological constitution and inherited characteristics play a major role in the etiology of psychopathology, particularly in the case of the more serious personality disorders and psychoses.
3. Ellis uses Green's reactions to REBT to get insight into Green's inner emotional and cognitive experience, which Green normally hides from others and sometimes even from himself.
4. Ellis's assessment of Green is mainly *instrumental,* in that it focuses on such assets and liabilities as Green can bring to bear on the tasks of REBT. The fact is that REBT views the diagnosis of Green's personality disorder as mainly a descriptive summary of his condition, which has instrumental value primarily within the context of rational emotive behavior therapy itself.
5. Ellis is careful to avoid what he himself has called "intellectual fascism" in his own relationship with Green. That is, he does not rate Green's totality or entire self simply on the basis of

Green's possessing a personality disorder. Rather, Ellis shows Green how he can unconditionally accept himself, despite any constitutional limitations he may possess, either physical or mental.

Therapeutic Practice

In terms of therapeutic techniques, the chapter illustrates the following methods:

1. First, Ellis teaches Donald Green the *main theoretical premise* of REBT: to wit, that **A**, Green's Adversity, does not usually *cause* his emotional consequences (**C**'s) by itself. Rather, it is **B**, consisting of Green's idiosyncratic evaluative beliefs about **A**, which mainly contributes to his disturbed emotional state.
2. Next, Ellis illustrates the difference between healthful rational beliefs (**RB**'s) and unhealthful irrational beliefs (**IB**'s).
3. Then, Ellis moves more directly to address one specific **C**—Green's shyness with women. Ellis immediately begins to investigate which IB's may be leading to Green's shyness.
4. When he discovers one possible IB, Ellis doesn't beat around the bush, or wait for Green to reinvent the wheel. Rather, Ellis immediately *shows* Green how he can attack his own IB and replace it with a more logical, empirically accurate, and pragmatic **RB**. The paradigm for accomplishing this change in REBT is to search for the "must" in the **IB**, and to change it into a preference.
5. Right from his first session, Ellis gives Mr. Green homework assignments. This shows Green from the very beginning that he need not depend on any one, including Ellis himself, to ameliorate his own emotional problems. The assignments are multimodal, including cognitive, emotive, and behavioral assignments.
6. At the beginning of the next session, Ellis *uses* Green's failure to carry out some of the homework as an opportunity to teach Green one of REBT's most important lessons—"unconditional self acceptance" (USA).
7. Next, Ellis introduces Green to one of REBT's most powerful and original emotive methods, rational emotive imagery. Although Green initially has a great deal of difficulty with this method, Ellis does not give in to his own "low frustration

tolerance" (LFT) with his client, but rather persists with Green until Green is actually able to *feel in his gut* that he, Green, has succeeded in changing his own emotional disturbance.

8. Then, Ellis shows Green how to use behavioral reinforcement to help him stay on track to achieve some of his long-range goals. Characteristically, REBT shows Green how to use both rewards *and penalties* to help him carry out the assignments.
9. Next, Ellis moves on to an entirely different **C**, Green's habit of arriving late to work. Again, Ellis doesn't wait for Green to diagnose his own **IB**, but immediately Ellis offers his own tentative hypothesis.
10. Next, Ellis shows Green another one of REBT's most original concepts, the idea of "discomfort anxiety," or "low frustration tolerance." Ellis shows Green how this secondary disturbance, Green's becoming anxious about *the threat* of experiencing his own anxiety, prevents Green from confronting his primary anxiety and disputing his anxiety-causing **IB**'s. Ellis shows Green how to work against this secondary disturbance *first,* in order to be able to then get at his primary disturbance.
11. Ellis decides to reveal to Green his diagnosis of a personality disorder, and to use the diagnosis to help Green achieve a more profound philosophical change, particularly with regard to *unconditional self-acceptance,* and *high frustration tolerance.*
12. When Green clearly exaggerates the probability of a particular disaster striking, Ellis doesn't disprove Green's prediction, but rather for the sake of argument *supposes that the worst thing that could possibly happen actually will happen.* This gives Ellis an opportunity to demonstrate quite dramatically to Green the profound philosophical difference between (conditional) self-esteem, and (unconditional) self-acceptance.
13. Finally, Ellis attempts to identify some of Green's more covert **C**'s, particularly his depression, and to show Green how he has defensively distracted himself from realizing how depressed he often feels.

Critique

Overall, Ellis does a fine job in demonstrating his own form of therapy on Donald Green, but I would add the following comments and suggestions:

1. Although I agree with Ellis's decision to inform Green that he probably has some form of personality disorder, I believe that Ellis's explanation to Green is not detailed enough. What are the main cognitive, emotional, and behavioral components of the personality disorder(s) that Green has?
2. Although the etiology of Green's personality disorder may be biological or genetic, it is presumably manifested through particular **IB**'s in particular situations. I would have worked with Green on identifying the specific **IB**'s that the personality disorder exhibits and in exactly those circumstances in which they tend to arise.
3. The human mind is almost endlessly creative, and it's possible that if Green were to have devoted his engineering skills to coping with his own biological predisposition to create refractory **IB**'s, he may eventually have been able to come up with some solutions that even Ellis couldn't predict at this point.
4. If Green were to benefit from drug therapy, presumably the drugs would reduce the frequency or refractoriness of some specific **IB**'s. Which **IB**'s? In response to which **A**'s? How will Green be able to assess the putative effectiveness of any pharmacological treatment?
5. After all, presumably Green will have a lifetime to deal with his own peculiar brand of personality disorder, and he had better be given as much information about it as possible. Ellis's therapy has given Green a good beginning on gaining more control over his emotional problems, but from now on, how he uses it for the rest of his life, and how far he progresses with it, will mainly be up to Green himself.

REFERENCES

DiGiuseppe, R., Terjesen, M., Rose, R., Doyle, K., & Vidalakis, N. (1998, August). *Selective abstraction errors in reviewing REBT outcome studies: A review of reviews.* Poster presented at the 106th Annual Convention of the American Psychological Association, San Francisco, CA.

Ellis, A. (1994a). Post-traumatic stress disorder (PTSD) in rape victims: A rational emotive behavioral theory. *Journal of Rational-Emotive and Cognitive-Behavior Therapy,* 13, 3–25.

Ellis, A. (1994b). *Reason and emotion in psychotherapy.* Revised and updated. Secaucus, NJ: Carol Publishing Group.

Ellis, A. (1994c). Rational emotive behavior therapy approaches to obsessive-compulsive disorder (OCD). *Journal of Rational-Emotive and Cognitive-Behavior Therapy,* 12, 121–141.

Ellis, A. (1996). *Better, deeper, and more enduring brief therapy.* New York: Brunner/Mazel.

Ellis, A. (1998). *How to control your anxiety before it controls you.* Secaucus, NJ: Carol Publishing Group.

Ellis, A., & Blau, S. (1998). Rational emotive behavior therapy. *Directions in Clinical and Counseling Psychotherapy,* 8(4), 41–51.

Ellis, A., & Dryden, W. (1997). *The practice of rational emotive behavior therapy.* New York: Springer.

Ellis, A., & Harper, R. A. (1997). *A guide to rational living.* North Hollywood, CA: Melvin Powers.

Ellis, A., & MacLaren, C. (1998). *Rational emotive behavior therapy: A therapist's guide.* San Luis Obispo, CA: Impact Publishers.

Lyons, L. C., & Woods, P. V. (1991). The efficacy of rational-emotive therapy: A quantitative review of the outcome research. *Clinical Psychology Review,* 11, 357–369.

Maultsby, M. C. (1986). *Rational behavior therapy.* Englewood Cliffs, NJ: Prentice-Hall.

McGovern, T. E., & Silverman, M. S. (1984). A review of outcome studies of rational-emotive therapy from 1977 to 1982. *Journal of Rational-Emotive Therapy,* 2(1), 7–18.

Meichenbaum, D. (1993). Changing conceptions of cognitive behavior modification: Retrospect and prospect. *Journal of Consulting and Clinical Psychology,* 61, 202–204.

Silverman, M. S., McCarthy, M., & McGovern, T. (1992). A review of outcome studies of rational-emotive therapy from 1982–1989. *Journal of Rational-Emotive and Cognitive-Behavior Therapy, 10*(3), 111–186.

Multimodal therapy (MMT) draws on the same principles of experimental and social psychology as do other cognitive-behavioral therapies. It emphasizes that for therapy to be thorough and comprehensive it must encompass seven discrete but interactive factors—behavior, affect, sensation, imagery, cognition, interpersonal relationships, and drugs/biological considerations. The first letters of the foregoing categories yield the convenient acronym BASIC I.D. This provides much broader assessment and treatment foci, distinctive instruments, and several unique procedures. Despite its greater breadth, MMT is basically a brief, short-term, highly focused, problem-solving treatment orientation. To mix metaphors, this therapy cuts to the chase without cutting corners.

The MMT approach was developed in concert with careful outcome studies that pointed the way to rapid, stable, and lasting treatment outcomes. Whenever feasible, MMT practitioners use empirically supported treatment methods. The therapeutic relationship is pivotal. Compatibility and rapport between client and therapist provide the soil that enable the techniques to take root. Thus, in MMT, emphasis is placed on skillfully applying the proper techniques of choice, within the context of appropriate relationship styles (e.g., styles that make adjustment in levels of warmth, formality, supportiveness, directiveness, and so forth).

MMT is a technically, but not theoretically, eclectic approach to treatment. It makes effective use of methods from diverse sources without relinquishing its theoretic base, which has a social learning and cognitive character. Fitting the requisite treatment to the specific client is an essential goal, and the ancillary use of several facilitators is also an integral component of this broad-spectrum but systematic orientation.

Alice Goodloe Whipple

4

Multimodal Therapy

SOMETHING ABOUT THE THERAPIST • *Arnold A. Lazarus*

Perhaps the seeds of my empathic responses and helping ethos are exemplified by an incident that took place when I was about 7 years of age. My elementary school was about a hundred yards from our house in Johannesburg, South Africa. It had been raining, was rather chilly. I waited in the classroom with several other children for the storm to pass before heading home. The rain soon subsided, and I was hurrying home with a friend when I came upon several kids taunting a little girl. She was in a lower grade, "developmentally delayed," and had obviously been caught in the rain. She seemed rather bewildered, had been drenched to the skin, and was shivering and crying her eyes out. I simply took her by the hand and led her to my house, where my mother promptly took care of her. She calmed her, ran a hot bath for her, and then wrapped her in a towel and blanket and brought her a cup of hot chocolate while her clothes were drying by the side of our wood-burning kitchen stove. Both my parents were kind and helpful people, and these qualities had been instilled in me from an early age.

When I entered the University of the Witwatersrand (South Africa) in 1952, my intent was to major in English with a view to becoming a journalist. As a teenager, I had published several short stories and articles in various magazines. The English department struck me as less than inspiring, and I switched majors to psychology and sociology, and ended up with a Ph.D. in clinical psychology in 1960. In 1957 I spent 3 months in London, England, as an intern at the Marlborough Day Hospital—an Adlerian institution headed by Dr. Joshua Bierer. I completed the remainder of my internship at Tara Hospital in Johannesburg.

My mainstream professors taught us the rudiments of Freudian, Rogerian, and Sullivanian theories, and I also learned what was then called "conditioning therapy" by joining Joseph Wolpe's followers off campus. I might mention that I had managed to get permission for Wolpe to chair my Ph.D. thesis committee. My dissertation compared systematic desensitization and insight-oriented methods on groups of phobic subjects. I became a certified psychologist and was in full-time private practice in Johannesburg until 1963, when I accepted an invitation to go to Stanford University in California as a Visiting Assistant Professor. (Professor Albert Bandura had read an article I had published in the *Journal of Abnormal and Social Psychology,* which was based on the experimental findings of my doctoral dissertation. He invited me "to see how the other half lives.") My wife, 4–year-old daughter, 2–year-old son, and I all flew almost half-way across the world. There were many reasons why I wanted to live in America, and after obtaining permanent resident visas, we subsequently all became American citizens.

My sojourn at Stanford broadened my outlook. For example, it was there that I first became familiar with the writings of Skinner and began to appreciate the nuances of operant conditioning. My training and outlook prior to that time had been pretty much confined to classical conditioning models. I did not see it as an either-or situation, and published an article with two of my Stanford graduate students—Gerald (Jerry) Davison (who became and remains a close friend) and David Polefka—on classical and operant factors in the treatment of a school phobia (Lazarus, Davison, & Polefka, 1965).

In 1967 I accepted a full professorship and joined Joseph Wolpe at Temple University Medical School in Philadelphia, which fulfilled one of my dreams at the time. I was very eager to work with my thesis mentor. Unfortunately, it soon became evident that our paths had diverged. I had already amplified a number of Wolpe's concepts and techniques (e.g., Lazarus, 1964, 1966; Lazarus & Abramovitz, 1962), which I regarded as too rigid and narrow. There seemed to be several useful techniques that nonbehavioral clinicians were employing that readily lent themselves to a learning theory explanation (I refer, for example, to the work of Gestalt therapists, transactional analysts, Adlerians, and especially rational-emotive therapists). I published a brief note to the effect that it is important to adopt promising techniques from diverse sources without necessarily subscribing to the theories or tenets that gave rise to them. To differentiate this approach from run-of-the-mill eclecticism, and to separate it from theoretical integration, I called it *technical eclecticism* (Lazarus, 1967). Wolpe viewed this as heresy, and it led to a severe disaffection, which grew into enmity. Consequently, in 1970, when I was offered a position at Yale University as a Visiting Professor and Director of Clinical Training, I was more than happy to leave Temple University Medical School.

In 1972, I went to Rutgers University as Distinguished Professor where I taught until the end of 1997 before founding a Center for Multimodal Psychological Services in Princeton, New Jersey, with my son, Clifford N. Lazarus, Ph.D.

The Setting for Therapy

In addition to my academic duties, I have always maintained an active psychotherapy practice. Since 1972, I have seen clients in my home office in Princeton. The living room serves as the waiting room, and my office-cum-study is a paneled room with built-in book shelves on three sides, recessed lighting, and an L-shaped formica desk that covers one entire side of the room. The placebo effect is deliberately accentuated by numerous diplomas and awards that adorn three of the walls. There is a mantelpiece, a fireplace, a recessed area with three filing cabinets, and a convenient bathroom. The furnishings consist of easy chairs and a sofa. There is no desk between my clients and me. There are two doors. The one leads from the living room (waiting room) and the other opens into a large den where I have run many groups and postdoctoral seminars.

Most of the people I see are referred by colleagues and former clients. I might mention that there are obvious advantages and disadvantages tied to seeing clients in one's home. Perhaps the biggest drawback is that some people see one as on call 24 hours a day. One of the biggest advantages for certain clients who were in sensitive political offices or professional groups is that they felt more secure than would have been true in a professional, and perhaps highly visible, office in a public building. Some have asked to park their cars in our garage in case someone should drive past, recognize their car, and infer (correctly) that they were in need of therapy.

Basically, over the years, my clinical practice and careful follow-up inquiries enabled me to develop the approach to psychotherapy I call Multimodal. (See Lazarus, 1995a, 1997.)

THE THERAPY FOR DONALD GREEN

Session 1

Don Green was referred to me as it was felt that multimodal therapy was an optimal approach for dealing with the multifarious assortment of problems he presented in intake. Although I had the details of the initial intake interview that preceded my first meeting with Donald Green, I had requested that he supplement this information by completing the Multimodal Life History Inventory (Lazarus & Lazarus, 1991) before we met. My usual procedure with literate clients who are not unduly distressed is to give them this inventory at the end of our first session, request them to fill it in at home, and bring whatever they had managed to complete to the second session. I recommend that they not attempt to fill out the 15–page inventory in one sitting, and I also suggest that they feel free to omit all identifying data (name, address, and so forth) if this would encourage them to be more candid.

Don arrives on time for our meeting carrying a small briefcase. We exchange hellos, he sits down and opens his briefcase. He appears to be more agitated than I expected from a reading of the case file. He takes out some papers.

GREEN. This is from my insurance. They have only approved six sessions. That means that after today we will only have five sessions left.

LAZARUS. I'm pretty sure we can get them to give us an extra four or five sessions.

GREEN. Even so, what can one accomplish in such a short time?

LAZARUS. The intake data indicate you said that the main thing you want from therapy is to get to work on time.

GREEN. Let me tell you. When I finished doing that questionnaire, I realized that I'm a basket case. Not getting to work on time seems to be the least of my problems.

LAZARUS. I don't think you're a basket case.

GREEN. (Going back to his briefcase and handing me the Multimodal Life History Inventory) Well just wait till you read this!

(I take the Inventory. It seems to be neatly and fully completed. I glance at the bottom of page 4 where I read Donald's response to the question: "What personal qualities do you think the ideal therapist should possess?" Interestingly, Donald had written: "A good therapist should be like Burgess Meredith in the movie 'Rocky'—the kind-but-tough trainer who cares for his fighter and works him real hard." Next I turned to page 8 and took a quick look at a 15–item questionnaire. Donald had rated the following statements "5," i.e., Strongly agree: "I should not make mistakes." "I should be good at everything I do." "I should not disclose personal information." "I am a victim of circumstances." "Other people are happier than I am." "It is very important to please other people." "Play it safe; don't take any risks." "I should strive for perfection.")

LAZARUS. I'll study this inventory carefully before our next session, but one obvious fact stands out like a beacon. You are way too hard on yourself. There's an interesting paradox here. You have developed an opaque and nondisclosing lifestyle. Yet, for therapy to be effective, it is most important that you disclose fully to me.

GREEN. I did something on Thursday night that surprised me. Instead of the usual chit chat with Jim and Mary I told them I was going into therapy, and we had an interesting conversation. Mary mentioned that she had been to a social worker for help with her own problems. I really don't know much about how therapy works, and Mary mentioned having a friend who has been seeing a shrink for years. I don't know much about therapy. Can you tell me something about it?

LAZARUS. I view therapy as education. If you realize that overcoming emotional problems is an educational process, the concept of *self-education* is easily understood. It is *crucial* to recognize that people who are willing to work and to make an effort to change are the ones who really improve their lives. This means reading certain books, keeping notes, and practicing prescribed techniques. I was struck by your analogy to boxing. I think it is appropriate. I will be your psychological trainer, and I will work with you for that championship fight—which means a happier and much more fulfilled life. You will be asked to carry out "psychological exercises" that consist of deliberately changing fallacious ideas and cultivating different behaviors. How does this sound to you?

(The foregoing orienting remarks set the stage for a treatment trajectory that will be active and collaborative. It also draws on the client's desire to be treated like a prize fighter by a hard-driving coach. If the client seems to be puzzled, uncertain, or confused, further clarification is called for.)

GREEN. I like the sound of it, and it differs from what I had expected.

LAZARUS. What did you expect?

GREEN. Like I said, I don't know too much about it but I guess my image is colored by Hollywood where you dig into the past and discuss dreams.

LAZARUS. I regard "psycho-archeology" as old fashioned. By that I mean treating a person's mind as if it were an archeological dig by probing the remote history of his or her personal life. If you want to change, you have to do different things and do things differently. I read something that I think is very clever. "If you keep on doing what you've always done, you will always get what you've always gotten. In order to get something different, change what you're doing." What do you think about what I have been saying?

GREEN. It makes sense. But I still don't see how we can really get anywhere in 10 weeks. I'm 42-years old and have been this way forever.

LAZARUS. First of all, we are not obligated to wrap things up in 6 weeks or 10 weeks. Even if we meet less than a dozen times we can stretch it out over several months, thereby giving you time to practice between sessions, to train really hard. Let me stress again that psychological growth and change, like any other form of learning and development, call for active participation on the part of the learner. Will you be a good pupil who will work really hard, or will you cop out or resist my training and instruction?

GREEN. Well, Dr. Lazarus, perhaps one of my weaknesses will turn out to be a strength. I am referring to the fact that I have always been *obedient*, but by following your instructions, this will be all to the good.

LAZARUS. Very good Mr. Green. So we understand each other.

GREEN. Please call me Donald.

LAZARUS. Sure Donald. But I believe in parity, so will you please call me, Arnold?

(At this juncture a general treatment plan for Donald is taking shape. I have emphasized my educational thrust and stressed that his active cooperation is imperative. By employing his metaphor of a boxing trainer, I know more or less how to structure our therapeutic relationship and how to facilitate rapport. I have led

him to realize that therapy is a two-way street and that his full cooperation is fundamental.)

LAZARUS. I reread the notes from the intake interview and made a little chart of what I saw as your main problems. Here let me show you. You will notice that I think in terms of seven interactive categories. Take a look.

Behavior:	Late for work
Affect:	Feels lonely and depressed; desires to have more friends; feels trapped; afraid of his subordinates at work; fears people in general; fear of barking dogs
Sensation:	No negative information. (Masturbates to pictures of women in men's magazines)
Imagery:	Fantasizes catastrophes; recurrent dreams of failure and of being lost; cannot picture himself getting married, having children
Cognition:	Has had thoughts of suicide; "I have been a failure in life;"
Interpersonal:	Shy; a loner; no confidants; no real friends; distant relationship with older sister; never dated; never had sex; obedient; people pleaser; unassertive with the foremen who report to him at work
Drugs/Biology:	Possibly overweight and physically unfit despite a thorough medical check-up

(In MMT vernacular, the foregoing list is termed a "Modality Profile." Seven discrete but interactive modalities are examined. The convenient acronym BASIC I.D. is derived from the first letters of each modality —Behavior, Affect, Sensation, Imagery, Cognition, Interpersonal, and Drugs/Biology—and provides an effective reminder to consider each dimension.)

GREEN. There's more as you will see when you read the questionnaire, but that pretty much captures it. Do you see what I mean about being a basket case?

LAZARUS. I've seen a lot worse. Generally, by changing several central or pivotal items, the rest may fall into place. You also have many positive attributes that could be listed under Assets. You are intelligent—what did the report say? "In the top decile of adult males." You are personable, honest, mechanically proficient, reliable (except for being late for work). Personality tests revealed no psychopathology, but showed that you are creative and imaginative.

GREEN. I guess it sounds okay when you put it all together like that. But let's face it. The debits far outweigh the credits.

LAZARUS. So we have our work cut out for us.

(This remark was intended to reinforce the collaborative context. The main question for me at this point is the extent of his readiness for change and his willingness to be a buyer instead of a window shopper. Given that there's no evidence of significant psychopathology, I'll be optimistic and move him along quite rapidly.)

GREEN. Where do we start?

LAZARUS. That poses a dilemma. Most therapists believe that before leaping into action it is essential first to establish rapport. You have to know that I care, that I can be trusted, that I have your very best interests at heart. The books contend that you will put me to the test to be sure that I am—to use our analogy—in your corner. This all takes time. When we finally create a working alliance, I can be really frank and outspoken with you. On the other hand, if I am premature, if I lay it on the line too soon, you will be offended, you will go on the defensive, you will feel criticized and attacked. So I'm not sure that I should take the chance of "wasting no time." Can I leap to the conclusion that we already have a sense of trust and rapport and I can be totally up front with you? It's quite a quandary.

(This semi-paradoxical statement is intended to obtain Donald's immediate cooperation. Notice the "right brain" assurances that I am indeed "in his corner.")

GREEN. I say we should go for it. I feel comfortable with you and am feeling confident that you can help me. (After a brief pause) I'd like to work with you.

LAZARUS. Great. But if I say or do anything that bugs you, please do not be an obedient puppy but tell me, be up front with me. Can I trust you to do that?

GREEN. I'll try.

LAZARUS. *Trying* is garbage. *Doing* is what counts.

GREEN. (Laughing) Okay Burgess.

LAZARUS. I'm going to jump in with my candid view of your coming late for work. I see that as a pseudo-problem. Let me explain. Let's say you've learned that a hit man has been hired to break your legs if you come late for work. Will you be on time? Or let's say that you will receive a million dollars tax free if you show up on time for the next 6 months? Will you still be "unable" to get to work on time?

GREEN. Under either one of those conditions you'd better believe I'd be there real early!

(If Donald had said that his inability to be punctual at work would not respond to either one of the aforementioned scenarios, but that he'd undoubtedly end up on crutches, and forfeit the million dollars, I would have stepped away from my short-term, intensive treatment trajectory and seen prognosis as far less rosy.)

LAZARUS. It's useful to think in terms of "push" and "pull"—like opposite poles of a magnet. The threat of broken legs, or the incentive of a million bucks is enough of a "pull" to override whatever is actually repelling you at work.

GREEN. But I like my job. I've been there for over 17 years.

LAZARUS. My hypothesis is that there is something disagreeable, unpleasant, distasteful going on for you at work. I want you to look for what it may be. Make notes when you are there of anything that displeases you or upsets you. Will you do this?

GREEN. Sure.

LAZARUS. I have some additional assignments for you to work on during the coming week. First, please continue being more open and self-disclosing with Jim and Mary. In addition, I want you to get into emotional risk taking. Instead of brown-bagging it at work, or eating alone in the cafeteria, I want you to go up to people each day and say "Do you mind if I join you for lunch?"

(I notice a fearful expression in Donald's eyes)

How does that grab you?

GREEN. That's scary!

LAZARUS. I know it is. But that's part of the training. It's the road work. It's like having a tough sparring partner. What's the worst thing that can happen? They can say, "Get lost, Creep. We don't want to eat with you!" They won't break your knee caps. Without emotional risk taking, there will be no change. "If you do what you've always done, you'll get what you've always gotten."

GREEN. I never expected to hear this.

LAZARUS. Perhaps I have screwed up. Maybe I have overestimated you. I'm going at a pace that is too fast. I should have obeyed my teachers and waited several weeks to establish rapport and all that. Should we change the treatment plan?

(This double-bind is a basic test of the treatment pace.)

GREEN. Let's go for it. I have more to gain than to lose.

LAZARUS. True. Finally, I am going to give you a book that I coauthored with my son. It is called *The 60–Second Shrink* (1997). If a picture is worth a thousand words, certain books are worth, not a thousand sessions, but maybe a dozen or two.

(I retrieve a copy from a carton, flip through it and place a check mark in front of several chapters before handing it to Donald. So-called "bibliotherapy" often expedites treatment. I find most self-help books too lengthy and complex, and that is mainly why I have written books that are succinct, easy to read, and to the point.)

DONALD. Thank you. How much do I owe you?

LAZARUS. It's all part of the overall fee.

DONALD. My insurance only pays you $80 an hour.

LAZARUS. No problem. Okay Donald, I look forward to hearing what you have done differently this coming week. Does the same time suit you next week?

DONALD. That's fine. Let me write it in my appointment book.

Session 2

I have perused the Multimodal Life History Questionnaire and emerged with a clearer sense of Donald's anticipation of aversive consequences. His answers clearly demonstrate the magnitude of his negative self-appraisal, his social anxiety and interpersonal skills deficits, and the extent to which he expects to be negatively evaluated and criticized by others—especially women. He fits the Axis II diagnosis on DSM IV of an Avoidant Personality Disorder.

Donald sits down looking rather edgy.

GREEN. You're going to be mad at me.

LAZARUS. You chickened out?

GREEN. Not really. It's been what you'd certainly call "educational." (He pauses) Well, let me not beat around the bush and get right to it. First of all, you're not going to believe this. I saw you last Tuesday, and since then I've gotten to work early each day. It seems that the magnet was to look for what you had called the distasteful or unpleasant forces you thought might be there. I think I found them. (He pauses and looks to me for a response)

LAZARUS. Well, that all sounds pretty good to me. Two things. First, please tell me what some of the negative forces are, and then let's see why I would be mad at you? So what did you discover that you don't like at work?

GREEN. I am not too clear about it, but I think my supervisor is a jerk, and the union is making life difficult for people in managerial positions. I need to think about it some more.

LAZARUS. Yes, I think that's important. Now tell me why I will be mad at you.

GREEN. (*He shifts around in the chair. Clears his throat. Scratches his lip.*) I kind of took the law into my own hands. You're not going to like this. Oh well. By Thursday I was feeling extremely uptight. I didn't want to retreat, throw in the towel, because I know what needs to be done. So I went to see my primary care physician and asked for a tranquilizer. He gave me a prescription for Xanax and I have been taking it when I get up in the morning and when I go to bed at night. It just seems to take the edge off my panic so I can do what I need to do.

LAZARUS. You're an enterprising fellow. If a small dose of Xanax helps you do what you need to do, I say that's just fine. I'm certainly not mad at you. But Xanax can be addicting. How much do you take?

GREEN. Only a quarter mg morning and night.

LAZARUS. Okay. Two things. Don't increase the dose, and do be sure to get off of it as soon as you feel comfortable doing so.

GREEN. I agree. It's just to tide me over in the beginning.

LAZARUS. So please tell me what different things you have done and what you have done differently.

GREEN. Well, the toughest thing, as I'm sure you know, was the thought of going up to people in the cafeteria and asking to join them for lunch. Last Tuesday night after leaving here, I had a vivid dream in which I was in the cafeteria and was unaware that I was stark naked. When I realized this, I tried to cover up and everybody was practically screaming their heads off with laughter. I woke up trembling and sweating. Talk about panic and anxiety! I thought of throwing in the towel. That's when the idea of taking a tranquilizer first came to me. I didn't want to disappoint you or myself. Anyhow, on Wednesday around 12:15 I went to the cafeteria, got some sandwiches and juice, and looked around. My heart was in my mouth. I saw two guys who work with me on waste disposal systems and I took the plunge. They were at a fairly large table and I walked over and asked if I could sit with them. I prayed I would not pass out from anxiety. The one guy said, "Sure. There's plenty of room." So I pulled out a chair and sat down. The gods smiled upon me because the other guy said something like, "We were talking about a second-hand car I bought and the troubles I'm having with it." I inquired if they knew about my hobby of fixing up cars, and they both said no. So I did a very atypical thing. I offered to check out the guy's car if he wanted to bring it to my place. He seemed very grateful, and on Saturday I spent a few hours fixing his car while he watched me work. He was most complimentary and was very appreciative when I said I would only expect him to pay for some parts I had installed. On Monday while I was in the check out line at the cafeteria, this fellow, his name is Joe, came up to me and said his car was running great. He was with another fellow and they invited me to join them for lunch. Again the gods smiled on me. We discovered that we shared an interest in chess, fishing, and walking, and he told me about a walking tour that starts two towns down from me which I did not know about.

LAZARUS. I'm impressed.

GREEN. Really?

LAZARUS. Yes really. But in a way I'm sorry it turned out relatively easy for you once you took the plunge. I wonder how you would have reacted if, instead of inviting you to sit down with them on Wednesday, they had rejected you—maybe by saying they were having a private conversation or something.

GREEN. I would have been devastated. My worst fears would have been confirmed.

LAZARUS. Yeah. That would have shown beyond a shadow of doubt that you are a loser, a worthless jerk, universally despised, utterly repugnant.

(I am exaggerating here for paradoxical reasons.)

GREEN. In truth, I honestly wonder if there is anyone who would consider me "lovable." I never felt any great love from my parents. My sister certainly had little time for me. I've never had a really close friend or confidant. No woman has ever loved me.

(I wonder at this moment whether or not I should be reassuring, empathic, supportive, and compassionate. I then recall his "kind but tough trainer" expectancy.)

LAZARUS. People who are regarded as lovable act lovably. They do loving things. They exude warmth, they smile, they ask caring questions, they express concern. They don't just sit on their butts and expect people to see them as lovable.

GREEN. So it's all one big act?

LAZARUS. Not at all. If they are phony and are just pretending, this will soon become apparent. But to be seen as lovable does not require one to possess a lovability gene. By the way, Donald, if you tell me that you would prefer to remain a loner, that would be fine with me.

(I say this to avoid placing myself in a position where I can be seen as being disappointed in him.)

GREEN. Is there, in your opinion, a possibility of my settling down, getting married and having children?

LAZARUS. You're not lovable enough for that. (I smile.)

GREEN. (Amused) I'm serious. Isn't it too late for me to start thinking of things that most people do in their 20s?

LAZARUS. No, you jackass! You can certainly do it if you can get it through your head that you have no fatal flaws, that you're a decent person, that you have lots to offer, and that despite your fear of people, if you stop living like a hermit and take emotional risks, you will amaze yourself.

(Another example of Arnold (Burgess-Meredith) Lazarus training Rocky for the Main Event.)

The remainder of this second session was spent asking Donald to clarify some ambiguous comments on the Multimodal Life History Inventory, followed by a brief discussion of some of the points he read in *The 60–Second Shrink*. Donald was particularly taken with Chapter 1 (What To Say When You Talk To Yourself), Chapter 14 (Rapid Relaxation Methods), Chapter 20 (The Tyranny of the Should), Chapter 28 (Avoiding Self Fascism), Chapter 40 (Don't Suppress Your Feelings), Chapter 60 (Receiving Criticism), Chapter 63 (On Being Extremely Private), and Chapter 114 (Two Common Mistakes in the Workplace).

Session 3

As Donald comes into the office, even before the door is shut, he says, "You were right!"

LAZARUS. Right about what?

GREEN. About hating my job.

LAZARUS. Do tell.

GREEN. As Jim and his wife Mary are fond of saying, "Too much is enough!" I didn't want to face up to the fact that after 17 years on pretty much the same job, one that my departed father had obtained for me, it was getting me down. In fact, in retrospect, it was at year 14 that the boredom became bothersome, and it was at that stage that the union made it such that although the foremen were under me, I had little if any power or say over them. It also dawned on me that my supervisor sees me as his lackey—like I'm his personal slave or something. Now it may seem strange to you that I was unable or unwilling to admit these obvious things to myself or to anyone else. But now that I'm on this emotional risk-taking thing, I say "In for a penny, in for a pound."

LAZARUS (Raising a glass of water) I'll drink to that!

GREEN. Wait till you hear this. What did you say last time? "Chutzpah maketh the man!" So I went to the head of Personnel and told him that I'm ready to quit my job but I hoped there was an opening for me elsewhere in the company. You will remember that it's a huge manufacturing company. So listen to this. He said there is an opening in the department that sells several industrial devices to other companies. They need someone with a background in engineering who can talk knowledgeably about the products. This is in a completely new building. I went there with him to be shown around. I can't tell you what a different atmosphere it has compared to the dumpy place I've been in for 17 years. The people seem more pleasant, the offices are great, and the likelihood is that if I do okay on the interviews I'll get the job. It comes with significantly more money. I have to give them a month's notice on my present job. I am struck by the fact that the test I did stressed my interest in sales—which made no sense to me at the time. Now I'm beginning to see why I probably answered the question as I did.

(The question refers to Donald's response on a vocational interest measure he had mentioned during the intake interview.)

LAZARUS. I think that's great. One thing we can do is some behavior rehearsal; we can role play various interviews. I want to be sure that you come across well and do not choke. How do you feel about that?

(I arrived at the role playing or behavioral rehearsal option by quickly applying the MMT spectrum BASIC I.D. I found no incongruities in any of the modalities—such as affective lapses, untoward tension in Donald's sensory mode, or any cognitive distortions such as unrealistic expectations or faulty attitudes. Hence, it seemed to make sense to try to ensure that Donald's style and demeanor would impress his interviewers.)

GREEN. That's a good idea.

LAZARUS. Okay let's go for it. I'm the interviewer. "Hi. My name is Buddy Smith. So Mr. Green, I understand that you've been with this company for many years taking care of pollution and emissions from smokestacks."

GREEN. "That's right Mr. Smith."

LAZARUS. Donald, how about jumping right in and saying something like, "I believe my talents can be put to much better use in this part of the company."

GREEN. Ah! You want me to lead with the jab.

(I'm not sure that the pugilistic analogy is apt in this context, but I decide to let it go.)

LAZARUS. I want you to appear strong, eager, and upbeat.

(Behavior rehearsal continues for about 20 minutes as we play different roles and reverse them. The remainder of the session is devoted to further discussion of The 60–Second Shrink, and Donald's misgivings.)

GREEN. So how am I coming along?

LAZARUS. Like a house afire. By the way, do you know about the Albert Ellis Institute in New York City?

GREEN. No. Why?

LAZARUS. I very much buy into their rational philosophy of life, and they have some excellent people there and some outstanding workshops. I happen to know that on this coming Friday evening, Dr. Ellis or one of his associates will be running a seminar in which people from the audience go up on stage and get treated.

GREEN. What? Now wait a minute. You're not suggesting that I volunteer for that?

LAZARUS. Not unless you want to. But I'd be very interested in your assessment of what some regard as the best educational entertainment in New York City for a mere pittance. You're only about 30 or 40 minutes from New York right?

GREEN. Is this an assignment?

LAZARUS. That's a good idea. Let's make it one. I'd be most interested in your opinion and you may even learn a thing or two.

(I happen to live and work in Princeton, New Jersey, which is midway between New York City and Philadelphia where there are many people, places, and excellent facilities I can draw on to expedite matters. Therapists in different regions who work the way I do will probably have access to resources in their own communities that can be used as adjuncts for their own treatment options. It is necessary to understand that MMT draws on many approaches that overlap with its fundamental social learning theory base. Multimodal therapists around the world are encouraged

to look for compatible professionals and institutes in their own localities.)

Session 4

Donald came to the session brandishing Albert Ellis's book *How To Stubbornly Refuse to Make Yourself Miserable About Anything—Yes, Anything* (1994).

GREEN. Have you seen this book?

LAZARUS. Indeed I have.

GREEN. What do you think of it?

LAZARUS. It's great. If you follow its rational-emotive prescriptions you'll be ahead of the pack.

GREEN. I think it's a good supplement to your *60–Second Shrink.*

LAZARUS. I agree.

Donald went on to say how much he had enjoyed the Friday night meeting at Ellis's Institute.

GREEN. I have a question. What do you think of my attending some groups at the Institute? They have an Anxiety Management Group coming up next week and an Assertiveness Training Group next month.

LAZARUS. I would encourage you to pursue those avenues.

GREEN. Oh, and by the way, my insurance runs out after our next session, but if it's all right with you, I can easily pay you out of pocket—especially if you stay with the $80 fee.

LAZARUS. That will be fine. (Pause) So tell me, did you have that interview yet?

GREEN. I sure did. It went just fine.

LAZARUS. Did you get the transfer?

GREEN. There's been no official word yet, but I'm pretty sure it's in the bag.

LAZARUS. I hope you are not setting yourself up for a disappointment.

GREEN. I don't think I am. But if I don't get the job, it won't be the end of the world. I won't like it but I can stand it and it won't be *awful.*

LAZARUS. Ah-ha, I see you've already swung into a new philosophy. Good going! By the way Donald, how about giving your sister a call—just to see what sort of reception you get. If she's pleased to hear from you, well and good. If not, still well and good.

GREEN. Yeah. I've thought of that.

LAZARUS. What's my response to that?

GREEN. Stop thinking about it. Just do it!

LAZARUS. (Pause) There are some areas we have not looked into. Barking dogs is one, nutrition and exercise is another, and perhaps most important is the issue of you vis-à-vis women and sex.

GREEN. Forget about the barking-dogs hang-up. It's not a big deal. Oh, perhaps I should mention that I've been going to work late every day—but now it's deliberate because I know I'm leaving and I don't give a damn.

(Some may see this as an expression of moral failure. He's still drawing a salary; he still owes a day's work for a day's pay; just because he's determined to leave doesn't mean he's entitled to short-change the company. I decide to test the waters.)

LAZARUS. So are you putting in 6–hour days at work?

GREEN. No. I'm simply making my own hours. I come late and stay late. I prefer it that way.

(I decided this was the point in my treatment plan where I would steer Donald into reflections on his sexual, romantic difficulties. The rest of the session was devoted to a discussion of Donald's fears of dating, his sexual inexperience, his negative body image, his basic fear of rejection, what it means to love and be loved, and the repetitive theme of his own intrinsic doubts about being lovable. He agreed to consult a nutritionist, to start an exercise regimen, and to respond to ads in the personal columns of several magazines. I suggested that he had a lot on his plate and that we should meet in 2 weeks.)

LAZARUS. So let's be sure we agree. When I see you next time, you will have attended the Anxiety Management Group. You will have phoned your sister, seen a nutritionist, started exercising, and responded to some personal ads.

Oh, I've been meaning to ask you if you are still taking the Xanax.

GREEN. No. I stopped that last week.

A week later I received an e-mail from Donald. It read: "I just wanted you to know that today was my first day at the new job. I think it will be terrific. The group meeting at Ellis' place was most helpful. I bought a bunch of videos, books, and audiotapes from them. But I've been too busy to answer any personal ads."

I replied as follows: "I have a hit man standing in the wings. Do you value your kneecaps? If so, you will have answered some personal ads before our meeting next week."

The following day I sent Donald another e-mail: "Why not let your insurance pay for some additional sessions if they will? Please send me their phone number so I can call and see about getting recertified—or whatever they call it." I subsequently called the company, spoke to a sympathetic representative, and was given six more sessions.

Session 5

GREEN. I decided not to call my sister. The more I thought about it the less point I saw in doing so. She was never an integral part of my life.

(I was pleased at what seemed to be an assertive response. Donald was not going to follow all my exhortations blindly and obediently.)

LAZARUS. I saw it as an experiment. Perhaps it is simply my own curiosity that lies behind it. I wonder how she will respond. I have little doubt that you are not copping out due to fear or anything like that. Given all the tough things that you have managed to do, calling her is no big deal for you. So let's drop it.

(The foregoing statement reflects my penchant for adopting a certain level of transparency with my clients. The parity of the client and therapist that I referred to in our first session is evident in my admission that I may have been motivated by a personal need or curiosity.)

GREEN. Also, I decided to get a book on nutrition instead of seeing a nutritionist. I know that my cholesterol is on the high side. I know that I have tended to eat junk. So I am now following the book's advice—less red meat, less fats and oils, more fiber, more fruits and vegetables, go easy on sugar and salt, take some vitamin-mineral supplements including antioxidants. I also take brisk 2-mile walks each day.

LAZARUS. Good for you! Now please tell me why you decided not to answer any personal ads.

GREEN. Surprise. Surprise. I sent off two letters replete with photos to a couple of ladies who sounded interesting.

LAZARUS. Great!

GREEN. I don't mind telling you that this area fills me with trepidation.

I directed the remainder of the session to discussing Donald's romantic and sexual fantasies, and his hopes and fears. He felt inadequate across the entire continuum—making simple small talk when out on a date to giving and receiving sexual gratifica-

tion. I moved into what I call a Second-Order BASIC I.D. analysis. This consists of taking a specified problem area and examining anticipated reactions and possible difficulties in Behavior, Affect, Sensation, Imagery, and Cognition. It also examines relevant Interpersonal reactions, and whether psychotropic Drugs may be indicated.

The item "Going Out On A Date" yielded the following Second-Order BASIC I.D. for Donald:

Behavior:	Fumbling and inept.
Affect:	Anxious.
Sensation:	Tension, perspiration, trembling.
Imagery:	Appearing stupid and awkward. He pictured himself failing and being ridiculed.
Cognition:	Self-talk to the effect that he is unlovable, unattractive, boring, and stupid. He also labeled himself unworthy and repulsive.
Interpersonal:	A deficient repertoire that would be appropriate for a 12–year old.
Drugs/Biology:	The need for a drink to calm him down, but the fear that alcohol might make him appear even more ridiculous.

The Second-Order BASIC I.D. work-up set the stage for the treatment emphasis and strategies that were applied for the next three sessions.

Sessions 6–8

These sessions were spaced over a period of 6 weeks and consisted of cognitive disputation in the mode of REBT; positive and coping imagery exercises (in which he pictured himself relating comfortably, openly, and lovingly to worthy women, as well as picturing himself discounting ridicule and rejection by others— "anyone who is that nasty is not really worth relating to.") Several female graduate students from a local university agreed to provide role playing scenarios (being out on a date) and offered frank sexual and romantic advice from the female perspective.

(Once again, I looked to others to assist me in achieving my treatment objectives. The female students certainly could provide a more authentic experience than I, alone, could offer.)

Donald's friend Mary had introduced him to a single and unattached woman, Sally Ann, with whom he went on several dates. He found the experience pleasant and relatively easy, but stated that he was not physically attracted to Sally Ann. There was, however, a woman at his new job, a paralegal assistant, Cindy, whom he found "extremely warm, friendly, helpful, and most attractive." Despite his trepidation he finally asked her out, and in Session 8 he announced that he had gone to a movie with her.

Session 9

This meeting took place 3 weeks after session 8 because Donald had called to say that he was still attending to his in vivo assignments and needed more time.

GREEN. I've been boning up on sex manuals.

LAZARUS. Pun unintended?

GREEN. (Laughs) God! When you first told me that therapy was education, little did I know how much studying I would be doing. I think I'm just about ready to hang up a shingle. Anyhow, I have seen Cindy every night over this past week, and all day Saturday and Sunday. By the way, our first connection was based on the fact that we both love Thai cuisine, and we found some great Thai restaurants in the city.

LAZARUS. If I may be so presumptuous, may I ask if you got laid?

GREEN. (Smiling and with irony) Why don't you get right to the point? We've kissed, fondled, touched, and all that. Let's say that we've done practically everything except have intercourse.

LAZARUS. Let's see how you can jump over that final hurdle.

We entered into a detailed discussion about sexual pleasuring via oral and digital stimulation. It appeared that Donald and Cindy had both been somewhat timid and reserved ("I liked that about her," Donald volunteered, "it gave me more confidence.") Nevertheless, what Donald called their "heavy petting" had culminated in orgasms for each of them. As might be expected, Donald was anxious about his erectile performance should they "go all the way." I expressed the view that I would be pleased if he failed to obtain or maintain an erection for two reasons: (1) it would test his anticatastrophizing skills, and (2) Cindy's reaction would tell us a good deal about her level of nondemandingness.

GREEN. I guess it's the same basic risk-taking theme.

LAZARUS. Right! Does Cindy know you have been in therapy?

GREEN. Yes. In fact, she'd like to meet you.

LAZARUS. I'd like to meet her too. Why don't we arrange for a threesome next time?

GREEN. Good idea. You can give her the clinical once-over for me.

TERMINATION OF THE THERAPY

Session 10

I had received an e-mail from Donald the previous day. He had written: "I'm not a virgin any more." I responded with "Touchdown!" He replied: "Don't you mean KO?" Indeed, I use different metaphors and analogies with different clients. In Donald's view he was a boxer and I was his tough-but-kind trainer.

He and Cindy arrived about 10 minutes late for their appointment. This was the first time Donald was not on time.

DONALD. So sorry we're late. We got into conversation and I missed the turn off from Route 1.

CINDY. (With outstretched hand) Hi. I'm Cindy. Nice to meet you.

LAZARUS. (Shaking hands with Cindy) Thanks for coming in.

(I was going to say something flippant, but she seemed a trifle nervous, so I played it straight.)

The three of us had an interesting discussion. Donald was surprisingly open and self-disclosing about his therapy. Cindy discussed a failed marriage that had lasted some 6 years. "Thank God there were no kids," she stated. As the session continued, I felt more and more strongly that Donald had done very well in his choice. Cindy was intelligent, attractive, and had a good sense of humor. Her long black hair matched her olive complexion. She volunteered, "Perhaps the things I like most about Donald are that, in contrast to my ex, he is a caring, sensitive, and gentle person."

I wanted to suggest that Donald and I meet one more time for a wrap-up session, one in which we would review his progress and try to determine if there are any unforeseen problems ahead that might derail him (I call this "antifuture shock"). But he had waxed

> *eloquent on his feeling that this, our 10th meeting, should be our final one. (It seemed that an even 10 held some positive symbolic meaning for Donald.)*

About 10 days later I received the following e-mail from Donald: "Just wanted to let you know that things are going very well. May we stay in touch this way? I will be glad to pay you for your time. If I need to, I'm sure I can set up an appointment to see you. Cheers, Donald."

I replied: "Good to hear from you. Please do keep in touch. If you need to see me you know where to find me. With genuine best wishes, Arnold."

A subsequent e-mail from Donald stated: "You will doubtless remember the catastrophic fantasies that used to bother me. I found a quote by Sophocles that described the way I used to be. "To him who is in fear everything rustles." I don't think I ever expressed my gratitude for all your help. Arnold, a million thanks! With profound appreciation, Donald."

In the 4 months that I had known Donald Green, he went from being an anxious, virginal, unhappy hermit, to an active heterosexual male, much happier at work, and with a coterie of male friends. He now satisfied the standard criteria for "adjustment"—love and sex, gainful work, friendship, and leisure activities. ■

CRITIQUE OF TREATMENT OF DONALD GREEN BY MULTIMODAL THERAPY
By Alice Goodloe Whipple

Introduction

The treatment of Donald Green by Dr. Arnold Lazarus as described in this case well illustrates the powerful therapeutic aspects of Multimodal Therapy (MMT), which delivers a comprehensive and systematic clinical assessment and treatment plan. The excellent "person-treatment" fit in this case is an integral feature of MMT. Because of its breadth and inherent appreciation of the many valid ways of helping, MMT draws on a rich storehouse of strategies and techniques from a variety of approaches. Furthermore, the distinctive aspect of

MMT, that which distinguishes it from other cognitive, behavioral, and affective approaches, is its emphasis on assessment and treatment across seven major discrete but interactive modalities of personality functioning (Lazarus, 1989, 1992; 1995a, 1997; Lazarus & Beutler, 1993). It provided a broad yet focused lens with which to view Donald's issues. Within MMT's framework, there is ample provision for a high degree of precision, but also flexibility and creativity, which were demonstrated by the therapist as he assisted Donald in remediating his problem areas and moving rapidly toward fulfilling his goals in life.

The Process of Multimodal Therapy

Assessment

The treatment in this case also illustrated the importance MMT places on a thorough clinical assessment. This was accomplished informally in the interviews, but also by utilization of the Multimodal Life History Inventory (Lazarus & Lazarus, 1991), which is comprehensive and yields valuable information across the seven discrete but interactive modalities of Donald's personality functioning. This assessment enabled Lazarus to form a well-founded conceptualization of problem areas and to plan with Donald for their amelioration. It also enabled Donald to gain more clarity concerning the personal issues that were crippling him. The therapist said, . . . "We have our work cut out for us," which implied not only that therapy is a collaborative endeavor, but that the work was well worth the effort. Later on, Lazarus zeroed in on one particular problem area—Donald's fears of and sense of inadequacy in dealing with women. For this he used a Second-Order BASIC I.D. process, which allowed a psychological magnification of all relevant dimensions of the problem.

It is important to emphasize that MMT has many additional assessment procedures that have not been included here. Clearly, one would rarely encounter a case in which all of the measures and assessment profiles created by Lazarus would be used. Nevertheless, the interested reader should be aware that other strategies do exist and may be found in other publications (see Lazarus, 1995a, 1997).

Therapeutic Relationship

The humanistic nature of MMT, which stresses parity in the relationship between therapist and client and also the collaborative nature of the therapeutic enterprise, makes for a nurturing psychological environment. In his writings on MMT, Lazarus (1989, 1992, 1995a) stated that the therapeutic relationship, that is, the bond between therapist and client and their mutual commitment to achieve the goals of therapy, is the soil in which the therapy takes root. He therefore believes this relationship is necessary albeit insufficient to help clients achieve the objectives that brought them into therapy in the first place. In the case of Donald, the relationship became not only an effective "milieu" for Donald's rapid growth and flowering, but also a vehicle for Donald's experiencing in vivo a new way of being in the world. It provided a fertile environment for the deployment of a variety of robust interventions (that have been empirically demonstrated to be effective).

The style and cadence of the therapeutic relationship stemmed from Donald's response to the question in the Multimodal Life History Inventory (Lazarus & Lazarus, 1991) that indicated that Donald' s ideal therapist would be similar to Burgess Meredith in the movie, "Rocky," a kind-but-tough trainer of boxers, who would be caring and ". . . work him real hard." This metaphor of the therapist as a boxer's trainer was applied by Lazarus in coaching Donald to go courageously into the arena of life and take emotional risks to achieve his goals.

The therapist used paradox to address underlying fears that Donald might have with regard to trusting him, mentioning that many professionals believe it takes a long time to establish rapport. He then asked Donald, "Can I leap to the conclusion that we already have a sense of trust and rapport and I can be totally up front with you? It's quite a quandary." This semiparadoxical statement encouraged Donald to become more quickly cooperative. The therapist had already also used right-brain assurances to enhance the relationship, for example, "You have to know that I care, that I can be trusted...." (the implication being that he was in Donald's corner).

Educational Model

The therapist took time and effort to instruct Donald in the educational treatment component of MMT, the treatment trajectory, and what Donald could hope to expect. This was especially important for Donald who thought he was a "basket case" with little or no hope for a better life. The therapist quickly assured Donald that he was not a basket case and proceeded to explain in greater detail how overcoming emotional difficulties was an educational process, and that self education was part of this endeavor. The therapist went on to state that people ". . . who work and make an effort to change are the ones who really improve their lives." He stressed Donald's assets and strengths, implying that he was really up to the challenge. In this way, Lazarus was able to impart the hope and optimism so important for a person to even begin to try to change. At the same time that he was affirming the necessity for Donald's full and active participation, he assured him that he would not be alone. They would work together, with the therapist as a trainer. He further used the analogy of boxing, which would involve several psychological exercises and other duties involved in training him for the "championship fight."

Although not explicitly stated in this write-up of the treatment of Donald Green, the seven interactive modalities of the MMT paradigm potentiate each other, and therefore there is often a positive cascading effect. This allows for a new and more positive configuration of behaviors to emerge once a change is experienced in one or two key areas.

Treatment Interventions

Many different types of interventions were brought to bear on Donald's problems, some of which have already been mentioned above. For instance, when he expressed his worst fears of being rejected by a group of people, Lazarus used paradox and exaggerated Donald's worst fears by saying, "Yeah, that would have shown beyond a shadow of a doubt that you are a loser, a worthless jerk, universally despised, utterly repugnant." With this kind of exaggeration, Donald could become more aware of his tendency to catastrophize. It would therefore be easier for him to identify and challenge his cognitive distortions. When Donald wondered if anyone could consider him lovable, some therapists would be tempted to reassure Donald, and inadvertently feed into his passive, avoidant lifestyle. However, Lazarus emphasized the proactive nature of people who ". . . act lovably. They do . . . loving things . . . exude warmth . . . smile . . . ask caring questions. They express concern."

There were not only psychological exercises within the sessions, but also psychological homework assignments outside of the sessions, which were designed to assist Donald to change cognitive distortions and learn new types of behaviors. Bibliotherapy was a helpful ongoing type of intervention and was congruent with the educational model of MMT. It greatly extended the range of therapeutic impact.

The range of therapeutic options was also greatly extended by the use of other resources outside of the one-to-one therapy sessions. For example, the therapist suggested that Donald go to the Albert Ellis

Institute in New York City, which is a bustling mecca on East 65th Street, at which there are always many different types of therapeutic activities taking place. Donald responded positively and decided to join an anxiety management group there. Another creative example of the use of outside resources was Lazarus' enlistment of several female graduate students to role play with Donald. In this way he gained realistic practice in socializing with women and an opportunity to absorb valuable information on sexual and romantic issues. When the virginal Donald ultimately established a relationship with a woman, "Cindy," and expressed concern regarding his erectile performance, the therapist assured him that if he failed to obtain or maintain an erection, it would " … test his anticatastrophizing skills;" and Cindy's reaction would yield information about her level of "nondemandingness." (In this way the therapist also took the pressure off Donald, an intervention that would be apt to facilitate erectile performance.)

There is a particular intervention in this case with which I take issue. When Donald revealed early in treatment that he was using Xanax, Lazarus offered a fair amount of positive reinforcement, calling him an enterprising fellow. I would have preferred a more neutral response, perhaps of a Rogerian nature, for example, "You really felt that you needed a chemical agent to feel comfortable enough to do what you needed to do?" Although Lazarus did offer cautionary statements, I believe it would have been more productive to examine why Donald was so eager to resort to a crutch of this nature.

Treatment Outcome

Donald achieved significant changes in the major areas of his life. He had made a group of friends, changed his work situation from one of unpleasant drudgery to one of exciting promise, and entered a satisfying relationship with the woman of his choice. The treatment of Donald Green demonstrated that Dr. Lazarus typically applies the multimodal therapy he has developed to vigorously engage in a collaborative endeavor for the healing and growth of the client…. or should we say, the training of Rocky for the "championship fight" of his life.

Additional Thoughts and Hypothetical Issues

Gender Issues: Female Therapist, or Donna vs. Donald Green

Had Donald gone to a female therapist, he might have found she was not compatible with his ideal image of a therapist as a boxing trainer. She might therefore have used this helpful information to determine that it would be in Donald's best interest to refer him to another therapist. A different set of expectations would have become evident, if one hypothesized that the client were a woman, say, Donna Green. How would this have affected the course of therapy? It is worth noting here that the flexibility of MMT would make ample provision for the special needs of many women, for whom relationships are often salient and form the core of their experiencing and decision making. This is indicated by the clinical experience of therapists and writers in the field of women's studies, such as Gilligan, (1982, 1993) and Brown and Gilligan (1992). This aspect of women's relating can be a great boon to them, as well as an albatross around their necks. Many women do not have problems of isolation, but rather ones of toxic relationships (McGrath, Keita, Strickland, & Russo, 1990). Conceivably a Donna Green with these problems could effectively extricate herself from an abusive relationship with the help of a therapist in the mold of a boxer-trainer. However, some other women might prefer metaphors connoting gentleness and nurturance, which a therapist such as Lazarus would then incorporate into the MMT treatment style. That would not be incompatible with the rigorous, active nature of the treatment. Nevertheless, if for any reason, he or Donna felt that she might find it more advantageous to work with a woman, he would refer her to a female colleague.

Hypothetical Treatment Impasse

Although the therapist was able to work with Donald to remove many road blocks to the progress of treatment, suppose there were an impasse? Suppose Donald had become really stuck. What other treatment strategies could have been used? In true MMT style, the therapist would have drawn upon any of a number of other alternative interventions or training techniques. For example, in a series of videotapes of distinguished therapists at work (Lazarus, 1995b), there is one showing Lazarus using quite a different type of intervention with a young man, Jim, in which he assisted him in engaging in a very vivid imagery process, with a somewhat psychodynamic flavor. In this process Jim remembered and reexperienced in the present what was to him a traumatic experience suffered as a child. The client was then encouraged to assert himself vigorously with his father in the imagery process and thereby gain a sense of mastery over a past situation. This sense of mastery was then transferred to more current issues.

MMT is exceedingly broad-based, and any individual case can but offer a snapshot of the most helpful procedures and processes that seemed especially applicable there. With another set of problems, the protean nature of MMT would be evidenced in a process that differed from the examples referred to above.

REFERENCES

Brown, L., & Gilligan, C. (1992). *Meeting at the crossroads: Women's psychology and girls' development.* Cambridge, MA: Harvard University Press.

Ellis, A. (1994). *How to stubbornly refuse to make yourself miserable about anything, yes, anything!* New York: Lyle Stuart.

Gilligan, C. (1982, 1993). *In a different voice: Psychological theory and women's development.* Cambridge, MA: Harvard University Press.

Lazarus, A. A. (1964). Crucial procedural factors in desensitization therapy. *Behaviour Research and Therapy, 2,* 65–70.

Lazarus, A. A. (1966). Broad-spectrum behavior therapy and the treatment of agoraphobia. *Behaviour Research and Therapy, 4,* 95–97.

Lazarus, A. A. (1967). In support of technical eclecticism. *Psychological Reports, 21,* 415–416.

Lazarus, A. A. (1989). *The practice of multimodal therapy: Systematic, comprehensive and effective psychotherapy.* Baltimore, MA: The Johns Hopkins University Press.

Lazarus, A. A. (1992). Multimodal therapy. In J. C. Norcross & M. R. Goldfried (Eds.), *Handbook of psychotherapy integration* (pp. 231–263). New York: Basic Books.

Lazarus, A. A. (1995a). Multimodal therapy. In R. J. Corsini and D. Wedding (Eds.), *Current psychotherapies* (5th ed.) (pp. 322–355). Itasca, IL: Peacock Publishers.

Lazarus, A. A. (1995b). *Multimodal Therapy.* APA Psychotherapy Videotape Series. Washington, DC: American Psychological Association.

Lazarus, A. A. (1997). *Brief but comprehensive psychotherapy: The multimodal way.* New York: Springer Publishing.

Lazarus, A. A., & Abramovitz, A. (1962). The use of "Emotive Imagery" in the treatment of children's phobias. *Journal of Mental Science, 108,* 191–195.

Lazarus, A. A., Davison, G. C., & Polefka, D.A. (1965). Classical and operant factors in the treatment of a school phobia. *Journal of Abnormal Psychology, 70,* 225–229.

Lazarus, A. A., & Beutler, L. E. (1993). On technical eclecticism. *Journal of Counseling and Development, 71*(4), 381–385.

Lazarus, A. A. & Lazarus, C. N. (1991). *Multimodal Life History Inventory.* Champaign, IL: Research Press.

Lazarus, A. A., & Lazarus, C. N. (1997). *The 60–second shrink: 101 strategies for staying sane in a crazy world.* San Luis Obispo, CA: Impact Publishers.

McGrath, E., Keita, G. P., Strickland, B. R., and Russo, N. F. (Eds.), (1990). *Women and depression; Risk factors and treatment issues.* Final report of the American Psychological Association's National Task Force on Women and Depression. Washington, DC: American Psychological Association.

Adlerian Psychotherapy is based on the personality theory, Individual Psychology, developed by Alfred Adler. This theory is teleological and represents a psychology of growth rather than one of instincts and libidinal drives. People are assumed to strive for personal competence and the achievement of meaningful goals, although these motives are often unconscious. All individuals attempt to reach their goals in a unique and creative manner, within limits set by heredity and environment. The developmental perspectives of this system are holistic and postulate that persons establish unique lifestyles that are normal and adaptive when they are consistent with the broader needs of the community in which they live.

Adlerian psychotherapy is educational rather than medical in its orientation. Clients are regarded as fundamentally healthy and creative rather than self-destructive; they are in need of instruction and direction to combat their discouragement, poor self-esteem, incorrect construals of their environment, flawed strategies in the pursuit of distorted goals, faulty attributions of guilt and responsibility, and unrealistic aspirations. The therapist's task is not to impose a theoretical template on clients' personal history and psyche, but to lead them through meaningful assignments, often of a social character, to a healthier lifestyle.

This socially oriented therapy, encapsulated in the principle of *Gemeinschaftsgefühl,* leads clients to become involved, socially, politically, and interpersonally, in the life of their immediate as well as larger communities. That orientation is the most important aspect of this therapy. It is a repudiation of the "navel-gazing" and purely intrapsychic approaches to therapy that preceded it and was ordained to integrate clients and students in the fulfilling human tasks of living in community with their fellows.

Raymond J. Corsini

5

Adlerian Psychotherapy

SOMETHING ABOUT THE THERAPIST • *Raymond J. Corsini*

When I received the master's degree from City College of New York (CCNY) in educational psychology in 1941, the only course that concerned any kind of clinical interaction was one in which we learned to administer individual intelligence tests. Nothing in the curriculum had anything to do with psychotherapy, which at that time we understood to be a medical procedure limited to psychiatrists who had undergone years of personal analysis. Psychologists were supposed to be specialists in testing, though they might do basic counseling such as vocational guidance. I took my first course in psychotherapy 14 years later, after I had treated clients with more than 1000 hours of individual and group psychotherapy.

My bachelor's and master's grades were always well below average, though I tried my best to earn good grades. In contrast to my mediocre academic career was my performance on objective tests. I had received a scholarship to CCNY based on my scores on the New York State Regents scholastic examinations, and on entering college I scored in the top percentile, 1 of 20 among 2000 entering students. Later, while enrolled in the master's program, I competed in a state civil service test for "junior psychologist." Even though I had the poorest grades of my academic cohort of 25 students, I scored No. 1 in my class on this test, and this led to an appointment as junior psychologist at Auburn Prison in New York.

While working at Auburn I was accepted in the Ph.D. program at Syracuse University. After 5 years of attending classes evenings, weekends, and summers, I was flunked out. At age 34, while working at the California State Prison at San Quentin as senior psychologist, I enrolled in the Ph.D. program at the University of California at Berkeley. Three years later, I again was flunked out. I finally earned the Ph.D. from the University of Chicago in 1955, at age 41. I mention my unusual academic history because it has meaning relative to my own psychotherapy.

At Auburn Prison I moved up from junior psychologist to associate psychologist and then was raised to the highest grade, senior psychologist. After a temporary transfer to the newly opened reception center at Elmira Reformatory, I was appointed as the chief psychologist at San Quentin. Three years later I became the supervising psychologist of the Wisconsin Department of Corrections, then the most prestigious and best-paid position in the field of prison psychology. After 3 years there, I left Wisconsin to study with Carl Rogers for a doctorate at the University of Chicago.

Once I had the Ph.D. degree, I worked at the University of Chicago as a psychometrist, became a partner in an industrial consulting firm for the next 5 years, and then taught for a year at the Illinois Institute of Technology and for another year at Berkeley (where I had flunked out some 10 years earlier). At age 50 I moved to Hawaii and established a private practice, from which I retired in 1988 at the age of 73. Along the way, in addition to my various jobs, I was always busy doing research and writing and editing books, several of which are devoted to psychotherapy.

Professional Experiences

At Auburn Prison one of my duties was to make sure every inmate's prison record included an IQ score. Since Auburn was a transfer prison, (receiving an overflow of prisoners from Sing Sing, where they had previously been tested), my main task was to interview inmates and write preparole reports. (Over the years, I wrote about 2000 such reports in the three state correctional departments that employed me.)

Eventually I established what amounted to a private vocational counseling practice at Auburn Prison. After 2 years of this practice, I decided to see how my clients had done relative to my vocational advice. I was able to get 100% follow-up with 50 inmates—after all, this *was* a prison. To my surprise, not a single prisoner I had counseled had followed my advice. I later published an article about this experience, with a postnote written by Carl Rogers (Corsini, 1947).

I had read Rogers' book, *Counseling and Psychotherapy,* in 1943 and, intrigued, had been looking for an opportunity to try his nondirective procedure (see Rogers, 1951). When an inmate in his twenties who had come to see me for vocational guidance indicated he would also be interested in personal guidance, I attempted to do formal psychotherapy in a nondirective manner for the first time. By the third session this client was in tears, wanting me to tell him whether he was a homosexual. I could only reply endlessly, in the Rogerian mode that he was *worried* that he might be a homosexual. He was in love with another inmate to whom he had never even spoken and for this reason he had concluded that he was gay. I wanted to give him reassurance that even if he was a homosexual, this was not necessarily bad, and at the same time I wanted to stay true to Rogers' method, so I suppressed my humanistic impulse and refrained from giving him the answer he was asking for. I wrote to Rogers, taking a long chance that I could get his opinion on how to handle this client. To my surprise he replied, and for several months he supervised me by mail.

While taking graduate courses at Syracuse University, I sat in on one taught by a Professor Wells whose specialty was hypnosis. Fascinated by his demonstrations, and with no other training, I decided to try hypnosis at the first opportunity. What happened was so traumatic that I did not "fool around" with hypnosis again for many years. A prisoner who had come to me for counseling about getting a divorce had an unusual criminal history. He was in prison for his first crime. At the age of about 30, he had assisted another man in an armed robbery, driving a stolen car to and from the scene, and then he had refused to accept his half of the stolen money. He had told his wife about the crime and his plan to confess it, leaving her in hysterics. He had gone to a police station, confessed, and pleaded guilty. He had been found guilty and sentenced to 15 to 30 years. Now, he told me, he wanted to give his wife a divorce so she could remarry.

Intrigued by the unusual circumstances of the crime, I asked him whether he might want to know the real reason for participating in a robbery and then giving himself up. He agreed to hypnosis and I began the procedure, imitating the professor I had seen. To my surprise, within minutes the client was in a deep trance. For over 3 hours I had him in and out of hypnosis, suggesting he would have amnesia when he came out of it. I tried all kinds of tests to make certain he was in a trance because I could hardly believe that my first attempt had been so successful. When I asked him, while he was hypnotized, why he had committed the crime, he said it was because he wanted to go to prison—which he later indignantly denied in his waking state. Finally I informed him that on coming out of the trance he would have a complete memory of all that he had told me. I gave him the signal to come to his normal state and, to my surprise and then to my horror, he got up from the chair, got on his knees, and started banging his head on the concrete floor, in an evident attempt to kill himself in this manner. I jumped on his back and put my hands between his face and the floor, and for minutes we struggled. When he stopped he went into a fetal position and sobbed "Eight more years, 8 more years," the time he still had to serve before he could see the parole board.

Since that time I have seldom used hypnosis except in private practice to help clients stop smoking. I believe that all psychotherapists should learn how to use hypnosis, but no psychotherapist should ever attempt what I did—using this powerful and mysterious technique without adequate training and safeguards.

At San Quentin, where I supervised four other psychologists, I was expected to do individual and group therapy as well as diagnostic work, including the certification of inmates on death row as sane or insane. As part of my assignment, I taught psychiatrists participating in rotating residencies how to do group therapy. I also maintained the equivalent of a private practice of psychotherapy in this prison, using the client-centered method for individual therapy and psychodrama for group therapy. Later, as the supervising psychologist in the Department of Corrections for Wisconsin, I supervised seven psychologists in five institutions and taught junior psychologists how to do group therapy.

When I took my first course in psychotherapy at the University of Chicago with Tom Gordon, I was older than he and had had more clinical experience, and I had already published more than the typical professor at the counseling center. But I was eager to learn as much as I could from the distinguished faculty that Carl Rogers had assembled, including, in addition to Gordon, John Butler, John Schlein, Jules Seeman, Rosalind Dymond, and Elias Porter. I asked Rogers for personal counseling soon after I arrived, but he informed me his counseling schedule was full. He said that when his schedule permitted he would see me, but meantime I might consider participating in a therapy group with one of his graduate students. This turned out to have unexpected benefits.

This group consisted of a student-therapist and six students, all younger than I. Within a few sessions our group was reduced to three: the therapist, another student, and myself. One day while I was talking, I suddenly, inexplicably, experienced a sharp pain or constriction in my throat, and I could no longer speak. Tears were running down my face. I grabbed the arms of the chair in an attempt to gain control, but it was no use. I could vaguely see the other two men in the therapy room looking at me in wonder. I could hear my mother's voice saying *"Sono contento che e morto senno sono sicuro che ti massavo"* (I am glad that he is dead, otherwise I am sure he would have killed you). She was referring to my father.

Embarrassed to be acting this way in front of two fellow students, I experienced the single most important moment of my life. I suddenly completely understood the reason for my miserable academic history.

My mother had borne twins in her first pregnancy. Both died in infancy. Then I was born. Then came another brother, who died in 1918 during the influenza epidemic. Another brother also died, a crib death). So, of my mother's first five children, I was the only survivor. Imagine her feelings when she saw her husband, my father, hitting her only child with enough force to knock him unconscious. Two of my early memories are of him knocking me out—and he died when I was 6.

In this moment of insight I realized that I had strung together a complex series of "logical" connections that went as follows: (*a*) I had been a bad boy, and (*b*) because I was bad, my father tried to kill me, and (*c*) because he tried to kill me, my mother wished him dead, and (*d*) he did in fact die because of her wish, but this was because of my being bad, and (*e*) since I was guilty of being the primary cause of my father's death, I should not succeed in academics.

As a result of this insight, I was finally freed of my unwarranted guilt. I had no further need to sabotage myself academically and got my Ph.D. degree without any difficulty. Among the side benefits of this incident was my conviction, which continues to this day, that psychotherapy is a genuine phenomenon and therapy often is an *Aha!* experience in which the beneficial insight comes suddenly, unexpectedly, and completely. My life changed sharply and for the better from that moment in other respects, too. I saw Rogers later in therapy, but actually I had already had my real therapy.

It may be of interest that I am an Adlerian after having had a successful personal, Rogerian, nondirective therapy, and that the cause of my problem had Freudian overtones. But life is complex and things are just not that simple, nor am I.

My Adlerian Background

I heard Alfred Adler speak before the Psychology Club at the City College of New York in 1935 and have written about my memory of that experience (Corsini, 1977). Nine years later, in Auburn, New York, I met my first Adlerian: Regine Seidler, a former teacher in Vienna who had participated in Adler's group parenting sessions. The director of a settlement house, she was taking graduate courses at Syracuse University at the same time I was. While commuting, we discussed psychology—I, Rogers; she, Adler. Then in 1953, when I gave a talk to the Chicago Group Therapy Association, I met in a single weekend three people to whom I was later to dedicate my textbook, *Current Psychotherapies:* Carl Rogers, J. L. Moreno, and Rudolf Dreikurs. At this convention I also met Harold Mosak, who was then working in Dreikurs' private practice.

After my talk in Chicago, a small, fat, bald-headed man came over to me and said, in a thick German (actually Austrian) accent, "My name is Rudolf Dreikurs. Have you ever heard of me? Your speech was excellent. Who are you?" On learning that I was planning to start studying for the Ph.D. at the University of Chicago, he offered me a scholarship at the Alfred Adler Institute, which I accepted.

The years 1953 to 1955 were busy ones. I was studying for the Ph.D., taking evening courses at the Alfred Adler Institute, and on weekends, whenever Moreno came to town, I would be on stage with him as an auxiliary ego. In addition, I was doing part-time teaching at a local college.

My first course on Adlerian personality theory was taught by Dreikurs and Mosak. Finally, after having examined a number of personality theories, having directly experienced Rogers' and Moreno's procedures, and having read their books, I had found something that really made sense to me. I was impressed by the concept that Adler's Individual Psychology is one of use rather than *possession,* and even more impressed by his notion of *Gemeinschaftsgefühl,* which has subsequently served as a philosophical guide to my personal behavior.

I became an Adlerian as the result of an incident during a course I took at the Alfred Adler Institute, which consisted of demonstrations of family counseling, Dreikurs' specialty. Dreikurs announced that he would be seeing for the first time a family about whom he had absolutely no information. Into the classroom came a woman and a man, the latter carrying in his arms a child about 6 years of age, emaciated, with a huge head, big, blank, blue eyes, and arms and legs like bare bones. The child was hanging limply in his father's arms, staring with open mouth, evidently mentally and physically retarded. He was put on a chair and stayed there like a rag doll, with his head at an angle. He never moved during the entire interview. My immediate diagnosis of congenital mental retardation was confirmed by the parents' account of his history.

The father was an attorney, the mother an accountant. They were about to put their son in a state institution for persons with retardation, and Dreikurs was the last professional they were going to see. The boy was their only child. When he was a baby they thought he was not developing normally, but their pediatrician reassured them that they were worrying unnecessarily. They consulted a pediatric neurologist when the child was unable to talk, feed himself, or walk by his first birthday. This doctor confirmed their fears that the child was developmentally retarded, and they began a series of visits to prestigious clinics, including the Mayo Clinic, and consultations with a number of neurologists, psychiatrists, and psychologists. All agreed that the boy was developmentally retarded, and they had concluded that nothing could be done to help him. One physician suggested trying electric shock, another suggested exploratory brain surgery, but all had concluded—as I had—that this was one of nature's mistakes due to a genetic malfunction, and the best solution was to put the child in an institution for mentally retarded persons.

After hearing this account, Dreikurs, to my surprise, got on his knees, faced the child, and began asking him questions. From where I was seated I could see only the back of the boy's head. Dreikurs asked the child the same four questions over and over, changing the order of the questions. This went on for perhaps 5 minutes. It seemed evident to me that this child, who never even moved his head or said anything, could not understand the questions put to him by this man who spoke with a thick accent. Finally Dreikurs stood up and stated, "There is nothing wrong with your son. He is normal." And then he began to give the parents explicit advice on what to do about their son.

My first impulse was to leave the room, to get away from this charlatan. Who did this arrogant psychiatrist think he was? A dozen experts had agreed that this was a child with mental retardation and developmental disability, and there was no hope that he could ever be normal. I had come to the same conclusion myself. Period. Place the child under custodial care.

Some 6 weeks later, when I saw this boy walk into the same room, albeit shakily, and heard him begin to talk, albeit haltingly, I felt electric shocks run up and down my back. I had been wrong, and so were all the other experts. Dreikurs had been right! There had to be something special in Adlerian theory and practice.

After the parents left, I demanded to know how Dreikurs had known that the child was normal and exactly what to advise. With a smile he explained how he had discovered, by means of his four questions, that this child was malingering, pretending to be incapacitated. Dreikurs then justified the logic of the advice he had given the parents, which I had thought at the time was criminally reckless.

This one incident, together with my personal comfort with Adlerian theory and philosophy, later led me to join Dreikurs' clinic and become an Adlerian. I worked for several years alongside Mosak and a number of other Adlerian psychologists and psychiatrists at this clinic, served for 2 years as Dreikurs' assistant at family education centers, and ran several parent education groups in Chicago. Later I started the Family Education Centers of Hawaii and served as senior counselor for 25 years, doing the kind of Adlerian parenting counseling that I had learned from Dreikurs. Eventually I became the editor of the *Journal of Individual Psychology.* I attend annual meetings of the North American Society of Adlerian Psychology and have written and edited a number of books based on Adlerian psychology, including a basic text (Manaster & Corsini, 1982).

The Setting for Therapy

I work in my home. My office consists of three rooms: a therapy room, a combined bathroom and storage room, and a room where I write and edit. The therapy room has easy chairs, built-in bookshelves, and several paintings of marine subjects. There is no desk, and no diplomas or other indications of my training and experience are in sight.

Most of my clients come from referrals. Ordinarily they call to make an appointment, and I interview them over the phone to find out why they want to see me. They usually have one of three major problems: marital discord, difficulties with children, or self-improvement issues. I refuse to see some people for a variety of reasons. I will not see a client if an agency expects a report from me. I will not even report how many sessions I see a client. I make notes, but after the client terminates I destroy them, a practice some agencies have questioned when they ask me for information. I reply that I work like a Catholic priest, keeping no records. If I have a former client's written permission to give information to a professional or an agency, I will do so, but only after I have read the report to my client for the client's approval. However, my procedure is illegal in some states. Practitioners of psychotherapy would do well to know existing local and state laws as well as the recommendations of professional organizations in regard to record keeping.

Generally, the first and last time I see a client we shake hands, and if a client wants to hug me, which sometimes happens, especially at our last session, I permit this. Mostly we talk; I vary my approach depending on the client. As a therapist I am "on the level," presenting an attitude of equality rather than acting like an expert. Sometimes, as a counselor, especially when dealing with parents who have problems with children or adolescents, I will be highly directive.

I usually refuse to see children alone or even with their parents, even though a good deal of my private practice involves parent-child problems. I believe it often does harm to such families to have an outsider intrude into their lives. I believe that the most ethical and successful method of dealing with parent-child problems is to train parents how to handle their children. I am a passionate advocate of nonpunitive methods of dealing with children, and for the past quarter century I have been teaching parents to use only logical and natural consequences of children's behaviors. I have also developed a novel educational system which is Adlerian in its concepts, the Corsini Four-R School System of Individual Education, which has been established in 12 schools around the world.

THE THERAPY FOR DONALD GREEN

Session 1

When Donald Green left following the intake interview, I began to ruminate about him—my usual custom, almost a habit. *Why does he continue to come to work late—his stated main reason for seeking therapy?* The answer is obvious: According to Adler, all behavior is purposeful, and for Mr. Green, coming to work late has a hidden goal. But what could that goal be? The most likely consequence of continuing this behavior, especially with a new supervisor once his present supervisor has retired, is that he would be fired from his job. And why does he go through all those futile attempts to get to work on time? Doubtless it's because he wants to impress himself with his earnestness. Everything he has told me adds up to the conclusion that he is playing games with himself although he seems on the surface to be open and aboveboard. He might well defeat me with a variety of ways to resist therapy. As a rule engineers are bright, and he might use numerous tactics to continue his behavior if I attempt to direct or control him. I will use my general Adlerian procedures, but I will have to watch myself that I don't give him reason to try to play tricks on me.

I am thinking along these lines while I wait for Donald Green to arrive for our first therapy session. In response to a soft knock on the door, I call out "Come in," and he enters, right on time. I smile at him; he looks about the room and finally sits down and looks at me. It is evident that he wants me to begin.

CORSINI. How are you?

GREEN. Fine.

(Evidently, Donald is not going to take any initiative. On the one hand, I do not want to generate the impression that he is to act like a schoolchild, and on the other hand I do not want to ask him to take over. I decide to ask a more or less neutral question.)

CORSINI. Been doing any thinking since the last time I saw you?

GREEN. Yes. Actually, I'm pleased I came to see you. I have been wanting to talk to a shrink for a long time, but you know how it is. Sometimes you keep on waiting, just letting things go . . . . By the way, how do you work? How does this therapy go? Are you a Jungian or something like that?

(This is a reasonable question. Often, especially if asked, I take the opportunity to explain my procedures. I decide to do this right now.)

CORSINI. I'm an Adlerian, and I follow a systematic way of operating developed by Rudolf Dreikurs, my teacher. Today we'll start with some personal history about yourself and your family. At the next session we'll use what is known as a projective technique. Then, at our third session, everything will be summarized. This will result in what we call a Life Style Analysis—a kind of overall summary of yourself in terms of your past and your present situation.

(Notice that I use the words "we" and "our." I want to convey that

I operate on the basis of equality. He is not expected to be passive, like someone coming in for a haircut.)

GREEN. I guess that's like a diagnosis? (I nod.) Makes sense. I thought you would have me lie down and just talk. Will you be asking questions?

CORSINI. Yes. I have a form here from which I'll ask you questions, and with your permission, I'll write down your answers.

GREEN. OK, fire away.

(Getting a Life Style has several advantages: [a] a good deal of important historical material is obtained, [b] the client begins to think of himself or herself objectively, [c] the therapy proper, which takes place after the Life Style has been obtained, can be focused on areas of greatest concern, which [d] can shorten the therapy.)

CORSINI. Are you ready? Any questions before I start?

GREEN. No, no questions. I'm ready.

CORSINI. I want to explain something about what we will be doing. When you go to a doctor or a dentist they may have X-rays taken to diagnose what is wrong. This is the same sort of thing we will be doing, except our diagnosis will be a collaboration. You are the expert on your life; you know yourself far better than I will ever know you. So we are like a couple of puzzle-solvers, trying to figure out why you have this work problem and other things, and then we may be able to figure out what to do about them. That is the purpose of all this preliminary material.

(I take out my notebook and begin the formal questionnaire [see Table 5.1]).

CORSINI. As I recall, you mentioned you had an older sister. Is that right?

GREEN. Yes—8 years older than me. Just her and then me in the family. Because of the 8 years difference I used to wonder whether I was an accident. . . .

(A therapist using a different system might want to stop at this point to discuss Donald's thinking that he perhaps was unwanted. I write on the side of the sheet "Unwanted?," to remind me to possibly explore that issue later.)

CORSINI. In what ways were you and your sister different?

GREEN. Like day and night . . . completely different.

CORSINI. Could you explain a bit more?

GREEN. She was social, had hundreds of friends. Everybody liked her. She was talented in everything: art, music. We had nothing to do with each other. She resented me.

TABLE 5.1 Protocol for Establishing Adlerian Life Style.

Family constellation
List all in family by dates of birth, including parents and dead siblings.

Self and sibling descriptions
Ask, if multiple siblings, who is most like and who is most different from client and in what ways. If only one sibling, ask how alike and how different. Then ask client to describe self and siblings as children. If only child, describe self as child.

Self and other ratings
Ratings desired in some manner, such as from O to 5, etc., or in rank order (who was the most critical?)

Brightness	Conforming
Energy	School grades
Helping around house	Rebelliousness
Pleasing others	critical
Considerateness	Selfishness
Sensitivity	Self-satisfied
Adjustment	Friendliness
Sports	Good-humored
Idealism	Ambitious
Morality	Getting own way

(Add any others that seem meaningful for client)

Sibling relationships
Ask which sibs paired off, which fought with each other, which ones did not like others, etc.

Parent-children relationship
Who was father's favorite? Mother's favorite? Who got punished most? For what and by whom?

Parent descriptions
Describe both parents, what their personalities were like, parental occupations, social attitudes, degree of harmony in the family, who was the boss and in what situations? Did they fight, and if so, who did the client think was right? Were the parents ambitious for the children? In what ways? Any close relatives, especially those who lived in home, or had effect on client?

Adapted from Rudolf Dreikurs's, "The Psychological Interview in Medicine," *American Journal of Individual Psychology,* vol. 10 (1954), pp. 99–122.

CORSINI. Were you alike in any way?

GREEN. Nothing that I can think of.

(I am starting to have some ideas about Donald. Living with a popular older sister who rejected and resented him and who was [at least in his mind] superior to him may be a partial explanation for his asocial behavior.)

CORSINI. What kind of kid were you?

GREEN. Quiet, invisible. I never volunteered for anything. Wanted to be by myself mostly. I did pretty well in school. I was in the Boy Scouts, but even there I didn't make any friends. I had a lot of hobbies; saved stamps, and I liked to make model cars. I guess you would have called me a good kid.

CORSINI. How about your sister? Can you tell me more about her?

GREEN. She was always with her friends—always singing, dancing, that sort of thing. She didn't want me around. Sometimes when my parents wanted her to baby sit for me, she made a big fuss. She never wanted to be seen with me. I don't know why she was ashamed to be seen with me. Maybe because I was fat—an ugly kid.

(I make a note, "Ugly as a child?" As Donald continues to talk about his sister and his parents, I list the ways he compares himself to her as they were growing up.

Donald says he believes that neither he nor his sister had a sense of humor; in fact, there was no humor in the family. From the next set of questions I learn that Diana was more athletic than he, attractive, and conventionally feminine. She was spoiled by their father but was punished more often by both parents, mostly by being confined to her room. She was popular and tended to be a leader in her social group. A frequent problem, according to the parents, especially the father, was that she wanted to be with her friends too much.

Donald was rarely punished, but when he was, it was often because his sister lied about him. Although he was pretty strong for his age he did not feel very masculine. His mother, whom he saw as weak, tried, usually without success, to protect him from his sister and his father. The father generally ignored Donald.

A childhood friend, Marcel, who was 4 years older than Donald, moved across the street when Donald was about 9. They maintained their friendship until Marcel's family moved away while Donald was in high school. Neither of them had any other friends. Mostly they talked, shared stamps, and played games such as checkers.

I then go into sibling relationships, but there is little new to be learned. The sister resented taking care of him. They rarely played games together, not surprising given the age gap, and when they did, she usually won. She often made fun of him. She was Father's favorite, while Mother had no favorites.

Both parents were now dead, Mother at 58, Father at 73. Father had been a quiet, solitary man, a hard worker, without humor. He had some friends at work but never brought them home. Mother was described as a hard worker, self-contained. She always spoke in a low voice, never lost her temper, and maintained her distance. The parents never showed any signs of affection to each other, and only Father showed affection to Diana. Donald thought that he was more like his father than his mother, but Diana was not like either parent.

Father was the boss in the house, but Mother sometimes could get him to change his ideas. Donald did not know whether they disagreed about bringing up the children. He saw his mother as a peacemaker, unwilling to fight openly about anything. The parents rarely quarreled; indeed, they rarely even spoke to each other. Donald was inclined to be on his mother's side if there was a conflict, because he thought she was more sensible, but he did not dare speak out. When Donald's father did punish him physically, using a razor strop, he did it silently, mechanically. His mother was ambitious for him and wanted him to go to college. Since he liked to make things and was good in mathematics, he decided to study engineering. No one else ever lived with them, but his father's mother visited the family a number of times. He was always happy to see his grandmother because she gave him attention and affection, which he never got from either of his parents.

CORSINI. Anything else I should know about your early life? Anything else important?

GREEN. I don't think so. My life has always been low-key. I always was—and I still am—a spectator on the sidelines rather than a player out on the field.

CORSINI. If I were only able to help you get yourself to work on time, would that be enough for you? Is that all you want from therapy?

GREEN. I was wondering about all these questions you ask me. I don't see how they relate to my job problem. You have not even asked me one question or made one statement about my getting to work on time. I'd like to know why you ask me all these questions.

CORSINI. That's part of the diagnosis I talked about earlier. If you went to a doctor with a cut on your hand, the treatment might just be to bandage it. But if you had some sort of pain that couldn't be explained, the doctor would most likely order X-rays and blood tests to get a diagnosis. Your major concern is to get to work on time in the morning, but this may be a symptom of something else. I don't know at this point if there is something else and, if so, what it is. So I'm trying to get an overall understanding of you, which should lead to changes in your life, including getting to work on time.

GREEN. Actually I'm pretty well satisfied with my life. I don't know if I would want any drastic change, like becoming a playboy. Perhaps giving up those crazy ideas I have about other people having it in for me would be important. I know the fears I have are silly, after I get over them, but at the time they seem real.

CORSINI. I take a holistic view of my clients. I want to help them become happier and more successful, both objectively and subjectively. This often means not only clearing up their specific complaints but also helping them get a new view of themselves and of life. For example, how would you rate yourself, on a scale of 10, on your job, family, and friends? First, how satisfied are you about your job?

GREEN. On a scale of 10, with 10 being highest? (I nod.) Well, I would say about a 7 for my job.

CORSINI. How would you rate your family life? I know you're not married and have no children and only one sister, but how satisfied are you about being single?

GREEN. Oh, I guess I would put that at about 5. I'm used to being alone, and I kind of accept it.

CORSINI. How about if you lived with someone, a wife or a lover, would that be better?

GREEN. That would depend on who it was. I suppose you want to know if I would prefer living with someone. I don't know, I really don't.

CORSINI. Well, let's keep your rating at 5 for family. How about a rating for friends?

GREEN. That would be low. I only have these two friends, and yet they are not really friends. More acquaintances, even though I have known them for many years. We have never really confided in each other. I guess I would give friends a rating of 2.

CORSINI. So it's 7 for job, 5 for family, and 2 for friends. (pause) I see our time is up. I'll see you next week at the same time.

GREEN. Right. See you then.

(At this point in the process of getting the Life Style, I try to keep an open mind, but I do have some preliminary hypotheses. Donald was a conformist in his youth, accepting his parents views of reality, while his sister Diana was a rebel. A serious, humorless man, he appears to have taken on the values and behaviors of his father. He seems to be a passive-aggressive type. I wonder about

his lack of a social life and the fact that in his early forties he is still a virgin. I have a feeling he has not really joined the human race. He should be an interesting client to work with.)

Session 2

As we begin our second session, Donald sits down, expressionless, avoiding looking at me. I decide to check his present mental status instead of immediately asking for his early recollections, the projective technique I use. I wait to see if he will say something, but he does not.

CORSINI. Is something bothering you?

GREEN (turning to face me). Yes . . . I came here just so I could be able to wake up and get to work on time. But it looks to me that coming here is just like if I go to a garage to have a new tire put on, and they want to repaint my car and put in a new clutch. That's what you are trying to do—make me over.

(This is a common reaction—I have run into this kind of thing before. I know how to react.)

CORSINI. You are right, of course. The reason for the Life Style interview is my concern with you as a whole person. If you simply want to solve this one problem, there are some therapists who may do that for you. A hypnotist perhaps . . . would you want me to refer you to someone else? We can cancel this session and I will only bill you for the two sessions that I've seen you.

GREEN. I didn't mean it that way. It's just that you haven't said a word about my sleep problem. All you've asked about is my family, my parents, and my sister. What do they have to do with my problem at work?

CORSINI. I thought we discussed this at the last session. I am much aware of your job situation. But my concern is with the total you.

GREEN. I suppose you are going to say. . .you know best; you are the therapist.

CORSINI. No, not quite. Remember, I said that we are cooperating, trying to figure out a puzzle. From your point of view the puzzle is your inability to come to work on time. But from my viewpoint the puzzle is not only why you are getting to work late but what other problems you may have experienced. I hope we can clear up a lot of things, including the job situation.

GREEN. I really don't know if I want a complete psychoanalysis.

CORSINI. This is not psychoanalysis. As I mentioned last time, this is the way I operate. . . .

GREEN. OK, then, let's get on with it. Is today some kind of a test? Do I have to write anything?

(I see Donald's concern about the Life Style procedure as evidence of anxiety. Perhaps he wants reassurance from me. Perhaps this is an attempt to sabotage the therapy, or perhaps this is a way of testing me. In any case, I will stay the course.)

CORSINI. No, I'll write down your replies. The first thing I'll ask about is your early memories. In the intake interview you spoke of being on the roof with your mother, and she could see your father while you could not. What I would like now is some more early memories.

GREEN. My earliest memory is that my parents and I used to go to the beach every Sunday....

CORSINI (interrupting). Sorry. That is not what I mean by a memory. We call that a report. For us a memory is something specific. Something that happened once. What is the earliest single, specific memory you can recall?

GREEN. The first thing I remember was that I was in the house with my mother and someone knocked on the door. I ran behind my mother. She went to the door to open it. I ran out of the room. Then she was talking to this man, and I was in the other room wanting to look in to see who it was, but I didn't go in. I could hear her talking to him.

CORSINI. How old were you?

GREEN. Maybe 2 years old.

CORSINI. Can you give me any details about the memory?

GREEN. Just wondering whether I should look in....

CORSINI. Anything else in the memory?

GREEN. Just that. . . me, on the outside looking in.

CORSINI. Are there any feelings associated with the memory?

GREEN. Scared and wondering. Feeling alone....

CORSINI. How about another memory?

GREEN. It was in 1952. We were in New York City. There was a parade for someone, maybe President Eisenhower. I was about 4. My father put me on his shoulders so I could see better.

CORSINI. What is clearest in the memory?

GREEN. The feeling of my father's clothes. His suit jacket against my bare legs. Like rough wool. It was such a feeling of . . . togetherness . . . intimacy. For once I was really close to him. I could feel his body.

CORSINI. It was a strong feeling—a pleasant one?

GREEN. More than pleasant. It was like real.

CORSINI. May I have a third memory?

GREEN. It's a sad one. I had been in the first grade for maybe a month. I'm seated on a bench-type chair with another kid—a boy. Suddenly, he puts his arm over my shoulder and I put my arm over his shoulder, and I know we're friends. At just this moment, a strange boy comes into the classroom and talks to the teacher. The teacher calls my name. I go up front and she tells me I have to go home because my mother is dying.

CORSINI. What is clearest about this memory?

GREEN. Touching him. I never saw him again.

CORSINI. What feelings were there in this memory?

GREEN. How good it was to be so close. And my shock at being separated from him.

CORSINI. Did your mother die?

GREEN. No, but they thought she was going to. She was very sick. Later, someone told me she had taken poison. We moved away, and I never went back to that school.

CORSINI. How about another memory?

GREEN. I walked over to a park across from the new house we moved to, and some kids were playing there. They tied me to a tree and left me. They just ran away. They made fun of me, called me "four eyes"—I was wearing glasses even then.

CORSINI. Any feelings about this memory?

GREEN. Anger, unfairness. What's the use? Sadness.

(I will not go into all 10 of the early recollections I obtained in this interview. Essentially, they all have more or less the same pattern. The early recollection process takes about an hour.)

CORSINI. Between now and the next session, I will be going over everything you have told me. I will go over your Life Style Analysis with you at the next session.

GREEN. Explain that again, please.

CORSINI. The Life Style Analysis is a tentative summary of you as an individual from a psychological point of view. It becomes the starting point of the therapy proper.

GREEN. I thought this was the therapy we're in. . . .

CORSINI. I said "therapy proper" because I want to separate the diagnostic part, which we have just finished, from the treatment part. Does that make sense?

GREEN. Yes, it's like an engineering problem. Diagnose why some piece of machinery doesn't work and then fix it.

CORSINI. Something like that. The analogy is not complete, though, since a person is a whole and not just a collection of parts. That's what is meant by holism. People are much more complicated than machines. Well, that's all we have time for today.

Session 3

Donald Green seems anxious at the beginning of this session. This is usual for people who begin Adlerian psychotherapy of the Dreikurs type because they know they are coming in for a diagnosis. I have written out the Life Style Analysis, and now I intend to read it to Donald. I'll go back to it and refer to it from time to time during the therapy.

CORSINI. Before we begin on the Life Style Analysis, is there anything you want to tell me?

GREEN. Yes! This past week I came to work on time every day! I had no trouble waking up. I'm even thinking of telling my neighbor he doesn't have to call me; I know it's a bother to him. And I decided to use only one alarm clock, and I'm going to tell the paperboy not to knock at the door.

CORSINI (laughing). And you were concerned that we would not work on that problem! And here it got cured, as it were, all by itself. How do you feel about that?

GREEN. What did you do to make it go away?

CORSINI. Nothing. I take no credit. You did it all.

GREEN. It makes no sense. Is the therapy actually working?

CORSINI. What do you think therapy is?

GREEN. I really don't know.

CORSINI. I'll tell you a secret; I don't know either. No one knows; it's a kind of mystery. Starting to wake up on time and getting to work on time tells me that you really want to change, even though, as you point out, we have not begun to work on that problem. So the fact that this happened to you is a kind of mystery—why are you making it happen?

> *(At this point I am optimistic about the chances for successful therapy. Donald's attitude now is quite different from what it was in the last session. Is it because he is now getting up on time? Is this an example of flight into health? He may be trying to escape from therapy, saying in effect: "Thanks, Doc, you cured me. How much do I owe you?" and then disappear. But later the symptoms*

may come back, and then he can take the attitude that therapy just does not work. Another explanation is that we had formed some kind of bond or working alliance, and this change was a gift to show me he liked me and wanted me to know he was a good client. This too would be a kind of trick. Another explanation is that he really wants to change, and this was a first attempt.)

CORSINI. Now, suppose we get to the Life Style. May I call you by your first name?

GREEN. Sure—and can I call you by your first name too?

CORSINI. If you wish. Call me Ray.

GREEN. Naw, I'll call you Doc. That's how I think of you.

(I am pleased by this apparently minor exchange. For the first time Donald is acting on the same level as I am, and he has injected a bit of humor into our relationship. It is a kind of test of me. I will continue with the Life Style Analysis, but perhaps he wants to avoid it. I will check this out.)

I take out Donald's Life Style Analysis and start to leaf through it. Donald looks at me and I can feel that he is frightened, as though he is going to hear bad news. This pleases me because I interpret it to mean that he will be paying attention to what he will hear. I begin reading from my prepared text.

> Mr. Donald Green, a 42–year-old, unmarried engineer, referred to therapy by his supervisor and also by an industrial psychologist, complains that he has difficulty getting to his job on time and says he would like treatment for this specific problem. He mentions that from time to time he fantasizes catastrophic situations that turn out to have no foundation. He presents a report on himself from an industrial psychologist that suggests that he seek counseling due to his asocial behavior. Apparently, practically his entire social life consists of a weekly dinner with a couple some 20 years his senior. He has never dated or had sex with anyone.
>
> He appears to be in good health, states that he has regular medical examinations, and there appear to be no biological causes for either the sleep problem or the social situation. He appears to be generally satisfied with himself and his life, and his main stated concern is getting to work on time.

I pause and look at Donald with a quizzical expression, as though asking him what he thinks. When he says, "You put it quite right; no comment" I continue reading.

> He is the younger of two children, with a sister, Diana, 8 years older. She ignored him as a child and apparently resented him. In the family he

played the role of Good Boy while she played Bad Girl. Diana, a rebel, was punished more than he was. While Donald did well in school and was cooperative in the family, his mother nevertheless appreciated the sister more and ignored Donald. Mother was supportive of Donald but she and her husband both were distant people. Father was dominant in the family. Apparently, Diana made an independent social life for herself and escaped from the narrow boundaries of the family, while Donald conformed more or less to the parents' expectations.

At this point I pause again and look at Donald, inviting his comments.

GREEN. Right on! She had the courage to go on her own. I didn't. I tried to please my parents, and I didn't succeed. I can now see it from Diana's point of view. Maybe she wanted me to be a rebel too, to be on her side. Maybe she felt that there were three against her—Father, Mother, and me. Maybe that's why she was angry with me. I never gave that any thought.

(Before I continue reading, I note that I am pleased that Donald has been able to empathize with his sister and see things from her point of view. This appears to be a new insight for him.)

As an adult, Donald continued his childhood pattern of behavior and became an amalgam of his father and his mother's more overt personality. Were they alive, they probably would approve of his lifestyle, in that he is a hard worker, conforming, a pleaser, with high standards. They might also approve of his being, like themselves, solitary.

(Again I stop to look at Donald, inviting comments.)

GREEN. You are right on the money. I keep thinking: "The child is father to the man" I can see the picture clearly. They were role models for me. I am now the person they made me become. I kind of sold out. Perhaps it was to gain their love . . . and I didn't succeed.

(After a pause, I continue reading the Life Style Analysis.)

And suddenly, something unusual has happened. Donald, the conformist, the good boy, starts to do something bad. He does not come to work on time! This seemingly minor variation from his whole life history of being a conformist, doing what others expect of him, is a puzzle to him, and now he states that he wants to be 'cured' of this problem. He follows the advice of two authorities, a supervisor and a psychologist, to get therapy for his problem. When I venture to discuss the possibility and perhaps the necessity of examining his whole life, it upsets him.

(I have a bit of concern about reading this last statement, since it seems to be unwarranted criticism. It was a judgment call, and perhaps I was wrong. But I did want it, and so l shared it with my client.)

GREEN. You're right about that, though. I know that getting to work late has a larger meaning.

After this comment from Donald I continue with my reading.

In his early recollections, five themes appear which are basic mistakes:

1. *He believes he is unwanted and unlovable.* This is an error. He is an intelligent, attractive, and successful person, and were he to give others the opportunity to know him, some people would like him.

2. *He enjoys contact with others but believes he can only get it in superficial or unimportant ways; he believes relationships are transitory and will not last.* This is also an error. Were he to open himself to others, he would be accepted.

3. *He believes he is not capable.* This is another mistaken concept. He is a capable and successful individual.

4. *He is unnecessarily fearful, reminding himself of the dangers of life by fantasizing.* This is a curious and totally unnecessary safeguarding mechanism.

5. *He does not face people problems directly. He is afraid of confrontations.* This is an error. He has the strength to meet and solve problems directly.

(After reading this list, I note Donald's facial expression. He seems to be in deep thought.)

GREEN. Would you read all of that again?

CORSINI. I have just a bit more to read, and then if you want I will repeat these themes. But first I want to discuss what strengths I think you have. So far, everything has been more or less negative. OK?

GREEN. *That* will be a relief!

Donald Green is an intelligent person, willing to learn, successful, in a good profession, and certainly someone others would like if he gave them the opportunity to know him.

After reading this final paragraph, I tell Donald that our time is almost up and I have someone else waiting. I promise to review everything next week. When I do a summary session I try to finish near the end of the hour, since I want the client to be left alone to ruminate on what he or she has heard.

Part of my technique is to find out at the next session how much is remembered of what I said.

Session 4

Donald opens the interview.

GREEN. I wonder, how accurate is the Life Style? And where did you get it?

(He is now taking charge.)

CORSINI. The Life Style statement comes from two major sources: what you have told me and the interpretations I make based on my training and experience. Another therapist might have come to different conclusions. Remember that it is a tentative statement and open to modification.

GREEN. I just wanted to make sure it wasn't engraved in granite. I have been doing a lot of thinking about what you said.

CORSINI. Good. What do you remember about the analysis?

(This is an important question. What I am most interested in is which of the basic mistakes did he remember, and which did he forget? Those that are forgotten are most likely to be difficult to deal with.)

GREEN. You said I didn't have courage to confront others—that I deal with life in a cowardly way.

(This was the last of the basic mistakes, and possibly the least important. This is an example of unconscious purposeful forgetting, a common phenomenon, a self-protective process.)

CORSINI. Do you remember any of the other basic mistakes?

GREEN. You said that I was intelligent.

CORSINI (laughing). That sure doesn't sound like a basic mistake.

GREEN. Let me see. . . something about intimacy, that I didn't know how to be intimate. (He thinks for a minute.) That's funny, I thought I remembered them all when I left. There were four, weren't there?

(Note that he has missed the essence of the second basic mistake, which emphasizes that he gets intimacy only from unimportant or superficial contacts, and he does not expect relationships to last. The discussion above is the reason for my writing down the five basic mistakes in summarizing the Life Style Analysis.)

CORSINI. There were five. Now, Donald, I have to explain something important. It has to do with psychological theory. Do you play chess?

GREEN. Yes, I used to, but I haven't played for some years.

CORSINI. Say that you and I are having a match. And say that you see me move a knight and you think it is a bad move, and you can't figure out why I moved it. Suppose you consider me to be a pretty good player. Then what would you think?

GREEN. Maybe you saw a better move, one that I cannot figure out.

CORSINI. Right! You would try to figure out why I moved that knight. You assume I had some reason for making the move. You try to figure out what I have in mind. Every move we make in chess has a purpose, and the purpose is to win the game. Now, when I examine your life situation, I wonder what the reason is for it. For example, you live like a hermit. You are fearful of other employees. You have practically no friends. You frighten yourself with all kinds of horror stories. You don't have someone to love or to love you, not even a pet.

I ask myself, why does a man with high intelligence, who is in good health and fairly attractive physically, act as you do? He must be acting this way for some purpose, or a series of purposes. What can that be? My only answer is that you are attempting to achieve some kind of goal, you want to obtain something, but I don't know what that can be.

Some psychologists go about figuring out a client by trying to understand the past. So they may say: Donald had a family that really did not accept him; his father was cold, his mother was weak, and his sister didn't like him. Therefore he is now a loner.

DONALD. Well that's true, isn't it?

CORSINI. Yes, but it does not explain your behavior. Your sister Diana had a similar heredity and environment, yet she went a different direction.

GREEN. Now you've got me confused. First you ask me a lot of questions about my past, and then you say that my personality does not come out of the past.

CORSINI. Bear with me a bit. Most psychologists take the position that the past determines behavior. Adlerians, among others, take a different point of view—that the future determines behavior. Your expectations about what will happen, as in chess, determine behavior, what you expect to achieve. Does that make sense?

GREEN. I don't know . . . . Let me think . . . . Yes, I think I see what you're saying. What I do, like being by myself, can't be explained by the fact that my family was full of loners, since my sister was always a social butterfly. I just took a different road.

CORSINI. Ah, but why did you do that, and what is the reason for continuing to do so?

GREEN. Beats me. I can't think why. . . .

CORSINI. OK, fair enough. Let's leave that. Maybe the answer will come to you. But let me ask you why you now have started to get up mornings? What in the past led to that? As you said yourself, I didn't even mention your sleep problem, but apparently you've conquered it, all on your own.

GREEN. But why did I do that? You tell me. Like you say, I must have had some goal, some reason for being late, but I can't figure it out.

CORSINI. I can only guess. Could it be that you gave up being late for some reason that has to do with me?

(My thinking at this point goes something like this: He has suddenly, dramatically changed the very reason for coming to see me in the first place. What of any consequence has happened in his life just before this unexpected change? The only thing has been meeting me. I watch him carefully, hoping that he might react with what Dreikurs called a recognition reflex [which is how Dreikurs knew that 6–year-old boy was playing his life-and-death game right from infancy]. I'm gratified to see Donald's startled reaction, so I know that I am probably right in my assumption.)

GREEN. I can't see where you're going, but it sounds OK to me. I'm still confused, though.

CORSINI. I'm going to confuse you still more. I believe that one of the few healthy things you have done was *not* getting up in the morning. Isn't that ironic? The very symptom that led your supervisor to suggest you see a therapist, and that you hoped I would cure you of, was probably *a healthy thing!* Had I tried to deal with it, you would have defeated me. As it was, you cleared it up on your own.

GREEN. Whoa there! Do you mean that my getting up late was good?

CORSINI. I think so. But let's see if you can find some explanation, no matter how fantastic, for first, not getting to work on time in the morning, and then for curing yourself.

(Donald shakes his head and then looks up at the ceiling, remaining silent for a while. I wait patiently, hoping he will be able to generate some insight into this apparently confused situation.)

GREEN. When I was a kid I used to pretend I was sick when I didn't want to go to school. My mother would let me stay home in bed. My father would be furious with her and say that I was shamming. Are you telling me that I am using the same technique?

CORSINI. I didn't tell you anything. All I did was guess that you had some secret goal to achieve by going to work late. But a good boy does not say, "Hey, I don't want to go to school" or "I don't want to work" What does a good boy do? He plays sick. What do you think?

GREEN. Makes sense. I'm still acting like a kid.
CORSINI. See you next week.

Session 5

GREEN. I want to tell you something strange I've been doing on the job. I usually eat lunch in my office. Sometimes, though, if I forget to bring my lunch, I go to the company cafeteria. At the door I look in to see if one of the small tables for two is vacant. If there is one, I then get in line at the counter, get my food, and sit down at an empty table. But if someone else takes the only empty table before I get to it, I leave the cafeteria, taking whatever food I can with me. Isn't that stupid?

CORSINI. What would happen if you went and sat at a table with others?

GREEN. They would fall off their chairs in surprise.

CORSINI. No they wouldn't.

GREEN. You don't know them.

CORSINI. Want to bet?

GREEN. You serious?

CORSINI. Absolutely serious. I'll bet you $10 that if you do just that, nothing of the sort will happen.

GREEN. I've never done anything like that in my life.

CORSINI. Do you really want to change your life?

Donald does not answer for a while. Then he looks at me in a pleading way. I wait, holding my breath. This is a crisis point. I have struck suddenly with a challenge, surprising him.

GREEN. Why $10?

CORSINI. That's about today's equivalent of what Dr. Dreikurs taught me to bet—never more, never less. Here is the bet. You will do exactly what we said: go to the cafeteria, look for a table where there is an empty seat, and ask if you can sit down. If they fall off their chairs I'll pay you $10. If they don't, then you pay me.

GREEN. But why should I do it?

CORSINI. Why did you mention the cafeteria?

GREEN. I suppose because I feel so stupid looking in and acting that way.

CORSINI. Well, then, there are two possible ways of solving that problem. One might be to keep talking about it. The other would be to take action and do something.

GREEN. I'll take the bet.

CORSINI. Good! But to help ensure that I'll win my bet, I want to role play something.

GREEN. I'm no good at play acting.

CORSINI. Even more reason to do it. Make believe that I am at a table and there is an empty chair at the same table. (I arrange a chair near me.) Now get up and come over and ask me if you can sit at my table. Let's see how it will work out.

After some initial hesitation and a number of questions, we role-play the same scene several times. At first, acting the role of a person at the table, I welcome Donald and initiate the conversation to make him feel comfortable. I vary this role several times until he begins to react in a relatively smooth and comfortable manner. Then I take a less friendly attitude and say the chair is reserved for someone else. He is now stymied. Next I change roles with him and have him be the one at the table. He is to treat me the same way I treated him, and I try to handle the situation as best I can. Then we change places, and we keep shifting roles for about a half-hour.

GREEN. That was interesting! I began to feel it was real, and after a while I was enjoying it. I'm looking forward to actually doing it tomorrow.

CORSINI. OK. I'm fairly sure that you'll do it, and that you'll succeed. But if you do succeed, what will you have learned?

GREEN. I suppose, knowing how to do things with others.

CORSINI. But is that important?

GREEN. For me, most important. Most important.

CORSINI. What do you imagine I think is more important?

GREEN. I have given up trying to figure you out. What? You tell me.

CORSINI. What was your first basic mistake, the most important one of all?

GREEN. Not feeling lovable, not being acceptable.

CORSINI. Ha! You remembered! Does it explain why you accepted my bet? Forget whether you will actually go through with it. Suppose the absolutely worst thing you can imagine happens when you ask for a seat at a table. Say that the people there make fun of you, laugh at you, ridicule you, throw a glass of water in your face. Suppose it is the most horrible experience of your life. From my point of view, while I would regret that this would happen to you and would also regret losing my $10 bet, nevertheless I would think you have made remarkable progress. You are actually willing to do something new *and* different *and* scary. I'm impressed.

GREEN. I think you are saying that I think I'm OK, that I'm lovable.
CORSINI. I think your taking my challenge means that you think so.
GREEN. As a matter of fact, I do. I *am* OK.

(From my point of view as a cognitive therapist, the therapy has passed another climax. Donald has remembered his first and most basic error, and he is willing to challenge it by direct action. I have prepared him through role-playing, and I am certain I will win my 10 bucks.)

Session 6

GREEN. You can't guess what happened.
CORSINI. Did I win my $10.
GREEN. Oh that, yes. Here's your money. (*I take the $10 and put it in my wallet.*) I have been eating every day with the fellows, five others, all foremen. I asked them if I could sit at their table and they said yes, and now we always eat together. They are a nice group. They look up to me because I'm an engineer—they say I have solved a lot of problems they couldn't figure out. I found I have a good reputation as an engineer. I could tell they were a bit nervous about me at first, and I figured out that maybe they felt inferior to me because I make more money than they do. One of the guys—Frank—restores old cars, too, and he invited me to his house, Thursday—the same night of the week I usually visit my friends, you know, the artist and his wife. Well, I accepted, and I called Jim to tell him I could not make it last week. Instead I went over to Frank's house, and we spent an hour or so looking at his cars, and I gave him some advice. His wife asked me to stay for dinner and afterward we had some drinks and did a lot of talking. Then we went back to the cars and I helped fix some wires he had misconnected on one of them. But that isn't what is good. Something else happened, more important. Can you guess?
CORSINI. You got engaged?
GREEN. Boy—are you a comedian! Well, in a way you're right. Frank's wife asked me to come to dinner again Saturday night, and when I got there they had another guest. Can you guess who it was?
CORSINI. Julia Roberts?
GREEN. You sure are in some mood today, Doc. No, but it was Francine, Frank's unmarried sister. We had a good time, the four of us, talking some politics, laughing, and telling jokes. I have never been good at that but I told a few and they about fell over laugh-

ing, not so much at the jokes as how I told them—usually forgetting the punch line. But they weren't malicious. Later, we all got serious, and they asked me why I had never married. All of a sudden, I decided to tell them everything: About my father and my mother and my sister and my job, and seeing you and how you had bet me $10 and took my money. They screamed over that. I suddenly felt like I belonged. Do you understand: *I felt like I belonged*!

(Had someone walked in, they would have thought that he was threatening me, standing up, shaking his fist at me, screaming at me. I looked at him with a smile on my face—a big, wide smile.)

CORSINI. I'll tell you what I think. I think you're on your way . . . nothing is going to stop you now.

GREEN. So fast? But this is only our sixth session together. I thought psychotherapy goes on for years.

CORSINI. Donald, there is an optimal time for therapy. Too little is a mistake, but so is too much. In my judgment you've decided that the basic mistake you made years ago, deciding that you weren't worthwhile, that no one wanted you, was an error. You checked it out by sitting at a table, accepting an invitation to work on a car, accepting two dinner invitations, and then opening up and sharing some of yourself. All these events indicate to me that you have now rejected the second basic error—that relationships have to be superficial, that they will not last, that you have to be careful of others. Remember your memory of being afraid to go into the room where there was a stranger? You had an associated mistaken belief that you are not capable. Having the guts to ask to sit at a table with strangers tells me that that mistake has been cleared up. And the fourth one, fantasizing all the dangers, seems also to have disappeared. You just went and did what you had to do, and it worked out right, as I guessed it would.

GREEN. Some other things happened, too, even more important. Two things that I did on the job. First, one of the foremen, not those I eat with, but another man who is a prime pain, has been on my case, always screwing up and acting like a wise ass about anything I tell him to do. Well he screwed up again so I gave him one grand bawling-out at the top of my voice, in front of everybody on the factory floor. All the other foremen and some of the workers heard me. And you know what? They were all on my side, and some of them told me so later on. And the second thing—I told my supervisor that I want to quit my job.

CORSINI. Wow! Looks like the worm is turning with a vengeance.

GREEN. I realized last week why I had been having trouble getting up in the morning. It was so simple and so logical. Were you able to figure it out, Dr. Analyst? (I shook my head.) Easiest thing in the world. I didn't like my job any more. I was tired of taking a lot of bull from foremen. That was one thing. But there was something even more important. I had gotten bored with the work. I just didn't want to work at that company and at that job any more, but I didn't have the guts to admit it, even to myself. So, I was trying to get fired by coming in late. One morning while shaving I asked myself, "Hey Donald, why are you not getting up mornings?" And then, out loud, I said to myself—I was looking in the mirror at the time—"Because I want to get fired" And then I answered myself, "Why wait? Go tell your boss you are quitting. Lots of people do it all the time."

So I went to see my supervisor and told him I wanted to quit, and he didn't think that was so big a deal. He asked me what I wanted to do instead and I said I didn't know. I just knew that I wanted to be free for the first time in my life. I have enough money to take care of myself for a couple of years. I can always find a job, maybe even make more money.

CORSINI. You sure are full of surprises today, aren't you? How do you feel?

GREEN. This may surprise you, but I feel calm—like things are working out just like they should. I feel content, safe, secure, at home. By the way, at the cafeteria now, I sit with a new group every day. And Frank and I see each other a lot. I go over to his place practically every night. He is starting to confide in me. Seems his wife can't get pregnant, and he is starting to tell me his problems. He wants to go on a weekend with me, his wife, and his sister, but I don't want to get involved with her. She is a nice person, but not my type. I have been talking to one of the women who works at the company with me. Matter of fact, I have a date with her tonight for dinner.

CORSINI. Donald, our time is about up. You are making such good progress that I would like to suggest that I see you only once every 2 weeks. OK?

GREEN. I don't know about that, Doc. We are making such good progress that I think of you as my lucky charm. I don't know whether it would be a good idea to break off so soon.

CORSINI. I am not talking about breaking off but about tapering off. If it doesn't work out, we can go back to the once-a-week schedule.

GREEN. OK. See you in 2 weeks, then.

This type of session, with a client suddenly making all kinds of unexpected progress in all directions, has been quite common in my experience as a therapist. To me, it is a sign that termination is called for. I don't want a client to become dependent on me. Sometimes I'm tempted to keep an interesting client, but since I must operate in the best interests of my clients, I must at least suggest tapering off, if not breaking off. The final decision is the client's, but it's my ethical obligation to tell the client my feelings and thoughts.

Session 7

CORSINI. Well hi, how goes things?

GREEN. I had a certain amount of anxiety—wanted to call you several times. But I decided to tough it out. I haven't turned in my resignation yet, on account of Cecile.

CORSINI. Cecile?

GREEN. She works in accounting, a computer expert. She's a couple of years younger than I am; was married, now divorced, no children. Real bright. We enjoy ourselves. We have dinner almost every night. Right after I see you I'll be seeing her today.

CORSINI. Sounds good.

GREEN. I have been giving a lot of thought to what I want to do. One thing is for certain. I want to change my job—even get out of that community. Start a new life. I feel restless, unsettled, wanting a change. Like a snake ready to shed its skin. I want to get into something different.

CORSINI. Well, you *are* moving along. Tell me about Cecile. Is everything going well there?

GREEN. Yes, but there is a problem with sex. Cecile and I have been doing a lot of kissing and petting. You know what I mean? I have gotten so excited that I get a big erection and then it becomes painful because I don't get any relief. You know what I mean? (I nod my head.) Well, Cecile has been married. She doesn't know I never had sex before. I wonder what to do about it. Should I go to a prostitute or see if I can get a sexual surrogate? Do you know one?

CORSINI. Donald, what do you think would be the best way to handle this problem?

GREEN. I guess telling Cecile.

CORSINI. I agree—but how about telling her after you two have sex, not before?

GREEN. That's an idea. . . . But what's your advice for me about sex?

CORSINI. Just enjoy yourself. It will all be very natural. I am sure that Cecile will be letting you know what is right for her.

GREEN. Suppose I can't perform? Then what?

CORSINI. Almost every man has had an impotence problem at some time. Often their first time. It's nothing to be ashamed of. Besides, if you couldn't perform, it would be a good thing. . . .

GREEN. Why so?

CORSINI. You would see how Cecile would react, whether she would be understanding and kind or what. Don't fake impotence for that reason, however!

GREEN (laughs). You can be sure of that. By the way, I have been talking with Cecile about quitting my job. She had an idea that perhaps the two of us might go into business together. I have been working on an idea of electrifying houses to make them more convenient, using a computer that will be programmed to perform a number of domestic functions automatically. This kind of thing has been done before, but she thinks she can actually make a cheap computer for the home by buying parts from various sources. I could then wire houses for the computer or hire people to do the work. I don't mean houses that are already built but houses under construction. Imagine—you buy a house and it includes a built-in computer you can program to do a lot of things, like turn off the phone, set the hot water heater at a certain temperature, that sort of thing. Cecile and I could set up a business together. What do you think?

> *(I have a problem at this point. Suddenly, the nature of our relationship has gone from one involving depth psychology, in which I hope I am an expert, to being a business consultant, at which I am no expert. How should I handle this?)*

CORSINI. Donald, I don't want to get involved in making any recommendation about business. I am no expert. However, you're thinking of having sex with this woman, whom you have known for less than a month, and at the same time having a business relationship with her. Isn't that going too far, too fast? Why not have one first, then the other? Which one first?

GREEN. Are you kidding? You know what will be first. (We both laugh.) You ought to meet her. Would you like to, socially, that is?

CORSINI. Have you told her that you are seeing me?

GREEN. Yes. She used to see a shrink—excuse me, a therapist—herself when she was getting her divorce. I've told her all about you.

CORSINI. Donald, I have no problem with socializing with you while you are in therapy with me. But I think, in view of the relatively short time we have known each other and the short time you have known Cecile, that it would be best for her to come with you to the next session.

GREEN. OK, she'll be happy to come. I figured that might be your response.

(Everything is working out well, but something is bothering me. On the one hand, Donald appears to have rather easily overcome the stupid basic mistakes he had accumulated, and this pleases me. His behavior indicates that the mistakes that had so screwed up his life have been overcome. But is he going too fast? Does he really have a good understanding of himself? I have more or less told him that he is ready for termination, but was I too impetuous? How about this woman in his life? Can this be a complication? Perhaps it is worth going back to examine again his basic mistakes.)

CORSINI. Donald, I'd like to go over your basic mistakes again, do you mind? (He nods indulgently.) First, I saw when we did your Life Style Analysis that you did not think you were lovable or that people wanted you. What do you say about that now?

GREEN. Cecile said she thought I was one of the nicest people she had ever met. I have introduced Cecile to Frank and his wife, and they think she is very nice. Frank had hoped I would like his sister, but I didn't care much for her. You know, the people at the plant like me. Some of them drop in to see me at my office, and I have a good relationship with most of the people I work with. I realize that you were right when you said that I was OK, but didn't think I was.

CORSINI. How about thinking you can only make contact with others on a superficial basis and that relationships will not last?

GREEN. That idea is gone! I've developed a friendship with the other fellows and, of course, Cecile. Our discussions have not been superficial. And I'm enjoying it! How long have these wonderful things been going on? Life is great!

CORSINI. So, on to No. 3. I said that you thought you were not capable.

GREEN. I used to think so. Now I *know* that I'm not capable—but only in certain things. Cecile, who likes to dance, has been trying to teach me how, and she has about given up. I may have to go to a dance school—but so what? I can't be good at everything, can I?

CORSINI. I can't dance either, so we're in good company. How about basic error No. 4, frightening yourself unnecessarily with those fantasies?

GREEN. I don't have them any more. Once in a while I get scared and then I test myself. And I have succeeded in everything I have tried.

CORSINI. And I guess I don't have to ask you about face-to-face confrontations. You really are doing well. Is there anything else on your mind?

GREEN. I didn't tell you—I called Diana.

CORSINI. Diana? Oh, your sister. Tell me about it.

GREEN. Was she surprised to hear from me! Told me she had been thinking a lot about me from time to time. We had more than an hour's conversation. She is a widow now, and I had a hard time finding her— kept calling people who I thought might know her. She is living in California with her two kids, 7 and 9. She wants to see me, and I promised to visit her at Christmas. She kept telling me that she had been crazy when she was young, how she hated our parents and how she hated me—what do you think for?

CORSINI. For being a good boy?

GREEN. According to her, she hated me for always being so perfect. She thought she never could be as good as I was. Isn't that the craziest thing? I told her how I felt about her and she told me she felt like a stranger in the home and that my father and mother and I were a unit, and she was outside. Can you believe all that?

CORSINI. Easily. Well, Donald, I guess our time is up, and I will see you in 2 weeks.

GREEN. How about a month? I have a vacation coming, and so does Cecile, and we'll be taking it together.

CORSINI. Fine, see you in a month, then. I hope you'll enjoy your vacation.

TERMINATION OF THE THERAPY

Donald and Cecile are waiting when I enter my office. Cecile is an attractive, well-groomed, dark-haired woman about 30 years of age. I wave toward the chairs, and they sit down. I look them over with a smile and wait to see who will start.

CECILE. I'm very happy to meet you, Dr. Corsini. Donald has been telling me a great deal about how you work. It's fascinating. He is quite a fan of yours.

CORSINI. Thank you. . . .

(Once again I wait, and again Cecile takes the initiative.)

CECILE. I knew who Donald was for almost a year before he started seeing you. It's really amazing how much he has changed! I never saw anything like it. He is like a new man—like a caterpillar becoming a butterfly.

GREEN (with a big smile). She likes the butterfly more than the caterpillar.

CORSINI. I'm curious. Would you tell me your impression of Donald before he came to see me?

CECILE. Well, you know, we work for the same company. I work in the main office and he's an engineer with a roving assignment. I always thought he was a very serious man—businesslike, no small talk. He was just interested in getting the job done—very competent and reliable. He was also self-sufficient, not at all sociable, but distant. Most people thought he was stuck up and didn't like to associate with ordinary people—a loner. But he always had a good reputation as an engineer; you want something done, he gets it done. For example, last summer, it was real hot and the air-conditioning in our office went out. I called about it on a Friday afternoon. Monday looked like a scorcher, and I dreaded coming in to work because the office would be like an oven. But when I got there the air-conditioning was on, and we found out that Mr. Green—nobody called him Donald—had come in on Saturday to work on it personally, even though it's not his responsibility. That's when I first became interested in him.

GREEN. Hey, you never told me that.

CECILE (to me). You don't know how hard it is to find a reliable man. Donald, do you remember I called you to thank you and suggested that we could have lunch together in the cafeteria, and you said you were too busy to have lunch? I felt rejected. The other girls in the office thought maybe you were gay. No one had ever seen you with a woman.

GREEN (teasing). Or with a man, for that matter. Now at least you know I'm not gay.

CORSINI. How did the two of you ever get together? Cecile, it looks as though you tried to meet him but he showed no interest.

CECILE (to Donald). Should I tell him, or will you?

GREEN. Well, dear, why don't you go first?

CECILE. It's the weirdest story. It had been about 4 months after I called him to ask him to have lunch and he said, "no." So I just gave up on him. Meantime, he had been seeing you. No one knew it, of course. Well, one day I'm at my desk and he runs into the office—and I mean runs in—and everyone looks up and sees him coming up to my desk. In a loud voice, he asks me whether I will have dinner with him that night, and when I say, "yes," he runs out again without another word. Now I *was* confused—all this out of nowhere. Everyone wondered what had happened, whether I had been seeing him. I didn't even know whether he meant it, or what. But when I left that night, there he was at the entrance to the plant. We did have dinner, and we had a good time.

CORSINI. What do you say, Donald?

GREEN. That day, I was working on a drawing for an electrical hookup, and I suddenly didn't want to continue with it. I was just thinking of Cecile, and how stupid I had been not to accept her invitation to lunch. I began to wonder how I could make it up to her and how to approach her, and then I thought of a fable my grandmother used to tell me. One day, the devil decided to go out of business, so he wanted to sell his tools: envy, anger, jealousy, deceit, and—the best of all— discouragement. I realized then that my fantasizing about catastrophes was based on discouragement. Nothing would ever work out—that was what I had been telling myself. Then I remembered how it had worked out when I took your bet and had the courage to ask to sit at a table with the other men. At that moment I said to myself, "To hell with the devil!" and I practically ran to Cecile's office. I knew, I knew, I knew she would say "yes" if I asked her to meet me for dinner. And she did.

CORSINI. Quite a story—a true romance! Tell me, how did your trip together work out?

GREEN. Marvelous—a real honeymoon.

CORSINI. But you had some misgivings about it, didn't you?

GREEN (to Cecile). He's a dirty old man. He's talking about sex. (He addresses me.) Really, it worked out perfectly—no problems. Now what I want to know is, how long has sex been around, and how come I found out about it so late?

CORSINI (to Cecile). I'd like to know something Donald and I talked about. When did you find out that this was his first time—before, or after?

CECILE. Right after the . . . first time. I couldn't believe what I heard! He had been such a great lover that it didn't seem possible that I was the first woman he had ever been intimate with.

CORSINI. And how did it go for you, Donald?

GREEN. It was all very natural. I just went with it and let happen whatever was going to happen.

CORSINI. Would you say you learned anything special from that experience?

GREEN. Later, thinking it over, I decided this would be my very last fantasy. You know something? I really feel I'm up to doing just about anything I am capable and interested in doing. Makes no sense, but that is how I feel. In our 2 weeks together Cecile and I got to know each other quite well. We are good companions, respect each other, like doing things together— and, we're planning to get married.

CORSINI. Congratulations! Sounds great to me. And it looks as though you two can become friends, which is more important in marriage than being lovers. Do you have the same interests?

GREEN. Yes. We both like the same kinds of things, being outdoors and so on. We enjoy talking to one another. We are comfortable together.

CORSINI. Everything sounds almost too good to be true. Donald, remember when we first started, I asked you how you felt about your work, family life, and friends? (Donald nods.) Let me check. Now, on the scale of 1 to 10, how satisfied are you relative to your work?

GREEN. I'd put that at about a 5 or 6. It is now just routine. I have less interest in my work than I did before. I just do it.

CORSINI. And your family life?

GREEN. Top of the scale. I've talked to my sister again, and I feel much closer to her than I ever did. And now I have Cecile. I would rate myself on family at 10.

CORSINI. And how about your social life, how satisfied are you with it?

GREEN. I would rate it about a 7. Cecile has met Jim and Mary, the couple I used to have dinner with alone. They love her, think she is the best thing that ever happened to me. We have been seeing them once a week, but now sometimes they come to my place, and Cecile and I entertain them. We see Frank and his wife, too, and I've met a couple of Cecile's friends and we've done some things with them. Also, Cecile and I go to church on Sundays together. I'm really enjoying relationships with new people, and I feel much more comfortable socially.

CORSINI. Well, job satisfaction has dropped from 7 to 5, family is up from 5 to 10, and friends have gone from 2 to 7. Everything looks good, except the job situation. What are your thoughts about it?

GREEN. Actually, I was thinking of quitting my job, but Cecile suggested that I wait a bit. I talked to my supervisor and told him I wanted to change jobs, do something different. He had nothing to suggest, so I went to see the personnel officer. She told me that I was in a kind of dead-end job, and all she could suggest was to wait until the chief engineer's job is vacant or look for something else. So it looks like I'm stuck where I am.

CECILE. I had an idea, but he didn't think much of it. What would you think if he became a technical salesman for the company?

CORSINI. How do you feel about that, Donald?

GREEN. I just don't know. I've never sold anything.

CORSINI. Your work, which you had rated 7, has gone down to 5; everything else has gone up. Your job no longer challenges you. May I make a suggestion, now that you're looking forward to meeting new people? Isn't that what a salesman does?

GREEN. Yes, you could say that. I guess I got salesmen confused with television pitchmen—I dislike them. Actually, I've been considering selling for the company. As a technical salesman, I would be talking to other engineers, and I know how to do that.

CORSINI. My guess is that you may find that work interesting. Remember that vocational aptitude test which showed you would like selling?

GREEN. Want to know something? Right now, I think of it as a challenge. With both of you on my side, I don't think I can fail.

CORSINI. Suppose you did fail?

GREEN. Wouldn't be the worst thing. The worst thing would be not trying. I'll give it a shot. You guys have sold me. But actually, I'd pretty much decided to take a crack at it. I'll go see the sales manager about it tomorrow.

CORSINI. I can't think of anything more I would want to ask you. Do either of you have anything else on your mind?

CECILE. If we get married, do you think we should try to have children?

CORSINI. Again, this is an area outside of my expertise. Why not wait until you are married, and until Donald is satisfied with his job situation? You're concerned about your biological clock ticking?

CECILE. No, I'm just wondering about it. I'm 34, and I don't know if I can get pregnant. Like most women, I want to have a baby sometime.

CORSINI. How do you feel about being a father, Donald?

GREEN. I'm scared, to tell the truth. Seems like such a big step. I'd wait, but if Cecile wants a baby right away, I'll go along.

CORSINI. If there's nothing else you want to take up, I think we can end our session.

GREEN. Would you want to see me again?

CORSINI. Only if you have a need to see me. I think you've made remarkable progress and don't need any more therapy. But I'm curious about how you experienced the therapy.

GREEN. I've been going over that in my mind. When I first met you I didn't have much feeling about you one way or another. You seemed competent and professional. I liked your common sense attitude, you didn't use fancy terms, and I liked your diagnosis of me in the Life Style Analysis. You talked with me frankly, one to one. I got to trust you. When I tried to argue that you were attempting to make me over, you stuck to your principles and told me to go somewhere else if I didn't like the way you were operating. I thought that took a lot of conviction. The big change occurred after the third session, when you read the list of my basic mistakes to me. What you told me was unbelievable, and yet I knew it was true. Essentially, you told me I was an OK guy, but I was operating on the basis of some unconscious ideas, fallacies about myself, and that I was discouraged. I realized that I was a grown-up child, a man but still acting like I had as a kid. I saw that I had taken sides with my parents against my sister. Oh, by the way, I called my sister Diana again, and we talked some more. Good talk.

So, I asked myself: What am I? Why am I like I am? And I decided that you really knew what you were saying and that I was playing a stupid game with my life. I think the real climax came then, when I decided to accept myself. And when you bet me that I would not make a fool of myself in the cafeteria, this meant to me that you believed in me.

CORSINI. And what about Diana? You said you had had a good talk with her.

GREEN. We had another long conversation. She sees me as a success and herself as a failure. She works as a salesperson in a store, and there's no man in her life right now. I told her about Cecile, and she said she was pleased and is looking forward to seeing us both. Cecile and I are planning on visiting her in California. I really want to see her and get some things straightened out.

Doc, I think this probably *will* be our last session. But can I come back sometime if I think it's necessary?

CORSINI. Of course.

We shake hands all around and suddenly, Donald hugs me. Then Cecile hugs us both and we remain close for a moment. With no further talk, they leave the office.

A FINAL NOTE

About 6 months later, I received a wedding invitation from Donald and Cecile. I was unable to attend because I had an out-of-town conference. I called Donald to explain, and he brought me up to date. He and Cecile had gone to California and had a real family reunion with his sister. Diana was coming to their wedding, and they were paying for her trip. Donald was now a technical salesman, loving the new work. As soon as they were married they would see if Cecile could get pregnant; if so, they would be moving to a larger home.

I closed the books on Donald Green as one of my better, most successful cases. But I reminded myself that any competent therapist, working in other ways, might have achieved exactly the same results I had. The credit went not only to me or to Adler or to my teachers, Dreikurs and Mosak; mostly it went to Donald Green. But without all of us, for all I knew, he would still be living by himself, working on his cars, seeing his two friends, and depending on the three alarm clocks, the neighbor, and the paperboy to wake him up. ■

CRITIQUE OF DONALD GREEN'S TREATMENT BY ADLERIAN PSYCHOTHERAPY

by Harold H. Mosak

Were Corsini an artist (and I would argue that he is), he would be another Honoré Daumier or Max Beerbohm. His talent reveals itself in his ability to highlight with several deft strokes the essential and most prominent features of Adlerian psychotherapy. This therapy description presents us with a picture that is instantly recognizable. Its basic theoretical assumptions, its commonsense outlook, and its ideal goal—*Gemeinschaftsgeftühl*, or social interest, as Alfred Adler defined it—are in immediate evidence. Among the assumptions are the following:

1. People should be seen as total human beings rather than fragmented into parts and part functions. All part functions are in the service of the whole person.
2. All behavior is purposive and is designed to move people toward their goals, rather than being the outcome of some preexisting cause.
3. While the past is of historical importance (one reason why we collect the life-style data), it is less important from a causalistic point of view.
4. People are seen as the creators of judgments and values rather than being seen as merely the outcome of causes or of a struggle with causes. People are proactive rather than merely reactive. In this perspective, people can assume responsibility for their lives. Problems that create distress in the person are almost always circuitous solutions to avoid meeting life tasks. These problems are unconsciously chosen by people in view of assuring their survival—physically, socially, and psychologically.
5. The preferred way of understanding people is through their subjective perceptions and evaluations of themselves and life. Adler indicated that the therapist must "see with the patient's eyes, hear with his ears, and feel with his heart." This is referred to by Carl Rogers as entering the client's internal frame of reference.
6. People can best be understood in a social context. For Adler, all problems were social problems. Adlerian therapists place considerable emphasis on the feeling of social belonging and on interpersonal relations and transactions.
7. Living in this world, people develop a characteristic "line of movement" in their goal-seeking behavior. Even when it seems that the person is pursuing contradictory goals, a closer look will reveal that underlying these apparently contradictory goals there is a common goal.
8. People are basically social "animals" whose highest ideal is *Gemeinschaftsgefühl,* a concept incorporating such traits as caring for others, the courage to be imperfect, and contribution to the common welfare (Dreikurs, 1971). All of these traits are alluded to in Corsini's therapy.

Corsini's contribution presents the flavor of how an Adlerian might conduct therapy with a client like Donald Green. Other Adlerians might proceed somewhat differently, but all would adhere to the basic assumptions noted above. Corsini's treatment also reveals the Rogerian training he received prior to embracing the Adlerian approach. He places considerable responsibility on the client and has an implicit belief in the client's ability to meet that responsibility. At one point in the Life Style Analysis, he remarks, "This is an error. He has the strength to meet and solve problems directly." Since Corsini does not inform us on what basis that assessment is made, he perhaps is referring to what Rogers taught him and me about the "growth forces" residing in the individual. While I do not negate the existence of such forces, my view, and that of other Adlerians, is somewhat at variance with his. A surgeon may rely on a patient's "growth forces," but nevertheless assumes responsibility for intervening in a directive way.

Corsini also portrays Adlerian psychotherapy as a cognitive psychotherapy. In his conversations with Donald he discusses "catastrophizing" and "awfulizing" much as Albert Ellis would. Ellis himself has pointed out many of the resemblances between Adlerian and Rational Emotive Behavior Therapy (Ellis, 1957). Corsini might reasonably be characterized as a theoretical Adlerian and a technical eclectic, although in the latter he is careful never to violate basic Adlerian assumptions.

Finally, independent of the influences of his training, there is a picture of Corsini, a person with long experience, who brings his own personality, his own style, to the therapy session. While I will not comment on Corsini's personality, he can best be described as a creative, innovative, risking therapist who always has the patient's welfare at heart.

Since I have written similar chapters myself, Corsini has my sympathies. I compare this form of writing to attempting to construct a budget. There are so many items we would like to include, but budgetary considerations do not permit it. *If only* there were more pages devoted to exposition of theory. Fortunately, that is taken care of in *Current Psychotherapies* (Corsini & Wedding, 1995) and in *Individual Psychology* (Manaster & Corsini, 1982). After all the figuring, something—many things—must be omitted because of the limits of the "page-budget allocation." Every omission feels like abandoning a loved, precious child.

In struggling to write such a chapter, the writer hears voices in his head lamenting, "I wish . . ." and "Wouldn't it be nice if . . ." and "If only . . . . ." My wish list for Corsini's chapter would include the following items:

1. *If only* he could have elaborated more on Adlerian psychodynamics, the therapeutic process, and the various techniques used. The description of Donald's Life Style helps us to understand "what makes Donald tick," but it does not explain the Life Style procedure. Shulman and Mosak (1988) have done so, if you want to learn more about this topic.
2. There are some brief allusions to such processes as interpretation, relationship, resistance, and "transference" in psychotherapy, but we could learn more about the roles of these processes in the treatment of Donald.
3. *If only* he could have demonstrated how many Adlerians have used multiple psychotherapy with their patients, as do Dreikurs and Shulman and Mosak.
4. Many Adlerians would have placed Donald in group psychotherapy, either as an adjunct to individual therapy or as the therapy of choice. Since Corsini is a pioneer in this area (e.g., Corsini, 1957; 1987), and since Donald requires both socialization and "feedback," I would assume that in actual practice Corsini would have considered doing so. If only we could have observed Donald in this setting!
5. Corsini does illustrate the use of action techniques with Donald. If only he could have illustrated the wide range of techniques available in the psychodramatic spectrum! (Corsini, 1965; Starr, 1977).
6. Corsini presents Donald as a compliant, perhaps overly compliant patient, and the client's final statement in the initial interview lends credence to this definition of him. However, defining Donald as an overly compliant patient hardly permits a demonstration of resistance, except insofar as overcompliance itself is considered to be a manifestation of resistance. Considering that a major Adlerian assumption centers about the uniqueness of the individual (Life Style), the approach an Adlerian therapist utilizes with one patient may not be applicable to others. Corsini's approach to Donald therefore should not be regarded as the way Corsini (or another Adlerian) might approach all patients. *If only* Donald had been another kind of patient, other views and techniques would have been utilized.
7. I am more than a bit surprised that Corsini does not do more with the psychological tests given by others. While Adlerians resort to testing less than some other therapists, they do make use of them. I am puzzled because Corsini has been in the

> forefront of the testing movement and has constructed a number of psychological tests himself. He does rely on one test—Early Recollections—which many have described as a projective technique (Mosak, 1958). Adler describes a person's early recollections as "the story of my life." Sought at the beginning of therapy, as it often is, it provides a quick picture of the patient's psychodynamics, without spending days conducting other psychological testing or spending months dredging up this material "on the couch." The economy of time and effort tends to keep Adlerian psychotherapy briefer than many others.

Corsini performs a service for us in introducing two ethical issues in his chapter. In the larger psychological field more attention is being devoted to such issues. However, the achievement of a unanimous viewpoint is a long way off. Many psychologists confuse legal and ethical issues. Others tend to blur the line of demarcation between what might be therapeutically contraindicated and what is unethical. Some studies of ethical opinion refer to minority opinions of unethical behavior (such as the opinion that it is unethical to shake hands with a patient). Therefore, some might take issue with Corsini's bet with Donald, although in another article Corsini (1979) rationalizes and justifies this technique on therapeutic grounds. And there are psychotherapists who socialize with their patients, while others may view this as a violation of their ethical principle of avoiding such a "dual relationship." Corsini apparently treats this as a psychotherapeutic issue and ethically warranted.

Throughout, Corsini presents us with straightforward commonsense. Adlerian psychology uses no jargon or esoteric concepts; its verbalizations are understandable by anyone of modest intelligence who has comprehension of the language in which the psychotherapy is conducted. We have to envy Corsini and Donald. Everything proceeds so smoothly, and change occurs almost immediately. Donald "catches on" and accepts without much question. Change, whether deliberate or unconscious, occurs with a predictability not regularly experienced by practiced therapists. If therapy ordinarily proceeded this effortlessly and smoothly, fewer therapists (and patients) would lose sleep at night, and complaints of therapist burnout would rarely be heard. But then, we must remember that this was (historically) one of his most successful cases.

Corsini has dropped the use of the medical model. At a theoretical level, Adlerian psychotherapy is a growth model of psychotherapy

(Mosak & Phillips, 1980). Patients are not seen as "sick," and the goal of therapy is not "cure." Patients are seen as discouraged, and therapy is designed to change their outlook and help them grow. Therapy is a matter of education or reeducation rather than a matter of cure. Corsini attempts to educate Donald with respect to his "basic mistakes," a term currently in disfavor with some Adlerians, although we retain the concept. He measures the success of the therapy in terms of whether Donald has succeeded in relinquishing these self-defeating "basic mistakes." So far all to the good, but many therapists also focus on the resources the patient brings to the therapy and to life. Through encouragement, especially the encouragement of risk-taking behavior, they endeavor to help the patient move into a more satisfactory relationship with the life tasks—the tasks of work, relationship to others, relationship to potential sexual partners, relationship to self, and relationship to issues of meaning and of the spirit (Mosak, Dreikurs, 1967; Dreikurs & Mosak, 1966, 1967). Using these criteria, Corsini has reason to feel the satisfaction he describes in his final paragraph.

REFERENCES

Adler, A. (1958). *What life should mean to you.* New York: Capricorn Books. (Originally published 1931.)

Adler, A. (1964a). *Problems of neurosis.* New York: Harper & Row. (Originally published 1929.)

Adler, A. (1964b). *Social interest: A challenge to mankind.* New York: Capricorn Books. (Originally published 1929.)

Corsini, R. J. (1947). Nondirective vocational guidance of prison inmates. *Journal of Clinical Psychology, 3,* 96–100. (Postnote by Carl Rogers.)

Corsini, R. J. (1965). *Role playing in psychotherapy.* New York: Aldine.

Corsini, R. J. (1977). *My memory of Alfred Alder.* In G. J. Manaster, G. Painter, D. Deutsch, & B. J. Overholt (Eds.), *Alfred Adler: As we remember him.* Chicago: NASAP.

Corsini, R. J. (1979). The betting technique in counseling and psychotherapy. *Individual Psychologist, 16,* 5–11.

Corsini, R. J. (1957). *Methods of group psychotherapy.* New York: McGraw-Hill.

Corsini, R. J. (1987). Adlerian groups. In S. Long (Ed.), *Six group therapies.* New York: Plenum.

Corsini, R. J., & Wedding, D. (1995). *Current psychotherapies* (5th ed.). Itasca, IL: F. E. Peacock Publishers.

Dreikurs, R. (1971). *Social equality: The challenge of today.* Chicago: Henry Regnery.

Dreikurs, R., & Mosak, H. H. (1966). The tasks of life I. Adler's three tasks. *Individual Psychologist, 4,* 18–22.

Dreikurs, R., & Mosak, H. H. (1967). The tasks of life II. The fourth life task. *Individual Psychologist, 4,* 51–55.

Ellis, A. (1957). Rational psychotherapy and individual psychology. *Journal of Individual Psychology, 13,* 38–44.

Manaster, G. J., & Corsini, R. J. (1982). *Individual psychology.* Itasca, IL: F. E. Peacock Publishers.

Mosak, H. H. (1958). Early recollections as a projective technique. *Journal of Projective Techniques, 22,* 302–311.

Mosak, H. H. (1995). Adlerian psychotherapy. In R.J. Corsini & D. Wedding (Eds.), *Current psychotherapies* (4th ed.) (pp. 51–94). Itasca, IL: F. E. Peacock Publishers.

Mosak, H. H., & Dreikurs, R. (1967). The life tasks III. The eighth life task. *Individual Psychologist, 5,* 16–22.

Mosak, H. H., & Maniacci, M. P. (1998). *Tactics in counseling and psychotherapy.* Itasca, IL: F. E. Peacock Publishers.

Mosak, H. H., & Phillips, K. S. (1980). *Demons, germs and values.* Alfred Adler Institute Monograph No. 3. Chicago: Alfred Adler Institute.

Rogers, C. R. (1951). *Client-centered therapy.* Boston: Houghton Mifflin.

Shulman, B. H., & Mosak, H. H. (1988). *A manual for life style assessment.* Muncie, IN: Accelerated Development.

Starr, A. (1977). *Psychodrama.* Chicago: Nelson-Hall.

Person-centered therapy, also known as client-centered therapy, and originally as nondirective therapy, is based on a relationship in which the therapist offers empathy. unconditional positive regard, and genuineness. *Empathy* is based on the therapist's interest in understanding the client's world of feelings and meanings, communicating that understanding in a natural and spontaneous manner, and ascertaining that the client feels understood. One aspect of *unconditional positive regard* is the therapist's willingness to allow clients to share their experience in the way they wish, to the depth they choose, and at their own rate. The therapist has unconditional positive regard for the uniqueness of the client's world and for the capacity of clients to resolve their problems, conflicts, and issues in the way that suits them. Thus the therapist respects the client's choice of school, course of study, occupation, marital partner, way of partnering, sexual orientation, and so on, though the choices might differ from the therapist's preferences. *Genuineness* means the therapist is congruent in using words that match thoughts and feelings and does not hide behind a professional façade.

The person-centered hypothesis is that when clients receive these conditions, they respond by thinking more highly of themselves, so they become willing to accept as part of their self-concept aspects that they formerly regarded as inadmissible. They become more self-reliant in their values and standards, and their mode of experiencing becomes more free, open, and spontaneous.

This approach was formulated in 1940 by the American psychologist Carl R. Rogers (1902–1987), a pioneer in psychotherapy practice, teaching, research, and writing. Rogers impacted thousands of people around the world. With gentleness and strength, he extended his therapeutic principles to education and international conflict resolution. (See Kirschenbaum & Henderson, 1989.)

Nathaniel J. Raskin

6

Person-centered Therapy

SOMETHING ABOUT THE THERAPIST • *Fred Zimring*

I entered graduate school at the University of Chicago because of my general interest in personality and emotions. In addition, I was interested in personal change because I had a strong feeling that I was not functioning as well as I wanted to.

At the time, in the 1950s, psychology was strongly oriented to animal behavior. It was thought that everything could be explained in terms of basic drives and instincts. Therefore it was with some skepticism that I first encountered Carl Rogers at the University of Chicago at an open meeting of the client-centered practicum. I had read some of Rogers's works, and his use of language seemed imprecise; the word *perception,* for example, was used in several different senses on a single page. In addition, because of the rigidly "scientific" and behavioristic nature of my first two graduate years, I thought Rogers would be impossibly "soft-headed." Everything changed for me in a few minutes of the open meeting during which a student acted as a client and Rogers acted as a therapist. In those few minutes of dialogue some small but definite changes occurred; some things came to exist for the client that hadn't existed before. This small atom of creation, occurring before my eyes, intrigued me. It seemed magical. *Where had the new material come from?*

Although this incident happened many years ago, I continue to experience this sort of creation, and it still intrigues me. When I am puzzled or bothered, and I talk to someone who knows how to listen, new thoughts, new possibilities mysteriously occur.

This incident led me to become a student in the client-centered practicum and then a member of the Counseling Center of the University of Chicago. The Counseling Center was an active group of client-centered therapists. It made little difference if you were a student or a member of the faculty. If you demonstrated competence at doing psychotherapy, or at research, or in training or administration, you assumed that responsibility and functioned in that position. I remained on the staff of the center for 5 years while I was a student and then continued for the 12 years I was on the faculty of the University of Chicago.

Carl Rogers, Jack Butler, and Tom Gordon, my therapists, supervisors, and teachers, were important to my development as a therapist. Not only did I learn about myself and about psychotherapy from them, I also learned something about the unabashed pursuit of excellence. Aside from the personal changes I underwent as the result of being a client, my interest in psychotherapy as a career was reinforced by the experience of seeing personal barriers crumble and new possibilities magically occur.

After leaving Chicago and coming to Case Western Reserve University in Cleveland, Ohio as director of clinical training, I initiated a year-long practicum in client-centered therapy. I still teach this practicum, and I have been more involved with training people to do client-centered therapy than with seeing clients myself. However, I do try to see at least two clients a week because I feel a loss when not seeing clients.

The way I do therapy has not changed much over the years. It seems to me that Rogers originated a fully formed, cohesive method of doing individual therapy. It is based on a few simple but profound hypotheses about what human beings are like and how change can be facilitated in them by the therapist. Over the years I have tried from time to time to alter what I do with clients in many ways. Whenever I try something different from client-centered therapy, however, I find that the changes I prize most for the client do not occur.

After a career doing individual therapy, I recently have begun to work with groups and have found that interesting. In a client-centered or person-centered group there is no leader, only a facilitator. The group goes where it wants to go and discusses what it wants to discuss. What seems to happen is a change in the nature of the group. At first the group is a collection of people who consider one another from an external point of view, and then it slowly begins to work within a more subjective framework. Finally the group comes to accept the participants' internal frames of reference as being of most importance.

In addition to training therapists, the main thrust of my professional activity has been to understand why changes occur as the result of client-centered or person-centered therapy. The status of Rogers's explanations of why change occurs has seemed to me to be quite different from the status of his descriptions of how therapy should be done. His explanations for why change occurs have seemed to be initial, tentative suggestions, rather than a finished product.

I have gone on from Rogers's rather general self-theory explanations to more refined explanations drawn both from self theory and cognitive theory. I have been involved recently with description of the self phases or states first proposed by George Herbert Mead, the "Me" and the "I," (Mead, 1934) and of how client-centered therapy alters these states. Explanation of what changes occur and why they occur seems to me vital.

In my opinion, many other kinds of therapy are trying to do what client-centered therapy does, but they do not do it quite so successfully. One of the main effects of many different kinds of therapy is to have clients appreciate the reality and importance of their subjective worlds. We are born into and develop in a world where objective/interpersonal realities are thought to be of primary importance and the personal/subjective world is considered less important. We learn about the reality of our subjective worlds in many different kinds of therapy. In client-centered therapy, very little of the therapist's world is intruded on the client, and the focus is on the client's internal framework. The client therefore can appreciate the reality and nature of his or her subjective world more quickly than if it were necessary to struggle with the therapist's frame of reference.

Another reason why client-centered therapy is more successful than other therapies is that resistance generally is less in client-centered therapy. Clients who are not pushed or led are not as likely to resist, and if they know that they can change the topic at any moment, they may feel more free to explore sensitive areas than they would in other kinds of therapy. The client is in complete control in client-centered therapy; there are no questions, no comments, no directions, and no advice from the therapist.

Training for Client-centered Therapy

It is surprisingly hard to learn to do client-centered therapy. Student trainees who meet once a week for 2 hours need 3 or 4 months before they are ready to see a client. Client-centered therapy is, in the main, empathic listening, and it may be so hard to learn to listen empathically because this skill involves the ability to hear the other person without intruding oneself. When we listen, we usually have a personal agenda that determines what we hear. Thus, when we listen to someone with a problem, our agenda includes the purpose of helping. With this purpose in the back of our minds, we frequently listen for the cause of the problem and are thinking of possible solutions. But when we do this, it is not possible to hear *exactly* what the person is saying.

Direct experience is the best way to train people in empathic listening, and role-playing is one way to obtain this experience. I have one person talk about some personal troubles (either the person's own or a friend's) for 5 minutes or so, while the other person, acting as the therapist, tries to understand and indicates what she or he understands about the situation. If this interaction is recorded, the person who acts as the therapist can review what the other person actually said and can check how accurate the understanding has been. It is in this active checking by the listener—the therapist trainee—that the learning occurs. This exercise can sometimes be done without an instructor present. In addition to role-playing, trainees listen to audio tapes, watch films, and read transcripts of therapy sessions. A surprising amount of material for this is available on the market. When I think a student is ready to see clients, I have an interview with the student in which I, acting as a client, talk about my concerns. If the student is facilitating and I, as client, feel I've made some progress, the student goes on to see actual clients.

Regardless of the type of psychotherapy in which a student is interested, practice in empathic listening should be a part of psychotherapy training. A therapist who doesn't know what a client is saying will find it hard to work with the client, even in the behavioral approaches. It is not easy to get this training, however, few academic programs have listening courses as part of their therapy training. Fortunately, teachers of the client-centered and person-centered approach have become more active recently. Summer institutes have been held in La Jolla, California since 1965. In addition to this program, there are a number of meetings and workshops every year through which counseling skills can be learned.

The Setting for Therapy

There is nothing remarkable about the faculty office in which I do therapy. I sit about 6 feet away from the client, and I do not sit behind a desk. The office furnishings do not seem to make much difference; once clients begin to talk, they are in their own worlds. I once had a blackboard put on a wall in my office and I was going to install a drape to cover it because I thought clients might be distracted by whatever was written on it. But the first client arrived before I had a chance to install the drape, and he noticed neither the board nor what was on it. Ten years later, when I moved, I noticed that I still had not installed the drape. In all that time, no client had commented about or seemed to be distracted by the naked blackboard.

Like most therapists, I suppose, I prefer to see people who come to me because they want help, not because they have been sent by others, such as courts or parents. It has been my experience that clients do best after having had several experiences with other forms of therapy. Many years ago we found that the most successful clients at the Counseling Center were in their third therapy experience. It is as if clients have to learn to do therapy. The severity of clients' problems has little relation to success; some of my most successful clients have had quite serious problems. For example, several people who were hospitalized for a number of years are now living independent lives as a result of client-centered therapy with me. But I also have had clients with seemingly little wrong in terms of their personality or background when they came in who did not change at all in therapy. Of course, the severity of the client's problem may have much to do with the length of therapy necessary to get to a satisfactory termination.

Clients have come to me from many sources. The most usual source is a recommendation from a former client, a friend, or relative. Years ago, when I started to do therapy, many clients came for therapy with an initial problem, but they had some awareness that, in addition to solving that problem, they wanted to change in a general way. Now most of my clients come because of a specific problem and leave after that problem is solved. In one case, a woman came because, some months after the death of her husband, she wasn't sleeping well and was having trouble leaving her house. She stopped therapy after two interviews because she had become aware of her anger at her husband for dying and leaving her. She was then able to sleep and could leave her house without trouble.

I am starting to see more elderly clients. Client-centered therapy, with its emphasis on the client choosing the problem and going at his or her own pace, seems ideally suited for working with elderly persons.

THE THERAPY FOR DONALD GREEN

Session 1

A unique characteristic of the Rogerian approach has to do with the importance of the client's internal frame of reference. It is a basic tenet of this approach that the therapist tries to understand what the client is saying from the vantage point of the client's frame of reference and only in that framework. I do not want to understand Donald Green in any way other than his present frame of reference. If I understood him from the report of a previous interview or from psychological testing, I might not understand his world *as he sees it at the moment.* In the present case, I do not want to know anything about Donald Green that he does not tell me directly. Therefore I do not acknowledge that I know anything about the intake interview. Donald begins the dialogue.

GREEN. Well, what do you want to know? Where should I start? What should I talk about?

ZIMRING. Talk about whatever is of concern to you, whatever is on your mind at the moment.

(This direct statement in reply to a question, which is intended to explain how to operate in client-centered therapy, is known as "structuring," or helping the client know how to function in this particular situation.)

GREEN. Should I talk about my childhood?

ZIMRING. I gather you are not sure how to begin. It would be most useful for you to talk about whatever is uppermost in your mind right now.

(A basic tenet of the client-centered or person-centered approach is that no material is the "right" material to talk about.

It is not more useful or therapeutic if some rather than other material is discussed. Because I genuinely believe this to be the case, the client will accept my answer. It is important for me to understand and accept the client's uncertainty if this is being experienced at the moment. At this point I think that Donald is saying, "What are the rules?" If he persists in asking questions, then I know uncertainty is central to him and my response then might be, "You feel uncertain about what to talk about.")

GREEN. The thing that is of most concern to me is getting up in the morning. I am having difficulty getting up. I am a good worker and a responsible person. I have done a lot of things to try to get myself up in the morning. I have set alarm clocks all over the house and had the paper carrier knock on the door, and it doesn't work. I still come in late.

ZIMRING. So no matter what you do, it keeps happening.

GREEN. Yeah, it's still a problem. And I do stay late after work to make up the time. But it still looks bad. I don't know what the other employees think about Donald Green always coming in late. After 17 years with the same company, I don't know why this is happening. I don't know what to do about it.

ZIMRING. Mhm. I gather there are two things here. One is you feel helpless about it all. Puzzled and helpless.

(This is a typical client-centered response. In 1957, Rogers named six "necessary and sufficient conditions" for change to take place in psychotherapy. One important condition is that "the therapist experience an empathic understanding of the client's internal frame of reference." Here, I am checking my understanding of Donald's internal frame of reference, of how he sees the world at this moment. I am not checking my understanding of what he has done to alleviate the problem. Thus I do not respond to what he did to avoid coming in late, and so on.)

GREEN I don't know what to do about it. Why can't I wake up?

(Instead of taking this as a question for me to answer, I understand this remark as being about his present frame of reference, that is, his present experience of puzzlement or helplessness.)

ZIMRING. Something you should be able to do and can't. And you don't understand why not.

GREEN. Right, right, I don't understand it. I've been there 17 years and I like my job. I've worked hard. I don't think it's that I don't want to go to work. So I don't know why I come in late.

ZIMRING. So it doesn't make sense.

(I make no attempt to reassure Donald that a solution is possible but rather stay with his feeling of puzzlement. You might think that a negative feeling like helplessness would get worse if we direct the client's attention to it, without any hope or reassurance. The opposite seems to be the case. If we stay with a negative feeling, the client will usually move from it, as Donald does in his next response.)

GREEN. I don't miss every morning; this morning I managed to make it to work on time. I didn't go back to sleep after the paper carrier woke me up, but maybe the only reason I managed to stay up was that I didn't feel well.

ZIMRING. You got up OK, but the reason wasn't anything you could count on.

(I respond to his reaction to what had happened, that he couldn't count on getting up, rather than to what had happened that morning. Responding to a client's reaction rather than to the circumstances of what happens is an important aspect of client-centered responding.)

GREEN. Yes, maybe it won't happen that same way tomorrow.

ZIMRING. You can't count on it....

(There could be some important material here. How was he feeling this morning? Was there any relationship between getting up in time and starting therapy? I could ask these and similar questions, but they are irrelevant at this point. As a matter of fact, they do not occur to me. All I am interested in is understanding what he means at the moment. If any of these questions did occur to me, they would be occurring from my framework and not from Donald's. If I were exploring my own framework, my attention would not be on him, and so I might not hear what he really means at that moment.

Listening in client-centered therapy is a most active and demanding process. The therapist makes hypotheses about what the client is saying and then checks the accuracy of these hypotheses by responding appropriately. When I am formulating questions from my own frame of reference, I am not formulating hypotheses about the client's frame of reference.)

GREEN. Yeah (pause). It was lucky how I got this job 17 years ago, right after college. My father had worked at the same company, and one of the owners recognized my name when I applied.

ZIMRING. It just sort of fell into your lap.

GREEN. Yes. I wish that man was still with the company, but he retired 10 years ago. The top management of the company changes so fast that half of them wouldn't know who I was if we passed on the street.

ZIMRING. Sort of anonymous.

GREEN. Yes. It didn't used to be that way. It used to be that the president went around the whole plant at least once a month and talked to most of the regular employees. He not only knew who you were, he knew whether or not you were married, and if you had children.

ZIMRING. It sounds as if it were more personal then.

GREEN. Yes. It used to be, when I sent a memo, I knew who was going to read it. Now I don't. We have a new secretary in our section at the plant. She was on the phone, chatting away with what sounded like a friend, and I gave her something to be typed. She snapped, "You're going to have to wait your turn"; she was rude. So I said, "Do it as soon as you can" and left it on her desk. I'll be interested to see how long it takes her to get it done.

ZIMRING. It's not quite clear to me. Are you saying that you want to see whether she is just ignoring you personally, or whether she is generally doing a sloppy job?

(I do not hesitate to tell Donald that I don't understand. My major responsibility to the client is to try to understand what is being said at the moment. When I don't understand, I ask questions. If something gets in the way of my understanding, it becomes my responsibility to remove the obstacle. If, for example, I fail to understand a client because I suddenly remember something I should have done, this internal intention can affect my understanding of my client.

Because of this kind of possible problem, I have learned to survey my internal landscape and concerns for a few minutes before I see a client, so as little as possible intrudes itself in my mind during the session. It almost never happens that I have negative feelings about a client or about our being together, but if it should, I would mention it to the client. One of Rogers's "necessary and sufficient conditions" is that the therapist be congruent in the relationship. This means that what the therapist is feeling about the client and the relationship should match what the therapist is expressing.)

GREEN. Yeah. A lot of people aren't working very hard today. Some people at the plant seem to treat it as if it was their home rather than a place to work, as if they didn't have to earn their pay.

ZIMRING. As if all they had to do was show up.

(This is an adequate but not exemplary response. I indicate that I understand Donald's opinion that a lot of people don't work hard at their jobs, but my response is about other people, not about his reaction. I focus on the client's external world and talk about it in the same way the client does. I communicate that I understand how the client sees the world, but the best kind of response would direct the client's attention to her or his own experience. However, if I had said, "It annoys you that people don't work very hard," I would have been directing Donald's attention to his annoyance. This would be an error, because he is not considering his annoyance at this moment.)

Session 3

In this report of the therapy for Donald Green, I will include only the odd-numbered sessions. This next session that follows is therefore No. 3.

We open this session in a typical way for a client-centered interview—I wait for Donald to begin talking. I usually do not engage in much social talk—the latest news, the weather, or whatever—although if the client begins that way I do not deliberately withhold my responses. My attitude is that this is the client's hour and I am interested in where he is and what he wants to explore, and this determines what happens at the beginning of the interview.

GREEN. Hi (pause).

ZIMRING. Hi.

GREEN. We hired a woman engineer the other day She seems OK so far. But things sure have changed; there were no women in my engineering class. Oh, there were a number of them at the college, but I didn't have much to do with them. Most of my time was spent studying, and on week-ends I worked as a waiter.

ZIMRING. Mhm. (I do not respond verbally and explicitly to everything Donald says. Frequently, understanding is conveyed by posture, facial expression, and so on. Understanding the client is important; explicit communication of that understanding is not so important.)

GREEN. There was this course called Human Factors in Design. I don't know, it was a real problem for me. No matter how hard I worked, I couldn't do well in it. The instructor gave me a hard time. Whatever I did, there was no pleasing him.

(At this point I could have said, "That must have been frustrating," or "you must have felt helpless," and Donald might have responded to either remark, that my observation was correct. Even so, in the client-centered framework, either one would have been wrong. Donald had not mentioned being frustrated or feeling helpless. My response would have focused him on frustration or helplessness, material that was not in his frame of reference at that moment. Many things are true of a client, but only a few are within the client's frame of reference at a given moment.)

GREEN (continuing). I don't know that he picked on me, but I could never say or do anything right in class.

ZIMRING. There was no pleasing him.

GREEN. Yes, no matter how hard I tried. He was one of those people who, once they make up their mind about you, they won't budge. One time, we had to do a project and I submitted it in plenty of time. Then I thought of something extra to do and did it and gave it to him, still within the time limit. He wouldn't accept it because it hadn't been turned in with the original project, even though the extra project was a good one.

ZIMRING. It didn't seem fair.

(Although Donald hasn't said he thought it was unfair, this seems to me to be what he is trying to communicate.)

GREEN. No, it wasn't (pause). You know, I've run into that a lot. Some people make up their minds, and you can't change them.

ZIMRING. Like running into a stone wall.

(Using a metaphor is a good way of responding to the client. Even if the metaphor is wrong, it refers to experience, and the client has to check with his experience to find out whether it is correct.)

GREEN. Yes, I'd have to put a gun to their heads to make them change their initial impressions. (He pauses briefly.) I usually don't make a good first impression, you know. Or rather, I don't make much of an impression. People don't seem to notice me.

ZIMRING. It's not so much that they have a bad opinion of you, it's that you don't seem to exist for them.

GREEN. That's right. The other day I was in line to order some food at a take-out place, and the woman at the counter started taking the order of the man behind me. I didn't know what to do for a second, and then I started to say something. The woman said, "I'm sorry," but she continued taking the other man's order. I just turned around and left.... The last time I was in Chicago I could hardly get a cab to stop for me.

ZIMRING. It's like you're invisible.

(This response focuses on Donald's experience of not being visible, which has a reasonable probability of being in his frame of reference at this moment. It is an adequate response, though it ignores his inconvenience at not being seen and his feeling that he would have to do something extreme to be noticed. A better response would have acknowledged these factors.)

Donald pauses for some time before continuing. Generally, I do not interrupt pauses. This is the client's opportunity to sense what else is of concern at the moment and to think in my presence. Beginning therapists often find that pauses make them anxious. Everyone is socially conditioned to make sure that long pauses don't occur; whenever there is a definite pause in a conversation, someone rushes in with a topic to keep it going. I allow Donald to continue when he is ready.

GREEN. Last week we were told what our salary increase for next year will be. My raise is lower than the rate of inflation was last year, so I'm really taking a pay cut.

ZIMRING. You're really going to be getting less money.

GREEN. Yes, and less than some other people are getting. I don't know whether to write a letter to my supervisor or go see him. I do know that I am not getting what I should. Last year was a good one for the company; I know they did all right and could afford to give us more. And even though I was late sometimes, I more than made up the time I missed, and my work performance has been good. My supervisor always gives me good ratings.

ZIMRING. So there's no good reason why you shouldn't get more money.

(You might infer that Donald is indignant or angry, but I do not mention these feelings because they are not in his frame of reference at this moment. He is not considering his feelings about the situation; he is concerned with his pay and is trying to communicate his opinion that he should be getting a larger raise.)

GREEN. The raise I got last year was a little larger than the average, and I performed better this year than last. I was sure my raise would be above average this year, too. I really don't know why it wasn't; it should have been.

ZIMRING. So you really expected a bigger raise and are puzzled that you didn't get one.

(In talking about "not knowing why," Donald may be beginning to consider his reactions to the situation. I choose to comment on his expectation and puzzlement, rather than on what he says about the situation itself)

GREEN. Yes (pause). It's as if I have to do twice as much as other people to get the same credit. I know I've done more than others who got bigger raises.

(At this point, my mind is actively generating hypotheses about what Donald means. He is saying that he doesn't count to others, perhaps to those in authority. He may mean that he is more invisible than others, a theme that has appeared before. Perhaps he is considering something about unfairness, although it is not clear that this is in his present frame of reference.)

ZIMRING. Somehow what you do doesn't seem to count as much as what others do.

GREEN. That's right. It's as if other people, and what they do, exist and are of the same stuff as the rest of the world. I'm different. I'm flimsier.

ZIMRING. Not as solid or real—you don't take up space in the same way.

GREEN. Yes, I don't know what it is about me. I don't have the same effect, can't make the same sort of impression as other people do.

ZIMRING. Somehow more powerless?

(I put this as a question, in a tentative tone of voice, because I am guessing that this is something he is experiencing at the moment and is trying to convey.)

GREEN. That's right! I don't know how to exist in the people world, the way others do. Other people seem to interact with each other with no trouble. I can't figure it out.

ZIMRING. It's both puzzling and darn hard.

(This interchange is a good example of how the client moves from considering the situation he is in to considering the self. One of the most puzzling aspects of client-centered therapy is why just understanding the client's frame of reference brings about change. Here my empathic understanding encourages Donald to give more consideration to his self.)

GREEN. Yes, and I don't know what to do about it.

ZIMRING. It's a real mystery.

GREEN. Yes, it is (pause). You know, I like to keep my place quiet....

(This is a sudden change of tone. What can it mean?)

ZIMRING. You like to have it peaceful?

GREEN. Well, when it's quiet it's more restful. In the evening I like to doze. But also when it's quiet, I know that nobody's outside the house.

ZIMRING. It feels safer when it's quiet.

(Though Donald does not choose to respond to my description of the quiet as "safer," he still may sometimes feel this way. Evidently, however, this is not central in his frame of reference at the moment. A correct response from the therapist not only describes the client's reactions but also is concerned with what the client is attending to and actively exploring at that moment. When the client does not respond to what I have said, I do not repeat it or explain what I mean. It is hard to drop or forget a hypothesis about what the other person means, but this is a skill the client-centered therapist has to acquire.)

GREEN. The funniest thing happened to me the other night. Just as I was falling asleep there was a noise outside, sort of a metallic crashing sound. Even though the door was locked and nothing could have happened to me, my whole body broke out in a sweat. Within half a minute I was wet from head to toe. It took me hours to get to sleep, and I felt sick most of the next day. Isn't that ridiculous? Nothing happened, and I still reacted like that.

ZIMRING. It was a pretty violent reaction you had, and it made no sense.

GREEN. Yes, I felt a lot like I did when I thought that a woman that I'd sold a car to had to get the car repaired and was sending someone to get even with me.

ZIMRING. Both times it felt the same, as if something terrible was going to get you.

GREEN. Yes, it was awful.

Session 5

GREEN. One of the foremen at the plant has to go to the hospital for minor surgery, and I'll have to supervise his unit until we know how long he's going to be off the job. I'll have to oversee manufacturing operations and make sure that the work is scheduled right. I hate this kind of work—I'm not a supervisor. I really dread it.

ZIMRING. Really hate the thought of it.

GREEN. Yes—I keep thinking about the people I'll have to supervise, going over the possibilities in my mind. The other night I woke up and couldn't get back to sleep thinking about it.

ZIMRING. On a real treadmill.

(There is some difference of opinion about this, but I find it useful to make metaphorical responses that have an experiential referent. Being on a treadmill involves the experience of doing something repeatedly without making any progress.)

GREEN. Yes (slight pause). I think I'm afraid of two things. On one hand, I'm afraid that when I tell them to do something I'll be ignored. I'll say something and they'll look at me and just keep on doing what they were doing.

ZIMRING. As if you were invisible.

GREEN. Yes, as if I didn't exist. On the other hand, I'm afraid they will criticize whatever I say or do. Whatever I do will make somebody angry.

ZIMRING. There'll be no pleasing them.

(Although Donald is experiencing apprehension about supervising, it would be wrong for me to mention this, since he is not focusing on his apprehension at the moment. Instead, he is focusing on others and how he thinks they will react.)

GREEN. Yes. I know I'm going to have trouble with some of those people. They can be so petty. Just selfish.

ZIMRING. Not caring about anything but themselves.

After a long pause, Donald volunteers a memory.

GREEN. I was thinking of my sister the other day, and how she was always mean to me. I remember once, oh, I must have been 10 years old, when Diana had a girlfriend at our house. They were trying on clothes in her room and she left her door open. Diana saw me looking and she really screamed and walloped me. It wasn't fair. I was in my own room, and if she wanted privacy all she had to do was close her door.

ZIMRING. It wasn't right to take it out on you that way.

GREEN. No—she was always doing that. I remember once when I was only 8 years old she asked me to tell the folks that she was home taking care of me when actually she was out with her friends. But I did tell them the truth when they asked me; I was too scared to lie to them. And when Diana found out I had told them, she was mad at me for weeks.

ZIMRING. She was very hard on you.

GREEN. Yes, and what made it worse was that Dad would always side with her (short pause). Well, I'm not sure he was always on her side; it was more that he was always critical of me. I remember once in high school when I was president of the Chess Club and I gave a talk on Parents' Day. My father was there. The faculty sponsor said I gave a good talk and was quite complimentary, but my father just told me about all the things I could have done better.

ZIMRING. He didn't give you much credit.

GREEN. I wasn't around him much; he was usually off by himself. But when he was there, I would always seem to mess up. I remember I was pretty good at Hi-Li, where you try to hit a rubber ball attached to a paddle by a piece of elastic. My father saw me doing it and said I should practice, that if I became good at one thing, maybe I would get good at other things.

ZIMRING (interrupting, while Donald is still talking). Sort of implied that you weren't much good at anything?

GREEN. Yes. The peculiar thing was that after that my score—the number of times I could hit the hall without missing—was always lower when he was in the house, even if he was in another room….

ZIMRING (interrupting). He didn't even have to say anything; just his presence made you worse.

(This interruption is not the best possible response. The fault is not that it is an interruption but that I am not responding to the main thing Donald is trying to tell me. When someone is telling you something, there is a present interest or intention in the communication. That is, the person is doing more than telling you a story or telling you about something. There is a purpose, a reason—often hidden—why they are telling this story at this moment. The best client-centered response combines a mention of this present interest of the person with an understanding of the content. What Donald is intending to communicate is the peculiar effect of his father's criticism.)

GREEN. Yes…. The other day I remembered a time when we were living in a summer cottage and I was supposed to get a new bathing suit. My father was angry with me about something. After he left the room and the door was shut, I waved my hand in sort of a dismissive way at him. Unfortunately, there was a frosted glass panel in the door. When he came home that night, he told me that I was not going to get a new suit because of my gesture. I was very disappointed and scared. How he saw it through the frosted glass, I don't know.

ZIMRING. It was scary and almost seemed magical.

(As in many responses, I mention both the feelings and the reaction Donald is talking about: "scared," and his present reaction to the incident, his puzzlement about how his father knew he made the gesture. He chooses to follow up on the latter.)

GREEN. Yes, he always seemed to know things about me.

ZIMRING. Always had you in view.

GREEN. Yes (pause). I met a man the other day whose father was working at the company while my father was working there. He said my father was at a company Christmas party he went to when he was a boy, and my father lifted him up so he could get something from the Christmas tree. You know, I can't remember my father ever holding me in any way.

ZIMRING. He didn't show you that kind of attention.

GREEN. I suddenly remembered something the other day that I haven't thought of for a long time. I was a small boy and I was taking a bath with my father. All of a sudden my father yelled for my mother to take me. He was disgusted and angry and I don't know why.

ZIMRING. Really a puzzle.

GREEN. Yes. I'll never forget how angry he was.

ZIMRING. It's really stayed with you.

GREEN. It wasn't fair. What could I have done that was so bad?

ZIMRING. Nothing could have been that bad.

GREEN (with emphasis). No, *nothing!*

Session 7

GREEN. I had an awful time last week. I told you I was going to have to supervise a unit at work, and it turned out the foreman was gone for 4 days. I found it very hard to do. I didn't want to talk to the workers on the line, but I had to.

ZIMRING. So you were really caught.

GREEN. Sometimes I actually felt like running. It was really difficult for me.

ZIMRING. Really awful.

GREEN. Yes, I knew that they were being critical, although nobody said anything to me.

ZIMRING. You knew it to be true.

(Psychotherapists from other orientations would argue that a major problem for Donald is his expectation of disapproval and criticism, and they might see my response as reinforcing this expectation. However, all that is important for me to do is to check my understanding of what he is saying. If Donald does have

incorrect or unreal expectations, as he gets to trust his own internal frame of reference he will rely less on an external frame of reference that contains expectations and perceptions of others.

One of the main goals of client-centered therapy can be seen here. Rogers proposes a continuum of types of knowledge, with subjective knowledge, knowledge of one's internal frame of reference, at one end. You have most subjective knowledge when you know your own frame of reference. At the other end of the continuum is objective knowledge, which involves no internal frame of reference. Pure objective knowledge exists when you know something that has no internal frame of reference, such as knowing how a gasoline engine works. Objective knowing also exists when you know something externally, even though it may have an internal frame of reference. Thus, if you think of yourself as being of a certain age, having a particular occupation, being married, and so on, you are thinking of yourself objectively or externally. Client-centered therapy should move the client closer to the subjective end of the continuum, where the self is seen less in external terms and more in terms of personal experiences and meanings.)

GREEN. Yes (pause). I had a dream last night....

ZIMRING. Oh?

GREEN. Yes. I dreamed I was talking to a professor about a paper that was due. It was hard talking to him, because he was looking down at his desk and making notes. I went away and worked on the paper, and when I finished I went back to the building where his office was. It was a big office building and the halls were dark. As I came to his office I thought I heard something down the hall. I put my assignment under his door and left in a hurry. I felt drained, like a balloon with the air escaping.

ZIMRING. You got it done and handed it in, but you were exhausted after your fright.

GREEN. Yes, I was surprised I could move.

ZIMRING. Also, was there something about hearing something down the hall?

GREEN. Yes, my heart started pounding fast.

ZIMRING. Very scary?

GREEN. Yes, but more than that. More like there was a monster down there.

ZIMRING. Terrifying and huge.

GREEN. Oh, yes. (Donald shudders slightly, closes his eyes, and moves his shoulders and arms as if he is shivering with cold.)

ZIMRING. Really awful.

GREEN. Yes.

(It does not occur to me, nor should it, that it would be "good" for him to understand what was so terrifying. It is enough for me to understand his experience. In Rogerian therapy, dreams are responded to as any other experience, without looking for symbolic material or probing for the dream's meaning. Donald's dream of going to the professor's office is treated in the same way that a report of actually going there would be. I concentrate on his experience of the dream, not on the experience implicit in the symbols of the dream.

Donald's shuddering behavior raises the question of whether, or how, the therapist should respond to the client's nonverbal behavior. The intention of the client is central. If a client should say, "I feel sad," and sit there and cry, the crying would be part of the communication of sadness. It would be telling how sad the person feels and so should be responded to. However, if the client sits and cries without saying anything, and if it is not clear what the crying means to the client, the therapist would accept the crying as an open communication and wait for the client to give some indication of its meaning before responding.)

There is a long pause before Donald continues.

GREEN. I remember that I told you I like things quiet around the house, but last night it was *too* quiet.

ZIMRING. *Too* much of a good thing?

GREEN. Yes. When I got home I picked up a magazine to read and couldn't stop, not even to go out for supper. I just couldn't get myself to move. I didn't talk to anybody all day yesterday, either, so I went for almost 48 hours without talking to another person.

ZIMRING. It was too quiet, eh? And you got stuck.

GREEN. Yeah. After a while I got to feel peculiar, like I was getting more and more invisible. This morning I found it hard to talk to the waitress. I was surprised when she responded.

ZIMRING. You sort of expected that she would not know you were there?

GREEN. Yes, this happens to me a lot. I wish I had more people in my life. But I don't know how to talk to people. It doesn't seem hard for others, but by the time I think of something to say, the interaction is over and the person I was going to talk to is already talking to somebody else.

ZIMRING. It's a real mystery how it's done.

(A slightly better response at this point would have been,

"You'd like to interact more but don't know how to do it.")

GREEN. Right. All my life I've been by myself. I've always felt all I had to do was get my job done, but now it's not enough.

ZIMRING. Just leaves a lot lacking.

(I understand the content of Donald's statement but not how he feels about it. While I decide to respond without guessing at his feelings, it would have been better if I had said, "At this point in your life you want more interaction with other people.")

GREEN. Yeah (pause). I can't seem to do anything right when it comes to other people.

ZIMRING. Always wrong somehow.

GREEN. I remember when my sister tried to teach me to dance. I wasn't very good at it and she made fun of me.

ZIMRING. She was hard on you.

GREEN. Yes. For months afterwards when she saw me coming she would cross her feet and pretend to stumble and fall down.

ZIMRING. Really cruel....

Donald agrees. Then he pauses and, speaking slowly, continues.

GREEN. I don't know what I am going to do. I'm always by myself.

ZIMRING. Always alone.

GREEN. Yes. . . and I don't know what to do about it.

ZIMRING. Feel powerless.

GREEN. Yes. I really can't do anything with people. Sometimes I don't feel like it is worth it.

ZIMRING. Sometimes it doesn't seem worth the effort?

GREEN. Right. You know, sometimes I wonder about going on.

ZIMRING. Things are just that awful sometimes.

(Clients who get to this degree of desperation test our faith in a basic client-centered premise: that, given a facilitating atmosphere, people will have the strength and resources to take care of their own lives. The therapist sometimes has an impulse to try to actively help such clients. However, a therapist who begins to worry about whether the client is suicidal or who considers reassuring the client is no longer working in the client's frame of reference. At the very moment when the client most needs to be understood, the therapist is not doing this. Over the years, it has been my experience that if we stay with clients and remain in their frame of reference while they are experiencing the bad part of life, they will come out of it on their own.)

GREEN. Yes, they are awful (pause). The other night I saw a movie that reminded me of my high school graduation. My father was angry with me; he thought I should have graduated with honors. My grades were OK but not that high, so he decided not to come to the graduation exercises. My mother said she felt bad about it but didn't want to antagonize my father, so she didn't come either. At the time it didn't bother me too much, but now I really think it was wrong.

ZIMRING. Really off base.

GREEN. Yes. They should have cared more. There was no reason for them not to attend. And everyone else was surrounded by their family. It was an awful thing to do to me.

ZIMRING. They really didn't do what they should have.

GREEN. No, they didn't. (Donald has talked about his parents several times over the past few interviews. My responses, however, are only to what he has just said, not to what has come before.)

Session 9

GREEN. I had a sad experience last week. My shop teacher in high school, Mr. Buck, died. He was the nicest man; he got me started rebuilding cars. I used to come back to school at night and over the weekend to work on cars. A lot of the time he would be there and we would talk together.

ZIMRING. It was a nice time.

(This response is superficial. A better response would have been, "He really helped you and you think of him fondly.")

GREEN. He was the first man who ever talked to me about himself and his life. He urged me to take advantage of my opportunities. He felt that he hadn't been very successful, ending up as a high school teacher. I remember how that startled me. Being a high school teacher seemed very successful to me.

ZIMRING. It surprised you.

GREEN. Both surprised me and was interesting. For the first time I began to see that adults are people like me and have feelings about success and failure like I do. I thought about those conversations for years.

ZIMRING. Very meaningful for you.

GREEN. Yes.... You know, I think it was the first time any adult treated me as an equal, as a person like himself.

ZIMRING. Do you mean that it was the first time anyone acknowledged that you were a person, too, or do you mean that it was the first time it occurred to you that you were a person like other people?

(My question is concerned with what Donald is saying, but it was prompted by a theoretical assumption that is important

to me: that client-centered therapy is successful because it facilitates the growth of an independent self. Thus it was no surprise to me that Donald chose this topic to discuss. I have to be careful that my theoretical assumptions do not guide much of my response to the client, because then I run a real danger of being outside the client's frame of reference.)

GREEN. I guess it was more the latter. I had always thought of children and adults as being very different, and I don't know if I had ever thought of myself as a person.

ZIMRING. It was a new thought.

GREEN. Yes (pause). Well, last week when I read in the paper that Mr. Buck had died and there was to be a memorial service at the high school, I decided to go. I was surprised at the number of people there I knew. I started talking to Ruth, a woman who had been in my class—in our senior year I had helped her with math. We had coffee after the service. I didn't find it too hard to talk to her. She's a widow, and both of us are interested in antiques. I asked her if she wanted to go to the antique show when it comes to town and she said she would like to. I'm sort of looking forward to that, but I hope I don't make a fool of myself.

ZIMRING. It could be a nice thing, but it does make you apprehensive.

(This response is correct in stating his ambivalence. It would have been more accurate, however, if I had mentioned the possibility of humiliation with which Donald is concerned when he says he is worried about making a fool of himself. The fact that he is apprehensive, while probably true, is not in his frame of reference, and I should not have commented on it.)

GREEN. Well, I'm not very good in social situations. Most people know what to say, but I'm just quiet most of the time. Maybe if there's something like antiques to talk about, I won't have so much trouble.

ZIMRING. Might make it easier.

GREEN. Yes, when there's a topic that I really know to talk about, like antiques, I don't feel so much that what I say will be foolish or inappropriate.

ZIMRING. It wouldn't be so dumb.

GREEN. Yes, but sometimes I feel like it's very hard.

ZIMRING. Talking to someone, you mean?

GREEN. Yes—I don't know what the other person is thinking.

ZIMRING. About what you're saying?

GREEN. Yes. Unless you're talking about a fact, how do you know the rule about what's right or wrong to say?

(Most of the time I can understand quickly what the client

says from my own experience. Here, I have to think. I can imagine myself in a social situation saying something inappropriate, something the listener might think was a foolish remark. For Donald, however, there is a mixture of abstract rules for the rightness and wrongness of conversations, which I do not quite understand, and a fear of what the listener might think, which is easy for me to understand. I choose to respond about the rules.)

ZIMRING. What are the rules?

GREEN. Yes. It's like a fantasy I had the other day, as I was going to sleep, of being a native who left his island for the first time and was wandering around in a strange, foreign city. It was like it was the first time I had ever seen a big city.

ZIMRING. Confusing and bewildering?

GREEN. It was like I didn't know how to talk to the people in the city. I started to ask directions of one man, and he just laughed at me and walked on. Another man just imitated my body movements and walked on without answering either. It was a bad time.

ZIMRING. I gather there were two things there. One was not to be able to communicate, the other was that they were making fun of you.

GREEN. Yes. As if, no matter how hard I tried, they thought I was an idiot.

(At this point the connection between Donald's wanting to know the rules for what should be said in a conversation and his fear of being criticized becomes clear to me. If you know and use the rules everybody else uses, they can't criticize you.)

ZIMRING. You didn't know the rules and couldn't find out what they were.

GREEN. Yes, exactly (pause). In talking to some people at Mr. Buck's funeral, I learned that an old schoolmate of mine from high school had died. I've been thinking about him. Neither he nor I was part of the crowd. We didn't play football or date much. We used to have chess games, and all one summer we worked on a Model T Ford. We finally finished it and took it out for a test drive, and after a half mile, while we were going through the park, it stopped. We couldn't figure out what was wrong until it finally occurred to us that we had forgotten to put gas in the tank. It was so funny! I laughed as hard as I can ever remember.

ZIMRING. It was a great time.

GREEN. Yes, but I lost touch with him after graduation. It was like after he left town to go to college he didn't exist.

ZIMRING. Sort of out of sight, out of mind?

(I choose to respond here because Donald may be begin-

ning a new theme about keeping contact with people. It would have been better, however, if I had waited until he indicated what his reaction was to losing contact with his friend.)

GREEN. I remember, in high school, playing chess with that friend on a Saturday night and thinking that everybody else was out on a date. It made me feel stupid. Like I was different.

ZIMRING. Not the same as everybody else.

GREEN. Yes . . . . I wonder what his life was like. Did he finally make some friends?

ZIMRING. Did he finally reach that goal?

GREEN. Yes, he was a nice guy, and I hope he did.

ZIMRING. He deserved it.

(When we discuss psychotherapy we tend to emphasize feelings and reactions and meanings. Values are equally important. Donald is talking about a value, an important goal; achieving friendship.)

GREEN. Yes (pause). I wonder if I am ever going to have any real friends.

ZIMRING. Is it ever going to work out?

GREEN. One good thing that happened last week is that I finally subscribed to cable television. It has a lot more variety, but I've got to be careful that I don't spend too much time watching TV. Too much time can be wasted that way.

ZIMRING. A real waste.

GREEN. There was a good program on gardening that my neighbor told me was going to be on, so I invited him over to watch it with me. That was pretty good.

ZIMRING. It was a nice occasion and you were pleased with it.

GREEN. Yes.

Looking back over this interview, several things strike me. Some of my responses were superficial, but this may not be as important as you might think. Frequently, the intent to understand the client is as important as, or more important than, the content of the therapist's responses. As I think about it, during this hour I was not aware of anything bothering me. If I had been, I might have said something to Donald like: "I'm not hearing you well today; would you mind telling me what you just said?" I would not hesitate to say something like this because my task is to understand, and I will do what is necessary to achieve this.

Several themes, such as Donald's increasing contact with others, emerge in this interview. I would not respond in terms of these themes unless they were the focus of his attention.

Session 11

GREEN. I spent more time with other people last week than I have in a long time. I've been working on a Model A Ford, and a couple of weeks ago I sent in my application to exhibit it next month at a show. Two other guys who are also working on the Model A called me, and I got together with them. It was interesting to talk with them. One has parts I need, and the other has some equipment I can use in the final assembly of the motor. I'm further along than either of them, so I can save them some time on what they still have to do.

ZIMRING. Sounds like it was a good thing all the way around.

GREEN. Yes it was (pause). Last Sunday I felt sort of down; I really couldn't move. Then it occurred to me that it was my mother's birthday. I miss her sometimes.

ZIMRING. It was really affecting you.

(This is not a good response; it focuses his attention on last Sunday. It would have been better to consider his more present feeling, missing his mother.)

GREEN. Uh huh. When I was young, my mother always knew where I was. It felt good working around the house when she was there.

ZIMRING. Comfortable, somehow.

GREEN. Yes, very much so. I remember sitting next to her and reading while she was sewing. You know, books always seemed more interesting when she was there.

ZIMRING. You just enjoyed things more when she was around.

(I do not probe for how things were better but simply stay with the fact that things were different when he was with his mother.)

GREEN. Yes I did, unless my father was there, too. I saw a film about rabbits on television the other night. When there is some threat, like another animal, the rabbit freezes. That's what used to happen to my mother and me. We'd be sitting there, each doing our own thing, maybe she'd be reading and I'd be working on a model. Then my father would walk in and we both would freeze. We would just sit there and stare at something until he left.

ZIMRING. Both of you would stop cold when he was there.

GREEN. Yes, I always had to watch myself when he was around. And you know, although I don't like it, I still get that same feeling sometimes. Like when someone I don't know is around.

ZIMRING. You don't like it, but it still happens.

(This response just repeats what Donald says. It might seem that the client would consider such repetition to be obvious and superficial. But this doesn't occur. If the therapist is understanding the client, the client is in his world and not much aware of the therapist.)

When Donald starts to talk again, he turns to another topic.

GREEN. I usually go to Jim's and Mary's on Thursday night to eat, but this week they were out of town. So I went last night instead (slight pause).

ZIMRING. Uh huh.

GREEN. After dinner, Mary usually goes to the family room and watches television while Jim and I talk. Last night it was different. She didn't leave, and we got into a long discussion, the only real talk we've ever had between the three of us. Jim started by saying that the only things people could really enjoy were those they had earned themselves. Mary said she thought that enjoyment is a personal quality that has to do with your ability to enjoy things, and it doesn't matter whether you have earned them or deserve them. Instead, she said, the question is whether you could relax and enjoy things in general. I took her side and said that if Jim was right, the wealthier the person, the happier that person should be, and that just didn't seem to be true. She and I sort of ganged up on Jim, and we had a boisterous argument. When I left to go home, Mary gave me a big hug and kiss. It was sort of an active evening.

ZIMRING. Sounds like a good time was had by all.

GREEN. Yes, but her display of affection sort of bothered me.

ZIMRING. It disturbed you in some way?

GREEN. Well, I thought it was a little much. After all, she is the wife of a friend. What if Jim had objected?

ZIMRING. You thought she stepped over the line, to some degree.

GREEN. Yes (pause). Last night wasn't a good night insofar as sleeping is concerned. I went to bed early and fell asleep fast. But then I woke up startled at every little noise. Finally, later in the night, I had an awful dream. It was one I've had before (slight pause). There was something looming in the dark. As long as I would stand and face in its direction, it would not move any closer. I knew that, even in the dream, and would try to keep facing it. But I could feel myself slowly turning away. I would shriek at myself, in my head, in the dream, not to turn, but I could feel it happening anyway. And all the time I knew that the menace was moving toward me as I turned away.

ZIMRING. So that somehow you ended up bringing the monster closer, and it was terrible not to be able to stop doing the thing that brought it closer.

GREEN. Yes, I couldn't help myself. It was the strangest thing. It was like I was standing on a turntable that just turned me, regardless of how hard I tried not to turn.

ZIMRING. Weird and uncontrollable.

(By "weird," of course, I refer to "the strangest thing." This is Donald's present experience of the dream, and so it takes precedence over his experience in the dream of not being able to control his motion. The present experience of something, even if it is a mild experience like being puzzled, is more important than the past experience being described, even if that experience was intense.)

GREEN. Yes, it was. I seldom have dreams that are that vivid, and I almost never have one where the feeling is that clear. But there was one dream I used to have when I was a kid that was vivid. I remember there was a goat in it, and the goat was in the backyard eating clothes hung out to dry on a line.

ZIMRING. Uh huh.

GREEN. Funny. I kept having that dream, but there wasn't much feeling in it.

ZIMRING. Just kept having it.

(I do not think about, or probe for, the meaning of the dream. Instead, it is up to Donald to use it as he will.)

GREEN. Yes (long pause). You know, I was thinking the other day about how I feel when people don't do what they should. For instance, I submitted a medical insurance claim 6 months ago. I called them 2 months ago when I didn't get the check and the woman said it had gone to the review committee. It still hasn't been paid.

(Considering his experience of the dream seems to have led Donald to consider his experience in another realm—anger.)

Session 13

GREEN. Something interesting happened the other day. I got a call from my engineering fraternity to take on a student in our program for tutoring inner-city kids in math and science.

ZIMRING. Mhm.

GREEN. So Saturday morning I went to the library and started working with a kid named Eric. He sort of surprised me and scared me a bit. He's taller and stronger than I am, even though he's only in high school. It's astounding what he didn't know, what he hasn't been taught. At first it was very hard. I would talk to him, and he wouldn't answer. He sat there with a sort of smile on his face, and I just wanted to call it off and go home. I thought I wasn't going to make a dent. But then I started to give him some math problems, using sports scores, and I found out that the problem was he didn't know much math. We had to start with third-grade math. After a while he began to enjoy what we were doing, and he really started participating. It made me feel good when he began to catch on.

ZIMRING. So it developed into a positive experience. It gave you a lot of satisfaction.

GREEN. Yes. I don't know what happened, but on the way home I stopped off for dinner at the usual place and talked to the waitress more than I ever have before. It was like somebody had oiled my talker. (He laughs.)

ZIMRING. All of a sudden it became surprisingly easy.

GREEN. Yes. Like the other day, when I oiled the hinges on my back door. Not only did it open more easily, it also stopped making all the noise it had been. Until then, I hadn't realized how hard it was to open and how much noise it was making.

ZIMRING. And I gather that talking to the waitress was like that, you sort of didn't realize how hard it had been to talk to her until somehow it became easy for awhile.

GREEN. Yes (pause). I don't know whether I told you, but we have a new production assistant. Jean's shy and finds it very hard to talk; she's still not confident. We were all having lunch in the cafeteria the other day and Mike, who is a bit of a blowhard, began to give her a hard time. He asked her about some novel he had just read and it was obvious that she didn't know anything about it. He just asked her more and more questions. I tried to change the topic to something we could all talk about, and then I asked him about something technical. That stopped the conversation. I don't like people like that. There he was, building himself up by tearing her down.

ZIMRING. Really left a bad taste in your mouth when he beat on her.

GREEN. I haven't talked much about the job recently. For a while there it was getting on my nerves. Recently, one of the foremen has been hanging around my office, talking to me, wanting my advice. The other day, I offered him a suggestion about a job in his department. We discussed it, and I think he is going to use my suggestion. Pretty good, him asking me.

ZIMRING. First you were annoyed with him, but now you are pleased that he liked your idea.

GREEN. Remember that neighbor I had in to watch television a couple of weeks ago? His property is in back of mine, and last week he was burning leaves and rubbish in a big bonfire. This is strictly illegal; there are not supposed to be any open fires in our neighborhood. I was afraid the fire would spread to my property and I reached for the phone to call the police, but I couldn't do it. It was peculiar. The police would not have told him who reported the fire, but I still couldn't complete the call. It was as if my hand wouldn't obey.

ZIMRING. I gather that what was peculiar was having your body sort of take over.

GREEN. Yes, and I don't know what to do about my neighbor; I guess I'll have to talk to him.

ZIMRING. You're going to have to do something about it.

(Donald agrees, and then there is a long pause before he continues.)

GREEN. The other day it was my turn to present a major part of the annual report to the staff before it's mailed out to the stockholders. I've been avoiding doing this for the last few years, but I had no excuse for not doing it this time.

ZIMRING. Had to do it.

GREEN. Yes. My part of the presentation was about 20 minutes long. I felt awful before I gave it; I bet I worried about it every night for a week in thinking about it in the back of my mind.

ZIMRING. It's always there.

(Donald nods in agreement before going on.)

GREEN. Well, I don't think I slept more than 2 hours Monday night. My presentation was the last one. When I got up to begin talking, I was afraid I wouldn't be able to speak, but finally I got started. One man kept looking at my left shoulder; I thought maybe my coat was ripped, but I didn't know what was the matter (slight pause). When I looked later, there was nothing wrong with my coat.

ZIMRING. Hard to figure.

GREEN Yes. I was surprised that I got through it. I actually delivered my part of the report without blocking and without making any bad mistakes. I was afraid that I was going to make a mistake and give them wrong figures without even realizing that they were wrong.

ZIMRING. Wouldn't even know that you had goofed.

GREEN. Well, I got through the report alright, much to my surprise. Didn't make any bad mistakes.

(Donald says something new, that he was surprised, and he also repeats something I did not mention in my last response: He did not make any serious mistakes. This tendency of the client to repeat when the therapist misses something, providing a second chance for a response, is very helpful.)

ZIMRING. So you were surprised that you got through it without anything terrible happening.

GREEN. Yes (pause). But the strangest, most surprising part was something else. The presentation was late in the morning, just before lunch, and mine was the last presentation. From the conversations I heard as the group was breaking up, people were talking about the new menu in the cafeteria and what they would have for lunch, not about the annual report.

(At this point I do not have the slightest idea of why it is surprising to him that people are talking about lunch. I remain quiet until he gives me more information.)

GREEN (continuing). When I remembered how they looked when I was presenting the report, I realized that most of them weren't listening to what I was saying. They were off in their own worlds.

ZIMRING. Not really hearing you at all.

(I am puzzled. He seems to be pleased, but he is talking about people not paying attention to him.)

GREEN. Right; most of them were in their own worlds and were not thinking of me at all.

(Donald smiles slightly, and I respond.)

ZIMRING. Not operating in respect to you.

("Operating" is perhaps a strange word to use here, but it is a neutral word. I do not want to use a word with any implication of what Donald finds pleasing about the absence of the attention of the others.)

GREEN. That's right. During my presentation, I don't think anybody was thinking of me or evaluating me. Astounding.

ZIMRING. Astounding that you could give a talk without their evaluating you.

GREEN. Yes, it's unbelievable.

(The realization that people live in their own worlds and are not critically evaluating him may have been a significant insight for Donald. If so, it will have an effect even though I do not highlight or emphasize it as an insight.)

Session 15

Donald sits rather slumped in his chair. He is quiet for a moment, and then he begins.

GREEN. This has been both a good week and a bad week (pause).

(At this point I do not say anything. To ask him, "Why, in what way?," might direct him to the content of the past week. However, his intention at the moment may be to stay with the badness; "One of the worst weeks I've had." Or his statement may be an expression of a present feeling, so his next statement could be, "I'm really down.")

GREEN (continuing). Early in the week I took Ruth to the antique show, and it didn't turn out so good.

ZIMRING. Not so great, eh?

GREEN. No. In the first place, I got to her apartment a half-hour early. I thought she said to pick her up at 7:00, but she said that our date wasn't until 7:30. Then, when we got to the show, it was not the kind of antiques in which she is interested. And I found it hard to talk to her. I was somewhat depressed afterwards.

ZIMRING. Felt down.

GREEN. Yeah. I felt like she must have thought that I made a poor choice of what to do when we went out. She tried to reassure me, but I thought at the time that she was just being polite. Now I'm not so sure.

ZIMRING. You felt down because you thought she would think that you had made a mistake in planning the evening, but now you're not so sure that she thought that.

GREEN. No, maybe she didn't, and that's good. I like her. But she's going away for a long vacation next week, and nothing's going on with anyone else.

ZIMRING. Sort of bleak.

GREEN. Sometimes I feel, "What's the use?" It doesn't seem like I'm able to lead a normal life.

(I am aware of the pressure to reassure Donald. There is both the social convention that reassurance should be given when the person talking to you feels bad, and my own desire to help Donald

avoid pain. I could subtly reassure him by saying, "After things didn't work out, you felt down"' indirectly telling him that his negative perception of himself and negative feelings were the result of the immediate circumstances. To be helpful in the usual way by offering reassurance would be responding from outside his internal frame of reference, which should be avoided in person-centered therapy. My response therefore does not try to reassure Donald.)

ZIMRING. Sort of seems impossible that your life will ever be normal.

GREEN. Uh huh. I don't know why I freeze so much when I'm with a woman. With men too, sometimes, but more so with women (short pause). When I got back from seeing Ruth, I couldn't stand to be by myself and went to the restaurant just to be with somebody. My neighbor was there. I talked to him for a few minutes. It was better than nothing, but....

ZIMRING. But not like what you had hoped for from Ruth?

GREEN. Yes. It wasn't a bad experience. I just wish it had gone better. I really would like some social life.

ZIMRING. Something you *very much want* (with emphasis).

GREEN. Yes! I feel like somebody who is trying to talk and finally comes out with a single word, while everybody else is rapidly conversing in complete sentences. If something doesn't happen soon, I don't know what I'm going to do (pause). The other day, I was going through some things of my father's and came across the certificate they gave him when he retired. You know, he worked at the same firm I'm with now. And (slowly), it has always seemed more like his firm than mine.

ZIMRING. That you are working more in his business than in one you can identify with yourself.

(This may be a significant insight for Donald. The perception of the business that employs him as being his father's firm may have been the source of some of Donald's negative feelings about work and partly responsible for his inability to get himself to work in the morning. Granted all that—and this is where client-centered therapy is very different from other psychotherapies—I would not lead him to explore the ramifications of the insight, that is, to consider that it may have been connected to his difficulty in getting to work on time.

Does Donald lose important learnings because I do not stimulate his exploration of the insight? Probably not. The insight, if indeed it is one, is really the description of an aspect of his world that has already become different. It was his increased attending to his feelings and reactions, stimulated by the earlier therapy sessions, that brought about this observation that we are terming an insight. He will use this observation in further understanding his world, if it helps him make sense of his world.)

GREEN. One good thing happened this week. I am on the committee to organize the annual company picnic. The plan was to have the picnic from 2:00 to 7:00 in the afternoon. We tried something like that years ago in my engineering fraternity, and it didn't work. Some people come early and then leave after an hour or so. Others come late. You don't have enough people to play games or baseball at any one time. I found myself explaining why the proposed times wouldn't work, and the others agreed and shortened them.

ZIMRING. So what you said was effective.

GREEN. It felt good to get the times for the picnic right, but the best part was that I was able to say what I thought without freezing. It just happened naturally because I was concerned about the issue.

ZIMRING. Focusing on the issue rather than the people involved?

GREEN. Yes. I didn't even think about what they might be thinking about me.

ZIMRING. Somehow this didn't exist for you at that moment.

Session 17

GREEN. Went on another vacation last week. That's the third long weekend I've taken in the last 2 months. Went to a state park in Kentucky and went through some caves with a group that explores caves. I know one of the guys in the group from the factory here. It was a pretty good weekend. On a weekend like that you are with people most of the time, but that didn't bother me. As a matter of fact, I rather liked it.

ZIMRING. It was a nice thing. It was rather good being around people.

GREEN. Yeah, I sort of hated to come back (slight pause). I don't know why I seem to get along better with people when I'm away from home. I drove down there with Joe, the guy who works with me. At the state park we stayed in cabins and Joe and I shared one with two other men. I did go for some walks by myself, but I was with everybody else most of the time, especially in the caves—when you climb around a cave you're never by yourself. There were times when I didn't have much to say and I wished I could be alone. But I didn't freeze once the whole weekend.

ZIMRING. It puzzles you why things go so much better with people when you are away than they do when you are at home.

(As mentioned earlier, in addition to the circumstances or substance a person is trying to communicate, there is also the person's present intention in the communication. The best client-centered response combines a mention of this present interest with an understanding of the content. Part of Donald's present interest is why he is more comfortable with others when away from home. My response focuses on that question without much concern for the content, that is, the circumstances of the weekend.)

GREEN. Yes. I actually initiated conversations a couple of times, and I never do that when I am here (slight pause). When I'm away, I feel less threatened by people, more able to think and talk.

ZIMRING. It's easier.

GREEN (nods). Somehow people don't seem as critical, as disapproving.

ZIMRING. Not as judgmental.

GREEN. People seem kinder when I'm away (pause). You know, talking to you *is* having some effect. (He chuckles.) I'm not sure it's a good one, though.

ZIMRING. Not an unmixed blessing, huh?

GREEN. Right. Like, I ordered an elementary algebra textbook for Eric, the pupil I'm tutoring. The bookstore promised they would have it for me 3 weeks ago. It wasn't there. Then they said they would have it 2 weeks ago. Again, it wasn't there. That was a real inconvenience; Eric and I had to do something else. Then the bookstore assured me it absolutely would be in last week. When I called and they told me they still didn't have it, I demanded an explanation and found out that they had lost the order and had never sent it in. I really got upset then; I talked to them about keeping their promises, being businesslike, the inconvenience they had caused. Finally I got the name of the president of the bookstore chain. There was a lot of adrenaline pumping, and it felt good.

ZIMRING. So you think our talks here had something to do with learning to stand up for your rights, and it feels good to do that.

GREEN. Yes, and. . . .

ZIMRING (interrupting). But I gather that maybe it wasn't entirely a good thing.

(This probably was not a good response. I am responding to what Donald said at the beginning of this part of the interview, to which I had already responded. Now, in the main, he is expressing his pleasure at what he has done. In client-centered therapy there is a tendency, which should be avoided, to concentrate

on what is troubling the client rather than on what the client is happy about. The effect of always concentrating on troubles may be that the client believes that bad feelings are more important than joys.)

GREEN. Well, I'd hate to be doing that all the time. It got in the way of going to bed at the usual time, but I must say I slept better. And it did feel good when the president's office called from Chicago to apologize and said they are sending a copy of the book express mail. We'll see if it gets here.

ZIMRING. You wouldn't want to make a habit of it, but it really seemed to have some effect on the world.

GREEN. Yes. (He chuckles.) My visibility seems to be increasing.

ZIMRING. No longer quite the invisible man, eh?

GREEN. Right. You know, I realized just yesterday that I haven't worked on rebuilding cars for a week. Instead I've been working on a squirrel feeder. The squirrel can only get the food if it figures how to work the latch. I figure that will make the squirrel population on my property smarter.

ZIMRING (smiles). Sort of survival of the smartest.

GREEN. Yes . . . . I've noticed something interesting. You know all the trouble I've had waking up in the morning? Well, the other Saturday morning, when I was supposed to tutor Eric, I woke up before the alarm went off. That's the second or third time that's happened. It seems that when my mind is working on something, I can wake up easily.

ZIMRING. It happens automatically when you're working on something interesting.

GREEN (long pause). It's not only that, it's not only that I am interested. It may also be that it is easier to get up when I don't anticipate criticism. And there doesn't seem to be any of that from Eric.

TERMINATION OF THE THERAPY

At the time of this interview, Donald Green and I have not seen each other for a month. I have been on vacation for 2 weeks, and Donald has been visiting a branch factory on the East Coast, where there may be an opening for him.

GREEN. Well, it came through . . . the chief engineer at the Stamford plant retired, and I was offered the job.

ZIMRING. Sounds as if that is a good thing.

GREEN. Yes, I thought I would not want to leave here, but they were very nice to me at Stamford. I stayed with the man who would be my boss, and I felt good. Usually that would have been a bad situation, but I found I could talk to him and his wife. I think I'll be able to work with him without much trouble.

ZIMRING. So it feels possible to you.

(I know this response is a little less positive than his feeling. It would have been better to match his feeling more closely, but I do not emphasize the positive because I want to give him the chance to talk about any negative aspects of the situation.)

GREEN. Yes. I told them that I would do it, that I would take the job. I've been waking up at night wondering if I am doing the right thing, but most of the time I feel good about it.

ZIMRING. So, even though there are doubts sometimes, mainly it seems like the right thing to do.

GREEN. Yes. Although I've been nervous about it at times, I haven't been nearly as nervous as I would have been a few months ago.

ZIMRING. A real change.

GREEN. Uh-huh. Not only will my salary be increased, I'll be doing more of what I want. I'll have a chance to design some new production techniques, something I've wanted to do for some time (pause). It will be hard to leave here, though.

ZIMRING. Although it will be hard to leave, it is something that you want to do.

GREEN. Yes. I have been hesitating to tell my friends, Jim and Mary, that I am going to leave. Every time I think to mention it, something else comes up.

ZIMRING. Somehow, you never get around to telling them.

GREEN. Yes. I almost never think about it until after I've left their house.

ZIMRING. It sort of slips your mind.

GREEN. Right (pause). I have a feeling that they will think I shouldn't go—that I should stay here.

ZIMRING. They'll think you're not doing the right thing.

Donald nods, then pauses. Finally he says:

GREEN. I wish there was some way I could tell them that it isn't them, that I'm not leaving because of them.

ZIMRING. Some way of telling them that.

(This fear of criticism and rejection has been a constant theme. Less of it has been heard recently, but it still surfaces at times.)

GREEN. Yes, I've been avoiding having lunch with the people at the plant, too. I sort of don't want to tell them about it, either.

ZIMRING. Would sort of rather not.

GREEN. Although there's some of them I won't miss; I'm glad to be through with them. Still, there's some that have been good to me.

ZIMRING. Some that have been helpful?

(This is said tentatively because I am not sure that "being helpful" is what he means by "been good.")

The next section of the interview is concerned with Donald's arrangements for moving. Not until the end of it does Donald discuss the fact that this is our last interview. In client-centered therapy, the final interview is not handled much differently from any other. Of most importance is what it means to the client that this is the final interview. Therefore I wait for him to comment on the fact that this is our last time together.

GREEN. I guess this is our last interview, since I'll be leaving next week. Do you think I'm finished with therapy?

ZIMRING. How do you feel about that?

(I ask this because it is not clear to me what he means by this question. He could mean anything from "What do you think about my progress?" to "Will I be able to go, to navigate on my own?")

GREEN (laughs). Well, I guess I'm as finished as I ever will be. I feel as if I've gotten some good things done here.

ZIMRING. You sound like it has been a good experience for you, and it has been for me also.

(My response is in accord with Rogers's "necessary and sufficient conditions" for successful psychotherapeutic change to take place, which calls for the therapist to be congruent in the relationship, expressing his or her feelings about the client and the relationship. I had had a good experience, and it was congruent to mention it.)

GREEN. I'll be coming back to town sometime. Would it be all right if I call and come to see you?

ZIMRING. Yes, please feel free to do so.

Frequently, clients will come back after terminating for one or two additional interviews. This decision is left in their hands. I have no problem with allowing them to choose their own pace at terminating.

Because Donald was moving, this was an involuntary termination. In a voluntary termination, the client may raise more questions about whether he or she is finished. I genuinely never have any opinion about a client's terminating, so it is easy to stay in the client's frame of reference. The whole question about being finished depends on the client's goals and how far she or he wants to go toward achieving them. Only the client can know this. Also, it is a mistake to assume that this will be the client's only chance at psychotherapy. Clients often leave therapy and then some time later, perhaps years, after it has become clear to them what more they want to achieve, they will get more therapy.

I frequently feel a sense of loss when a client leaves. I have been with clients in some touching and dramatic moments of living. It is sometimes quite painful when they terminate. I have to deal with this pain as my problem and make sure it doesn't influence, even subtly, the client's decision to finish therapy. With the exception of clients leaving town, it is surprisingly easy to keep a client in therapy. All the therapist has to do is choose client material that has to do with problems rather than with strengths and weaknesses. The therapist also can lean forward when the client talks about problems and lean backward and be less attentive when the client talks about feeling stronger. If the goal is to keep a client in therapy, it is helpful if the therapist believes that it takes a long time for therapy to be successfully completed. In the late 1940s the average client-centered case lasted about 10 interviews. Ten years later, the average was perhaps twice as long. This change probably came from a change in therapists' beliefs rather than as the result of a deliberate strategy.

I did not do several things at the end of the therapy for Donald Green. I did not review the progress we had made. I was not concerned with what he still had to accomplish. I was not concerned with any strategy for making sure that the gains of the therapy would be lasting. The benefits from therapy will last because of the changes that occur during therapy. There have been a number of changes in Donald Green. By the end of therapy, Donald is putting more reliance on his subjective world than on the external, objective world of logic. He is paying more attention to his feelings and to his experience. There has been an increase in the degree to which he trusts himself to make decisions that will be right for him. These changes will not be affected by what I do in the final interview.

Over the years, I have found that there are a number of subjective criteria, that is, criteria drawn from my experience, which seem to be correlated with a client's objective progress. One is how the therapy sessions felt to me. Were the hours barren and dull, without much happening, or did they flow easily? With Donald, the first hours of therapy seemed somewhat slow and difficult, but then the flow started, and both Donald and I were surprised at how quickly the end of each session arrived. Seeing Donald never felt like work to me, and I was glad that he hardly ever canceled a session.

Another subjective criterion is the ease of difficulty I have in staying in the client's internal frame of reference. Occasionally it is difficult to stay with a client without my mind wandering more than I would like. This was not the case during the interviews with Donald Green. I found myself working easily to try to understand him. Clients who are not understood will frequently repeat what they have said before changing the topic. That this seldom happened indicates to me that Donald was understood much of the time.

All in all, I was pleased with the way the therapy went. It was an enriching experience and a significant relationship for both Donald and myself. I will miss him and wish him well. Despite the closeness and intimacy we experienced, I will probably never see or hear from him again. This is sad, but it is necessary in this facet of life.

We ended therapy the way we began. It was Donald's internal frame of reference that was of primary importance, not my support and encouragement, or my external evaluation of his progress, or my estimation of the problems that still existed. ■

CRITIQUE OF DONALD GREEN'S TREATMENT BY PERSON-CENTERED THERAPY

by Nathaniel J. Raskin

Although changes in overt behavior are the primary expectations relative to the results of therapy, they are not the only ones. Changes in individuals' phenomenology—that is to say, changes in how they experience life—may be of equal or greater importance. Thus, from the point of view of an observer, a person who has had successful therapy may not have changed at all in behavior. Nevertheless, the person may experience greater internal peace, feelings of satisfaction, new attitudes toward the self, and other covert changes in thinking and feeling (Rogers, 1980). In the case of Donald Green, the person-centered therapy provided by Fred Zimring produced obvious behavioral changes, but perhaps of even greater significance is how Donald now experiences life.

Before psychotherapy, life may be dull and repetitive. After successful therapy, life may be experienced more fully and richly, with more color and variety. This certainly seems true of Donald in his sessions with Zimring, who used Carl Rogers's person-centered therapy as he understands it (Rogers, 1951).

As a therapist I am pleased when there is positive behavior change but am even happier when there is a positive change in how the person experiences the world. Many events in a person's life, in addition to psychotherapy, can change behavior: a new job, meeting new people, a new relationship, and so on (Mead, 1934). Few things other than psychotherapy, however, can change how a person experiences life. And if a person is able to experience life more fully, it is highly likely that that person will be better able to cope with whatever occurs in the future.

Donald Green's behavioral changes after therapy are marked. When he begins to see Zimring he is isolated and has little to do with people. By the end of therapy, although he is hardly gregarious, he has much more people contact, and social interactions and assertiveness are easier for him. He finds it possible to initiate contact with people and is beginning to have a social relationship with a woman. Donald's major stated problem is his inability to awaken and get to work on time. Although he does not spend much time in therapy working on this problem, it disappears over the course of the therapy. On the job, he becomes more assertive, and he starts to interact more creatively with people whom he previously regarded as authority figures. As therapy goes on, he begins to engage in a greater variety of leisure and social activities.

The changes in how Donald experiences life include changes in his relation to feelings and meanings. These are a group of dimensions of experience that frequently change as a result of client-centered therapy. One dimension of a person's relation to feelings has to do with awareness of feelings. Some people start therapy with little awareness of their emotional states. Progress for them is simply becoming more aware of their feelings. At the beginning of therapy, Donald is aware of very little feeling in his life. As therapy progresses, he reports having more feelings outside therapy as well as in it. He reports some dreams and the feelings that went along with them (Rogers, 1961).

Another dimension has to do with the degree to which clients acknowledge feelings as belonging to them. It may seem strange, but people may display what look like feelings (say, give the impression of being angry) and yet not acknowledge or be aware of having these feelings. When Donald begins therapy he acknowledges past feelings to a small extent but has few feelings in the present, and he does not own these emotions. As therapy progresses, he is able to express and to accept the anger he felt when he did not receive a book when it was promised.

A third dimension of this relationship has to do with presence of feelings. Some people, at the beginning of therapy, discuss only feelings and problems of the past. A person may talk only about mistakes made in choosing a school, or relationships with parents, or anxieties in childhood. The person will not bring up how she or he feels right now (Rogers & Dymond, 1954).

Some clients, and this was particularly true of Donald, strenuously avoid contact with others whom they see as dangerous. This view usually changes with successful therapy, as it did with Donald. This was apparent in his lunches with others at work, his relationship with the student, Eric, his interactions with other men rebuilding automobiles, and his date with Ruth.

A question often asked about client-centered therapy goes somewhat as follows: How can you help a client if you do not know the cause of the problem and do not help the client solve problems? An assumption of principal importance for Carl Rogers was: *The organism has one basic tendency and striving—to actualize, maintain, and enhance the experiencing organism.* Rogers saw this as true for all life forms (1961).

Donald had learned early in life that it is good not to cause a disturbance, not to express feelings. He may also have learned that a good person keeps things going smoothly by not having strong reactions. He mentions, early in therapy, his reactions to being judged negatively for being late getting to work. Because Zimring unconditionally accepts this reaction, Donald may have begun learning that he was not unworthy because he had this strong reaction. Over the course of therapy, as he continues to talk about his reactions, more and more of these "conditions of worth" that had been imposed by his parents disappear. He then is able to acknowledge his reactions.

Another explanation for the effects of client-centered therapy rests on Zimring's empathy. A stream of reactions continually occurs within us. We get into trouble when we do not attend to this stream and if we do not act in terms of our subjective reactions. Client-centered therapy is empathic with this stream of experiencing as it enters the awareness of the client. By responding appropriately, the therapist directs attention to it. In continually commenting on and discussing the nuances of Donald's experiences and reactions, Zimring has the effect of directing the client's attention to his own reactions (Rogers, 1957).

At the beginning of therapy, Donald almost never refers to or uses his reactions as a source of data about the world. Instead he focuses on logic and circumstance. Zimring does not focus on or respond to the realities or content of the statements made by Donald, as some therapists might. Instead he focuses on Donald's experience and reactions, sticking closely to the client's subjective world—his internal frame of reference.

Some of my responses to Donald might have been different from Zimring's. For example, in response to Donald's expression of uncertainty as to what to bring up at the beginning of the second interview, I might have replied: "You are not sure how to begin" rather than Zimring's structuring response, "Talk about whatever is of concern to you, whatever is on your mind at the moment." My purpose is not to direct the client but rather to attempt to convey my awareness and appreciation of the client's attitude at the moment. But the important thing is that Zimring relates to Donald with the attitude that the client has the capacity to change, that he can direct the change, and that the nature and quality of the change are up to him.

From the outset of the therapy, Zimring is quite clear about what he has to offer Donald. He accepts it as true that if Donald receives the "necessary and sufficient" conditions implicit in client-centered therapy, he will expand his whole process of growth. To accomplish this, Zimring does not see his role as intervening, motivating, clarifying, teaching, or as making the process occur in any way at all. His function is to free his client by removing blocks to the client's experiencing processes.

In this facilitating role the client-centered therapist is implicitly demonstrating a great regard for the client. The therapist's expression of belief that the client can take charge of his or her own life helps the client to enhance self-regard and gain courage to expand awareness and to embark on new directions.

Could Zimring have predicted the specific content of Donald's new perceptions and experiences or the specific nature of his behavioral changes? I believe that he would have regarded such predictions as quite irrelevant or even as interfering with his primary task of focusing on Donald's cognitions and affections while moving from moment to moment of experiencing in therapy.

This unusual nondirective manner of relating to Donald also frees Zimring to deal with what is most meaningful to the client as he goes along in the therapy. For example, Donald might concentrate on the presenting problem of getting to work on time, or he might focus on job satisfaction or dissatisfaction, his early life, his current relationships, or whatever. Zimring is ready to go along with Donald, whichever way the client decides to go, and so he is respectful of Donald.

Zimring demonstrates a constant regard for Donald's particular pattern of change and growth. I found the therapy to be quite believable, different in some details from how other clients change, but similar in the quality of feeling or tone that accompanies self-directed growth. In following the way changes occur in person-centered therapy, you may find them unremarkable because they emerge so easily and naturally. But if you step back, you may have the perception of an aesthetic and spectacular process—the appearance of an emerging, flowering person.

Interacting with a person in the manner of a person-centered therapist is conceptually simple. In practice it is not so easy because the belief in the client's capacity and respect for individuals, feelings that are necessary, are profound and not easy to come by. As Zimring states, it is surprisingly hard to train students in this approach.

Zimring's extensive comments accompanying his responses to Donald also bring out the thoughtfulness that went into his work, as it does in the work of all successful client-centered therapists. He clarifies the fact that becoming a good listener requires shedding attitudes and behaviors associated with other ways of trying to help people with problems.

Of course, client-centered therapists differ in their operations. Each of us brings to the therapeutic process special qualities as well as theoretical conceptions that are personally meaningful. In Fred Zimring's career as a therapist, researcher, and educator, the notion of subjective experience is a dominant one. He emphasizes this in his work with Donald Green and his explanations of what happens within the client. In so doing, he helps to show why experience is such a central concept in the person-centered theory of personality reorganization.

REFERENCES

Kirschenbaum, H., & Henderson, V. L. (Eds.). (1989). *The Carl Rogers reader.* Boston: Houghton Mifflin.

Mead, G. H. (1934). *Mind, self and society: From the standpoint of a social behaviorist.* Chicago: University of Chicago Press.

Rogers, C. R. (1951). *Client-centered therapy: Its current practice, implications and theory.* Boston: Houghton Mifflin.

Rogers, C. R. (1957). The necessary and sufficient conditions of personality change. *Journal of Consulting Psychology, 21,* 95–103.

Rogers, C. R. (1961). *On becoming a person.* Boston: Houghton Mifflin.

Rogers, C. R. (1980). *A way of being.* Boston: Houghton Mifflin.

Rogers, C. R., & Dymond, R. (Eds.). (1954). *Psychotherapy and personality change.* Chicago: University of Chicago Press.

EDITORS' ADDENDUM

Following are several references that the editors think would be useful supplementary readings in the Person-centered school of psychotherapy.

Barrett-Lennard, G. T. (1998). *Carl Rogers' helping system: Journey and substance.* London: Sage.

Bozarth, J. (1998). *Person-centered therapy: A revolutionary paradigm.* Ross-on-Wye: PCCS Books.

Brodley, B. T. (1993). Some observations of Carl Rogers' behavior in therapy interviews. *Person-Centered Journal, 1*(1), 37–47.

Raskin, N. J. (1996). Person-centered psychotherapy: Twenty historical steps. chapter 1. In W. Dryden (Ed.), *Developments in psychotherapy: Historical perspectives* (pp. 1–28). London: Sage.

Cognitive Behavior Therapy is based on the principles and procedures of experimental psychology, particularly social learning theory. According to this theory, normal behavior—and most abnormal behavior—is maintained and modified by environmental events. The influence of these external events on individuals is largely determined by cognitive processes, which in turn are affected by the social and environmental consequences of behavior. Cognitive-Behavior Therapy theory emphasizes the constant reciprocity between personal actions and environmental consequences in the analysis and development of methods for self-directed behavior change.

In Cognitive-Behavior Therapy, treatment involves a detailed, continuing assessment of each client's problems, focusing primarily on current determinants of behavior. The assumption is that people are best described by what they think, feel, and do in specific situations. Once therapists form an understanding of the determinants of a client's problems, they typically select several different techniques to be included in a multimodal treatment program designed to modify all aspects of the problem. Treatment methods are precisely specified and based on results of controlled research, wherever possible.

Aside from technical expertise, behavior therapists should possess the clinical and interpersonal skills essential to any effective treatment method. These therapists function as problem-solvers who provide emotional support and engage clients in mutually agreed upon efforts to change their behavior.

G. Terence Wilson

7

Cognitive Behavior Therapy

SOMETHING ABOUT THE THERAPIST • *Barbara McCrady*

I always knew I'd be a professional. In fourth grade, my career was to be law; by high school it was medicine; in college, it was neuroanatomy research. I completed an undergraduate degree in biological science, and in my last year of college and for a year after that, I worked in a neuroanatomy research lab. The work was difficult, stimulating, and was the kind of basic research that would clearly contribute knowledge that would benefit people. But as a child who came of age in the 1960s, the sense that my work would affect the world someday, in the distant future, was not satisfying enough. That was how I came to psychology.

As an undergraduate at Purdue University, I took only two psychology courses—introductory and abnormal. The professor who taught abnormal psychology, Robert Toal, was a community-oriented psychologist who devoted many lectures to concepts of community activism and change. His lectures fired my imagination, and when I became dissatisfied with basic research, I came back to them. I also was devoted to a television series called "Bronson's Way," which featured a man who rode his motorcycle from town to town, involving himself in people's problems in each place he visited. One week he worked with an emotionally disturbed child, and in the way of all television shows, he touched this child profoundly in the course of the hour. My restiveness with biology, the inspiration of Professor Toal, the success of a fictitious television character, and my high school memories of teaching swimming to children with mental retardation culminated in my rather impetuous decision to enter clinical psychology. Although I knew absolutely nothing about this field when I entered it, this was a decision I have never regretted.

When I applied to graduate programs, I planned to become a community psychologist, organizing and helping to empower community groups for change. My husband and I wanted to go to California (another dream of children of the 1960s), so I applied to and was accepted at the University of California at Los Angeles. However, he was able to obtain a draft-deferral job in Rhode Island, which was a consideration during the Vietnam War, and we decided to move to the East Coast.

The University of Rhode Island (URI) had just begun a doctoral program in clinical psychology, after having had a master's-level program for many years. After we moved East, I went to talk to the department chair at URI. Being naive probably was helpful, because I thought I could just begin graduate school that fall. Instead, the department chair, Stan Berger, told me that they had admitted their first-year class, but he encouraged me to take undergraduate psychology courses and then apply for the following fall. After the first semester, a graduate student in the experimental psychology program had to leave, resulting in an open assistantship. Some of the faculty who knew me through coursework suggested that I be admitted to fill the assistantship. With that, I became a graduate student in clinical psychology, still not really knowing what I had begun!

The orientation of the URI clinical psychology program in 1970 was primarily humanistic/interpersonal. The core themes of the program, human potential and sensitivity, resonated with my own values. Personal growth experiences were integral to the program, and students were given feedback about their interpersonal styles. I experienced much of this as dislocating, as it was so different from my previous academic experiences in biology, chemistry, and physics. While I was attracted to the humanistic approach, the courses in behavior therapy and operant methods appealed to me as a scientist. However, since the department emphasized the importance of experiential methods, I felt that the more cognitive and analytic approach of the behavioral courses was less "genuine," and therefore less valuable.

I saw a number of clients through the psychological clinic at URI, working particularly with couples with marital or sexual problems. I liked couples therapy and learned behavioral and systemic couples techniques through supervision with Jim and Jan Prochaska. Jan also became my first role model for a woman professional who was married and had a child. Jim was fairly behavioral in his orientation, and I learned behavioral approaches from him, but I did not view these as central to my thinking as a therapist.

My two practicum placements during graduate school did much to broaden my thinking about clinical psychology. My first placement, at a child and family services agency, exposed me to people with limited personal and economic resources. I did individual and couples therapy and taught sex education to inner-city Black teenagers. My second placement was at a private psychiatric hospital, where I did traditional psychological testing and outpatient therapy and functioned as a treatment team leader for a limited number of inpatients. I learned about severe psychopathology and the complexities of working within a treatment team milieu. I also began to work with two people who were important to me for years to come—Tom Paolino, a psychiatrist, and Dick Longabaugh, a psychologist.

Even though I saw a good number of clients in therapy, read about and discussed therapy frequently, and had close supervision, my ideas about therapy remained fairly unformed during graduate school. I had some sense that the relationship between the client and therapist is critical to the therapy process, that respect for the intrinsic potential of a human being is essential, and that being open and genuine would create a climate that would allow the client to change and grow. My formulation of therapy was unsatisfying, however, because it lacked the kind of scientific rigor that I had grown to respect as a biologist and a biological researcher.

When I applied for internships, I wanted community experience. I accepted a clinical internship at Worcester State Hospital, where community experiences and individual, couples, and family therapy training were combined with responsibility for an open psychiatric unit at the state hospital. The associate director of the internship, Larry Peterson, was a talented and devoted behavior therapist who had the absolute conviction that behavior therapy is the most successful and reasoned approach to treatment. His conviction infuriated me; we debated regularly, and I resisted his certainty. At the same time, he was a superb supervisor, and the clients I saw under his supervision did well, a bit to my surprise. I also found that when I would ask for references to approaches or techniques Larry recommended, he was able to refer me to research publications as well as clinically descriptive material. As my clients did well and I began to read more widely in behavior therapy, I began to rethink my opinions of behavior therapy. Our most notable success was with a lesbian in her 40s, who had had years of unsuccessful therapy for problems with depression and anger. Larry encouraged me to focus on relaxation and assertiveness skills with her, and she responded wonderfully. She worked out several difficult issues with her lover and her job and became much less depressed. She terminated therapy successfully, leaving me with the sense that what we had done in therapy had made sense, to her and to me.

I did not become a "convert," however, until I began to work with a young woman client under the supervision of Susan Vogel. Susan provided the kind of intense supervision in interpersonal therapy that I was seeking. The client, Lisa, responded, to a point, but finally she said rather plaintively, "Now I *know* what I'm doing in my relationships, but I don't know *how* to change." That single sentence represented the moment for me that I became a cognitive-behavior therapist, for at that point I realized that cognitive-behavior therapy could be used to help clients achieve their goals and actualize their potential as human beings. Before, I had perceived cognitive-behavior therapy as mechanistic, without a value base, and as manipulative. Lisa's comment helped me realize that I could use the methods of behavioral assessment, that were also cognitive, to help clients clarify their own goals, and I could use cognitive-behavioral treatment techniques to provide them with the competencies necessary to achieve these goals. When it became clear to me that I could effect an integration between my humanistic values and my scientific hardheadedness, my transition to being a cognitive-behavior therapist was an easy one.

After I completed my internship, I took a position working with Tom Paolino and Dick Longabaugh at Butler Hospital in Providence, Rhode Island. Tom had been awarded a grant from the state to study an innovative method of treating alcoholic couples through joint hospitalizations. I was hired to develop and implement a research study to evaluate the effectiveness of the joint-hospitalization approach. I had virtually no background in alcoholism but had fairly extensive experience with couples, and I had good research experience from my days as a biologist. I took the position for pragmatic reasons—I needed a job while I completed my dissertation—but the position became formative for my career. I worked in the research position for a year, completed my dissertation, and was offered a position at Butler and as a faculty member in the Brown University Program in Medicine. I was hesitant, due to my continuing desire to work in the community, but I decided that I could spend a few years as a medical school academic psychologist.

During the 8 years I was on the faculty at Brown, I began two major programs—a psychological consultation and assessment program for the hospital and a treatment program for problem drinkers. I became heavily involved in alcoholism treatment research while continuing my interest in couples, aspects of treatment, obtaining research grants, and publishing my work. I also saw a wide range of clients in both inpatient and outpatient treatment, including schizophrenic, manic-depressive, anorexic, and alcoholic patients; women with issues of independence and identity; distressed couples; and people who were just unhappy.

When I first joined the faculty, David Barlow had just come to Brown and Butler Hospital. He began a clinical psychology internship training program with a strong behavioral orientation. I supervised interns, and, through seminars, reading, supervision, research, and experience, I solidified my skills and identity as a cognitive-behavior therapist.

Three clients stand out most clearly in the large caseload I had over these 8 years. I think each of them taught me a special lesson as a therapist and helped me to develop and expand my skills as a cognitive-behavior therapist. Lou was a 50–year-old alcoholic man who also had a serious driving phobia. He went through our alcoholism treatment program and did well. He continued in outpatient treatment with me, and we worked hard on his driving phobia and on his continued abstinence from alcohol. After about 6 months he was doing well enough to stop treatment, but he asked if he could "check in," periodically. We began to meet on a gradually decreasing schedule, first monthly, then every 3 months, then finally every 6 months for a 15–minute appointment. About 2 years after Lou had left the day hospital, his son, who was also an alcoholic, fell asleep in a chair with a lit cigarette in his hand. Lou's house burned, and his son was burned to death. Lou stayed sober through this horrible experience, saying simply "drinking won't change what happened." I remember Lou because of his courage and the lessons he taught me about the importance of long-term contact with some clients and how important people's thinking is in determining their behavior.

The second client who stands out in my Butler memories is Jaynie. A young professional woman, she had significant problems in her relationships at work and with men, as well as with her chronic anxiety. For the first 2 or 3 months I saw her, she refused to have the door to my office closed. Only several months later did I learn that she was strongly attracted to me sexually and that she was confused about her sexual identity. She taught me much about handling extremely uncomfortable feelings as a therapist and the need to tailor the pace as well as the content of the therapy, and she taught me that clients may have problems that they do not reveal to a therapist for a long time.

The third client was a 62–year-old woman who was admitted to the inpatient hospital with severe depression. She felt utterly hopeless, was acutely suicidal, and wept in a way that was painful for all of us to hear. She did not respond to antidepressant medication or to intensive, cognitively oriented treatment for her depression. Finally we decided that electroconvulsive therapy (ECT) was the most appropriate treatment for her and transferred her to the care of a psychiatrist who specialized in ECT. For me, this was a terribly difficult decision, because I felt fairly negative about ECT, and my client was terrified. However, after three or four treatments, her depression lifted dramatically. The woman who felt hopeless became animated and began to care about herself and her life again. She sought me out to thank me profusely for recommending the ECT to her. My shock at her response sent me back to the library, where I looked more thoroughly at the quite respectable literature on the effectiveness of ECT, particularly for the pattern of depression she had experienced. From her I relearned the lesson that I need to be informed about the effectiveness and indications for a treatment, even if I do not particularly like the treatment. I also developed a healthy respect for the role of physiologically based treatments, under some circumstances.

In 1983, I left Rhode Island to join the faculty at Rutgers University. My position at Rutgers combines several of my passions as a psychologist. I am a member of the faculty of the psychology department, teach graduate courses, and supervise graduate students in their research and clinical work. I also am the clinical director of the Center of Alcohol Studies (CAS), the oldest alcohol research center in the world. At CAS, I conduct research on issues related to alcoholism treatment and have developed a series of innovative alcoholism treatment programs in the local community. I spend part of my time in the development and administration of these programs, which also serve as sites for clinical training for our students and for our research on alcoholism treatment.

Now, 13 years out of graduate school, I am firmly a cognitive-behavior therapist. For me, this therapy combines my respect for science with my respect for people. As is evident from Terry Wilson's (1989) writing, the data on the effectiveness of behavioral approaches are impressive, supporting its equal or superior effectiveness in the treatment of the majority of psychological problems. It is also important to me that the approach of cognitive-behavior therapy places responsibility on the therapist for developing a plan for treatment and for continually evaluating the effectiveness of that plan. The constant evaluation and modification of treatment allow for a flexible and self-critical approach to therapy, which I believe challenges the therapist and does not blame the client, unlike trait-theory-oriented treatments. Also important is my sense that cognitive-behavior therapy is highly respectful of people's capacities and dreams. We respect the client's ability to say "I would like to become X," and we become a consultant who can provide the client with tools to try to become "X," rather than an omniscient or all-knowing therapist who manipulates or maneuvers the client to change. I also think that cognitive-behavior therapy is eminently teachable and that the treatment can be well enough specified that it lends itself particularly well to research. Finally, this therapy fits with my worldview—that human behavior is a product of the interaction between the person and the environment, rather than a function solely of forces within or outside the individual.

Training to Become a Cognitive Behavior Therapist

It is probably clear from the discussion of my own path to becoming a cognitive-behavior therapist that I would recommend serious consideration of this therapy to any student who wants to become a therapist. In the next 20 years I think cognitive-behavior therapy will become ascendant because of the strong research base for the approach and the serious efforts to curtail the costs of health care. Cognitive-behavior therapy is well suited to briefer interventions, and, because goals of treatment are well specified and progress is well documented, insurance companies are likely to be more amenable to reimbursing the costs of treatment.

There are several important components in the process of becoming a cognitive-behavior therapist. A firm academic grounding in psychological theory and research, plus personal experience with clinical research, will provide training for the kind of rigorous and critical thinking skills I believe the cognitive-behavior therapist should acquire. The student should also learn to turn to the scientific literature as a source of answers for questions, rather than relying solely on personal experience and clinical supervision. However, close supervision that pushes the student to formulate cases, monitor progress, and evaluate outcomes is crucial. In addition to this rigorous kind of training, therapists need to be exposed to a range of life experiences, both to become familiar with problems outside their own experience and to become humble about the limited range of knowledge and experience any individual can have. Additionally, in becoming therapists students need to develop a level of self-awareness and to come to understand how they cope with personal problems, react emotionally to situations, and think about problems and people. Some students develop this self-awareness and understanding through life experience, some through clinical supervision, and some through their own therapy.

The Setting for Therapy

At this point in my career, I occasionally see private clients in my office at the Center of Alcohol Studies. The building is a rather typical two-story, red-brick structure on the campus. My office looks like a combination of traditional professor's office, with piles of papers, journals, and computer printouts, and a private practitioner's office, with comfortable chairs and a low table. The overall impression is probably one of comfortable chaos.

I see most clients under certain special circumstances. One is in a consultation and outpatient substance-abuse treatment program at one of the community hospitals in New Brunswick, New Jersey, run by a clinical team consisting of a physician, psychologists, a nurse who is also a certified alcoholism counselor, and graduate students in clinical psychology. Here I see hospitalized medical patients who have or are suspected to have problems as a result of their alcohol or drug use. Evaluations and treatment are conducted at bedside, while these patients are undergoing medical treatment. They are an unusually challenging group to work with because most of the patients have not labeled themselves as having an alcohol or drug-use problem, and none of them is seeking psychological help. Thus my challenge as a clinician is to help them begin to label themselves as having problems and to help them consider the notion of changing some aspects of their behavior, either through treatment or on their own. Since I had previously worked only with clients who were seeking treatment, this aspect of my work is unusual. As part of the outpatient program at this hospital, I also run a couples clinic that serves as a base for my continued research on couples' approaches to alcoholism treatment.

In addition to my consultation work, another psychologist and I run an employee-assistance program for the New Jersey Dental Association. Through this program, I see dentists with alcohol, drug, or psychological problems. My primary roles are evaluation, referral, and monitoring of treatment and progress, rather than direct treatment. These clients present some of the most complicated problems I have seen, including serious drug abuse, legal problems, and concurrent emotional, family, and financial problems.

We recently opened a unit for college students with alcohol and drug problems. Students live in the inpatient unit of the student health center at Rutgers and continue to attend classes and maintain other aspects of their student identity while participating in an intensive treatment program. This new assignment has allowed me to return to a familiar role, as therapist for patients in residential treatment.

THE THERAPY FOR DONALD GREEN

Session 1

There are a number of differences between the way I normally conduct an initial interview and the intake interview done by Ray Corsini, presented in chapter 1. I would have spent more time obtaining detailed information on the client's presenting complaints. I would have informed him how I work as a therapist and shared some of my expectations about his role as a client. In an initial session, I would not have asked about his dreams. At the end of the interview, I would have given him a brief homework assignment to bring to the next session. Because of these differences from my usual way of beginning therapy, my first session with him will seek information that I normally would have looked for in an intake session with him. Donald Green enters my office putting out his hand rather tentatively.

GREEN. How are you today, Doc?
MCCRADY. I'm OK, how about you?
GREEN. Oh, OK.
MCCRADY. Last week, in the intake session that you had with Dr. Corsini, you discussed a number of things that were bothering

you. I was wondering if you had any reactions to that session or if there were any other concerns you had that you didn't present.

GREEN. Well, I guess I felt kind of embarrassed after I left. I figured that Dr. Corsini probably thought I was kind of a jerk, with no friends, no wife, and all those strange things that I worry about. I thought about not continuing with therapy, but my boss is really concerned that the new supervisor who will take his place when he retires will not put up with my being late so much.

MCCRADY. It sounds as though you have done a lot of thinking about how a therapist might react to you. I'll tell you—my strongest reactions on reading the report on your intake interview were that you seemed pretty unhappy, and it took a lot of courage to tell so much about yourself to a stranger.

(I think Donald probably does a lot of "mind reading," where he decides on what another person thinks and then acts on that belief, and this probably has contributed to his discomfort around people. I want to begin right away to challenge his assumptions by correcting any mind reading he has done with me. I plan to introduce more specific interventions later that will help him with this problem if my initial guess is correct.)

MCCRADY. Did you think of any other problems that might be important to bring up at this point?

GREEN. No, not really.

MCCRADY. OK then, I'd like to spend some time this session in getting a clearer picture of your problems with being late for work. I also want to make sure that we discuss your overall goals for treatment, so we can agree on what we're trying to accomplish during our sessions.

GREEN. Sounds fine to me.

MCCRADY. Then let's begin with the lateness at work. When did you say this started?

GREEN. Oh, about 3 years ago, I think.

MCCRADY. Can you tell me something about your life at that time—were there any changes in your work or personal life around then?

GREEN. No, not really. Nothing I can think of. It just seemed to come out of the blue.

MCCRADY. OK, then, lets look more at the present. Can you tell me more about your usual morning routine? I'm interested specifically in knowing when you get up, what you do between the time you get up and the time you leave for work, and something about your commute, since you live fairly far out in the country.

GREEN. I don't really do anything unusual in the morning—just what everyone does. I get up, shower, shave, eat breakfast—you know, things like that. I don't think you'll find anything in that to really *explain* my problems.

McCRADY. I guess right now I'm not trying to completely explain your problem, Donald. But to help you make any changes, we need to start with a careful description of what's happening right now. The approach I take in therapy may be a little like your work—first we have to carefully describe and understand how something is working right now, figure out what is wrong with it, and then we can begin to develop a plan to make changes. My job with you is kind of like that of a consultant—I'll help you learn how to discover what patterns in your life are contributing to the things you are unhappy about, and then I can help you learn ways to change some of those patterns. Does that make sense to you?

(Donald has given me a natural opening to describe a bit about my behavioral approach to treatment. I like to emphasize two parts of treatment—assessment and change—as distinct components of the therapy. I define myself as a consultant because I believe that captures the cognitive-behavioral therapist's role well—not an omnipotent stranger in a "one-up" position, but rather a colleague in a sense, who has special expertise to be shared with the client. I do not use the term "psychotherapy," but rather use terms such as "therapy," "cognitive-behavior therapy," or "learning-based treatment.")

Donald thinks a moment before he replies.

GREEN. You know, what you're saying is a lot different from what I thought therapy was supposed to be. I thought I would just have to talk a lot, and eventually I'd feel different. I thought that in therapy you have to talk about your parents and your childhood. I think I like your approach better, if I understand it. It seems to make sense to me.

McCRADY. I'm glad I could clarify things for you. Keep asking me questions as we go along, and I'll do my best to keep explaining to you what and why I'm suggesting the things I do. Now, let's go back to your morning routine. Start with the time you get up.

GREEN. Well, as I mentioned last week, I'm a really heavy sleeper, and I have this elaborate routine to make sure I do get up. I go to bed at 11:00 every night, read for about a half-hour, and turn out the light. My first alarm goes off at 6:30, and the paper carrier comes at 6:45.

McCRADY. Does the wake-up routine work for you, or do you end up going back to sleep after all the alarms, neighbors, and paper carriers get you up?

GREEN. Sometimes it works, but sometimes I go back to sleep after everyone's gone. But if I get up on time, I still may be late for work. I'm just in a fog in the morning and can't seem to get going.

McCRADY. So sometimes you get up on time, but that doesn't really help you in getting to work on time?

GREEN. That's right. I just don't understand it.

McCRADY. Could you tell me more about how you feel when you first get up?

GREEN. I'm sleepy and seem to move very slowly. I've always been that way—that's not any different than it ever was.

McCRADY. Do you ever feel like you don't know where you are when you're first getting up or have no idea what day it is?

GREEN. Well, maybe when I first wake up, but I just lie there for a minute, and then I remember what I have to do that day.

McCRADY. Do you ever have trouble with your balance when you first get up?

GREEN. No, that never happens to me.

(The questions about disorientation and ataxia [poor balance/coordination] are relevant to a diagnosis of hypersomnia disorder. Donald does not have symptoms consistent with hypersomnia. If he did, I would have referred him to a sleep lab for a formal evaluation, because about 85% of hypersomnia cases seen in sleep disorder centers have a physical cause as contributing factor. A routine physical examination by an internist or general practitioner would be insufficient to diagnose such a disorder. Since he does not appear to have a primary sleep disorder, I can continue with more specific behavioral interviewing.)

McCRADY. OK. What do you do after you get up?

GREEN. Well, I, ah, I go to the bathroom first. That usually takes me a while. I subscribe to a couple of auto mechanics magazines, and I read those while I'm in the bathroom. Sometimes the articles are really interesting. Anyway, then I shower and shave, and then I go to the kitchen to eat breakfast.

McCRADY. What do you usually have?

GREEN. Usually just a cup of coffee and a couple of sweet rolls. I usually read the front section of the paper then. Then I brush my teeth and check to make sure everything's OK around the house. Then I leave.

McCRADY. What kind of things do you check?

GREEN. Oh, you know, I make sure that all the windows are closed, that the oven and stove are off, that the pilot lights are burning, that all the lights are off—things like that.

McCRADY. How long does all this take after breakfast?

GREEN. Not too long, but it varies. Sometimes after I leave I'm not sure if I turned off all the lights or something, so I go back to be certain.

McCRADY. OK, that gives me a general idea of your usual routine. Does it vary on any mornings?

GREEN. No, not really.

McCRADY. Good. I'd also like to know a bit about your commute, and your schedule first thing once you get to work.

GREEN. It takes me about a half-hour to get to work. Usually the traffic's not too bad, but once in a while if there's an accident or something it'll take me longer. I used to leave the house an hour before I had to be at work, so that even if there was a tie-up I wouldn't be late. Now, I'm just happy if I'm not too late. Did you ask me something else too?

McCRADY. Yes, I was interested in your schedule and routine when you first get to work.

GREEN. When I come in, I go past my supervisor's office, but I don't usually see him. His secretary, Miss Donahue, is really nice to me and always says "Good morning." I say "hello" to her, too, but we never talk much after that. I think she'd keep on talking if I ever stopped by her desk. When I'm late, though, she's usually not there, because she's already attending meetings. Then I go to my office and review reports from the day before. If there were any problems, in pollution ratings or whatever, I have to go talk to the plant foreman who is responsible for each one. They get kind of angry when I say anything—that's definitely the worst part of my job.

(For a behavior therapist, defining the antecedents, consequences, and thoughts and feelings surrounding a problem is essential to developing a plan for change. I am using behavioral interviewing to look for specific details rather than the kind of global information Donald first gave when I asked about his routine.)

McCRADY. I think I'm beginning to get an image of what your morning is like. Often, some of the variations in a person's routine are also important to figuring out how to bring about change in a problem. So what I'd like to have you do for the next week is to begin to keep careful track of your morning routine. Let's put together a time log on which you can keep track of your daily activities. For now, I think you should include the time you get up, what devices you use to get up, and the time you spend on each part of your routine at home. Include your commuting time and then a log of the first hours at work—where you are, who you see, and what you do. Also, you should mark down anything different that happens. I'd like you to fill it out each day. Keep the form with you as you go through your routine, and mark down each thing as you finish it. On your morning break at work, write down any additional things that happened. Does this make sense to you?

(By careful questioning, I've begun to get an idea of some of the factors that may be contributing to Donald's lateness. I suspect that he spends excessive time reading and engages in obsessional checking routines about the house. I also suspect that his eating and exercise habits may be contributing to his logy feeling in the morning. It sounds as though his lateness may be partially an avoidance of uncomfortable interpersonal situations at work—with the secretary and with the people Donald is supposed to work with. I suspect that he is minimizing the time devoted to certain activities and is unaware of any possible link between his lateness and the social situation at work. Therefore, to get a clearer picture of his routine, I need to develop a way to collect day-to-day information about his functioning. The Self-Recording Form for comfort-discomfort in various activities will provide a format for doing this.)

I give Donald the Self-Recording Form for Daily Routine (see Figure 7.1), along with specific instructions for daily recording of his degree of comfort-discomfort. Donald looks over the form before commenting.

GREEN. This makes a *lot* of sense. Do you think it will really help?

MCCRADY. I'm sure it will give us a better picture of the lateness problem. From there, we can begin to decide how to help you change it. Is it fair for me to assume that you want to go back to being on time for work?

GREEN. Absolutely. I like my job and want to keep it.

MCCRADY. OK, I just want to be sure that we are working toward the

SELF-RECORDING FORM FOR DAILY ROUTINE

Time		Primary	Other	Subjective Rating
Start	End	Activity	Activity	Completely Comfortable / Extremely Uncomfortable 0------------------------100

FIGURE 7.1 Self-recording form for daily routine.

same goal here. You reported many of your other concerns last week, too, and before we run out of time today I'd like to review some of these other problems. We won't be able to go into each of them in the same detail as we did with the lateness, but I'd like to see if we can agree on the problem areas you'd like to work on during treatment. During the week, I'm going to pull together some questionnaires to use that will help me understand these problems better, and then we can develop plans for dealing with each of them. By the beginning of our fourth session I hope we can set fairly specific goals for each of these other problem areas. Then we'll agree on an initial number of sessions for treatment.

(As a cognitive-behavior therapist, I want the client to participate fully in defining problems and setting goals for treatment. Treatment involves an explicit contract, either verbal or written, which includes specification of the goals of the treatment and expectations for the client and the therapist. With Donald, because he presents several rather major problems that encompass much of his life, I think a problem-specific focus is particularly important. If we do not define and agree on priorities in his treatment, it would be easy to jump from one area to another, without really effecting any significant changes in any area.)

GREEN. OK, Doc.

MCCRADY. It seems to me there were four other major problems you talked about in our first session. You spoke about feeling isolated, lonely, and uncomfortable around other people, and you seemed to have a rather negative view of yourself. You also said you were concerned about those catastrophes you imagine, and I think you mentioned a fear of barking dogs. Are these basically the other major things you're feeling unhappy about?

GREEN. Yes, but the barking of dogs isn't really a major problem. The other things you mention are real problems to me. Do you think I can actually change? I've been this way my whole life.

MCCRADY. I think you have a good chance of making some changes. Even with me, you seem to be able to talk easily and tell me about yourself. A good part of being able to get to know other people is being able to share something of yourself, and I think you already have some of what you need to do that. We must learn more about what makes it hard for you to share, and then I can try to help you learn how to do it. I can't promise that you'll become the life of the party, but you don't have to live out your life in a room by yourself, either.

(I want to give Donald some feedback and a sense of hope about therapy, based on the information I have so far. As a behavior therapist, I try to reinforce positive behavior of the client, rather than maintaining the more neutral therapeutic posture characteristic of psychodynamically oriented therapists.)

MCCRADY. As you think about these problems, and the problem with lateness that brought you to see me, do you have any idea about what is most important for you to work on first? I'm not asking you to decide what's most important to you as a person, or to say what bothers you the most—just to say where you want to start.

GREEN. I *have* to start getting to work on time. If I can do that, I'll feel much better. I hate feeling like I'm so weak that I can't control something so simple. Maybe then we can talk about some of these other things, but I'm still not sure that there's any point to it. I think my personality is pretty well set. I'm worse than my father—I'm afraid I'll always be alone.

MCCRADY. OK, so our first goal will be to get your work schedule back on track. We'll begin to work on that and also to assess these other problems more carefully. I understand how hopeless you feel because you've been this way a long time. But let's see how we do together and whether some of these problems begin to appear more manageable. We have to stop for today, but be sure you fill out your forms each day this week. We'll look at them together at our next session.

GREEN. Thanks, Doc.

Donald and I shake hands, and he bumps into the comer of a low table as he turns around to leave.

Session 2

Donald arrives early for our second session and comes into my office with a serious look on his face.

GREEN. I did those forms all week, Doc, and things aren't any better.

MCCRADY. That's OK, Donald. The forms are just to help us see the patterns that are keeping you in this habit of being late. Just writing things down won't change things very much.

GREEN. I guess I know that you didn't promise anything, but I kind of hoped things would change anyway. But let me show you what I did.

Donald hands me his filled-in report forms (for Thursday and Friday mornings, see Figure 7.2). For the next 20 minutes, we go over each day of his work week. Our appointments are on Wednesdays, so we review the week from Thursday to Wednesday. Thursday morning, Donald had gotten up on time, was ready to shower by the time the paper carrier arrived, and left for work early. He arrived on time and was greeted warmly by Miss Donahue, who commented that she hadn't seen him in 2 weeks and tried to engage him in conversation. He went to his office and did solitary work for the first hour of the day. Thursday night there was a thunderstorm, and on Friday morning Donald got up only when the paper carrier came to the door. After breakfast he checked every electrical appliance in the house to be sure that nothing had been damaged by the storm. Five minutes after he left the house, he returned because he had forgotten to check the pilot lights on the stove (they were all on). He arrived at work about 20 minutes late but still was greeted by Miss Donahue, who told him how nice it was to see him 2 days in a row.

Monday morning was a disaster. Donald had received a new magazine in the mail and stayed up until midnight Sunday reading it. He was tired in the morning and went back to bed after the paper carrier delivered the paper. When he finally did get up, 45 minutes late, he scanned two articles before he even showered. He decided to skip breakfast and left the house without checking anything. Ten minutes

SELF-RECORDING FORM FOR DAILY ROUTINE

Time: Start	Time: End	Primary Activity	Other Activity	Subjective Rating (Completely Comfortable 0 — Extremely Uncomfortable 100)
THURS.				
6:30		GOT UP		15
6:30	8:00	SHOWER, DRESS, EAT, CHECK HOUSE		15
8:00		LEFT HOUSE		20
8:30		ARRIVED AT WORK	SAW MISS D.	70
8:30	9:30	WORKED IN OFFICE		35
FRI.				
6:30	6:45	GOT UP		15
6:45	8:00	SHOWER, DRESS, EAT		15
8:00	8:10	CHECK HOUSE (STORM)		20
8:10		LEFT HOUSE		20
8:15		RETURNED HOME		80
8:15	8:20	RECHECKED HOUSE		20
8:20		LEFT AGAIN		
8:50		ARRIVED AT WORK	SAW MISS D	75
8:55	9:45	WORKED IN OFFICE		45
9:45		TALKED TO FOREMAN		80

FIGURE 7.2 Example of Donald Green's self-recording form for daily routine.

from the house, he realized that he had left his bedroom window open and returned. He then decided he should check the whole house, in case he had forgotten anything else, and ended up arriving at work more than an hour late. By then, Miss Donahue was not in sight, and he had missed most of the Monday morning engineers' meeting. Tuesday and Wednesday mornings, he got up when the paper carrier arrived, spent only a few minutes reading and checking the house but longer showering and having breakfast, and arrived at work about 40 minutes late.

The objective information on the forms yielded several hypotheses about the nature of Donald's lateness. However, the comfort ratings on the forms for each activity provided even more information. Donald rated his interactions with Miss Donahue at 70 and 75, at the uncomfortable end of the scale, despite their brevity. He rated arrivals when he did not interact with Miss Donahue at 30, closer to comfort than discomfort. His discomfort at the engineers' meeting rated 90. In addition, his discomfort rating when he left in the morning without checking the house was 80, but it dropped to 20 after he returned and completed his checking ritual. If he checked before leaving, his discomfort ratings were also 20.

McCrady. Well, Donald, as we look these sheets over, a couple of things strike me. It looks as though you got pretty uncomfortable on those mornings when you ran into Miss Donahue and at that engineers' meeting. Can you tell me more about what makes those situations uncomfortable for you?

Green. I don't think Miss Donahue has much to do with my problem. I think that I just have trouble getting going in the morning.

McCrady. That may be so, but it does strike me that you are much more comfortable on days when you get to work and don't see her. Let's just try to explore this a little more. It is possible that she has nothing to do with your lateness, but that's what we're trying to do—to see if there are factors that contribute to your being late but that aren't immediately obvious. Besides, you have already said that you're pretty uncomfortable around people but would like to change that, so by talking about Miss Donahue and the meeting I can get a better understanding of what makes those situations so uncomfortable.

Green. I still don't think she's my problem, but I'll tell you that I feel very awkward around her. I never know what to say, and I know that she's never been married, so I think she wants to go out with me. She's nice, but I can't imagine going out on a date or kissing her or anything. I don't know if she really wants to go out with me. I don't know why she would—she's very stylish—always has her nails and hair done real nice. I'm not much to look at.

McCrady. So you do a lot of thinking about what she thinks of you, why she's talking to you, and you feel pretty tongue-tied? Is that a fair summary of what you're saying?

GREEN. Exactly.

MCCRADY. How about at the engineers' meeting—what kind of thoughts and feelings do you have there?

GREEN. I just hate those meetings. Each engineer is supposed to give a 5–minute update on what he's doing. I get all sweaty and nervous before it's my turn and don't even hear half of what they say. Then I worry that someone will ask me a question and I won't know what they're talking about. By the time it's my turn, I'm a wreck. They all know it, which doesn't help much. Sometimes the chief engineer just skips me, and then I'm even more embarrassed. I know he does it just because I get so nervous.

MCCRADY. It sounds as though you do similar worrying in the meeting and with Miss Donahue. You worry so much about what other people think of you that it interferes with your own ability to think. It also sounds as though you get physically uncomfortable—is that right?

GREEN. Yeah, you're right, I shouldn't get so nervous all the time.

MCCRADY. I'm not trying to evaluate you, I'm just trying to describe what I think happens to you. It seems clear to me that you face some pretty uncomfortable situations every day at work, and some days are more uncomfortable than others. I could see how these situations would lead you to want to dawdle in the morning, but, as you said, we don't know yet if they are an important part of your being late.

GREEN. I notice that I spend a lot of time checking the house every day. As a homeowner, I think I should do these things—what would happen if there was a gas leak or something? I could lose everything, and innocent people would get hurt if the house exploded.

MCCRADY. And I can see that the checking seems to take up a lot of time, especially on those days that you return to the house. Do you ever find anything out of place while you're checking?

GREEN. No, never. I'm pretty careful. Are you telling me not to check things any more?

MCCRADY. No, Donald, I'm not trying to give you any instructions right now, just trying to see what's been happening. I notice that you rate yourself as pretty uncomfortable when you first get up in the morning. Is that discomfort the same as the discomfort about checking or those situations at work?

GREEN. No, not at all. In those other situations I feel real nervous inside. When I first get up, I just feel kind of lousy and tired, like

I just can't get moving. I keep thinking that my bed feels so good, and there's nothing really to look forward to, nothing to get up for.

McCrady. Can you describe your thoughts in the morning a little more?

Green. Well, I don't want to keep complaining all the time to you, but I don't think my life's very, well, you know, right. I'm over 40, no friends, no wife . . . . I mean, look at me. I'm not much to look at. Sometimes it's just very hard to get up and face another day. There's nothing to look forward to, and it seems as though nothing will ever change. I guess I get pretty down on myself. I shouldn't complain so much—I have a good job and even have my own house.

McCrady. It sounds as though you get to thinking about all the things you're dissatisfied with. That also makes it hard to want to get up.

Green. That's right.

McCrady. It seems to me that we can sort out at least four different things that are contributing to your problems with getting to work on time. First, you've said that you're a heavy sleeper and always have been. You've handled that by relying on more and more external things to wake you up. Second, your unhappiness with many things in your life sometimes seems to slow you down in the morning. Third, you do lose a lot of time checking and rechecking things in the house, and sometimes that makes you late. And my hunch is that some of the things that make you uncomfortable at work also slow you down in the morning, like having to face people you don't feel comfortable with.

Does that sound like a fair summary of what we've talked about and what's on the sheets?

Green. Well, it sure does sound complicated. Do I have to change everything in my life before I can get to work on time again? That would be pretty hopeless.

McCrady. No, I think we can tackle some of these things slowly and still help you with your schedule. I think the place to start with this is to just pick one thing that's responsible for making you late and try to make some changes in that. Then we can see what happens . . . OK?

Donald nods in agreement.

McCrady. Now let's shift gears for a few minutes. I want to give you some questionnaires to fill out to help me get a better picture of some of the other problems we discussed last week. I have several here that I'd like you to spend some time on this week. This first one is called the Thought Inventory. It was developed to help us understand the kinds of worries you have when you fantasize catastrophes. I just want you to fill out the second half, from question 23 on. The first half is more for people who are consistently afraid of one thing, which they try to avoid.

(I give Donald the Thought Inventory, which describes many of the thoughts associated with rituals, as well as many irrational fears people have. To get a sense of the types of things he worries about, I ask him only to complete the section on irrational fears. The inventory asks a respondent to indicate what "unpleasant consequences" he or she is worrying about, such as "Contracting a serious disease," "Having a bad accident happen to me," and "An intruder breaking into my home, car, etc." (Steketee & Foa, 1985, p. 128).)

GREEN (pointing to the form). So I should just answer this part?

MCCRADY. Right. These other three questionnaires ask you about your feelings around other people and how you feel about expressing your feelings and opinions. I think filling them out will be pretty straightforward.

(Next I give Donald the Social Avoidance and Distress Scale and the Fear of Negative Evaluation Scale, both developed by Watson and Friend (1969). These two questionnaires should give me a good picture of his thoughts about interpersonal situations. In addition, I give him the Assertiveness Inventory, which asks him to describe how likely he is to behave assertively in a variety of situations [Gambrill & Richey, 1975]).

MCCRADY. Finally, I'd like you to complete this questionnaire to help me understand better how you've been feeling in general. The instructions are here at the top.

(I give Donald the last questionnaire, the Beck Depression Inventory, a simple self-report questionnaire that evaluates symptoms of depression. Although I do not think that Donald is clinically depressed, I believe it is important to evaluate his depression more fully [Beck, Rush, Shaw, & Emery, 1979]).

GREEN. So you want me to fill all these out this week?

MCCRADY. That's right. I also want you to keep using the Self-Recording Form to keep track of your morning routine. Don't feel that you have to change anything yet because we want to be sure that we haven't missed anything major that's affecting you. Next week, we'll go over these questionnaires and your forms, and then we'll get a clear plan for treatment.

GREEN. OK, I'll see you then.

Sessions 1 and 2 have been crucial to my development of a behavioral formulation of Donald's presenting problems. The detailed interviewing has given me a clear picture of the variety of antecedents to his lateness problem, and I have provided him with the assessment tools I will use to evaluate this and his other problems. This data collection method is at the heart of the behavioral approach. I want Donald to feel fully involved in this so he will become a cooperative partner in the change process. In the next session, I plan to provide him with detailed feedback about the problems and my proposed treatment plan. Normally I am able to do this by the end of the third session because I would have begun the self-recording after the initial interview, and the questionnaires after the following session. However, even without these questionnaires, I have a fairly good idea of what has contributed to some of Donald's major problems and how I think they relate to one another. Between this session and the next, I want to develop a case formulation. In connection with this I will also prepare a problem list, a DSM-IV diagnosis, and a plan for treatment for Donald.

Case Formulation

At this point, I have a fairly good picture of the problems Donald is experiencing and some hypotheses about the relationships among these problems. Donald's problems seem to include (1) behavioral deficits in terms of skills needed to interact with other people; (2) behavioral excesses in terms of his house-checking behavior; (3) cognitive problems, which include negative self-evaluative statements, anticipations of aversive consequences in a range of situations, and ruminative, distorted thoughts; (4) physiological problems with anxiety; and (5) problems with weight, eating habits (which I only infer at this point from his description of his breakfasts), and lack of exercise. It seems to me that Donald's lateness at work is related to several factors, including his heavy sleeping, social anxiety, general physical condition, and checking rituals. His social anxiety and lack of social skills contribute to his social isolation, which enhances his negative image of himself. I also think that his weight and general physical appearance are both a result of and a contributing factor to his social isolation.

A theme that seems to pervade much of his functioning is a fear of negative evaluation and a fear of criticism or punishment by others. This is most evident in his work situation; he is uncomfortable in social situations that require confrontation, or even extended conversations on his part. It also fits with his relatively isolated lifestyle, his few friends, and his solitary hobby of repairing cars. The "catastrophes" he imagines also seem consistent with this theme; the two he has described relate to the concept of doing something wrong and expecting to be caught or punished. His dreams are also consistent with this theme, with the major elements including fear of failure, looking foolish, or being punished. I do not think that this hypothesized experience of fear of negative evaluation occurs in all situations, but it does seem to occur across a range of situations. This formulation, which focuses on both specific problems and hypothesized themes that occur across a variety of situations, is similar to the approach that Turkat and Maisto (1985) take to the behavioral treatment of clients diagnosed as having personality disorders.

Although I do not focus much on the historical roots of clients' presenting problems, it seems clear that Donald's parents were poor models for positive social skills. His father was socially isolated, and his mother never appeared to express her feelings or desires directly. His memory of his parents suggests that they did little to enhance his feeling of being valuable or lovable. He describes his father as avoiding him and his mother as caring for him but providing no physical affection. His memories suggest that his father allowed little room for imperfection, and he reports being criticized or punished by his father for his mistakes.

Problem List

After completing my case formulation, I always develop a problem list for clients and establish a DSM-IV diagnosis. The problem list provides a vehicle for weekly case notes and helps me keep my focus clear during treatment. Donald's initial problem list is shown in Table 7.1.

TABLE 7.1 Problem List for Donald Green

GREEN, DONALD	
1.	Lateness at work
2.	Social anxiety
3.	Social skills deficits
4.	Social isolation
5.	Ruminative thoughts
6.	Negative self-image
7.	Fear of barking dogs

TABLE 7.2 DSM-IV Axes for Diagnosis of Mental Disorders

The *Diagnostic and Statistical Manual of Mental Disorders*, fourth edition (DSM-IV) uses a multiaxial approach to diagnosis, which assumes that a client must be assessed and understood along multiple dimensions of functioning. There are five *axes* for diagnosis:

Axis I: **Clinical Syndromes.** These represent acute emotional or behavioral problems for which people seek treatment.

Axis II: **Developmental Disorders and Personality Disorders.** These are problems that usually begin in childhood or the adolescent years and continue fairly unchanged into a person's adult life.

Axis III: **Physical Disorders and Conditions.** This axis shows the clinician to note any physical problems that might be relevant to the client's emotional or behavioral problems.

Axis IV: **Severity of Psychosocial Stressors.** This axis allows the clinician to indicate the amount of stress that the client has been experiencing in the last year. Ratings are from 1 (no stress) to 6 (catastrophic stress).

Axis V: **Global Assessment of Functioning.** For this axis, the clinician makes an overall rating (from 1 to 90) of the client's overall psychological, social, and occupational functioning.

DSM-IV Diagnosis

Establishing a diagnosis is less consistent with a behavioral approach to assessment because it focuses primarily on symptoms and makes the assumption that clients have "disorders." Behavioral approaches focus instead on presenting problems, without attempting to decide whether they fit a pattern that suits a particular diagnostic label. However, diagnosis is important for communicating with other health care professionals and for determining whether a client does have a diagnosable problem for which there is a known treatment of choice. Moreover, it is required for insurance purposes. My diagnostic formulation is based on the *Diagnostic and Statistical Manual of Mental Disorders* published by the American Psychiatric Association (see Table 7.2). For Donald, the diagnosis is as follows:

Axis I: V71.09 No diagnosis or condition of Axis 1.
Axis II: 301.82 Avoidant Personality Disorder, characterized by be-

ing easily hurt, having none or only one close friend, avoiding social or occupational activities that involve significant interpersonal contact, and being reticent in social situations for fear of saying something inappropriate.

Axis III: None.

Axis IV: Psychosocial Stressors: Work pressure.
Severity: 2–Mild

Axis V: Current Global Assessment of Functioning (GAF): 65
Highest GAF past year: 65

The other diagnoses I considered for Donald include hypersomnia, occupational problem (not attributable to mental disorder) and schizoid or schizotypal personality disorder. His sleep problems are not sufficiently severe to warrant a hypersomnia diagnosis, and it appears that his work problems are related to his problems with social avoidance and to a minor compulsive checking ritual. The other two personality disorder diagnoses I considered are more appropriate for clients who lack a desire for social interaction and who are aloof and withdrawn. Donald, in contrast, appears to want more interaction but is too uncomfortable to seek it out. It is important to note, however, that Morey's (1988) research suggests a large degree of overlap between the avoidant and schizoid personality disorder diagnoses, and many clients, such as Donald, present features of both.

Plan for Treatment

My complete plan for Donald's treatment includes the following points:

1. Lateness at work
   a. A mild exercise program to increase the immediate positive value of getting up in the morning.
   b. Imagery techniques to increase the ability to get up without so many external agents.
   c. A response-prevention program to decrease the time involved with checking rituals.
   d. A social skills training program to enhance ability to talk with Miss Donahue without undue anxiety.
2. Social anxiety
   a. Relaxation training.
   b. Cognitive-restructuring techniques to increase positive self-

statements about social interactions and to decrease fear of negative evaluations by others.

3. Social skills deficits
   a. Further role-playing to evaluate his social skills deficits.
   b. Social skills training, including the elements emphasized by Hollin and Trower (1988) as optimal components of social skills training, such as instruction, modeling, rehearsal, feedback, and homework.
   c. A specific emphasis on assertion skills, especially as related to work situations.
4. Social isolation
   a. Gradual exposure program to decrease social isolation.
   b. Some clarification of interests and identification of optimal settings for meeting people with similar interests.
5. Ruminative thoughts
   a. Monitoring for the appearance of any new "catastrophic thinking."
   b. Cognitive restructuring with exposure if any new ruminative patterns develop.
6. Negative self-image
   a. Treatment primarily through plans for dealing with social anxiety, social isolation, and social skills deficits, as well as exercise program.
7. Fear of barking dogs
   a. No treatment planned, unless Donald decides later that he wants help with this problem.

Session 3

At the beginning of this session, I collect Donald's questionnaires and Self-Recording Forms. After reviewing them and scoring them quickly, I ask a number of follow-up questions to obtain more detailed information about some of his responses. On the Beck Depression Inventory he scores a 7, which suggests that he is only mildly depressed. He endorsed items such as, "I am so sad or unhappy that it is very painful." "I feel that I won't ever get over my troubles," "I am disappointed in myself," "I am critical of myself for my weaknesses or mistakes," and "I have thoughts of harming myself but I would not carry them out." These answers are consistent with his self-presentation as being unhappy about his life situation.

The three measures related to social skills make the nature of some of his social-interpersonal difficulties clearer. On the Gambrill and

Richey Assertiveness Inventory he reported that he rarely does things that require assertiveness. For example, he said he never asks others for favors, rarely expresses his feelings or opinions, and usually gives in to other people's requests or demands, even if he thinks they are unreasonable. This inventory also asks clients to rate how uncomfortable various situations would make them, and Donald indicated that he would experience a "fair amount" or "much" discomfort in almost all the situations. The only behaviors that did not make him very uncomfortable were such things as apologizing if he feels he is wrong or admitting his ignorance about something. His answers on the Social Avoidance and Distress Scale (SAD) and the Fear of Negative Evaluation Scale (FNE) indicate that he feels uncomfortable in many social situations and worries intensely about others' evaluations of him. His score of 24 on the SAD suggests an extreme degree of social avoidance (the mean on the SAD is 9.00, with a standard deviation of 8.07). He scores 25 on the FNE, also well above the mean of 15.47 (standard deviation of 5.62).

These questionnaires and the interviewing have given me a fair picture of Donald's problems in social situations. However, I also want to be able to observe how he interacts in different situations that involve other people. I decide to try some role-playing with him but to postpone that part of the assessment until we begin to work directly with his social discomfort.

On the Thought Inventory, he indicated that he worries most about being criticized or ridiculed by other people, being responsible for making a serious mistake, or ruining his reputation. He is relatively unconcerned about other types of catastrophes, such as illness, death, or accidents.

After discussing the results of the questionnaires with Donald and clarifying some of his answers, I ask him for his reaction to them.

McCrady. You did a nice job with these questionnaires and the recording sheets. Did you have any thoughts as you went through them?

Green. They really got me thinking more and more about myself. These two (pointing to the FNE and the SAD) in particular seem to be made just for me. They describe exactly how I feel when I'm around other people.

McCrady. I'm glad they seem so relevant to you. Now let's take a little time to agree on some goals for the treatment. Let's try to make the goals as specific as we can for each of the problems you'd like some help with. I'd also like to tell you a little about some of the things I think we will do during treatment.

INITIAL TREATMENT CONTRACT

1. We will meet for ten sessions, then evaluate our progress.

2. The goals of treatment for Donald are:

   a. To begin arriving at work at the scheduled time.

   b. To be able to carry on brief conversations with people at work without becoming excessively anxious.

   c. To begin to learn how to give directions to people at work.

   d. To improve how he feels by exercising.

3. Donald agrees that his responsibilities in treatment are to come to scheduled appointments on time, to call at least 24 hours ahead if he has to change or cancel an appointment, to pay bills on time, and to do homework assignments to the best of his ability.

4. Dr. McCrady's responsibilities are to be at scheduled appointments on time, to provide the most effective treatment that she is aware of for Donald's problems, to be available for emergencies, and to arrange appropriate coverage when she is not available.

Signed: ______________________ ______________________

Donald Green Barbara McCrady, Ph.D.

____

Date

FIGURE 7.3 Initial treatment contract for Donald Green with Barbara McCrady.

GREEN. OK, Doc.

After some discussion, Donald and I agree on an Initial Treatment Contract (see Figure 7.3), which embodies several elements that are important to a behavioral approach. First, it is time-limited. I do not expect to complete treatment with Donald in 10 sessions, but breaking down the treatment into smaller segments emphasizes the need to evaluate progress in some regular fashion. Second, the contract sets specific, small goals, the ones I think can be achieved in a relatively brief time. This should enhance Donald's feelings of self-efficacy about change. Also, the goals are specific, so we will know if we have achieved them or not. And the goals are directed toward the major problems Donald presented.

Up to this point, Donald and I have spent most of the session discussing the questionnaires, the treatment contract, and the treatment goals. I leave some time at the end to begin to implement the plan for dealing with the problem of lateness at work.

McCRADY. Now we can begin to put into effect the plan for dealing with your lateness. I think the place to start is with helping you develop some new techniques for getting up on time and having something to do right away that makes it more worthwhile for you to get up—something you can really look forward to in the morning.

GREEN. What do you have in mind?

McCRADY. Two things. First, I'd like to see if we can help you become more reliant on yourself to get up. We can use some imagery techniques to help you learn to get up without all the help from neighbors and paper carriers. And, I'd like to see you develop some kind of mild exercise program for when you get up.

GREEN. That doesn't sound like me—I'm not a weightlifter or long distance runner—look at me.

McCRADY. I don't mean that. What I was remembering is that in the intake interview you mentioned how much you liked walking tours on vacations. Well, what about a 2- or 3-mile walk each morning?

GREEN. I don't know—I have enough trouble getting up. Won't that just make it worse? I'll have *more* to worry about instead of less.

McCRADY. Maybe, but tell me how you feel about walking.

GREEN. You're right—I like walking. When I'm on vacation, I do get up early and take walks. It's quiet then, and no one's around, and you can notice everything.

McCRADY. All right, then, can we agree on beginning by working out a walking program and trying the imagery techniques?

GREEN. I guess.

McCRADY. I also suspect that we'll have to develop some kind of program to help you get your checking of the house under control, but let's hold off on that for now.

GREEN. OK, maybe I can just cut that down. I have never really thought about how much time I waste doing that.

McCrady. Well, don't try to take on too much at once. Let's start with the plan for the walking program. Is there a walk you'd enjoy that originates near your house?

Green. Yes, there's a park about a half mile away. I could walk there and walk around the park for a while.

McCrady. Let's set a small goal for starters—how about just walking to the park and back?

Green. That'd be no problem—it would only take me about 20 minutes.

McCrady. Can you make changes in your wake-up routine to get up 20 minutes earlier?

Green. I'm not sure, but I'll try.

McCrady. Well, see how this works out. Next week we'll begin to work on some imagery to help you with getting up in the morning without so many external aids. Keep track on your Self-Recording Form of the walking you do, along with everything else you've been recording.

Green. OK. You know, I'm beginning to feel pretty hopeful about this therapy. It seems like things really could get better.

Sessions 4–11

Now that I've given some specific examples of how I work as a cognitive-behavior therapist, I will shift to a more narrative format to describe most of the remainder of the treatment. My approach remains fairly consistent throughout—working at a very detailed level to specify actual behavior, thoughts, and feelings; reinforcing progress; and trying to effect changes in small steps. Each session begins with a review of homework and any important events of the week and ends with the assignment of new homework.

In the next several sessions, we focus on Donald's lateness problems at work. He takes to the exercise program immediately and complies faithfully. Over the next 6 weeks he gradually increases his walks to 3 miles each morning.

I then introduce some imagery or covert rehearsal techniques to help Donald get up without so many external aids, I have him sit back in his chair, close his eyes, and imagine his alarm clock. First he imagines himself setting the alarm for the time he wants to get up in the morning. Then he imagines the clock again, with the morning time displayed, and then I have him imagine the clock ringing. The imagery continues with his turning off the clock, getting up immediately, and feeling pleased with himself for getting up so easily.

Donald becomes quite anxious when I initially have him close his eyes. He cannot keep them closed and begins to breathe rapidly and to perspire. I have to discontinue the covert rehearsal to discuss his discomfort. He indicates that he feels foolish with his eyes closed and is certain I am looking at him and thinking about how stupid he looks and how stupid his problems are. I try to reassure him by telling him that my main concern is to help him get through this problem. Then I tell him that I am not sure this approach will work, so I also have some anxiety about it. This revelation surprises him; he says he thought that I was always completely self-confident. It helps him become more comfortable with the covert rehearsal procedure, and then he can go through it, though he still is somewhat anxious.

We rehearse this technique six to eight times during the session and I assign it as homework, to be practiced at least three times a day, with the last rehearsal when he goes to bed. We make no immediate change in his use of external aids.

Although in the first week of the rehearsal Donald notices no changes in his awakening pattern, by the second week he begins to awaken when the alarm goes off. In Session 6, he decides to tell his neighbor and the paper carrier not to call him or wait for him any more, because he feels confident that he can get up without them. However, he continues to set the three alarm clocks and place them at strategic points around the house. Then, in the first week Donald tries to get up without the neighbor and paper carrier, he oversleeps the first 2 work days and skips his morning walk. He is surprised at how much he misses the walk. After that, he is able to get up when the alarm goes off.

Other reasons for Donald's lateness still have to be addressed, however. After Session 4 he tries to eliminate his checking rituals on his own and is successful for 3 days, but he is extremely anxious when he does not return to check things and cannot sustain this pattern. I address the checking ritual directly in Session 6, and we spend some time identifying its behavioral and cognitive components. His checking is rather predictable—he would check that all the windows are closed and locked, the faucets are all turned off, the pilot lights on the stove and oven are lit, all the lights are off, the heat is turned down, and the doors are locked. Once he gets in the car, he would begin worrying that he had forgotten to check something. Sometimes he could remember what he had checked and could continue on to work; other times he could not reassure himself and would return to the house.

The treatment of obsessive-compulsive rituals, including checking, is discussed by Steketee and Foa in David Barlow's (1985) handbook on the treatment of psychological disorders. They emphasize that the most effective treatments include exposure to the feared object or situation, combined with response prevention in which the client is not allowed to engage in the ritualistic behavior. The response-prevention procedure usually results in high client anxiety at the beginning, with the anxiety gradually reducing over time. The procedure is based on the learning principle of extinction. Because of the high client anxiety associated with the procedure, response prevention usually needs to be done under the direct supervision of a therapist.

It is difficult to determine how to implement response prevention for Donald unless I make many trips to his home, which is impractical and probably would elicit a great deal of anxiety from him. I ask Donald about checking in general, and, as I expect, he checks in other situations as well. Therefore I arrange a situation at my office that will allow us to implement a response-prevention program. Since I am seeing Donald in the evening, the kitchen in my building is not being used. Before he comes in, I make sure that both coffee makers and all the lights are on, the faucet is dripping, and one burner of the stove is still hot. We make it Donald's responsibility to turn off the coffee makers and lights, shut the faucet, and check the stove and oven. After he does that, he is to come to my office for our appointment.

For the first part of the session, Donald discusses his thoughts about the kitchen and his desire to again check on what he has already checked. We discuss ways he can talk to himself about the desire to check, such as, "It's OK to be anxious, I don't have to do anything about it" or "It will be just fine even if I don't check." I have him rate his anxiety at 5–minute intervals on a 0 to 100 scale, similar to the subjective comfort-discomfort rating on the Self-Reporting Form. When we graph the anxiety ratings, we see that in each session his anxiety peaks and then decreases. We also construct a list of situations in which he has checked and arrange them in hierarchical order, from least anxiety-provoking to most anxiety-provoking. Between sessions, I have Donald use response prevention on his own, beginning with less difficult checking situations, such as turning off the lights in his office and locking his car, and gradually moving to more difficult situations. We schedule two response-prevention sessions each day. He uses the back of his daily recording sheet to write down his anxiety rating at 5–minute intervals.

After three sessions of response prevention in the office, Donald is ready to try something at home. I begin by having him check everything in the house once and then agreeing that he can recheck anything except the lights, the least difficult item for him to check at home. After a few days his anxiety about checking the lights begins to decrease, and we gradually add other items he is to avoid checking. By Session 11, I assign him to implement the response-prevention program for all checking when he leaves in the morning. We agree that he will call me if he feels that he must return to the house. He has 2 days the first week where his anxiety is very high, and he calls both mornings. We deal with the anxiety on the phone as we had in the office, and after that he is able to resist the impulse to return to check.

The combination of imagery techniques, exercise program, and response prevention to deal with the checking is effective in decreasing Donald's lateness. This is evident in a graph we have been constructing during our sessions that shows his discomfort rating on arriving at work, his discomfort on leaving home, and his record of being late getting to work (see Figure 7.4). We get the data from the Self-Reporting Forms he has been filling out. However, his discomfort level is still high when he arrives at work, and I am concerned that he will begin to be late again as an avoidance response to the uncomfortable situations at work.

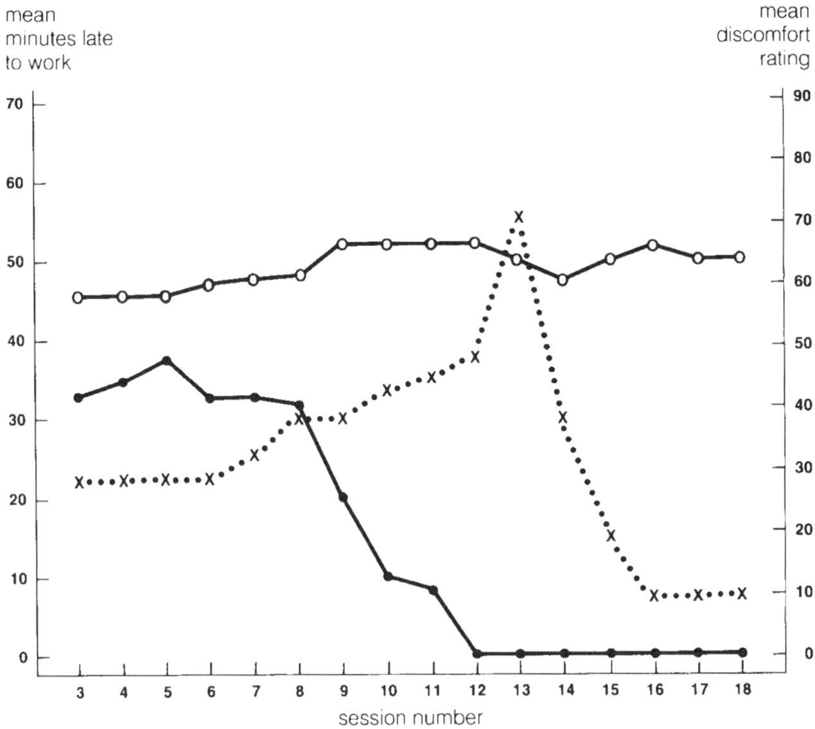

FIGURE 7.4 Graph of lateness and discomfort ratings for Donald Green.

Sessions 12 and 13

At the beginning of Session 12, we review Donald's progress with the lateness problem. We look at the graphs of discomfort ratings we have been constructing each week and discuss his feelings about his progress.

McCRADY. It looks as though you've made good progress toward being on time for work. How are you feeling about it?

GREEN. I guess I feel OK. My supervisor seems happy that I'm on time, and I like it that I can get up and out of the house when I want to.

McCRADY. So do you feel as if this problem's pretty well resolved?

GREEN. I guess so, although I don't feel very confident about it yet.

McCRADY. That's understandable—you were late for 3 years and have only been getting to work on time for a couple of weeks. We'll keep working on the imagery, your exercise, and watching the checking for a while. But there's something else that might be

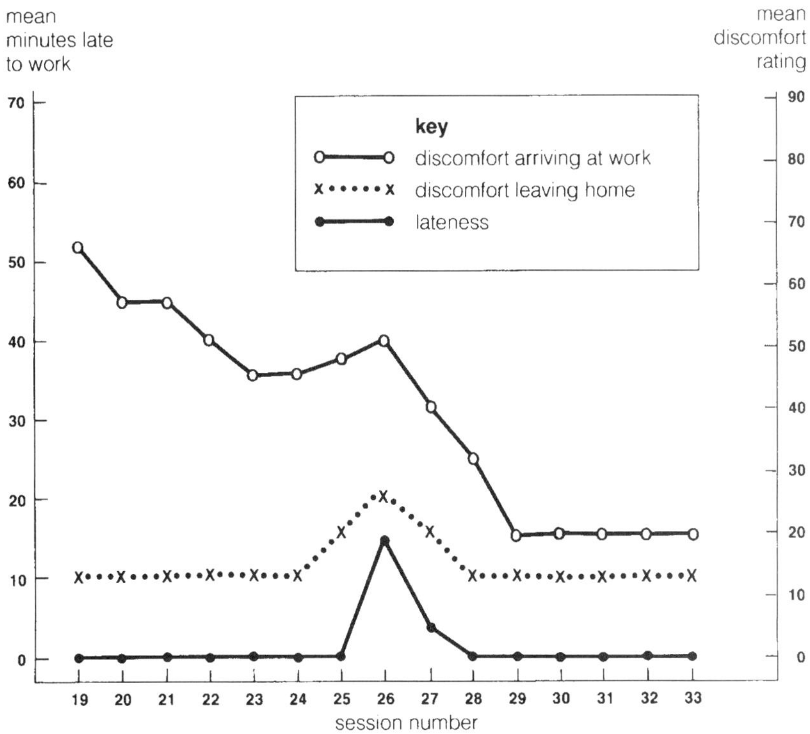

keeping you uncomfortable. I've noticed that your discomfort ratings when you get to work are still pretty high.

GREEN. Yeah, I noticed that too.

MCCRADY. It seems to me that your feelings when you're around people may be making it difficult for you at work. Remember that another of the goals we set was to help you learn some ways to interact with other people more comfortably than you do now.

GREEN. I was wondering when you were going to get around to that.

MCCRADY. Is it something you've been thinking about for a while now?

GREEN. Uh-huh.

MCCRADY. Why didn't you ask me about it?

GREEN. Well, I figured you knew what you were doing, and. . .

Donald hesitates and looks at the ceiling, clearly uncomfortable.

GREEN (continuing). I was afraid that now that you know me better, you've decided that there is no point in trying to help me with people.

MCCRADY. You mean that you thought I had decided you were hopeless or something?

GREEN. I guess so. (Donald looks at his hands, obviously embarrassed.)

MCCRADY. Are there things I've said or done that made you decide I thought you were hopeless?

GREEN. I guess just your attitude—you're always nice to me and encouraging me, like I'm pitiful or something. And I don't even think you like me.

(Donald has just demonstrated the way his thinking and anxiety inhibit him with other people. He had tried to read my mind and had concluded something quite erroneous—that I thought he was hopeless—and then he was acting on that belief: As his therapist, I can help him see what he does, which should set the stage for beginning to deal with his social anxiety. I also think I should be fairly careful of Donald's feelings; my sense is that he can be hurt easily and doesn't recover from it very well. So my task is to help him see the irrational nature of his thinking and also to support him. There is an awkward aspect of this conversation, because I don't feel close to Donald in the way I do with some clients, and I don't want to give him false feedback about my personal feelings.)

MCCRADY. Let's go back a few sessions, Donald, to when you filled out those questionnaires about social situations. I remember that you told me you felt as though they were written just for you—they described your feelings so well.

GREEN. Uh-huh.

Donald isn't even looking at me at this point.

MCCRADY. I think what you've done with me is just what you described in the questionnaires. You started reading my mind, without any definite information, and came to some conclusions about how I was thinking and feeling without even checking it out with me. It sounds as though you've been making yourself miserable about something that's not even true!

GREEN. So I guess it's my fault?

MCCRADY. No, not really your fault. You've gotten into this pattern of expecting the worst from other people and avoiding dealing with them, so you don't have to hear what you're afraid they're going to say. It seems like a pattern you learned a long time ago—neither of your parents seemed to express their feelings to other people much at all. So I'm not trying to *blame* you, but I do want you to see how your thinking puts you into these unhappy situations. If you start to become aware of how you do this, then you can make a choice to learn to think differently.

GREEN. I don't know if that's possible.

MCCRADY. It's difficult, but something that I think you have the ability to do. You've made a lot of progress already, and with difficult problems. There's no reason you should be unable to change.

GREEN. Well, I don't know.

MCCRADY. To me, you still seem to be kind of uncomfortable and unhappy.

GREEN. I guess so.

MCCRADY. I can't read *your* mind, either, but is it because I haven't said anything about my feelings about you?

GREEN (looks away). Um.

MCCRADY. Well, let me try to answer you. I like working with you—you have a lot of courage, you've talked about things that obviously are hard or embarrassing for you to bring up, and you've really worked hard to make changes. I don't feel as though I know you real well, but my sense is that you have a lot of warm feelings and creative thoughts kind of locked up inside you. I'd like to help you be able to share more of yourself with me and with other people.

Donald sits up a bit straighter and finally looks at me again.

GREEN. You really feel that way about me?

MCCRADY. Absolutely.

GREEN. I can't believe that you actually like me. You've got so much going for you, and I'm such a blob.

MCCRADY. You're doing it again—thinking negatively about yourself. Let's begin to look at how you get your thinking into these negative cycles.

(This has been a very uncomfortable conversation for both of us, but I think it will be critical in helping Donald begin to deal with his problems with people.)

For the remainder of Session 12 and part of Session 13, we discuss the concept of cognitive distortions. I give Donald a copy of Burns's (1980) list of these distortions (see Table 7.3). We start by looking at the list and trying to identify which types of distortions Donald used when he decided that I think he is hopeless, interpersonally. He says that he was

TABLE 7.3 Definitions of cognitive distortions (Adapted from D. D. Burns's *Feeling Good: The New Mood Therapy* (New York: William Morrow, 1980).

1. **All-or nothing thinking**. Seeing things in black-and-white categories.
2. **Overgeneralization**. Viewing a single negative event as a patter of defeat.
3. **Mental filter**. Picking a single negative detail and dwelling on it exclusively.
4. **Disqualifying the positive**. Rejecting positive experiences by insisting that they "don't count."
5. **Jumping to conclusions**. Making negative interpretations of equivocal events.
   a. *Mind reading*. Arbitrarily concluding that someone dislikes you.
   b. *the fortune teller error.* Anticipating that you will not succeed.
6. **Magnification (catastrophizing) or minimization**. Exaggerating the importance of things or inappropriately minimizing your good features and others' faults.
7. **Emotional reasoning**. Assuming that your negative feelings are correct.
8. **Should statements**. Motivating yourself with shoulds and shouldn'ts, musts and oughts.
9. **Labeling and mislabeling**. Attaching negative labels to yourself.
10. **Personalization**. Seeing yourself as the cause of events which in reality are not your fault.

(1) "disqualifying the positive" by focusing on one aspect of my behavior that he thought was negative but ignoring the positive aspects of my interactions with him, (2) "jumping to conclusions" by making an interpretation of my thinking without asking me about it ("mind reading"), and (3) engaging in "emotional reasoning" in that he felt hopeless and concluded that therefore it was true that he was hopeless.

After discussing these cognitive distortions that Donald has about our interaction, I give him as homework the task of identifying the distortions he experiences when he gets to work each day. He is to write these down on the back of his daily Self-Recording Form.

Session 13 is also our 10th treatment session, when our Initial Treatment Contract expires. I bring that up with Donald, and we review the goals we had set at the beginning of therapy. Donald and I agree that he has met his first goal, being on time for work, and that he does feel better when he takes his daily walks. It is clear that we have not made progress on the other two goals (carrying on brief conversations at work without excessive anxiety and learning how to give directions). We decide to contract for an additional 15 sessions, with the following goals for Donald:

1. To be able to carry on brief conversations with people at work without becoming excessively anxious.
2. To be able to give directions to people at work, when appropriate.
3. To be more comfortable in the weekly engineers' meeting.
4. To get involved in some activity or situation outside of work where he could meet people.
5. To develop skills to carry on conversations with people without excessive anxiety.
6. To decrease negative and distorted thinking about people's opinions of him and to increase his positive thinking about social interactions.

I ask Donald about his fear of barking dogs, and he again says that he does not want to bother with that. I also ask him if he has begun to imagine any catastrophes, but none were concerning him at that time.

Sessions 14–18

In the next five sessions, we do intensive work on Donald's cognitive distortions. His daily log of thoughts at work is helpful in describing in more detail the ways he makes himself uncomfortable. I teach him a simple technique to deal with this kind of thinking. First, he is to use his discomfort as a signal that he is probably thinking in a distorted way. Second, he is to identify what he is thinking. Third, he is to assign the thought to one or more of Burns's categories. Fourth, he is to generate an alternative thought that will allow him to feel more comfortable. We first use this technique, writing down each of the steps, on situations that had occurred during the past week. As homework, he is to use the same technique at the end of the day to analyze one situation that has made him uncomfortable during the day. Finally, he is to use this technique at least once a day.

Cognitive restructuring is difficult for Donald, and he is only partially successful. I estimate that his anxiety is so high that it inhibits his ability to use cognitive skills. Therefore, in Session 17, I introduce him to progressive relaxation. I have Donald close his eyes and sit back in the chair, and then I give him systematic instructions to tense and then relax different muscle groups in his body. I include instructions on breathing techniques to facilitate relaxation. The relaxation instructions take about 20 minutes, and Donald is able to relax fairly well. His discomfort with evaluation inhibits his relaxation somewhat, because he worries about what I think of how he is doing, but this is not a major factor. I assign the homework of practicing relaxation twice a day. We repeat the relaxation process during Session 18, and he is to continue to practice it at home.

Sessions 19–23

These sessions represent a period of successful work with Donald. He learns the relaxation technique well and begins to apply it at work. Once he is able to relax more, he can use some of the cognitive-restructuring techniques that he was less successful with previously.

We then construct a hierarchy of increasingly difficult interpersonal situations. These include brief conversations with Miss Donahue, sitting with other people at lunch, talking to people in the halls and at the company picnic, giving directions to people who work under him, and meeting new people. We role-play a number of these situations so that I can begin to get an idea of how he handles them, and then we practice how to handle the least difficult situation—the conversations with Miss Donahue.

When we role-play a situation, we first discuss what he could say, and then I pretend to be Donald and Donald pretends to be the other person, to give him a model of how to handle the situation. Then he tries out the behavior himself, with me taking the role of the other person. I then give him feedback about how he does, and he tries again. As homework, he is to rehearse each situation at home three times (to his mirror) and then try it out at work. By the end of Session 23, he is able to chat briefly with Miss Donahue in the morning, without any particular discomfort, and is sitting with other people at lunch. We have begun some specific practice with assertiveness, to help him in giving directions to employees, but he has not yet tried this skill out.

Sessions 24–28

During these sessions we continue the role playing and cognitive restructuring. Donald has begun to try to give instructions to foremen and has encountered a fair amount of negative feedback from them. Upset by these reactions, he has begun to feel hopeless again about being able to change. We discuss how he is thinking about the foremen's reactions, and we identify several types of distorted thinking. I emphasize that he cannot control how other people react, and therefore he will not always get the results he wants when he is assertive. He needs to focus more on how he feels when he does and does not speak out, rather than on whether others are cooperative. I also suggest that he has the right to feel angry at them for reacting negatively because his instructions are not unfair or excessive. This restructuring seems to help him. However, he is late for work 2 days during this time period (see Figure 7.1).

We also begin to focus directly on the engineers' meeting. Initially, I had Donald practice his relaxation skills during the meeting and focus on his cognitive distortions. This decreased his anxiety somewhat, but he still spent much of the meeting dreading when he would be asked to speak. We finally decide to have him ask if he can give his report at the beginning of the meeting, and he rehearses his speaking about it with the chief engineer. When he finally is able to make this request, although with considerable anxiety, the chief engineer is quite receptive. Donald continues to experience some anxiety before he speaks, but he is able to relax after he has spoken and finds the rest of the meeting less uncomfortable.

Although Donald is making a good deal of progress at work, his social life continues to be limited to his weekly dinner with Jim and Mary. I bring up the idea that, to feel less lonely, he needs to take some risks to meet people in other settings. He feels very uncomfortable with the idea but continues to express his desire to have a "normal" life. Therefore we begin to brainstorm where he might be able to meet people. Donald quickly says that he doesn't want to go to bars, he doesn't know how to dance, and he's not athletic. I observe that he is engaging in pretty negative thinking again and ask him to try to think about things that he likes instead.

We use brainstorming techniques to identify possible activities or places where Donald might meet people. In brainstorming, the client is encouraged to think of a range of ideas without censoring any ideas, and I write these down as we talk. Donald's final list includes: house tours, nature lectures, hiking club, adult education classes, volunteer work, Big Brothers, auto collectors clubs, square-dancing classes, chess clubs.

By Session 28, Donald has investigated some of these activities and decides to do some volunteer work at the local Boys' Club, where he can teach boys some of what he knows about auto repairs and restoration. I am concerned that this activity will not put him in contact with adults, and especially not with adult women, but since he is quite enthusiastic about the program, I do not want to discourage him.

We also review the treatment contract again, since we have nearly completed 15 more sessions. Though Donald has met almost all of his goals, he still feels limited in carrying on conversations and is just beginning to involve himself in an outside activity. Therefore we contract for three more sessions to attempt to achieve these last two goals. I also decide to space these sessions at 2–week intervals, to begin to prepare Donald for termination from treatment.

Sessions 29–31

Donald spends most of each of the last three sessions reporting on events at work and at the Boys' Club. We continue to discuss how to handle some work situations and talk about his volunteer work at the Boys' Club, which turns out to be extremely satisfying. His expertise with cars makes him an instant hit with the boys. He takes a car that he has purchased for restoration to the club, and they work on it together. A number of other adults, volunteers and staff, also are interested, and Donald begins to interact with them. Because they all want to help the boys, conversation with these adults seems easy for Donald.

At session 31, we review the progress Donald has made through treatment. He reports that he feels much better about himself and is enthusiastic when he gets up in the morning. He is getting to work on time and is interacting with the people at work. He has to deliberately use the relaxation and cognitive-restructuring techniques, especially in the engineers' meeting and with the foremen, and he occasionally falls into negative thinking. He is excited by his volunteer work. Though Donald still is living alone and has not made any progress toward meeting women or dating, he decides that he is ready to discontinue treatment and see how things go for a while. We schedule one more session to discuss termination. I give him the four major questionnaires that we had used at the beginning of treatment and ask him to complete them again as a way of formally evaluating his progress.

TERMINATION OF THE THERAPY

Termination in behavior therapy is designed to maximize the ability of clients to apply what they have learned and the probability that they will maintain the gains they have made in the therapy. Much of therapy can be considered preparation for termination, because it focuses on teaching a skill and then applying it in the client's real world. My intent in terminating therapy is to help my clients consolidate what they have learned and to improve their ability to continue to use these skills. As a guide for termination, I use the relapse prevention model first proposed by Marlatt and Gordon (1985) as a way to deal with addictive behaviors. This termination process includes several specific elements.

1. Instead of abruptly ending the treatment, I spread out the last few sessions so the client has more opportunity to apply what he or she has learned, as contact with me becomes less frequent.
2. I schedule some follow-up sessions after the end of the regular therapy. These sessions are sometimes called "booster" sessions, but I prefer to think of them as a way to review and consolidate progress and to identify any new problems before they become major or continuing problems.
3. I help the client identify the major changes that have been made and what the client considers most important to maintaining these changes.
4. I make a formal evaluation of the client's progress by reviewing

the data collected during treatment and readministering any formal assessment devices.

For Donald, the last session of his regular treatment is Session 31.

MCCRADY. Last week you said you felt ready to stop treatment.

GREEN. Well, yes. I feel much better, and I think I can use what you've taught me. I don't want to keep depending on you every time I have a problem.

MCCRADY. I agree that you've made tremendous changes. I think you've really used therapy well—bringing up problems, trying out the techniques we've worked on here, talking about things that are pretty uncomfortable to discuss.

GREEN. I'm going to miss seeing you.

MCCRADY. I do appreciate that, Donald, and one thing I like to do is to schedule a couple of follow-up sessions to see how you're doing and if there is anything else you want to discuss. Usually my clients find these follow-ups helpful, but I must admit that I have a selfish reason to schedule them as well—I want to see what happens with you later.

GREEN. I like that idea a lot. When will I see you again?

MCCRADY. Let's schedule our first follow-up for a month from now. If all is going well, I'll see you next in 3 more months, and then 6 months after that.

GREEN. OK.

MCCRADY. For the rest of the session today, I'd like to spend some time discussing what you think of the therapy, what things were most helpful, and what you think is most important for you to do to keep the positive changes going.

GREEN. Well, this was very different from what I expected. As I said before, I thought that I'd lie on a couch and talk a lot, and you wouldn't say much. I guess I was surprised when I saw you, because you're not only a woman but you look pretty young. But I like how you work—everything made a lot of sense to me, and I felt like you respected me. I mean, I did get embarrassed, but then I always do—or at least, I always used to!

MCCRADY. I hope that's a thing of the past!

GREEN. Well, maybe not completely, but it is a lot better.

MCCRADY. It sounds as though you like the approach we took. Of all the things we did, which ones seem most important to you now?

GREEN. I liked the role-playing a lot. Sometimes when I'm getting uncomfortable now I can picture you in my mind, asking me how I could handle the problem, and then I see us role-playing, and that helps. I don't use the relaxation stuff too much now, but it's nice to know how to use it. I like the walking—it gives me a lot of energy and starts the day out better. And I guess the cognitive distortions list is helpful, although I still feel pretty foolish when I use it and see what I'm doing to myself.

MCCRADY. So, some of the specific techniques, like the cognitive restructuring and role-playing, are helpful and you still use them, at least in your imagination, but others aren't so important now.

GREEN. That's right.

MCCRADY. Do you find self-recording helpful?

GREEN. Not so much now, but it sure helped you figure out what was wrong at the start.

MCCRADY. I like to think that it helped *us* figure that out! Anything else we did that was important to you?

GREEN. Not really. You did help me a lot, though. I feel better about myself in general now—I just have more confidence about things, and I haven't thought about any catastrophes at all.

MCCRADY. I think that's another sign of the progress you've made. Now let's look at your latest answers on the questionnaires, to see what they can tell us.

Donald hands me the four questionnaires, and I score them. His score on the Beck Depression Inventory is down to a 2. On the Fear of Negative Evaluation Scale he scores 15, which is just at the mean for that scale, and on the Social Avoidance and Distress Scale he scores 14, still somewhat above the mean but much improved from his initial score. On the Gambrill and Richey Assertiveness Inventory, he rates his discomfort as lower in most situations but still describes himself as unlikely to be assertive in several circumstances. Overall, the questionnaires reflect progress for Donald, though some discomfort and difficulty with social situations persist.

MCCRADY. It seems that the way you've answered these questionnaires goes along with the way you've been feeling—much better, even though you still get uncomfortable or uncertain of yourself.

GREEN. That's what I thought when I was filling them out.

MCCRADY. One other thing I'd like to do today—let's see if we can make a list of things that would be warning signs that your old problems might be coming back. Can you think of any specific occurrences that should tell you things are going wrong?

GREEN. If I started being late for work again, that would be one bad sign. And if I stopped going to help at the Boys' Club, that would be another.

MCCRADY. (writing these down). Anything else you can think of?

GREEN. I'm not sure.

MCCRADY. What about if you started getting into a lot of negative thinking again?

GREEN. That absolutely would be a bad sign.

MCCRADY. OK, then, I'll put that on the list. What about any of your patterns of behavior at work—like eating alone, or doing work rather than assigning it to the foremen?

GREEN. I guess those wouldn't be very good signs either. You might as well add them to the list.

MCCRADY. OK. And, how about the daily walks—are they important enough to put down here?

GREEN. Yes, I didn't think of them, but I can't imagine not taking them.

MCCRADY. OK, then, do you think this list is complete enough now?

GREEN. Yes, I think so.

MCCRADY. (handing him the list). Think of this as a list of warning signals—if any of them starts happening, you need to take immediate action.

GREEN. What do you mean?

MCCRADY. Let's talk about that. The first immediate action would be just to notice that one of these things is happening, and then you would need to ask yourself why it is happening. Then you can remember the skills you've learned in therapy and see which ones will help you get back on track. Let's try an example. Say you cut back on the number of hours you are spending at the Boys' Club.

GREEN. I wouldn't even want to think about that, but OK.

MCCRADY. I wouldn't either—you seem to be enjoying it so much. But let's just pretend for a minute.

GREEN. OK.

MCCRADY. What might be some reasons for you to cut back on your time at the club?

GREEN. I'd probably start thinking that someone there didn't like me—you know, like those catastrophes I used to imagine.

MCCRADY. OK, how could you go about handling that kind of thinking?

GREEN. I'd have to figure out if it was true or not, or if I was using one of those distortions in thinking again.

MCCRADY. Sounds like a good plan, but what if it doesn't work?

GREEN. Could I call you?

MCCRADY. Sure, that's always a possibility. Anything else you could do?

GREEN. I'm not sure.

MCCRADY. What about trying to talk to the other person to see if you're mind reading or not?

GREEN. That would be pretty hard for me to do, but it's an idea.

MCCRADY. The most important thing is to take the approach that it's a problem you want to solve, rather than just accepting that things are going wrong. You can try a lot of different ways of handling it.

GREEN. Kind of like therapy, huh?

MCCRADY. Right.

GREEN (looking uncomfortable again). Look, I want to thank you for helping me. I, uh, brought you a present. It's not much, but I just wanted to thank you.

Donald hands me a pair of earrings shaped like small roses. They are congruent with my taste and style and quite attractive. It is a thoughtful gift that really touches me. That he is able to thank me so directly also is an indicator of how far he has come in therapy.

MCCRADY. The earrings are beautiful. Thank you. I really have enjoyed working with you.

We confirm the appointment for our first follow-up session in a month, and then we say good-bye.

Follow-Up

Donald had a total of three follow-up sessions with me over the next year. During that time, some positive things continued to happen in his life. A group of volunteers and staff at the Boys' Club began to socialize together—going out for dinner occasionally, or chaperoning Saturday-night dances for the boys and getting together before or after them. Donald became particularly friendly with one of the female volunteers who also was somewhat shy, so he felt comfortable around her. The last time I saw him, they had begun to date. Donald was anxious about dating, since he never had done so before, and he was extremely anxious about displaying physical affection or having a sexual relationship. He did not want to return to therapy, however, because he knew that she was equally inexperienced, and, he thought,

"Things will work out." My sense was that he was embarrassed talking with me about sex, and he seemed a bit uncomfortable telling me about his affection for this woman. We agreed that he'd call me if there were any problems, but I did not hear from him again. ■

CRITIQUE OF DONALD GREEN'S TREATMENT BY COGNITIVE BEHAVIOR THERAPY

by G. Terence Wilson

The case report of the treatment of Donald Green by Barbara McCrady provides a representative and informative description of the classical practice of cognitive-behavior therapy. The report highlights several distinctive features of this therapy, the therapist-client relationship, clinical assessment, and multifaceted treatment.

Therapist-Client Relationship

McCrady wisely took pains to develop a good therapeutic relationship with Donald. A good therapist-client relationship is a necessary but insufficient ingredient of effective cognitive-behavior therapy in complex cases such as his. This is one of the commonalities that cognitive-behavior therapy shares with other systems of psychological therapy, although there are distinctive features about the way in which cognitive-behavior therapists relate to their clients.

McCrady deliberately tried to make Donald feel like a cooperative partner in the task of helping him change his behavior. She explained the reasons for asking him to record his daily activities and thoughts, and she was careful to check that he understood this and other assessment and behavior-change strategies and that they made sense to him. Actively involving clients in the treatment plan and in the assignment of therapeutic activities between sessions (often called "homework assignments") is critical in ensuring that clients actually engage in them. Findings from experimental social psychology as well as clinical research show that clients are more likely to adhere to therapeutic instructions (they will resist less) when they are allowed to feel part of the behavior-change process and not simply given "doctor's orders."

Donald responded well to McCrady's various requests to keep records and practice treatment techniques. I attribute this in large part to McCrady's careful and sensitive handling of the therapeutic relationship. Recall that Donald entered into treatment with quite different expectations about what therapy would be like and what he would have to do ("lie on a couch and talk a lot"). Had these initially unspoken expectations about what therapy would be like gone unaddressed, it is likely that treatment would not have proceeded as smoothly. Clients do not always comply with therapeutic prescriptions as readily as Donald did. Behavior therapists frequently encounter resistance to behavior change on the part of their clients. Their conceptualization of resistance, and how they cope with it, has been detailed elsewhere (Lazarus & Fay, 1982; O'Leary & Wilson, 1987).

McCrady's style of inviting Donald's feedback about her understanding of his problems and how to treat them was vitally important in identifying some of his apparently typical self-defeating cognitive distortions. She uncovered how he engaged in "mind reading"—how he jumped to the inaccurate and dysfunctional conclusion that she really "didn't like him" and that she thought he was "hopeless." McCrady was able to use this information effectively in introducing the technique of cognitive restructuring. Here is a good example of a behavior therapist focusing on the in-session interaction between her and the client to provide the client with an important interpersonal learning experience.

The mind-reading example shows how behavior therapists work to have their clients see treatment as credible and relevant to their particular needs. Developing trust in the therapist is another goal of treatment. To this end McCrady was open, direct, genuine, and selectively self-disclosing. She shared with Donald her true feeling about him in a way that was both genuine and emotionally supportive. She even shared some of her concerns about the probable effects of a treatment strategy she had adopted. Clients, as a whole, respond well to this therapeutic style and typically rate behavior therapists highly on dimensions of warmth and caring (O'Leary & Wilson, 1987).

Clinical Assessment

The case exemplified both the goals and methods of assessment in cognitive therapy. The major goal is to identify the different factors that are currently causing the client's problems. Complex or relatively diffuse cases such as that presented by Donald Green are broken down into separate, albeit interconnected, parts. Notice that in arriving at her formulation of Donald's case, McCrady did not limit herself to a piecemeal analysis of specific behaviors. Rather, she focused on specific problems as well as a theme or common thread, which she hypothesized to occur across different situations. She developed an integrated and clinically consistent analysis of Donald's problems. The focus was not only on his overt behavior but also on his thoughts and feelings. In other words, McCrady was concerned with understanding and then treating the "whole person."

Cognitive Behavior therapists use a variety of assessment methods, as this case shows. A detailed clinical interview is fundamental, but it is complemented by self-recording by the client, role-playing, and the use of selected questionnaires. Assessment in cognitive-behavior therapy is a continuous process in which the therapist constantly monitors the effects of treatment as a means of confirming the validity and utility of her formulation of the case. Hypotheses about the nature of a client's problems are tentatively framed and must be open to revision, based on response to intervention. Notice how McCrady constantly referred to Donald's self-recording to assess his progress and to identify pitfalls. This information provided specific guidelines for the strategies she used.

Behavior therapists typically do not rely on traditional personality tests for assessing clients and developing treatment strategies. These tests derive from personality trait theory and rest on the assumption that an individual's behavior is relatively consistent across different situations. Cognitive Behavior therapists are more interested in assessing behavior in the context of specific situations. They select self-report questionnaires that measure relatively focal areas of clients' functioning. The assertiveness inventory and social anxiety scales McCrady used are examples of this emphasis on focal assessment within specific domains of functioning.

Multifaceted Treatment

Cognitive Behavior therapists have at their disposal a wide range of different cognitive and behavioral treatment strategies. In part, the personal skill of the therapist rests in selecting appropriate methods and implementing them at the right time in therapy. McCrady's report illustrates the use of several of the most important, commonly used cognitive-behavioral techniques, such as self-monitoring, progressive relaxation training, cognitive restructuring, social skills and assertion training, and response prevention. Different techniques are usually required to overcome different dimensions of a client's problems. McCrady did not assume that one or two methods would necessarily have broad, generalized effects across all of Donald's problems. Rather, she tailored specific methods to each facet of his problems. However, it must be emphasized that cognitive-behavior therapy is a way of thinking about clinical problems, rather than simply a collection of different treatment techniques. McCrady's selection and use of different techniques followed logically from her overall assessment of the interrelationships among specific facets of Donald's problems.

What is especially useful about the report is McCrady's discussion of her thinking behind choosing each technique and the specific effects she hoped to achieve. Notice that in selecting techniques McCrady took into consideration the degree to which they are supported by empirical evidence. A good example is the choice of response prevention to overcome Donald's obsessive-compulsive checking rituals. Obsessions and compulsions are among the most difficult of all clinical disorders to treat. Exposure plus response prevention is the only psychological method that has been shown to be effective in controlled clinical research (Riggs & Foa, 1993). More generally, it should be emphasized that all of the techniques employed by McCrady have been shown to be effective in one or another controlled clinical outcome study (O'Leary & Wilson, 1987).

The learning principles on which specific techniques are based are more important than the techniques themselves. Cognitive Behavior therapists often have to improvise—to adapt particular techniques to the specific needs of individual clients. Therapeutic versatility of this sort requires an understanding of underlying principles of behavior change. McCrady provides a revealing example of therapeutic ingenuity in her use of exposure and response prevention. It was impractical for Donald to be supervised directly in his home. Instead of simply relying on instructions that he may well have found too anxiety provoking and that he would not have followed properly, McCrady exposed Donald to a situation that elicited his checking compulsion in the kitchen of her building. This creative arrangement allowed her to monitor his progress in following through on what is an emotionally threatening task for most clients, at least initially.

McCrady's treatment approach exemplifies another key characteristic of cognitive-behavior therapy, namely, graduated behavior change. In the use of exposure and response prevention, for example, she constructed a hierarchy of situations ranging from the least to the most anxiety-eliciting.

The choice and sequencing of particular treatment techniques are a dynamic process in which there is a constant interplay between the therapist's judgment and the observed outcome. For example, shortly after introducing the technique of cognitive restructuring, in which she asked Donald to identify and then alter his distorted cognitions about social interactions, McCrady ran into difficulty. The technique proved only partially successful. Apparently, Donald was unable to adhere to her instructions about how to use cognitive restructuring. McCrady inferred that severe anxiety was responsible for this therapeutic impasse. To cope with the anxiety she then introduced progressive relaxation training, which reduced Donald's anxiety and facilitated his use of cognitive restructuring.

Alternative Treatment Formulations and Strategies

In my view, McCrady's formulation of the case and her selection of assessment and treatment strategies were well-founded. The picture one gets is of a seasoned and highly competent cognitive-behavior therapist at work. Most important, the outcome was satisfactory. Donald showed marked improvement in different aspects of his functioning that had seriously interfered with his life and brought him to therapy. Moreover, this improvement was not short-lived. He continued to function well 1 year after treatment had ended. Donald's success is not surprising. The treatment-outcome literature shows that the types of problems he presented reliably respond well to cognitive-behavioral treatment. Nonetheless, as in any case report, it is possible to take alternative viewpoints and to speculate about how treatment might have been different.

It seems clear that Donald suffered from severe social anxiety and was lacking in assertiveness. His interpersonal functioning was significantly impaired, and he led a lonely life. McCrady included these deficits in her formulation of the case and began to address them systematically in Sessions 12 and 13. Some other cognitive-behavior therapists might plausibly have tackled Donald's social anxiety and unassertiveness earlier in treatment, on the assumption that these problems were focal to the case. They seem related to his social isolation, his negative self-image, and his late arrival at work. The cognitive restructuring and role-playing strategies used by McCrady might have been implemented sooner.

At the end of treatment, Donald was still living alone and had not made any progress toward meeting women or dating. He chose to discontinue therapy at that point, although he did subsequently return for three follow-up sessions. It is unclear how readily McCrady accepted Donald's decision to end therapy, or whether the decision to end treatment reflected a mutual agreement between therapist and client. Some cognitive-behavior therapists might consider treatment incomplete without greater progress in this important domain of interpersonal functioning. Lack of change or improvement in a critically important area such as heterosexual relationships would mean not only that his functioning was still limited but also that he would be more vulnerable to relapse or a recurrence of his problems in the future. There are several different treatment interventions cognitive-behavior therapists might employ in such a case. One area of exploration would be Donald's apparent anxiety about sexual functioning. The therapist might probe Donald's knowledge and feelings about this more directly. It might be speculated that in part Donald's interpersonal anxiety and difficulties were motivated by an underlying fear of physical intimacy and sexual functioning. One of the strong suits of cognitive-behavior therapy is its proven success in reducing sex-related anxiety and enhancing sexual adequacy and satisfaction. In this case, of course, Donald continued to improve after termination. The fact that during the 1-year follow-up period he did begin to date a woman suggests that termination was not untimely.

REFERENCES

American Psychiatric Association (1987). *Diagnostic and statistical manual of mental disorders* (3rd ed., rev.). Washington, DC: Author.

Barlow, D. H. (Ed.) (1985). *Clinical handbook of psychological disorders: A step-by-step treatment manual.* New York: Guilford Press.

Beck, A., Rush, A.J., Shaw, B. F., & Emery, G. (1979). *Cognitive therapy of depression.* New York: Guilford Press.

Burns, D. D. (1980). *Feeling good: The new mood therapy.* New York: William Morrow.

Gambrill, E. D., & Richey, C. A. (1975). An assertion inventory for use in assessment and research. *Behavior Therapy, 6,* 550–561.

Hollin, C. R., & Trower, (1988). Development and applications of social skills training: A review and critique. In M. Hersen, R. M. Eisler, & P. M. Miller (Eds.), *Progress in behavior modification* (Vol. 22). Newbury Park, CA: Sage Publications.

Lazarus, A. A., & Fay, A. (1982). Resistance or rationalization? A cognitive-behavioral perspective. In P. L. Wachtel (Ed.), *Resistance: Psychodynamic and behavioral approaches* (pp. 115–132). New York: Plenum.

McCrady, B. S., Longabaugh, R., Fink, E., Stout, R., Beattie, M., Ruggieri-Authelet, A., & McNeill, D. (1986). Cost effectiveness of alcoholism treatment in partial hospital versus inpatient settings after brief inpatient treatment: Twelve-month outcomes. *Journal of Consulting and Clinical Psychology, 54,* 708–713.

Morey, L. (1988). Personality disorders in DSM-III and DSM-III-R: Convergence, coverage and internal consistency. *American Journal of Psychiatry, 145*, 573–577.
O'Leary, K., & Wilson, C. T. (1987). *Behavior therapy: Application and outcome*, (2nd ed.). Englewood Cliffs, NJ: Prentice-Hall.
Riggs, D. S., & Foa, E. B. (1993). Obsessive compulsive disorders. In D. H. Barlow (Ed.), *Clinical handbook: of psychological disorders: A step-by-step treatment manual* (2nd edition) (pp. 189–239). New York: Guilford Press.
Turkat, E. D., & Maisto, S. A. (1985). Personality disorders: Application of the experimental method to the formulation and modification of personality disorders. In D. H. Barlow (Ed.), *Clinical handbook of psychological disorders. A step-by-step treatment manual.* New York: Guilford Press.
Watson, D., Sr., & Friend, R. (1969). Measurement of social-evaluative anxiety. *Journal of Consulting and Clinical Psychology, 33*, 448–457.
Wilson, G. T. (1995). Behavior therapy. In R. J. Corsini and D. Wedding, *Current psychotherapies* (pp. 197–228). Itasca, IL: F. E. Peacock, Publishers.

EDITORS' ADDENDUM

The reader interested in the treatment of personality disorders that enlist strategies that transcend strictly cognitive behavioral paradigms may wish to consult the following publications:

Linehan, M. M. (1993). *Cognitive-behavioral treatment of borderline personality disorder.* New York: guilford.
Persons, J. (1989). *Cognitive therapy in practice: A case formulation approach.* New York: Norton.
Persons, J. (1997). Dissemination of effective methods: Behavior Therapy's next challenge. *Behavior Therapy, 28*, 465–471.
Young, J. (1994). *Cognitive therapy for personality disorders: A schema-focused approach.* Sarasota, FL: Professional Resource Press.

The following articles can also be consulted with profit:

Glass, C. R., & Arnokoff, D. B. (1992). Behavior therapy. In D. K. Freedheim (Ed.), *History of psychotherapy: A century of change* (pp. 587–628). Washington, DC: American Psychological Association.
Gortner, E. T., Gollan, J. K., Dobson, K. S., & Jacobson, N. S. (1998). Cognitive behavioral treatment for depression: Relapse prevention. *Journal of Consulting and Clinical Psychology, 66*, 377–384.
Jacobson, N. S., Dobson, K. S., Truax, P. A., Addis, M. E., Koerner, K., Gollan, J. K., Gortner, E., & Prince, S. E. (1996). A component analysis of cognitive-behavioral treatment for depression. *Journal of Consulting and Clinical Psychology, 64*, 295–304.
Patterson, C. H., & Watkins, C. E. (1996). Cognitive-behavior modification. In *Theories of psychotherapy* (pp. 247–267). New York: HarperCollins.
Wilson, G. T. (1998). Manual-based treatment and clinical practice. *Clinical Psychology: Science and Practice, 5*, 363–375.

Index

Note: Page numbers followed by letters *f* and *t* indicate figures and tables, respectively.

D

S